Despite their increasing importa[...] standing of why nation-states initiate economic sanctions, or what determines their success. This book argues that both imposers and targets of economic coercion incorporate expectations of future conflict as well as the short-run opportunity costs of coercion into their behavior. Drezner argues that conflict expectations have a paradoxical effect. Adversaries will impose sanctions frequently, but will rarely secure concessions. Allies will be reluctant to use coercion, but once sanctions are used, they can result in significant concessions. Ironically, the most favorable distribution of payoffs is likely to result when the imposer cares the least about its reputation or the distribution of gains. The book's argument is pursued using game theory and statistical analysis, detailed case studies of Russia's relations with newly independent states, and US efforts to halt nuclear proliferation on the Korean peninsula.

DANIEL DREZNER is an Assistant Professor of Political Science at the University of Colorado at Boulder. He is the author of a number of articles in scholarly journals, and has acted as a research consultant for the RAND corporation.

CAMBRIDGE STUDIES IN INTERNATIONAL RELATIONS: 65

The Sanctions Paradox

CAMBRIDGE STUDIES IN INTERNATIONAL RELATIONS

Series list continues after index

The Sanctions Paradox

Economic Statecraft and International Relations

Daniel W. Drezner

CAMBRIDGE
UNIVERSITY PRESS

CAMBRIDGE UNIVERSITY PRESS
Cambridge, New York, Melbourne, Madrid, Cape Town, Singapore, São Paulo, Delhi

Cambridge University Press
The Edinburgh Building, Cambridge CB2 8RU, UK

Published in the United States of America by Cambridge University Press, New York

www.cambridge.org
Information on this title: www.cambridge.org/9780521644150

First published 1999

A catalogue record for this publication is available from the British Library

Library of Congress Cataloguing in Publication data
Drezner, Daniel W.
The sanctions paradox: economic statecraft and international
relations / Daniel W. Drezner.
     p.   cm. – (Cambridge studies in international relations: 65)
ISBN 0 531 64332 5 (hardback) – ISBN 0 521 64415 1 (paperback)
1. Economic sanctions.   2. International economic relations.
3. Economic sanctions – Case studies.   I. Title.   II. Series.
HF1413.5.D74   1999   327.1'17–dc21   98–39105   CIP

ISBN 978-0-521-64332-0 hardback
ISBN 978-0-521-64415-0 paperback

Transferred to digital printing 2009

This book is dedicated to my parents,
Esther and David Drezner.
For feeding me a steady diet of carrots and very few sticks.

Contents

Figures

Tables

Acknowledgments

The genesis of this book came from when I was a Civic Education Project lecturer in Ukraine, and witnessed first-hand the dynamics of economic coercion. Five years later, this book has traveled with me across the Atlantic, from coast to coast, and into the mountains. At each way station, I have racked up significant intellectual debts.

The origins of this book are my doctoral dissertation, "Are carrots and sticks good for you? The utility of economic statecraft," which was written at Stanford University. First and foremost I must thank my advisor, Stephen D. Krasner. Steve's strength as an advisor is to force his students to think about international relations with almost as much lucidity as he does. His guidance turned an amorphous idea into a concrete piece of work. Bruce Bueno de Mesquita, Kurt Taylor Gaubatz, John Ferejohn, Judith Goldstein, and Paul Krugman performed yeoman service on my oral and written committees. I am also grateful to Aaron Belkin, Nora Bensahel, Alex George, Michael McFaul, Kira Nam, Saule Omarova, Tonya Putnam, Doug Rivers, Evan Feigenbaum, Jeremy Buchman and Scott Sagan for their comments and suggestions.

The dissertation was rewritten into something resembling a book when I was a postdoctoral fellow for the 1996/97 academic year at the Olin Institute for Strategic Studies at Harvard University. I am grateful to Sam Huntington and Steve Rosen for giving me the ideal intellectual environment for this task. Kurt Dassel, Mike Desch, Drew Erdmann, Page Fortna, Jeff Legro, William J. Long, Pauline Jones Luong, Lisa Martin, Laura Miller, Robert Paarlberg, James McAllister, Carol Porter, Eric Reinhardt, and Mary Elise Sarotte were all kind enough to read over portions of my draft and constructively critique it. Their advice was keenly felt.

The final revisions were completed in my first year as an assistant professor at the University of Colorado at Boulder. I thank Mark Lichbach, Claudia Dahlerus and Jeff Kopstein for their insights on various sections of the manuscript. I owe a special debt of gratitude to Steve Chan for reading over my penultimate draft and providing me with his astute commentary.

John Haslam at Cambridge University Press tolerated my boisterous e-mails with grace and economy. Hilary Scannell's swift and spare copy editing saved me from a number of unintended gaffes. The two anonymous reviewers for the press provided excellent suggestions for revisions. Many thanks.

I thank Paul Diehl, Kurt Dassel and Eric Reinhardt, who were kind enough to let me use some of their data in chapter 4. Parts of previous drafts of chapters 2, 4, and 6 have appeared in *Security Studies* (volume 6, number 3) and *International Studies Quarterly* (volume 42, number 4). I thank the editors of those publications for releasing their copyright.

Everyone mentioned above is absolved from any errors contained in this book. This includes the two computers that I used to compose this work: the Macintosh Powerbook 160, serial number MFC322D2J450, or the Compaq Deskpro, serial number 6731BPM5Q888. These machines were kind enough never to crash on me.

Finally, I am and will be eternally grateful to my wife, Erika Drezner. Through listening to my complaints, and proofreading my chapters, she has heard enough about this project to give an excellent two-minute summary of it to anyone who asks. I could not have written this without her constant support and devotion. As she is so fond of pointing out, when I first met her, I was but a lowly graduate student fumbling with the first crumbs of a theory. I now have a doctorate, a tenure-track job, and a book. How's that for causality?

1 Introduction

A tale of two cases

On August 6, 1990, the United Nations Security Council voted to impose multilateral economic sanctions against Iraq in response to Saddam Hussein's invasion of Kuwait. By any conventional measure, these sanctions achieved the greatest degree of international cooperation in modern history. Iraq suffered damages equal to roughly half its pre-war gross national product, a cost far outweighing any other sanctions attempt in this century. Despite the severe economic dislocations suffered by the Iraqi regime, it refused to surrender any Kuwaiti territory. Ignoring claims that the sanctions would have worked with time, the US-led coalition decided to retake Kuwait through military force. On April 3, 1991, the Security Council voted to extend the sanctions regime until Iraq complied with additional demands to reveal its weapons of mass destruction program, recognize the border with Kuwait, and pay reparations. An unstated but desired demand was the removal of Saddam Hussein from power. Iraq has labored under the UN sanctions regime for eight years. As a result, infant mortality rates have increased sevenfold, annual inflation rose to over 4,000 percent, and per capita income has fallen to less than half pre-war levels. In the face of continued economic losses and bellicose US rhetoric, the Iraqi regime has only acquiesced to UN demands when additional military threats have been made. On every issue area, when the only pressure is economic sanctions, Iraq has not budged. Domestically, Saddam's regime shows no signs of falling; if anything, the sanctions regime has strengthened it. Despite the most potent sanctions in history, economic coercion has failed to produce any significant Iraqi concessions.[1]

In late August 1991, the United States was trying to cajole all the relevant players in the Middle East into a multilateral peace conference in Madrid. A blocking point was the Israeli construction of new housing in the occupied territories of the West Bank and Gaza. The Israeli government of Yitzhak Shamir sought to acquire US-ensured financing to cover additional expenses. The Bush administration responded by delaying and then refusing to grant $10 billion in loan guarantees until the Israelis froze the building of all new settlements in the territories. Shamir agreed to the delay before the Madrid peace conference, but refused to concede on the issue of new housing. US Secretary of State James Baker told the Israeli government that the loan guarantees were conditional on the freeze in housing construction in the occupied territories. With Shamir reluctant to yield, Washington used economic pressure to force a change in government. US and Israeli authorities agree that Shamir's refusal to concede cost him and his Likud party the June 1992 elections. In August of 1992, the new Labor government, led by Yitzhak Rabin, acquiesced to the US terms and agreed to freeze the building of all new settlements in return for the loan guarantees. Shamir's Defense Minister and campaign manager later described the episode as an unprecedented example of US interference in Israeli domestic politics.[2] Nevertheless, the Israeli government acquiesced to US economic pressure, paving the way for the historic 1993 accord between Israel and the Palestine Liberation Organization.

Although the Iraqi case has been the focus of more attention, both episodes are examples of economic coercion. I define economic coercion as the threat or act by a nation-state or coalition of nation-states, called the *sender*, to disrupt economic exchange with another nation-state, called the *target*, unless the targeted country acquiesces to an articulated political demand. The disrupted exchange could include

---

[1] See Hufbauer, Schott, and Elliott (1990a), pp. 283–98 on the pre-war UN sanctions. On the postwar sanctions regime and its effect on Iraq's population, see Reuther (1995) and the *Economist*, "Iraq: more medicine please," March 7, 1998. On how the sanctions have strengthened Hussein's grip on power, see "CIA says Saddam Hussein emerged stronger," *Boston Globe*, September 20, 1996, p. A2, and Robert Wright and John Daniszewski, "Hussein may be main beneficiary of UN aid effort," *Los Angeles Times*, March 4, 1998, p. A1.

[2] See Arens (1995), pp. 1, 301. See Baker (1995), pp. 540–57, for the US take on the episode.

trade sanctions, boycotts, aid suspensions, freezing of financial assets, or the manipulation of tariff rates.[3]

The two cases suggest several puzzles that need to be addressed. First, why did unilateral US pressure on Israel succeed where multilateral UN pressure on Iraq failed? The existing explanations about economic coercion are of little use. Experts predicted that the sanctions against Iraq would be successful.[4] The case had all the attributes traditionally associated with successful sanctions: the target incurred significant economic damage; the sanctions effort was backed by an international institution; all major trading partners cooperated with the UN resolutions; and the threat of military force behind the sanctions effort was clearly signaled. Yet the coalition leaders believed that economic statecraft would not be enough to extract the desired concessions; sanctions failed to achieve their goals without the additional use of force. By contrast, the Israeli case involved unilateral sanctions that imposed smaller though still significant costs on the target and no threat of military force. Unlike the Iraqi case, Congress was reluctant to threaten economic coercion, and in taking action President Bush incurred the wrath of the American–Israeli Public Affairs Committee, one of the most powerful foreign policy lobbies in the United States. Despite all this, coercion was still successful. What accounts for the extent of the target country's concessions?

A second, less obvious, question is what prompts the initial attempt at economic coercion? In both cases, the target governments had taken actions that conflicted with the policy preferences of the United States. While that is clearly part of the answer, it fails to explain why the United States chose to use economic coercion as its preferred policy option. It could have done nothing; it could have tried traditional diplomacy; it could have offered economic inducements; it could have responded with immediate military intervention. Indeed, in the Iraqi case, the United States eventually showed a preference to use force

---

[3] I will use the terms economic coercion, economic statecraft, and economic sanctions interchangeably in the interest of style, but they are technically different. Economic statecraft includes the use of inducements as well as sanctions. In the public perception, economic sanctions are associated with trade-disrupting measures. The definition of economic coercion includes cases of economic sanctions such as those against Iraq, but it also includes episodes such as the Israeli one, which is not commonly thought of as a sanctions case.

[4] Gary Hufbauer and Jeffrey Schott testified before Congress in December 1990 that sanctions would compel Iraq to withdraw from Kuwait, although it could take more than a year. See Pape (1997), n. 3.

instead of relying on economic coercion. In the Israeli case, it could have offered a carrot, as it had done in the past. How do senders choose among their policy options in an international crisis? Under what conditions will a sender attempt economic coercion?

The argument

This book is about the role of economic coercion in international relations. It creates a model to explain the behavior of senders and targets by taking into account their opportunity costs of deadlock and expectation of future conflict with each other. Coercion alters the allocation of benefits by imposing costs on both the sender and target countries. The short-run costs of sanctions imposition are important to the target and sender, but they are not the only factor. Conceding in the face of economic coercion implies a redistribution of political assets between the target and sender. Nation-states care about this redistribution if they think it will harm their bargaining position in future conflicts. This expectation of future conflict is translated into a short-run concern for relative gains and reputation that varies with the expectation of future threats or conflicts in the bilateral relationship between the sender and target.

The expectation of future conflict has a contradictory effect on economic coercion. On the one hand, it makes senders more willing to threaten economic sanctions. The greater the concern for relative gains and reputation, the more likely the sender will prefer a "stalemate" or "deadlock" outcome of disrupted economic exchange and attempt to coerce. *Ceteris paribus*, senders will be eager to coerce adversaries, and reluctant to coerce allies.

The sender's enthusiasm does not translate into greater concessions. The second effect of conflict expectations is paradoxical and surprising. While a robust anticipation of future disputes might make the sender prefer a coercive strategy, it also reduces its ability to obtain concessions. The target's conflict expectations determine the magnitude of concessions. Facing an adversarial sender, the target will be worried about the long-run implications of acquiescing. Because it expects frequent conflicts, the target will be concerned about any concessions in the present undercutting its bargaining position in future interactions. The sender might exploit the material or reputation effects from these concessions in later conflicts. When relative-gains concern is prominent, a concession represents a gain for the coercer

Table 1.1. *The predicted pattern of economic coercion*

	Minimal conflict expectations	Heightened conflict expectations
Large gap in costs	Significant concessions	Moderate concessions
Small gap in costs	No coercion attempt	Minor concessions

and a loss for the coerced. When reputation is important, acquiescence bolsters the sender's credibility as a tough negotiator while weakening the target's reputation. With allies, this concern is less prominent, because the target anticipates fewer zero-sum conflicts. *Ceteris paribus*, targets will concede more to allies than adversaries. Ironically, a sender will obtain the most favorable distribution of payoffs when it cares the least about the relative distribution of gains.

Table 1.1 summarizes the predictions of a conflict expectations model. Between adversaries, senders will be more willing to sanction, even if a target's costs of deadlock are only slightly greater than the sender's own costs. Despite these preferences, it will not be able to extract significant concessions from the coercion attempt. Because the target is also concerned with the future implications of backing down, any concession is a double blow; not only does it lose in the short run, it grants the sender greater leverage in future disputes. While the presence of conflict expectations might make the sanctioner prefer deadlock, it also makes acquiescence less palatable to the sanctioned. Thus, between adversaries, I expect to see sanctions that are frequently costly to the sender and produce only marginal concessions.

Between allies, the sender will be unwilling to threaten economic coercion unless the gap in the costs of sanctions imposition is large. The target's costs of deadlock must be significant and the sender's own costs must be small for the sender to prefer a coercion attempt. Once this threshold is met, however, economic sanctions will be fruitful. Because the target does not anticipate many future conflicts, it will care less about the material and reputational implications of conceding, and more about the immediate costs and benefits. It will concede more to avoid the costs of deadlock. Thus, between allies, I expect to see sanctions that are less costly to the sender, with more productive results.

A conflict expectations model can explain the dynamics of economic coercion with more accuracy and parsimony than any existing explanation. A problem with the existing literature is that it has focused too much on the most publicized cases of economic sanctions, which usually involve adversaries. Because of this sample bias, alternative explanations overlook less contentious but more successful coercion attempts between allies. In focusing on a limited subset of coercion cases, these writings have painted a distorted picture of economic sanctions. These arguments are not necessarily wrong, but their effects are much smaller than their proponents claim. In contrast to a conflict expectations model, they explain fewer cases, and less of the variation in outcomes.

Why economic coercion matters

Why should anyone care about economic statecraft? Two reasons, one for the pragmatist and one for the theorist. The practical reason is that the incidence of economic sanctions has multiplied since the end of the cold war, without a similar increase in policy analysis. The esoteric reason is that an examination of economic statecraft can illuminate the nature of power in international relations.

The use of economic statecraft in international relations has a long pedigree. The Athenian boycott of Megara helped to trigger the Peloponnesian war. The trading empires of Venice, Portugal, and the Netherlands used economic warfare to limit the power of their rivals. Early Anglo-American relations were consumed with issues of economic diplomacy; a chief complaint in the Declaration of Independence is the "Cutting off our Trade with all Parts of the World." Woodrow Wilson believed that the "economic, peaceful, silent deadly remedy" of economic sanctions could be used by the League of Nations to police international society. Nazi Germany was particularly aggressive at cultivating economic dependency from its eastern European neighbors. The US embargo of Japan in the late 1930s contributed to the Japanese attack on Pearl Harbor.[5]

[5] On the Athenian boycott, see Thucydides, *History of the Peloponnesian War*, p. 73; Ellings (1985), pp. 17–18, and HSE (1990a), pp. 4–5. On the uses of economic coercion

The end of the cold war has sparked a renaissance in the use of economic statecraft. The United States has been the most prominent and prolific actor to employ economic coercion. The National Association of Manufacturers asserts that between 1992 and 1996 the United States imposed or threatened economic sanctions sixty times against thirty-five different countries, affecting 42 percent of the world's population.[6] These sanctions are estimated to exact an annual cost of close to $20 billion in lost exports.[7] Richard Haass, writing in *Foreign Affairs*, goes further, observing: "What is noteworthy ... is not just the frequency with which sanctions are used but their centrality; economic sanctions are increasingly at the core of US foreign policy."[8]

The United States is the most noticeable actor employing economic statecraft; it is hardly the only one. The United Nations Security Council implemented sanctions seven times in 1994 alone, as opposed to mandating sanctions only twice in its first forty-five years.[9] The Russian Federation has employed economic coercion as a way of extracting political concessions from the Baltic republics and the Commonwealth of Independent States. Lesser powers such as Greece, Turkey, and Nigeria have used economic coercion as an element of their regional foreign policies. Even non-state actors are employing this tool. In December 1996, De Beers threatened to boycott all purchases of Russian diamonds unless the government acquiesced to granting the South African company monopoly control over its raw diamond exports.[10]

There is every reason to believe that the prominence of economic coercion will increase in the future. Over the course of the past century, major powers have been increasingly reluctant to use or threaten force, while at the same time demonstrating a growing eagerness to employ economic coercion.[11] Bosnia, Chechnya, and Somalia have highlighted the costs of military intervention for the

---

between 1400 and 1800, see Ellings (1985), pp. 18–21 and Irwin (1991). On the Anglo-American economic warfare, see Renwick (1981), chapter 1. For Wilson's belief in the power of economic sanctions, see Daoudi and Dajani (1983), p. 26; for cases of League of Nations sanctions, see Doxey (1980), chapter 4. Hirschman (1945) provides the best account of Nazi economic statecraft in the 1930s. The US embargo of Japan is discussed in HSE (1990b), pp. 53–61.

[6] Schlesinger (1997), p. 8.
[7] Hufbauer, Elliott, Cyrus, and Winston (1997).
[8] Haass (1997), p. 74.   [9] Pape (1997).
[10] *OMRI Daily Digest*, "De Beers issues ultimatum to Russia," December 19, 1996.
[11] Pollins (1994).

great powers. Unless the use of force is quick and successful, militarized disputes sap a nation's resources and create a domestic political backlash against the sender government. As public resistance to military interventions increases, and as foreign aid budgets are slashed, policy-makers are turning more and more to economic coercion as an attractive substitute to advance the national interest.[12]

With the increased popularity of this policy tool comes the need for a better understanding of how it works. Analyzing foreign policy is like honing a knife. A sharper knife makes a cleaner cut; a well-understood policy option makes for well-executed policies. However, as the next section will show, the existing literature is of limited use to policy-makers. Most of the scholarly and policy discussions of economic sanctions consist of debates about high-profile cases. Policy-makers have a disturbing tendency to ignore explicit theory but to use analogies to celebrated cases as a poor substitute. A clear model of coercion can provide statesmen with a strategic knowledge that, combined with their knowledge of the specific dispute, allows them to bridge the gap between theory and policy.[13]

The second reason for studying economic coercion is to address the relationship between power and interdependence. Power is the currency of world politics. International relations theorists have always appreciated the power of the sword, but disagree about the importance, utility, and definition of economic power. Modern realism developed in reaction to the Wilsonian faith in economic power to regulate international politics. Not surprisingly, realists tend to denigrate the utility of economic statecraft. Neoliberal institutionalism developed in reaction to the realist paradigm; neoliberals believe that economic interdependence can affect the behavior of nation-states for the better.[14]

This debate is not trivial. If economic sanctions are a potent tool of diplomacy, then world politics can be much less violent than it was in the past.[15] Neoliberals argue that increased interdependence in the modern world will cause states to act in a more cooperative fashion, because it increases the costs of defection. The prisoner's dilemma shows the importance of sanctions to neoliberals. In a world full of

---

[12] Rogers (1996).   [13] George (1993).

[14] Keohane and Nye (1978).

[15] This is not meant to imply that economic coercion has no human costs. The UN sanctions imposed against Iraq have had a serious humanitarian impact on that nation's citizenry. See Lopez and Cortright (1997) and Buck, Gallant, and Nossal (1998).

prisoner's dilemmas, states will go it alone unless they expect to be punished for defecting. Increased levels of economic interdependence, it is argued, make punitive but peaceful strategies possible in a number of different arenas. Joseph Nye notes, "Interdependence does not mean harmony. Rather, it often means unevenly balanced mutual dependence. Just as the less enamored of the two lovers may manipulate the other, the less vulnerable of two states may use subtle threats to their relationship as a source of power."[16] For cooperation to be a stable outcome, countries must believe that it is best to avoid being the target of sanctions.[17] Robert Axelrod and Robert Keohane note: "When sanctioning problems are severe, cooperation is in danger of collapse ... To explain the incidence and severity of sanctioning problems, we need to focus on the conditions that determine whether defection can be prevented through decentralized retaliation."[18] Axelrod and Keohane use the term "sanctions" to mean a variety of punitive measures, but economic coercion would certainly be a prominent example.

Neoliberals assume that potent economic sanctions provide an incentive for cooperation. That assumption cannot go unexamined. If neoliberals are correct, then it is possible for the power of the sword to be trumped by the power of gold. If they are not correct, then states may blunder into war because their faith in economic statecraft is misplaced, and the description of the world as a manageable prisoner's dilemma is inaccurate. The better we understand the dynamics of economic coercion, the better we can evaluate the effect of interdependence on international interactions.

The literature

In 1945, Albert Hirschman argued in *National Power and the Structure of Foreign Trade* that great powers could use economic coercion to extract concessions from weaker states. Hirschman's analysis capped two decades of writings that thought of economic coercion as a potent diplomatic tool.[19] That belief faded quickly with the onset of the cold

---

[16] Nye (1990), p. 158. See also Crawford (1994).

[17] See Oye (1986), Axelrod (1984), Rosecrance (1986), and Buzan (1984).

[18] Axelrod and Keohane (1986), p. 236.

[19] Hirschman (1945); Daoudi and Dajani (1983). See Wagner (1988) for a sophisticated evaluation of Hirschman's approach.

war. Since then, pundits and policy-makers have disparaged the use of sanctions in foreign policy:[20]

> George Kennan: "There have been suggestions that we should withhold m.f.n. treatment, and indeed discourage trade itself, as a means of extorting political concessions generally ... This idea seems to me to be quite unsound; it is in any case impracticable."

> Richard Nixon: "Some people think of economic leverage as the punitive use of economic sanctions, with highly publicized conditions set for their removal. This is highly ineffective, and sometimes counterproductive."

> George Shultz: "As a general proposition, I think the use of trade sanctions as an instrument of diplomacy is a bad idea ... Our using it here, there and elsewhere to try to affect some other country's behavior ... basically has not worked."

> Milton Friedman: "All in all, economic sanctions are not an effective weapon of political warfare."

> *Time*: "Economic sanctions have rarely been successful."

> *US News and World Report*: "The problem with sanctions is that, more often than not, they fail to achieve results."

> *Far Eastern Economic Review*: "Of the many arguments against economic sanctions, we have always found the most persuasive is the simplest: they don't work."[21]

This disdain mirrors the scholarly community's consensus about sanctions. David Baldwin, who provides the most authoritative survey of prior work, observes, "The two most salient characteristics of the literature on economic statecraft are scarcity and the nearly universal tendency to denigrate the utility of such tools of foreign policy."[22] A first cut of this literature would seem to confirm this assessment. Consider the following statements:

> Johan Galtung: "In this article the conclusion about the probable effectiveness of economic sanctions is, generally, negative."

---

[20] Even Hollywood is derisive; in the 1997 movie *Air Force One*, Harrison Ford, playing the President, denounces a policy of applying economic sanctions to terrorist states as "cowardly."

[21] Nixon, Shultz, Friedman, and *Time* quotations from Daoudi and Dajani (1983), pp. 47, 184–7; Kennan (1977), p. 220; *US News and World Report*, "Sanctions: the pluses and minuses," October 31, 1994, p. 58; *Far Eastern Economic Review*, "Sanctioning Burma," May 8, 1997, p. 5.

[22] Baldwin (1985), p. 51.

Peter Wallensteen: "[T]he general picture of the sanctions is that they are highly unsuccessful in bringing about the compliance desired."

Henry Bienen and Robert Gilpin: "With very few exceptions and under highly unusual sets of circumstances, economic sanctions have historically proven to be an ineffective means to achieve foreign policy objectives."

Margaret Doxey: "The record of international sanctions of a non-military kind, even when applied within an organizational frame-work, suggests that on their own they will not succeed in drastically altering the foreign or domestic policy of the target."

Makio Miyagawa: "Notwithstanding such serious impacts upon the target countries, economic sanctions have only rarely achieved the declared goals."

Abram Chayes and Antonia Handler Chayes: "When economic sanctions are used, they tend to be leaky. Results are slow and not particularly conducive to changing behavior."

Robert Pape: "[E]conomic sanctions have little independent useful-ness for [the] pursuit of noneconomic goals."[23]

These are strong statements from a profession accustomed to hedging.

A second cut at the literature reveals two distinct strains of analysis of the sanctions issue. One set of explanations, the domestic politics approach, focuses on the politics within the sender and target coun-tries. The decision to initiate sanctions is caused by the domestic pressure within the sender country. The outcome of a sanctions effort will most likely be failure because of the domestic politics within the target country. The second set of arguments, the signaling approach, focuses on systemic variables to explain why economic coercion is often imposed but rarely profitable.

According to the domestic politics approach, if the target country's behavior violates international norms, citizens in sender countries will feel compelled to "do something." Even if the foreign policy leader agrees with public opinion, the costs of effective military intervention may be too high. On the other hand, the domestic political costs of doing nothing are substantial, because it creates the image of a weak leader. The lack of options leaves the sender regime hamstrung.

[23] Galtung (1967), p. 409; Wallensteen (1968), pp. 249–50; Bienen and Gilpin (1980), p. 89; Doxey (1987), p. 92; Miyagawa (1992), p. 206; Chayes and Chayes (1995), p. 2; Pape (1997), p. 93. For other pessimistic observations, see Knorr (1975), pp. 205–6; von Amerongen (1980), p. 165; Blessing (1981), p. 533; Willett and Jalalighajar (1983), p. 718; Lindsay (1986), p. 154; Hendrickson (1994), pp. 22–3; Barber (1995), p. 29.

Senders will turn to economic statecraft as an imperfect substitute for forceful action. Economic coercion can deflect domestic pressure and register the sender regime's disapproval of the target's actions without going to war. The sanctions themselves might be ineffective, but their implementation allows the foreign policy leader to avoid accusations of do-nothing leadership.

Many authors have proposed all or part of this rationale. James Barber observes: "The purpose of sanctions here is to demonstrate a willingness and capacity to act. Negatively, the purpose may simply be to anticipate or deflect criticism."[24] M. S. Daoudi and M. S. Dajani concur: "The imposition of sanctions absorbs the initial public reaction that something needs to be done."[25] Ivan Eland concludes:

> Bluntly stated, most of the times a nation imposes sanctions on another country, it has few policy options. The target nation usually has committed an unacceptable act and intense domestic pressure, particularly in democratic states, to "do something" can persuade the government in the sanctioning nation to respond by imposing sanctions to meet goals other than target compliance."[26]

The literature is rife with assertions like these.[27] From a foreign policy perspective, rational calculation plays a limited role; from a domestic politics perspective, economic statecraft serves as a steam valve to relieve governments from the pressure of their populace. In this explanation, sanctions are symbols; their effectiveness is of secondary concern.

Domestic-level explanations provide three factors working against the utility of economic coercion. First, given the causes of sanctions imposition, their implementation will be erratic and haphazard. Thus, the target country may not be inconvenienced at all. Second, even if the sanctions are potent, target governments can use the specter of international coercion to create a "rally-round-the-flag" effect. Domestic groups line up behind the government in reaction to an external threat. To do otherwise would smack of disloyalty. There are psychological factors which reinforce this effect. Johan Galtung's study of Rhodesia noted that the mutual sacrifices created by the sanctions led

---

[24] Barber (1979), p. 380.
[25] Daoudi and Dajani (1983), p. 161.
[26] Eland (1995), p. 29.
[27] See Renwick (1981), p. 85; Schreiber (1973), p. 413; Hoffman (1967), p. 154; Daoudi and Dajani (1983), appendix II; Haass (1998).

to an *esprit de corps* among the citizenry and a closer identification with the government.[28]

The third reason is that target governments may, for domestic reasons, *prefer* to be sanctioned. In the long run, sanctions hurt the trade-oriented sectors of the economy by depriving them of income. At the same time, an embargo strengthens import-substitution sectors by giving them rent-seeking opportunities. Since export sectors will prefer the target government to acquiesce, a lengthy sanctions dispute can politically weaken the foreign policy leader's domestic opponents. This is particularly true if the target regime is authoritarian. Sanctions permit target regimes to strengthen state control over the economy, and readjust the impact of sanctions policies away from its most powerful supporters. For example, when the UK-led coalition imposed sanctions against Rhodesia, household incomes for black families fell, while white incomes rose. Serbian leader Slobodan Milosevic used the United Nations embargo to reward crony enterprises with scarce goods, while punishing his political rivals. United Nations aid to Iraq has freed up funds for Saddam Hussein to reward his inner elite.[29]

general sanctions hurt population/opposition & allow leaders to shift rents to elite

For economic coercion to work, target elites must suffer as much as target populations. Case studies of Uganda have shown that the sanctions to remove Idi Amin became more effective when Great Britain halted the export of luxury goods. This hurt the Ugandan army elite, which relied on the "whiskey runs" for creature comforts. Accounts of the sanctions against Haiti after 1990 revealed that the Haitian military regime was willing to negotiate only after the Clinton administration prevented the Haitian armed forces from acquiring oil or weapons on the global market.[30]

smart sanctions can hurt regimes & bring to negotiating table

The half-hearted motivations of sender governments, combined with backlash effects within the target country, make it extremely difficult for economic sanctions to generate concessions. A domestic politics approach produces several hypotheses, as seen in Table 1.2. Sanctions are more likely to be initiated when the sender is a

---

[28] Galtung (1967).

[29] On Rhodesia, see Losman (1979), pp. 112–13, and Rowe (1993). On Serbia, see Woodward (1995), p. 148 and Licht (1995), p. 158. On Iraq, see Wright and Daniszewski, "Hussein may be main beneficiary of UN aid effort," p. A1, and more generally, Reuther (1995), pp. 125–7.

[30] On Uganda, see Miller (1980), p. 124, and Ullman (1978), pp. 532–3; on Haiti, see Werleigh (1995), p. 168. More generally, see Morgan and Schwebach (1996).

Table 1.2. *Existing approaches to economic coercion*

	Domestic politics	Signaling
Causes of coercion attempt	1. Domestic pressure on the sender regime 2. Lack of palatable alternatives	1. Desire to signal future actions
Causes of coercion outcome	1. Ability of target regime to use sanctions to its own political advantage	1. Cost of the signal to the sender 2. Implicit threats of power projection or military force 3. Ability of the sender country to attract multilateral cooperation
Coercion is more likely to be attempted if:	1. The potential sender is a democracy 2. The target is geographically distant from the sender	1. No predicted pattern
Coercion is more likely to generate concessions if:	1. The target regime is domestically unstable 2. Sanctions hurt the target elites as much as the general population	1. The sanctions are costly to the sender 2. Military force is also threatened or used 3. The sender attracts international cooperation

democracy. Public opinion to do something should resonate more with foreign policy leaders facing electoral pressures. It is also argued that sanctions will be used primarily when the sender cannot use more persuasive means of statecraft. Therefore, states will use economic coercion when the costs of military intervention are too great. If the target is physically distant, power projection becomes a more difficult enterprise, and sanctions are therefore more likely.[31]

[31] This hypothesis does not test domestic-level variables, but still comes from a domestic-level approach. An implicit assumption of this level of analysis is that international factors constrain the sender regime from acting more forcefully. Therefore, this hypothesis must be true for domestic factors to have an appreciable effect.

Two predictions can also be made about the likelihood of sanctions success. First, if the target government is domestically unstable, it may lack the means to convert a sanctions dispute into political support. Such a government would be more likely to acquiesce so as to hold on to power, or be removed in favor of those who prefer accommodation. Second, if target elites are made to suffer as much as target populations, there is no opportunity for rent-seeking, which puts elite pressure on the target government to concede.

The signaling approach to economic statecraft has little to say about the initiation of sanctions, but pays more attention to variables affecting the outcome. Two factors are frequently cited. The first is the background assumption that without a high degree of international cooperation, sanctions are useless. International trade theory suggests that for a homogeneous good with a high substitution elasticity, only a sender coalition responsible for more than half the supply of that good can influence the terms of trade.[32] Few individual sender countries have this capability, and when they do it is usually ephemeral. Therefore, for sanctions to have any influence, international cooperation is necessary. This explains the overwhelming focus in the literature on multilateral cases of economic coercion. Obtaining international cooperation is exceedingly difficult, however.[33] As more countries join in the coercion attempt, the sanctions coalition gets more unwieldy. There is a greater incentive for individual countries to free ride, permit illicit trade, and pocket increased profits.[34] Because of the difficulties in sustaining multilateral cooperation, the signaling approach is skeptical about the prospect of economic coercion succeeding on its own merits.

While sanctions rarely generate concessions, they can function as effective signals. This argument rests on the assumption that states conduct foreign policy in a world of imperfect information. If states are uninformed about other states' preferences, there is always an incentive to bluff in international crises. For example, if the United

---

[32] Gardner and Kimbrough (1990).

[33] See Bayard, Pelzman, and Perez-Lopez (1980), Doxey (1980, 1987), Martin (1992), Mastanduno (1992), Mansfield (1995), Kaempfer and Lowenberg (1997), and Drezner (1998) for more on cooperation and economic sanctions.

[34] Even if states nominally comply with multilateral sanctions, individual firms may be tempted. This was certainly the case with Yugoslavia's neighbors in the early 1990s. See Raymond Bonner, "How sanctions bit Serbia's neighbors," *New York Times*, November 19, 1995, section 4, p. 3.

States threatens to use force against a target country and the target acquiesces, it has won without having to carry out its threat. The possibility of a costless victory creates an incentive to make even empty threats. Unless the target country knows the extent of US willingness to use force, it will have difficulty distinguishing between a credible threat and cheap talk.

Because of imperfect information, states frequently engage in signaling techniques to demonstrate credibility. Some acts, such as the mobilization of troops, can signal that rhetoric will be translated into action if the sender's demands are not met. Economic sanctions can be thought of as another type of signal. The key to a successful signal is to take an action that will separate credible threats from cheap talk. For this reason, a costly signal is better than a cheap signal. If a signal is costly, a bluffing sender is less likely to use it because of its price.[35]

According to this argument, economic sanctions are ineffective as coercive tools, but may be useful as signals. Their value as a signal comes not from the damage inflicted on the target, but the cost to the sender. David Baldwin notes in *Economic Statecraft*: "Other things being equal, it is always desirable to minimize costs; but other things are not equal. The selection of a costly method of conveying a signal may add credibility to the signal. Thus, a statesman interested in demonstrating resolve may want to avoid the less expensive means of communication."[36] In a world of cloudy signals, policies that prove costly to the sender can be an excellent means of conveying information.

Lisa Martin makes a similar argument about the relationship between the sender's costs and acquiring multilateral cooperation for sanctions. She observes that potential allies in the sanctioning effort need to be convinced of the sender's commitment. Costly sanctions by a great power can convince other states to join in the sanctioning effort; the high costs act as a signal of the great power's seriousness of intent.[37] Thus, a costly signal of sanctions helps to send a credible signal to other possible senders as well as the target.

Note the implicit argument that runs through this entire line of reasoning. According to this logic, unilateral economic sanctions cannot work on their own. They are only effective if they act as a signal that stronger measures, like multilateral embargoes or military

[35] Schelling (1960), Fearon (1994).
[36] Baldwin (1985), p. 372.   [37] Martin (1992), pp. 36–8.

intervention, will be taken in the future. The causal argument in this school of thought is that what appears to be a sanctions success is actually the product of an implicit military threat. Sanctions, therefore, are not a true cause of concessions, but merely an observable signal of military power.[38]

This logic is consistent with empirical claims that the few successes ascribed to economic coercion are really examples of successful military threats.[39] Recent examples also provide support. US sanctions against Haiti from 1990 to 1994 were successful in removing the military junta in power and reinstalling Jean-Bertrand Aristide as president. Through the fog of history, it would be easy for future scholars to argue that the sanctions caused the outcome. That would obviously overlook the crucial role of the US military threat. The Haitian leadership acquiesced when they were told by American negotiators that the US 82nd Airborne Division was on its way. Sanctions may have assisted in the return of Aristide, but the chief cause was the threat of force.

Table 1.2 shows the empirical tests that can be derived from a signaling explanations. There are clear hypotheses about the likelihood of sanctions success. First, if the sender incurs significant costs in its sanctions attempt, the credible signal is more likely to produce concessions. If the signal fails to work, then economic coercion will only work if it is associated with companion policies that genuinely produce concessions. Multilateral cooperation in the sanctions effort is expected to generate concessions. Also, if there are threats of military or quasi-military intervention in the dispute, the target is more likely to acquiesce for obvious reasons, even though economic coercion is not the cause.

Reviewing the literature, one can see a confluence of domestic and international factors leading to the same conclusion: economic statecraft rarely works. Sanctions are initiated because other options are not feasible, and the sender regime wishes to placate domestic pressures to take action. They have little chance of success. Domestic politics within the target country will lead to defiance. Unless sanctions attract significant multilateral cooperation, and hurt target elites as much as the population, they will not force acquiescence. Since these conditions are difficult to achieve, economic pressure will rarely

[38] Lenway (1988), and Morgan and Schwebach (1997) also make this observation.
[39] Knorr (1975), Schreiber (1973), and Pape (1997).

be the causal mechanism for target concessions. More likely, costly sanctions act as a signal of stronger measures and convince the target to back down.

Flaws in the literature

And that, it would appear, is that. It would be comforting to think that political scientists have successfully described at least one corner of the foreign policy arena. It would also be wrong.

Economic sanctions are more effective than the literature claims. Gary Hufbauer, Jeffrey Schott, and Kimberly Ann Elliott have created a database of 116 sanctions cases.[40] They code the success of the episode, as traditionally defined, into one of four categories, ranging from outright failure to complete success. If the most stringent definition of success is used, more than 35 percent of the cases qualify as a success. Less than 30 percent of the cases listed fall into the category of complete failure. In many of these successes, there was no observed threat of military force, no multilateral cooperation, and nor were the sanctions particularly costly to the sender. This evidence hardly suggests that sanctions always work, but it calls into doubt the hypothesis that they always fail.

Why is there such a discrepancy? The first problem is one of definition. The question phrased in the literature is "do sanctions work?" This is too simplistic. M. S. Daoudi and M. S. Dajani comment: "Most studies have assumed that the objectives of economic sanctions were to return to the status quo that prevailed prior to the act of aggression which brought the sanctions about. In reality, the aims of sanctions have been consistently less ambitious."[41] Scholars compare the sanctions outcome with the status quo ante (i.e. before the action that prompted sanctions) to determine the success of a coercion event. This is the wrong counterfactual; the hypothetical alternative is the outcome if coercion was not attempted in the first place. If the targeted country does not change its policies at all, then the event should be judged a failure. If there is some compromise, however, and the value of the concession outweighs the sender's costs of coercion, then the episode counts as a partial success.

The degree of success also depends upon the type of demand.

[40] HSE (1990a, 1990b). Pape (1997) argues that many of these cases are miscoded.
[41] Daoudi and Dajani (1983), p. 2.

Baldwin notes: "A moderate degree of success in accomplishing a difficult task may seem more impressive than a high degree of success in accomplishing an easy task. In assessing statecraft, as in judging diving contests, scores should be adjusted for the level of difficulty."[42] These nuances are overlooked in the simple dichotomy of success/failure made in the literature.

The second problem is the tenuous link between international relations theory and the sanctions literature. Most of the recent contributions on economic statecraft consist of well-crafted theories that lack empirical support,[43] or well-crafted case studies that produce generalizations of dubious quality.[44] The literature often overlooks theoretical developments that blunt the utility of their causal mechanisms. Consider the effect of domestic politics on both the sender and the target country. It is theoretically unclear whether the sender is more likely to succeed if there is domestic support for sanctions or if there is some political opposition. On the one hand, the two-level games approach argues that unanimous domestic support enhances the sender's bargaining position because it reduces the likelihood of the sender reversing its strategy.[45] On the other hand, an incomplete information approach would make the opposite claim: domestic audience costs send an effective signal of resolve to the target country. Now consider the effect of domestic politics within the target country. The domestic politics approach argues that the more vulnerable target elites are to sanctions, the more likely that they will acquiesce. A rational choice perspective would suggest an alternative outcome, however. If sanctions narrow the ruling coalition within the target country, it could force the decision-maker into a more hardline bargaining position. A weakened leader who cannot afford to alienate a narrow coalition of hardliners will stand firm. A leader with a broader base of support, or one insulated from public opinion, has the luxury to concede without fearing the collapse of the target regime.

These contradictory effects within the target and sender countries suggest that the sanctions literature exaggerates the absolute effect of domestic politics on economic coercion. It is possible that both the two-level games approach and the audience cost approach are correct, but that in most situations, the effects cancel each other out. Similarly,

---

[42] Baldwin (1985), p. 372.
[43] See Tsebelis (1990), Eaton and Engers (1992), Smith (1996).
[44] Cortright and Lopez (1995), Klotz (1996).
[45] Moravscik (1993), pp. 29–30.

the opposing effects of sanctions within the target country's ruling coalition could lead to the overall insignificance of domestic politics. Empirically, this would mean that although isolated cases would show the importance of domestic politics, the aggregate effect would be minor.

Finally, the sanctions literature is also guilty of numerous methodological sins.[46] First, almost all of the arguments use an inductive approach; theories about economic statecraft are developed only after an examination of case studies. Under Arend Lijphart's typology, most of these works are interpretive case studies.[47] The concern is not with theory, but with explaining the specific event. As such, few of the derived propositions have the necessary fecundity to be useful in other issue areas. The inductive approach causes researchers to ignore important variables or questions raised by broader approaches to international relations. Case selection exacerbates these problems. Most of these writings focus on the more celebrated cases of sanctions. Open a book on economic sanctions and most of its pages will be devoted to the following cases: the League of Nations sanctions on Italy; CoCom's strategic embargo of technology exports to the communist bloc; and UN sanctions against Rhodesia, South Africa, Iraq, and/or Serbia. Several theories of economic coercion have been developed almost exclusively from these cases.[48]

Certainly these sanctions cases are well known, but they do not necessarily represent the universe of observations. Their very celebrity suggests they are atypical; they are important because they stand out in some unusual way. In most of the cases, the primary sender had multilateral assistance and backing from an international organization. The demands made of the target country were non-negotiable. The primary sender and target were adversaries. The sanctions policy usually failed. By choosing cases that take on extreme values of both the dependent variable and several independent variables, the literature commits two errors. First, there is a tendency to underestimate the main causal effects on the universe of events. Second, these

---

[46] In many ways the problems are similar to the extensive literature on deterrence theory. The criticisms presented here also have a parallel in that literature. See Achen and Snidal (1989).

[47] Lijphart (1971).

[48] See Adler-Karlsson (1968), Losman (1979), Renwick (1981), Doxey (1987), Leyton-Brown (1987), Mastanduno (1992), Cortright and Lopez (1995), Haass (1998).

studies will overestimate effects that are unique to the extreme set of cases.[49]

The conflict expectations model predicts this sort of sample bias. Since disputes between adversaries are noisier than coercion attempts between allies, the best-known cases are more likely to look like failures. By developing arguments inductively from a biased set of observations, the existing theories can at best explain a subset of the data on economic coercion. Consider the two cases at the beginning of this chapter. There has been plenty of attention devoted to the United Nations sanctioning of Iraq. There has been much less scholarly literature on the US economic coercion of Israel.

These definitional and methodological problems do not mean that the existing explanations are incorrect. They do suggest that the empirical evidence marshaled for their arguments is insufficient. The ideal way to evaluate alternative theories is to tease out contrasting hypotheses, and then test the hypotheses against the appropriate sample to see which explanation has more validity. This book will test the conflict expectations model against alternative domestic and systemic approaches using a variety of different methodologies.

The methodology

This book will use game theory to develop the conflict expectations model. Instead of words and sentences, symbols and equations are used to develop theoretical results. Game theory is valuable as a modeling tool, but it can also be off-putting. For many political scientists, it seems like an attempt at obfuscation rather than clarification. Game theorists talk in their own language, have their own unstated assumptions, and seem much more comfortable with algebraic manipulation than the rest of the political science community. This is a tragedy, because the goal of formal modeling is to clarify, not confuse.

There is a motive to the mathematics. It lays bare all of the assumptions made in the theory. It makes plain the causal mechanisms that drive the model. It is easier to critique and evaluate a model which is explicit in its assumptions than to deconstruct more opaque verbal treatments on the same subject. Game theory explicitly compares and contrasts equilibrium outcomes with counterfactual possi-

---

[49] Collier and Mahoney (1996).

bilities. In writing this book, I have tried to keep the use of technical language to a minimum. The aim is for international relations theorists to understand intuitively the dynamics of the model without wading through pages of equations.

To test the conflict expectations model against alternative explanations, I will use a variety of quantitative and qualitative methodologies. As noted previously, one of the problems with earlier work on economic sanctions is the tendency to draw conclusions from one big case, even though there exists a sufficient number of recorded sanctions episodes to permit statistical testing.

There is an ongoing debate in international relations on the validity of statistical tests versus case studies. This debate overlooks the common-sense idea of "triangulation"; a robust explanatory model should find empirical support using different testing methodologies. Statistics, comparative analysis, and case studies all have their advantages in hypothesis testing. Statistics can demonstrate significant correlations across a large number of events. Usually, however, the data are far too coarse to permit any serious examination of the causal mechanisms. Charles Ragin's comparative method uses the logic of Boolean algebra to test for combinations of causes.[50] His approach has the benefit of allowing for a greater causal complexity, and can generate significant results with far fewer cases. On the other hand, this method is extremely vulnerable to measurement error and oversensitive to outliers. Structured, focused comparison and the process-tracing of individual cases has the singular advantage of identifying causal mechanisms with a smaller chance of producing spurious results.[51] The small sample inherently limits the generalizability of the results. Each of these methodological approaches has flaws. Used in concert, however, they can offer compelling support to bolster or reject a hypothesis. Increasing the diversity of testing procedures show that large-N and small-N approaches can complement each other in the testing of international relations theory.

The rest of the book

Chapter 2 outlines the conflict expectations model of economic coercion and spells out the testable implications of that model. The key variables are the opportunity costs of imposing sanctions for the

---

[50] See Ragin (1987).   [51] See George and McKeown (1985).

target and the sender, and the bilateral expectations of future conflict. The model predicts that as the sender's costs of deadlock increase, economic coercion is both less likely and less fruitful. As the target's costs increase, sanctions are more probable and more profitable. The model also shows that conflict expectations have a contradictory effect on the dynamics of economic coercion. On the one hand, an adversarial relationship will make the initiation of a coercion attempt more likely. On the other hand, it limits the usefulness of the attempt. Between adversaries, economic pressure should be common but of marginal use. Between allies, economic pressure should be less frequent, but also more successful.

These hypotheses will be tested in the later chapters by using a combination of statistical, comparative, and process-tracing methodologies. Chapter 3 is a plausibility probe. It reviews the results of earlier statistical studies to see whether existing explanations in the literature have any explanatory power relative to the conflict expectations model. Several well-known cases of economic coercion will also be looked at to see if they support the conventional wisdom or the model presented here. Chapter 4 proceeds with new statistical tests of the conditions under which a sender will threaten sanctions, and the eventual size of target's concessions. These results provide strong support for the conflict expectations model, and call into doubt the general applicability of the alternative arguments.

The rest of the book uses comparative case studies and process-tracing of individual cases to see whether the causal mechanisms of expected costs and the concern for relative gains are present. Chapters 5, 6 and 7 chronicle Russia's use of economic coercion against the newly independent states of the former Soviet Union. The breakup of the Soviet Union provides a "natural" experiment to test models of economic coercion. Russia possessed several economic levers over the other post-Soviet states, and Russia's formal demands were constant across the newly independent states, yet the concessions varied by country. Chapter 5 looks at Russia's ability to coerce. Chapter 6 details the instances of economic coercion used across all fourteen of the newly independent states. Chapter 7 uses Boolean analysis to explore the variation in attempts and concessions across all fourteen of the newly independent states.

Chapter 8 compares the role of sanctions and inducements in economic statecraft. I argue that the expectation of future conflict limits the usefulness of both carrots and sticks in negotiating with adversaries. Only under a narrow set of conditions will the sender be willing to use economic inducements with adversaries. Therefore, senders are often forced to choose between belligerent threats of military conflict or economic statecraft that is limited in its productivity. This hypothesis is tested by process-tracing United States economic diplomacy in two instances: South Korea's efforts to acquire nuclear weapons in the mid-1970s, and North Korea's efforts to acquire nuclear weapons in the early 1990s. Both countries faced roughly equal costs of not acquiescing to US pressure. Because North Korea anticipated far more future disputes than South Korea, however, it was worried about the material and reputational implications of acquiescing. It would not concede without the carrot.

Chapter 9 summarizes the theoretical and empirical results. The robustness of the conflict expectations model provides some suggestions for both theory and policy. Theoretically, the results suggest that interdependence does not necessarily lead to enhanced economic power. Furthermore, economic power is not a universally applicable tool of diplomacy. These results also question the role that international organizations play in regulating economic exchange. Pragmatically, the results suggest that economic coercion has a place in the tools of statecraft, but that place is narrowly defined. In particular, it is of limited use against adversaries. The model developed here also sheds some light on three current policy debates in the United States: the engagement or containment of "rogue states," the madating of sanctions by the US Congress, and the use of extraterritorial sanctions to ensure multilateral cooperation.

I   Theory and data

2   A model of economic coercion

This chapter develops a theory of economic coercion that incorporates conflict expectations. The goal is to answer the questions raised in chapter 1. When will countries threaten economic coercion? When will the targeted countries concede? How large will their concessions be?

All models start with assumptions. This chapter starts by elaborating the two substantive assumptions made in this book. First, governments act as rational unitary actors. Second, states that anticipate frequent political conflicts will be more concerned about the distributional and reputational effects of influence attempts in the present. When actors expect future disagreements, they will care more about the relative distribution of political assets, and more about their reputation for toughness. Because adversaries anticipate more clashes than allies, alignment is a useful empirical measure of conflict expectations.

The chapter then develops a simple extended-form game of economic coercion. The model shows that the strategies of the two countries depend on the opportunity costs of a stalemate outcome and the expectations of future conflict. As the target country's opportunity costs of deadlock rise, sanctions are less likely and less useful. Conflict expectations have a contradictory effect on economic coercion. On the one hand, when both countries anticipate numerous disputes, the sender will be more likely to use economic sanctions as a foreign policy lever. On the other hand, the target's expectation of frequent conflict will reduce the magnitude of its concessions.

The rest of the chapter considers the implications of relaxing some of the model's technical assumptions. What happens when states realign their position in the international system, altering conflict expectations? The model predicts that it will increase the likelihood of a coercion event, but reduce the sender country's ability to extract meaningful concessions from the target. What happens when demands become non-negotiable? The model predicts that stalemates over indivisible issues are more likely to occur between adversaries than allies, leading to prolonged sanctions imposition. How do senders choose between economic coercion and economic inducements to influence the target. The model argues that senders will be far more willing to use inducements with allies than adversaries. Carrots as well as sticks are of limited use against adversaries; only under a narrow set of circumstances will the sender prefer to offer a carrot over accepting a stalemate outcome. This result suggests that without the willingness to use brute force, even great powers are constrained in their ability to influence an adversary's behavior.

The assumptions

It is impossible to talk about strategic behavior without first delineating who is acting strategically and what motivates their decisions. For the purposes of this model, the actors are the foreign policy leaders of nation-states. It is assumed that the foreign policy regimes within these states act as a unitary, rational actor.

This assumption has been made repeatedly in international relations theory, and the justification for it will not be delved into here.[1] What should be stressed, however, is that this assumption is not as sweeping as would first appear. It implies two things. First, there is a foreign policy leader who has final decision-making authority over a country's foreign affairs. Second, that leader will act strategically to maximize the regime's utility and interests over outcomes. Decision-makers are instrumentally rational; given a set of preferences, leaders will make choices in order to reach their most preferred outcome, as constrained by the decision-making environment.

Once the principle of rationality is accepted, a second, more substantial assumption must be made; how do nation-states order their preferences? I argue that states fashion these preferences in reaction to the capabilities and intentions of the other states in the international system. Foreign policy leaders conceive of a national interest defined as maximizing their welfare and the security of that

---

[1] For more thorough discussions of this argument, see the first chapters in Bueno de Mesquita (1981) and Krasner (1978).

welfare. To further their interests, states will usually act to increase their own income and wealth. A nation-state will care more about the short-run distribution of payoffs if this affects its long-run welfare.

Conflict expectations influence how willing a state is to stand firm in a conflict in two ways. First, states are concerned that concessions can be used later to threaten their security. This possibility leads to an explicit concern for relative gains. This concern becomes more important if states expect frequent disputes. Second, states prefer to have a reputation for tough bargaining. The importance of reputation increases as the likelihood of repeated conflict increases.

The debate about the role of relative gains concern in international relations is a familiar one. For the past decade, it has been couched in terms of the debate between the neoliberal and neorealist paradigms.[2] Realists argue that states must be wary of gaps in gains because of the ever-present possibility that those gaps will be exploited in a future military attack. Neoliberals, by contrast, argue that these factors are salient only under extreme circumstances. This debate is concerned with variables such as polarity and the offense–defense balance to determine the extent of relative gains. The logic developed here sidesteps this debate. It argues that states will care about relative gains if they anticipate that those gaps will reduce their absolute utility in the long run.[3] This could arise from the possibility of a future military conflict, as realists argue. It could also arise from the possibility that a small concession in the present could lead to the long-run disintegration of a state's position on a particular issue. The issue could be the control of a disputed piece of territory, access to raw materials, weapons nonproliferation, or the constraints on controlling a restive population. Whatever the proximate issue area, foreign policy leaders will care about relative gains if they expect that an unequal distribution of gains in the present will lead to reduced benefits in future conflicts.

Concessions made in the present can be translated into future leverage. Robert Keohane observes:

> For relative gains, rather than simply the desire to maximize utility to account for tough negotiations, there must be some plausible way by which one's partner could use advantages gained from the

[2] See Gowa (1986, 1994), Grieco (1988, 1990), Powell (1991), Mearsheimer (1995), and Rousso (1996) for the realist argument. For neoliberal responses, see Snidal (1991), Keohane (1993), Keohane and Martin (1995), and Liberman (1996).
[3] See Viner (1948) and Matthews (1996) for previous arguments along these lines.

international agreement to hurt oneself in a future period, and a significant motivation to do so. Only if the advocate of a relative gains interpretation can show that these conditions are met, is it plausible to entertain this hypothesis.[4]

The subject matter of economic coercion is well suited to Keohane's criteria. When sanctions are imposed, economic leverage is used to extract political concessions. A successful sanctions episode results in an explicit transfer of political assets from the target to the sender. States will be concerned about relative gains due to the possibility of today's concessions becoming tomorrow's leverage. A variety of demands could be used in this fashion. A great power may use economic coercion to secure military basing rights, and those bases are used in a later coercion episode to threaten the targeted country's territory. A demand for greater liberalization within the target regime might permit the sender country to exploit domestic divisions in a later dispute. The importance of the transfer increases as the likelihood of future conflict increases. When a country makes a political concession to a potential aggressor, the decision to acquiesce has a greater probability of coming back to haunt the country in the future.

How important are these transfers? The standard realist argument assumes that between states of unequal power, the concern for relative gains is unimportant, because the distribution of power is already lopsided. Such an argument assumes that all power is fungible, and therefore great powers can readily impose their will on smaller states. Any transfer is of little importance in the overall distribution of power. There are two flaws in this logic, however, that suggest that unequal adversaries will care just as much about material transfers as equal adversaries.

First, some types of concessions have very poor or expensive substitutes. Political assets are more heterogeneous and less substitutable than economic assets. Concessions that transfer information, institutional access or asset-specific investments alter the local distribution of power in a way that other power resources cannot without serious political externalities. For example, in the US dispute with North Korea over its nuclear weapons program, the North Koreans were extremely reluctant to allow special inspections of certain installations. From their public statements, the North Korean leadership believed this concession would have provided the United States

[4] Keohane (1993), p. 281.

with strategic military information that could not have been obtained elsewhere. The United States could have acquired this information through more forceful means, but the repercussions from this sort of power projection would have affected the entire region. This concession was a transfer of asset-specific resources that North Korea perceived as hurting them in future conflicts, despite the differences in power at the aggregate level.[5]

Second, the assumption of fungible power is not necessarily true in the short run. It may be possible to redirect power resources towards a particular target, but it cannot be done immediately, and there are associated opportunity costs with it.[6] While states must keep the aggregate distribution of power in mind, they will be more concerned about the local correlation of forces and policy levers. For example, while the United States holds an overwhelming military and economic advantage over North Korea in terms of aggregate power, that advantage rapidly diminishes when looking only at the military balance of power on the Korean peninsula. Over the long run, the United States could focus more of its power to deal with North Korea, but this would take time and draw resources away from other foreign policy concerns.

The importance of relative transfers depends on the expectation of future conflict. If the concession is significant but the number of expected disputes in the bilateral relationship is small, the relative distribution of payoffs will matter less. Previous game-theoretic models have highlighted the importance of conflict expectations. Robert Powell argues that relative-gains concern is salient when a military attack is expected. The logic developed here includes instances beyond military force, but is consistent with Powell's argument.[7] Duncan Snidal's model concludes that relative gains will be salient when the foreign policy leader's attention is focused on the bilateral dispute.[8] A high expected probability of future confrontations and threats from another state will lead to an enhanced concern for relative gains in bilateral dealings with that state.

Conflict expectations will also affect states through their concern over their bargaining reputation. In a future conflict, foreign policy

---

[5] See chapter 8.
[6] See Nye (1990), for why this is particularly true after the cold war.
[7] It should be noted that Powell himself believed that the model was applicable to instances beyond the fear of a military attack.
[8] Snidal (1991).

leaders will consider the history of prior bilateral negotiations in developing conjectures about the other state's behavior. For example, if a country has a history of acquiescing in the face of deadlock, the other country will have the incentive to act tough in crises, so as to obtain a better outcome. By contrast, if that state has a history of refusing to fold even if that action is costly, the other foreign policy leader will take that history into account in later rounds of negotiations.

The importance of reputation in international relations is as old as the concept of economic sanctions. In the Athenian debate over how to handle the Spartan ultimatum to end the Megarian boycott, Pericles stressed the reputational consequences of backing down:

> Let none of you think that we should be going to war over a trifle if we refuse to revoke the Megarian decree ... for you this trifle is both the assurance and the proof of your determination. If you give in, you will immediately be confronted with some greater demand, since they will think that you only gave way on this point through fear. But if you take a firm stand you will make it clear to them that they will have to treat you properly as equals.[9]

If a nation-state demonstrates that it prefers to incur a costly outcome, provided it hurts the other side even more, it can affect the outcomes of those future conflicts. Furthermore, reputations are interdependent; one state's boost in reputation will come at the expense of the other's.[10] In a crisis, whichever side backs down is perceived to have lost credibility. At the same time, the side that triumphed will find its credibility enhanced. Therefore, leaders must be concerned that backing down in the present will raise the other state's expectation of success in later episodes. A state will care about the distribution of payoffs in the present because this will alter its perceived reputation in other states.

It has been argued that the importance of reputation in international politics is exaggerated.[11] According to this strain of thought, a reputation formed by one set of interactions will not carry over into another confrontation. In other words, if the United States has a reputation for tough negotiations with Japan, this will not affect later conflicts with France. Whatever the merits of this argument, it does not affect the theory presented here. A conflict expectations approach argues that

---

[9] Thucydides, *The History of the Peloponnesian War*, p. 119.
[10] Leng (1983).   [11] Mercer (1996).

reputational concerns are particularly salient because the expected conflicts involve the same actors, as opposed to a diffuse reputation for all international interactions. For example, it could be questioned whether US toughness in the Persian Gulf during Desert Storm translated into reputational benefits in later conflicts in other parts of the globe. In dealing with Iraq, however, the reputation of the United States was enhanced. For five years after the Gulf War, Saddam Hussein acquiesced to a number of United Nations demands in the face of US military threats.

Reputation becomes more important as the expectation of repeated play, and the shadow of the future, increases. If players anticipate that a game will be played often, they will be more willing to sacrifice current gains for a larger payoff in the future. Countries will always have some incentive to be concerned about their reputation. Nevertheless, the incentive will be much stronger when they expect a greater number of potential conflicts. States have both tangible and abstract reasons to factor in conflict expectations when crafting their existing strategies.

Causal empiricism suggests that the expectation of future conflict varies with the dyad. For example, during the cold war, the United States clearly expected more zero-sum disputes with the Soviet Union than with West Germany. At present, India can anticipate a greater number of disagreements with Pakistan than with Bangladesh. For the foreseeable future, the United States is more concerned with the possible North Korean nuclear program than the probable Israeli nuclear program. In each of the cases where more future conflict is expected, one or both states perceive a significant threat from the other. In relationships where threat perception is high, so is the expectation of future zero-sum conflicts.

A logical extension of this argument is that the concern for relative gains and reputation is inversely correlated with the degree of alignment. Allies will anticipate few disputes, and care less about relative gains and reputation. Adversaries will anticipate frequent threats of conflict, and therefore care a great deal about relative gains and reputation.

It is often unclear what theorists mean when they talk about allies, adversaries, or alignment. My definitions are as follows. States are allies if they share a history of cooperation and mutual trust on security and other issues that is not disrupted by shifts in the international distribution of power. States are adversaries if they have a history of discord and conflict on security and other issues that is not disrupted by shifts in the international distribution of power. By allies I do not mean states that temporarily join coalitions to fight a common enemy, such as the United States and the Soviet Union in World War II or the United States and Syria in the Gulf War. By adversaries I do not mean states that have highly public but ephemeral spats over a single issue, such as the dispute between France and the United States over the Uruguay Round.

The use of alignment as a measure of conflict expectations is consistent with balance-of-threat theory. Stephen Walt, for example, observes: "Joining a defensive alliance to oppose a potential threat will protect you if the state in question is in fact aggressive. Such an alliance will be superfluous – but probably not dangerous – if the state in question turns out to be benign. By contrast, bandwagoning may fail catastrophically if one chooses to ally with a powerful state and subsequently discovers that its intentions are in fact hostile."[12] Walt's empirical evidence supports this trend towards balancing against threats.[13] Alignment is therefore an observable measure of how much states expect to be in conflict with each other.

Walt argued that states will tend to balance against their *greatest* threat. In an international system where anarchy is the ordering principle, all states represent potential threats. Even among allies there is some concern about the future implications of an existing concession. Still, threats are a combination of capabilities and intentions. If the intentions are benign, as between long-standing allies, the perception of threat will be less. Adversaries will adopt more antagonistic positions on multiple-issue areas. It is more likely that adversaries will clash in the future about different issues. In conflicts with adversaries, states will be more concerned about the possibility of concessions made in the present being used against them in the future. Because of a greater expected probability of future conflict, they will care more about their past reputation as a predictor of future outcomes.

A balance-of-power critique would argue that alliances or alignments are worthless measures of conflict expectations. According to neorealism, alliances are temporary structures that change with the

---

[12] Walt (1987), pp. 179–80.

[13] Walt (1987) found that of the alliances formed in the Middle East between 1950 and 1985, 93 percent of them were made in response to a threat. All of the alliances that lasted longer than three years balanced against an external threat.

distribution of power in the international system. Indeed, it is possible that an attempt at economic coercion could trigger a realignment between the sender and target. There are two responses to this criticism. First, power is only one component of threat. Nations must also incorporate the aggressive intentions, geographic proximity, and offensive capabilities of other states into their alliance decisions. [14] The literature on enduring rivalries suggests that bilateral conflicts endure far longer than realists would predict.[15] Alliances are more durable than previously thought; the persistence of cold war alliances into the next millennium suggests that bilateral amity also endures longer than realists would predict. Second, there is little empirical evidence of states realigning during a coercion attempt. Obvious exceptions exist, such as the US sanctions against Cuba in 1960, or the Soviet sanctioning of Yugoslavia in 1955; but less than 15 percent of the sanction events include any sort of balancing behavior. This is another example of how focusing on a few well-known cases can bias a theory.

To sum up: the model will assume that states act as rational, unitary utility-maximizers. National preferences are partially motivated by conflict expectations. There are two effects of this expectation. First, states will have some concern for relative gains, because concessions made in the present can be used against nation-states in the future. Second, countries are concerned that conceding in the present will damage their reputation in future interactions. Both of these concerns vary with the expectation of future conflict. Therefore, states will care more about relative gains and reputation effects when their perception of threat is palpable. Because states balance against their threats, conflict expectations will be greatest between adversaries. Disputes will also be anticipated between allies, but to a lesser degree.

The model

There are two ways to formalize the conflict expectations model. The first is to assume that states are egoistic utility-maximizers with an expectation of a future dispute where the outcome depends on relative capabilities. The second is to create a reduced-form utility function, incorporating the conflict expectations into the actors' utility functions in the form of a concern for relative gains. As Robert Powell has observed, there is no *a priori* answer as to which approach is

---

[14] Walt (1987).   [15] Diehl and Goertz (1993).

better.[16] For this chapter, the reduced-form model will be used for two reasons. First, this version of the conflict expectations model is easier to present and analyze.[17] Second, the primary focus of this book is the effect of conflict expectations on economic statecraft, and not on the causes of those expectations.

All games must have players, strategies, and payoffs. The coercion game has two actors: Sender and Target, labeled S and T for notational convenience.[18] These actors are rational and are assumed to have full information about the possible strategies and payoffs. The game is played only once.

The structure of the game can be seen in Figure 2.1. Sender moves first; it can elect to do nothing and end the game at status quo ante (SQA), or it can choose to make a demand (D), attached to a threat of economic coercion.[19] Sender determines the magnitude of the concession. It might represent a shift in Target's policy on an international issue, a shift in one of Target's policies towards Sender, or a change in one of its domestic policies that has international ramifications. The demand is an action that hurts the target regime and benefits the sender regime.

If Sender chooses to make a demand, then Target must decide between backing down or standing firm. If it chooses to back down, the outcome is acquiescence (AQ); Target agrees to Sender's demand. If it chooses to stand firm however, Sender has the last move. It could choose to back down and accept the status quo (SQ), or carry out the threat of disrupting economic exchange, which produces an outcome of deadlock (DL). The deadlock outcome means that Sender disrupts some bilateral economic exchange. This could include suspending aid, imposing trade barriers, freezing financial assets, or reducing investment flows. This action would obviously be painful to Target, and presumably painful to Sender. The opportunity costs of such an action would be the scarce resources needed to compensate for the interrup-

---

[16] Powell (1994), p. 336.

[17] Versions of the model that are more explicit about the future implications of present concessions produce results that are substantially similar to the reduced-form game presented here. See Drezner (1998).

[18] It could be argued that many high-profile coercion efforts do not have just one sender, but many. An examination of these events shows that most sanctions episodes have one dominant sender who persuades and cajoles other states into cooperation. For more on this, see Martin (1992).

[19] Another variant could be that Sender implements sanctions and threatens to keep them in place unless Target meets its demands.

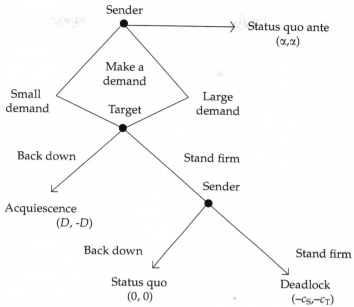

Figure 2.1   The coercion game

ted exchange. Small opportunity costs imply that the costs of substitution are low (i.e., few investments where the value of the asset is specific to the bilateral relationship).[20] The deadlock outcome is essentially a stalemate; Sender and Target both incur costs, but Target makes no concessions.

Figure 2.1 also shows the payoffs for each outcome. All of the payoffs are relative to the status quo outcome. Sender and Target payoffs in the status quo are normalized to zero. Status quo ante produces the same outcome, plus a small increase (α) for both actors. The difference between SQ and SQA is that Sender's threat temporarily freezes the bilateral relationship, preventing further increases of trade or investment. Even if the threat is not carried out, the crisis is sufficient to cast a pall on the economic relationship. Acquiescence also delivers the status quo payoffs, but there is also a direct transfer; Sender gains and Target loses the demand D.[21] Finally, the deadlock

---

[20] See Klein, Crawford, and Alchian (1978) for more on asset-specific investments.
[21] The results do not change appreciably if Sender and Target place different values on the demand.

outcome disrupts the bilateral relationship. Both actors suffer costs from the loss of economic exchange. Sender and Target receive penalties of $-c_S$ and $-c_T$ respectively.

If the sender and target cared only about their short-run absolute benefits, backwards induction solves the game quickly. Sender, choosing between backing down or standing firm, will always back down; it will prefer the benefits of continued economic ties to the costs of economic disruption. That is to say, $0 > -c_S$. Moving backwards, Target, at its decision node, knows that Sender will back down. Therefore, its strategic choice is between acquiescing to Sender's demands, or standing firm and reaching a status quo outcome. Since Target must concede in an AQ outcome, it will always prefer the status quo payoff and elect to stand firm. Finally, Sender must decide between doing nothing and arriving at status quo ante, or making a threat and reaching the status quo. Because Sender always prefers the additional benefit from the SQA payoff, it will do nothing. Therefore, if one assumes that Sender and Target care only about their own payoffs, the unique equilibrium of this game is status quo ante. Because the sender will not prefer to carry out a costly threat, it will opt to do nothing. If the utilities correspond to the payoffs, this is the only subgame perfect equilibrium in the game.[22]

If one assumes that only immediate absolute gains matter, the game is, frankly, boring. Even if Target suffers much greater costs than Sender, Sender cannot credibly threaten coercion, because it will always prefer to back down and incur fewer costs. The only way Sender's threat to coerce can produce concessions is if it genuinely prefers deadlock to the status quo.

I now introduce conflict expectations into the model. Sender's and Target's utility functions (U_S and U_T) are a linear, weighted function of absolute and relative preferences:

[22] A subgame perfect equilibrium consists of strategies that are fully rational at every decision node of the game, even if the decision is not on the equilibrium path. This is a more refined solution concept than a Nash equilibrium. A Nash equilibrium would consist of Sender and Target strategies such that, holding the other player's strategy constant, it is impossible to improve one's utility using another strategy.

There is one other Nash equilibrium in this variant of the coercion game. If the sender committed itself making a demand and standing firm at a confrontation, then the target's optimal strategy would be to acquiesce if the demand was less than the costs suffered from deadlock. This is not a subgame perfect equilibrium because Sender's strategy off the equilibrium path (to stand firm if Target also stands firm) is not the optimal choice at that decision node.

$$U_S = \beta(P_S) + (1 - \beta)(P_S - P_T), \tag{2.1}$$

$$U_T = \beta(P_T) + (1 - \beta)(P_T - P_S), \tag{2.2}$$

where

P_S = Sender's payoff from the outcome;
P_T = Target's payoff from the outcome;
β = Mutual expectation of harmonious relations.

β, by definition, lies between zero and one. By extension, $(1 - \beta)$ is the mutual expectation of the likelihood of future conflict. For perfect allies, $\beta = 1$; for perfect adversaries, $\beta = 0$.

This utility function adds only one wrinkle. It assumes that countries place some emphasis on their distributional performance by directly comparing their payoffs. β is the measure of how this concern is apportioned, and represents the expectation of future conflict. If the two states anticipate few political conflicts, then $\beta \rightarrow 1$, Sender and Target care only about absolute gains, and the utility function collapses back into the simple case of the utilities equaling the payoffs. If the two actors anticipate endless political conflicts, then $\beta \rightarrow 0$, Sender and Target care only about relative gains, and view the game as a strict zero-sum negotiation. As conflict expectations increase, so does the concern for the material and reputational effects of any concession by either actor.[23]

Incorporating conflict expectations makes the game slightly more complex. Backwards induction does not provide a unique solution. At its final decision node, Sender does not necessarily prefer Status Quo to Deadlock. To be sure, there are still conditions under which Sender still prefers to back down. When this happens, the outcome of the game is still SQA. If Sender prefers DL to SQ, however, then the game could have a different outcome. Moving backwards, Target would

---

[23] There are two ways to incorporate concerns about reputation into this model. The first is to argue that reputations are formed from outcomes; a country's bilateral reputation for negotiation is determined by how well that country's payoff compares to the other actor's. This means that reputational effects are felt through the concern for relative gains. The second way is to argue that reputations are formed by strategies; a country's reputation is formed by the consistency to which its foreign policy leaders stick to their positions. Actors would be penalized when they go back on a strategy: in this case, when Target acquiesces, or when Sender backs down after threatening sanctions. I have chosen the first approach for reasons of tractability. Modeling reputation effects using the other approach does not affect any of the results in this chapter; it only *reinforces* the hypotheses.

face a choice between acquiescence and deadlock, and this choice is less clear cut than between acquiescence and the status quo. Target's decision depends on the size of Sender's demand.

Finally, it is unclear whether Sender will prefer acquiescence to either deadlock or the status quo ante. If it prefers the status quo ante, then it can simply choose not to make a threat. If Sender prefers deadlock to all other outcomes, it can make its demand request so large that Target would never acquiesce, guaranteeing an outcome of DL.

In order to determine the outcome of the game, the following questions must be answered:

1 When will Sender prefer deadlock (DL) to status quo (SQ)?
2 For what demands will Target prefer acquiescence (AQ) to deadlock (DL)?
3 Given those values of D, will Sender prefer acquiescence (AQ) to deadlock (DL) or status quo ante (CSQA)?

To answer the first question, Sender's utility from the status quo outcome must be compared with its utility from the deadlock outcome. If $U_S(DL)$ is greater than $U_S(SQ)$, then Sender is willing to stand firm:

$$U_S(SQ) = \beta(0) + (1 - \beta)(0 - 0),$$

$$U_S(DL) = \beta\{-c_S\} + (1 - \beta)\{-c_S + c_T\}.$$

$U_S(DL)$ is greater than $U_S(SQ)$ if and only if:

$$\beta\{-c_S\} + (1 - \beta)\{-c_S + c_T\} > 0,$$

$$c_T - c_S > \beta c_T.$$

$$\beta^* < 1 - \frac{c_S}{c_T}. \tag{2.3}$$

I will call equation 2.3 the *coercion condition*. If $\beta < \beta^*$, then $U_S(DL) > U_S(SQ)$; Sender prefers standing firm to backing down, and the coercion condition is satisfied; if $\beta > \beta^*$, then Sender prefers backing down to standing firm; $U_S(DL) < U_S(SQ)$, and the coercion condition is not satisfied.

The coercion condition is not a fixed point. As conflict expectations recede (i.e. β increases) the coercion condition becomes more difficult to satisfy. If both states anticipate a great deal of future conflict, and therefore are extremely concerned with relative gains and reputation effects, the coercion condition is not a difficult threshold to meet. The opportunity costs would have to be close to parity (c_S approaches c_T in value) for Sender not to coerce. However, even if Sender views the game only as a zero-sum contest, Sender will not threaten coercion unless Target suffers the greater costs. Conversely, if the two countries are allies and few disputes are expected, then the gap in opportunity costs needs to be significant (c_T must be high and c_S low) for Sender to prefer deadlock over status quo.

This result shows that the sender will rationally threaten sanctions if and only if there is some concern about relative gains and reputation effects. Even if conflict expectations are minimal, there can exist a set of circumstances under which Sender would prefer deadlock. This would happen if the difference between the relative opportunity costs were significant, or if the price of sanctions to the sender were small. This does not imply that the existence of conflict expectations automatically leads to sanctions. If Sender's opportunity costs are greater, then it would prefer to back down even if it viewed the relationship with Target as strictly conflictual; it would be worse off in deadlock. The coercion condition represents a blending of short-run and long-run concerns. Foreign policy leaders must balance the short-run costs and benefits with the repercussions that present actions will have in future clashes. Unless states are perfect allies or perfect adversaries, it is a world of mixed motives. Even if Sender is facing an allied target, there could still exist a set of circumstances in which threatening sanctions is the rational course of action. Likewise, even if Target is an adversary, Sender might still prefer not to disrupt exchange. Figure 2.2 shows the relationship between the cost and alignment variables and the decision to coerce.

The coercion condition generates two testable hypotheses.

> Hypothesis 1: No coercion event should generate greater opportunity costs for the sender country than the target country.

At first glance, this hypothesis borders on the banal. As noted in chapter 1, however, some theorists argue that sanctions which incur heavy costs on the sender are more effective at displaying commitment credibility to the target nation. By that logic, sanctions that are costlier to the sender than the target should be extremely effective in demonstrating sender commitment, and therefore increase the likelihood of acquiescence. Furthermore, the attention to big cases, particularly the US grain embargo of the Soviet Union following the

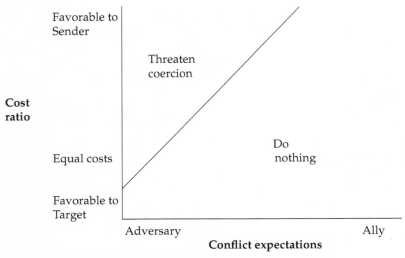

Figure 2.2   The sender's coercion decision

1979 Afghanistan invasion, has encouraged the perception that sanctions are frequently more costly to the sender than the target.[24]

A more sophisticated hypothesis can also be derived from the coercion condition.

> Hypothesis 2: Within the set of coercion events, the alignment between Target and Sender should be negatively correlated with the cost to Sender, but positively correlated with the cost to Target.

This is not the first hypothesis that comes to mind in testing the coercion condition. The ideal test requires comparing the actual set of coercion events with situations where the sender considered sanctions but elected to accept the status quo ante. Unfortunately, it is tricky to observe nonevents, and trickier to measure variables observed in events but not nonevents. Using random dyads that include events where coercion is not imposed, as well as the observed coercion attempts, would be loaded with methodological roadblocks. For example, there is no appropriate measure of expected costs that could be used for both sets of data on a large-N sample.[25]

---

[24] See chapter 3 for more on this case.

[25] Morgan and Schwebach (1997) conduct an interesting test using cases of extended deterrence as the null set of situations where sanctions were not imposed. Sislin (1994) compares cases where the United States has proffered carrots of military aid to situations where sanctions were imposed. Neither study, however, measures the potential costs of sanctions in the cases where alternative policies were pursued.

The goal is to develop testable propositions. Sample bias makes it difficult to test when states will attempt to coerce. While it is empirically impractical to compare events with nonevents, it is possible to observe correlations among variables within the set of observed events. The coercion condition becomes a tougher threshold to satisfy as the two countries anticipate fewer conflicts. If the two countries are allies, the gap in the opportunity costs of deadlock needs to be large in order for Sender to still satisfy the coercion condition. Therefore, an increase in β should cause a concomitant increase in c_T and a decrease in c_S in situations where sanctions are observed. Hence the second hypothesis.

If the coercion condition is not satisfied, backwards induction shows that the game will end as before: the sender will not threaten sanctions because it knows it will back down in the end. However, if the coercion condition is satisfied, the next step is to determine the range of concession values for which Target prefers acquiescence to deadlock. Target must now choose between acquiescence and deadlock. Its choice depends on the magnitude of Sender's demanded concessions. Sender will maximize its utility by demanding as large a concession as possible. The concession size is constrained, however. If the Sender asks for too many concessions, Target will prefer a stalemate over backing down. Therefore, the demand size is endogenously determined. Sender needs to calculate the range of values of D such that Target prefers acquiescence to deadlock, or when $U_T(AQ)$ is greater than $U_T(DL)$:

$$U_T(AQ) = \beta(-D) + (1 - \beta)(-D - D),$$

$$U_T(DL) = \beta\{-c_T\} + (1 - \beta)\{-c_T + c_S\}.$$

$U_T(AQ)$ is greater than $U_T(DL)$ if and only if:

$$\beta(-D) + (1 - \beta)(-D - D) > \beta\{-c_T\} + (1 - \beta)\{c_S - c_T\},$$

$$c_T - (1 - \beta)c_S > (2 - \beta)D.$$

$$D^* < \frac{c_T - (1 - \beta)c_S}{2 - \beta}. \tag{2.4}$$

I will call equation 2.4 the *concession function*, and D^* the *optimum possible concession*. The concession function indicates how c_S, c_T, and β affect D^*. Not surprisingly, as the gap in opportunity costs increases, so does the optimum possible concession. An increase in the gap makes deadlock less appetizing for Target; it will be willing to acquiesce to a larger demand. More intriguing is the effect that conflict expectations have on D^*. By inspection, one can see that as β increases, the numerator unambiguously increases in value while the denominator unambiguously decreases in value. Partial differentiation confirms that a decrease in conflict expectations *increases* the optimum possible concession, D^*.

This result, at first glance, seems counterintuitive. The concession function implies that Sender will extract a larger transfer from Target when it cares less about its relative performance. Therefore, the optimum possible concession is maximized when the two countries have no conflict expectations. Ironically, it would seem that Sender maximizes its relative gain when it cares about those gains the least.

The intuitive explanation rests on correcting the attention bias international relations theory places on great power preferences. Senders are usually great powers, and it is frequently assumed that their preferences and power guide international events. This is true only in their ability to increase the costs to Target without incurring significant costs themselves. The concession function shows that the target state's preferences also affect the outcome. While the target's preferences do not affect whether economic sanctions are threatened, they do affect the size of the concessions if the coercion condition is satisfied. If Sender's demands exceed the optimum possible concession, Target will prefer to stand firm and go to deadlock. This is a suboptimal outcome for Sender. Thus, in crafting its demand, Sender must be sensitive to Target's preferences. Its power is expressed in this model through the ability to make Target incur significant opportunity costs. This influences the demand size. That power, however, is still constrained by Target's preferences.

Seen from the target country's perspective, it is not at all surprising that, *ceteris paribus*, it would acquiesce to a larger demand if it was less concerned about future disputes. In the model, if Target surrenders demand D^*, Sender automatically receives the same benefit. Acquiescence implies a transfer; the sender gains and the target loses some political asset. In the calculus of conflict expectations, the agreement to accede to the demand is doubly negative. In acquiescing, not only does Target lose, but Sender wins, increasing the likelihood of its winning in future disputes. By contrast, both countries suffer losses in a deadlock outcome. A stalemate outcome is not as damaging from a conflict expectations perspective, because Sender does not acquire what Target loses; it suffers some costs as well. If the concerns for relative gain and reputation are significant, Target will acquiesce only to smaller demands to avoid deadlock. As conflict expectations fade, Target is less concerned with how much its acquiescence in the present will affect bargaining in future disputes. Acquiescing to Sender's demand looks preferable to the alternative of deadlock. As the target country's preference function moves from distributional to egoistic concerns, its grudge about conceding wanes, so the sender country can ask for more.

From the concession function, I can obtain the following hypotheses.

> Hypothesis 3: The target's concessions will increase when the difference between Target's and Sender's opportunity costs of deadlock increases.

> Hypothesis 4: The target's concessions will increase when Target and Sender are more closely aligned with each other.

The logic of these hypotheses flows directly from the optimal concession function.

The final question is whether, if the coercion condition is satisfied and the optimum possible concession is requested, Sender will prefer acquiescence to either deadlock or status quo ante. It can reach any of those outcomes through its strategy selection, so it will choose the outcome that maximizes its utility. Evaluating the effect of D^* on $U_S(AQ)$, it turns out that Sender will always prefer acquiescence to deadlock given the optimum possible concession. This is shown in the first lemma in the appendix. Comparing $U_S(AQ)$, with $U_S(SQA)$, it is clear that unless the payoff from not disrupting the relationship at all (α) outweighs the magnitude of the concessions, AQ is preferred to SQA. Indeed, even if the gains from not threatening outweigh the expected demand, Sender will still threaten if the expectation of future conflict is sufficiently high. This is shown in second lemma in the appendix.

Combining the implications from the coercion condition and the optimal concession function, two conclusions can be drawn. First, the expected costs of coercion have a monotonic affect on the outcome. As Target's opportunity costs of deadlock increases, *ceteris paribus*, Sender's utility from the equilibrium outcome is nondecreasing. As Sender's opportunity costs of deadlock decreases, *ceteris paribus*, Sender's utility is nondecreasing as well. The effect of conflict expectations is not monotonic. *Ceteris paribus*, if the coercion condition is

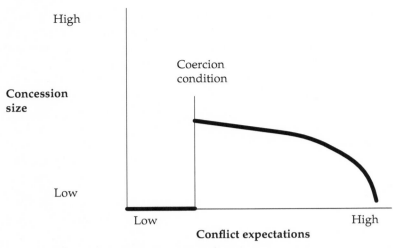

Figure 2.3   The effect of conflict expectations on concession size

satisfied, a less adversarial relationship increases the size of the concessions Sender can successfully extract from Target. As the conflict expectations decrease, however, the coercion condition will not be satisfied, and Sender cannot extract any demand from Target. The outcome is the status quo ante. Figure 2.3 captures the contra- dictory effect of conflict expectations.

In summary, the dynamics of the statecraft game are as follows:

1   If $\beta > \beta^*$, Sender prefers status quo to deadlock. The stick is of little use. In this situation, the optimal strategy for Sender is to do nothing and accept the status quo ante.

2   If $\beta < \beta^*$, Sender prefers deadlock to the status quo. This allows it to coerce successfully, obtaining as many concessions as the optimal concession function permits. Sender knows that if it chooses the stick strategy, the outcome is acquiescence.[26]

---

[26] These solutions are predicted because they are the only subgame perfect equilibria. As mentioned in note 22, however, there is another Nash equilibrium. If the sender country commits to standing firm prior to playing the game, then the target's optimal strategy is to acquiesce if the demand size is not too large. It is possible, therefore, to force the target country into acquiescing without relying on the concern for relative gains. This equilibrium solution is the game-theoretic equivalent for those who argue that hard bargaining can explain what appears to be relative gains concern.

Comparing these equilibria is important in considering the role that the concern for relative gains plays in economic coercion. Some theorists argue that it is impossible to distinguish between the concern for relative gains and the desire to maximize one's share in a distribution of payoffs. The second Nash equilibrium could be considered

The model indicates that variables can have a consistent or a contradictory effect on economic coercion. Target and Sender opportunity costs have a consistent effect. As c_T increases and c_S decreases, economic sanctions are more likely, and the optimal possible concession gets larger. Conflict expectations have a contradictory effect on economic coercion. The greater the concern for relative gains and bilateral reputation, the more likely that Sender will employ economic sanctions. At the same time, however, the optimum possible concession decreases, because the target country is more resistant to transferring concessions to the sender. The condition which makes the sender wish to threaten coercion in the first place also makes the target more reluctant to concede to large demands.

A caveat: switches in preferences

Until now, the model has implicitly assumed that the source of an economic coercion attempt was a single policy conflict between Target and Sender. It further assumed that the policy disagreement was independent of the long-term alignment between the two actors. This is not always true. For example, since the early 1960s the United States has used economic pressure against Cuba because of the latter country's switch in political alignment following Fidel Castro's rise to power. Since the 1979 Iranian revolution, the United States has economically coerced that country; it anticipated more conflicts with a Cuba led by Castro than Batista. Similarly, the United States had fewer conflicts with Iran ruled by the Shah than with Iran ruled by Khomeini. In these cases, Sender might be motivated to attempt coercion because of a shift in Target's entire foreign policy. This shift would certainly change both states' conflict expectations, affecting the utility of a sanctions strategy.[27] If Target radically restructured its foreign affairs so as to oppose Sender's policies, their relations would naturally become antagonistic. These changes would affect the game structurally by changing the extent that Sender and Target anticipate future political conflicts.

---

supporting evidence for this contention. This solution concept is less realistic, however; it depends on the sender country acting irrationally off the equilibrium path, and could only work if Sender was able to credibly commit to its strategy before the game was played. Whereas the equilibrium discussed in the text uses a more robust subgame perfect equilibrium solution, this argument relies on a more fragile solution concept.

[27] Another possibility is that Sender's threat of coercion would change the value of β.

If Target decides to realign its national interests, the result would be a change in the expectation of future conflict between the two states. The previous section shows the contradictory effect an increase in conflict expectations would have on the coercion game. This leads to the fifth hypothesis.

> Hypothesis 5: If Target realigns against Sender during the coercion dispute, Target's concessions will be smaller.

Conflict expectations, as observed earlier, has a contradictory effect on the coercion game. A decision by the target to balance against the sender implies a greater expectation of conflict and therefore more concern for relative gains and reputation effects. This makes it more likely that Sender will prefer deadlock to the status quo, and thus makes a sanctions event more likely. On the other hand, the increase in distributional concerns also makes acquiescence a less appealing outcome to Target. In order for AQ to be the equilibrium outcome, Sender must reduce its demand to make it more palatable for Target. Balancing behavior only reinforces the effect of conflict expectations; the result is more events of economic coercion, but fewer concessions made.

Another caveat: non-negotiable demands

The coercion game assumed that the demand was a continuous variable, and could be calibrated to any value. This is not always true in international politics. If the issue in question involves a strong international norm, it may not be possible for the sender country to adjust its demand. The sanctions against South Africa, for example, were not lifted during the early 1990s, despite numerous steps by the South African government to end white minority rule. The strong norm against apartheid made it difficult for any of the sender countries to settle for anything less than complete abolition.[28] Most of the sanctions were not lifted until multiracial elections were held in 1994. Norms concerning nuclear nonproliferation and human rights could also make demands non-negotiable.

What are the effects of indivisible demands on the coercion game? As already observed, the optimum possible concession is constrained by the costs of coercion and the expectation of future conflict. If

---

[28] Nelson Mandela, in his first speech upon release from prison, emphasized that sanctions should be maintained until apartheid was completely dismantled.

Sender asks for concessions greater than D^*, Target will stand firm and prefer deadlock. For Sender to threaten economic coercion in the first place, it must prefer deadlock to the status quo, so it will also stand firm. If the coercion condition is satisfied, and the demand is greater than the optimum possible concession and cannot be compromised, the equilibrium outcome is deadlock; sanctions are imposed indefinitely.

This leads to the following hypothesis.

> Hypothesis 6: Sanctions will be imposed for a longer duration when the two countries are adversaries.

It is logical that if Sender and Target share heightened conflict expectations, the likelihood of a deadlock outcome increases. If Sender and Target are adversaries, Sender is more likely to coerce, but it will also be forced to ask for smaller concessions. By contrast, if Sender sanctions an ally, the odds are better that it can extract a concession big enough to satisfy even a non-negotiable demand. A greater concern for relative gains and damage to reputation will constrain the magnitude of Target's concessions; this, combined with an inflexible demand, leads to deadlock.

There is one other reason why deadlock is more likely between adversaries, although the intervening causal mechanism is outside the formal model. Demands can become immutable through public diplomacy. If the sender country articulates the firmness of its demand in the public domain, the reputational cost of any compromise increases. By contrast, if the sender and target negotiate behind closed doors, without stating their positions publicly, the price of compromising is less. Publicity leads to bigger audiences, and thus to higher stakes in the battle for reputation. If public negotiations can lead to inflexible demands, then conflicts between adversaries are more likely to produce lumpy demands. Allies have multiple channels of communication with each other, and those channels are more routinized and less public. This lowers the transaction costs of negotiation. Adversaries often lack these routinized channels, and have an incentive to keep information private. This raises the costs of bargaining and makes it more difficult to keep negotiations private. Negotiations become a public spectacle, making demands inflexible. Although this explanation is outside the scope of the formal model, it reinforces its conclusions.

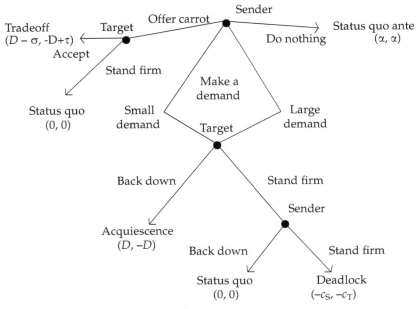

Figure 2.4   The statecraft game

Choosing between carrots and sticks

One objection to the notion of inflexible demands is that if side-payments are an option, it is always possible to cut a deal to avoid a costly deadlock.[29] Until now, the conflict expectations model has ignored the other options in the policy-maker's tool kit. This section introduces a strategy of economic inducements to see how states choose among their policy options.

Figure 2.4 displays a modified version of the coercion game that I will call the statecraft game. In this variant, Sender has the additional option of proffering a carrot to an attached demand. If the target rejects the carrot, the outcome is the status quo.[30] If the target accepts, the outcome is tradeoff (TO). Target surrenders demand D, but gains the value of the carrot, τ. Sender gains D, but loses the cost of the carrot, σ. The values of σ and τ are not necessarily equal. If, for

---

[29] See Fearon (1995), pp. 381–2.
[30] Allowing Sender to threaten the stick after the carrot has been rejected does not affect the results.

example, the carrot is expanded trade concessions, or loan guarantees, the sender's cost is less than the target's benefit.

Given this new game structure, two questions need to be asked:

1 What is the optimum possible concession using the carrot option?
2 Under what conditions will Sender opt for the carrot?

Sender will maximize the demanded concessions to the point where Target is indifferent between tradeoff and status quo. Setting $U_T(TO)$ equal to $U_T(SQ)$:

$$U_T(TO) = \beta(\tau - D) + (1 - \beta)\{\tau - D - (-\sigma + D)\}.$$

$U_T(TO) = U_T(SQ)$ if and only if:

$$\beta(\tau - D) + (1 - \beta)(\tau - D + \sigma - D) = 0,$$

$$\tau + (1 - \beta)\sigma = (2 - \beta)D.$$

$$D' = \frac{\tau + (1 - \beta)\sigma}{2 - \beta} \tag{2.5}$$

Equation 2.5 shows that the dynamics of the carrot are similar to those of the stick. The concession size increases with the value of the carrot to the target; it also increases with the sender's costs of paying it. Conflict expectations reduce the concessions that a carrot can obtain. The logic is identical to the dynamics of economic coercion.[31] *Ceteris paribus*, the more adversarial the relationship, the more lucrative the carrot must be for Target to accede to the same demand.

This result shows that the expectation of future conflict constrains the ability of carrots to work in the same way it constrains the stick. Both economic coercion and economic inducements will be of limited use in dealing with adversaries.

Given the optimum possible concession for the carrot, under what conditions will Sender choose to use inducements instead of coercion? Sender's decision rests on what the equilibrium outcome would have been if the carrot was not an option. There are three possibilities:

1 Sender cannot satisfy the coercion condition, and otherwise the outcome is status quo ante.

---

[31] If the cost of the carrot to the sender equals the benefit to the target ($\tau = \sigma$), conflict expectations become irrelevant. The coercion condition becomes $D' = \tau = \sigma$.

2 Sender can satisfy the coercion condition, and otherwise the outcome is acquiescence.

3 Sender can satisfy the coercion condition, the demand is non-negotiable, and otherwise the outcome is deadlock.

The mathematical results comparing these equilibria are presented in the appendix. The results can be summarized in one observation and one hypothesis. The observation is that carrots will be used more frequently between allies than adversaries. If economic coercion is not a rational strategy for the sender, it must choose between doing nothing or using the bribe. In almost all cases where the coercion condition fails, the sender will be willing to use the carrot rather than do nothing. Since the coercion condition is more likely to fail with allies than adversaries, there should be more instances of carrots between allies. This observation is straightforward, and will not be explored further.

The last hypothesis concerns the cases when carrots will be used between adversaries.

> Hypothesis 7: If the sender is observed offering a carrot to an adversarial target, the following is likely to be observed: (1) The demand is non-negotiable. (2) The carrot is very lucrative for the target. (3) The carrot is virtually costless for the sender.

It was shown earlier that when conflict expectations are salient, the target will concede less to the sender because the transfer of resources produces a double loss of utility. Just as the concern for relative gains and reputation makes Target more reluctant to acquiesce, it makes Sender more reluctant to offer the carrot. Because it anticipates future conflicts, the sender is reluctant to surrender its own resources and strengthen the target at the same time. Given the right set of conditions, the sender will prefer the tradeoff option even if the target is an adversary. This outcome is more likely if the demand is non-negotiable and the carrot is cheap to the sender but valued by the target. If the demand is non-negotiable, then Sender's alternative to the carrot is deadlock rather than acquiescence. If the carrot is cheap to the sender but lucrative to the target, the utility of the carrot option increases.

The inclusion of a carrot option in the coercion game does not affect the earlier results or hypotheses. The opportunity costs of coercion and expectations of future conflict have the same effect on the initiation and outcome of coercion events. Even if the sender can use carrots instead of sanctions, their use will largely be restricted to circumstances where the sender cannot use economic coercion as a rational threat. When both options are possible, the sender will choose to use the carrot instead of the stick only under a narrow set of conditions. Those conditions are at their most stringent in dealing with adversaries.

Conclusions and implications

This chapter has used the tools of game theory to model the dynamics of economic coercion. I assume that states act as rational unitary actors and are concerned about whether their present actions will materially or reputationally affect their bargaining position in future interactions. Because of this, foreign policy leaders will have some concern about the distribution of gains in international political conflicts. Nation-states will care more about the distribution of payoffs and reputation effects when conflict expectations are great. Because states will balance against their perceived threats, they anticipate more future conflicts with adversaries than with allies. The more closely two countries are aligned, the less their interactions will seem like a zero-sum game.

Economic coercion is an attempt to extract political transfers, and those transfers may undercut bargaining positions or bargaining reputations in future conflicts. Given this, a sender country will decide to threaten coercion if it prefers a stalemate of long-term economic sanctions over backing down from a threat and accepting the status quo. The sender will prefer deadlock if the target's opportunity costs of deadlock are sufficiently greater than its own costs, and there is some expectation of future conflict. There exists a coercion condition that links the cost terms with the concern for the distribution of payoffs. If the sender faces an adversarial target, it will prefer deadlock even if the target's costs are only marginally greater than its own. If the target is an ally, then the gap in costs must be extremely high for the sender country to attempt to coerce. As the concern about the relative payoffs declines, the gap in costs must be greater for the sender to threaten sanctions.

While states must care somewhat about the distribution of payoffs in order to threaten economic sanctions, it has a paradoxical effect on the magnitude of the target's concessions. As conflict expectations increase, the target will be more resistant to concessions, because the

Table 2.1. *The predicted pattern of economic coercion*

	Ally	Adversary
Large gap in costs	Significant concessions	Moderate concessions
Small gap in costs	No coercion attempt	Minor concessions

sender will benefit from whatever losses it incurs. The sender must reduce its demand in order for the target to prefer acquiescence. Conflict expectations have a contradictory effect on the game. If the bilateral relationship is amicable, then the sender will be less eager to attempt coercion, yet if it still prefers sanctions, it will obtain more significant concessions from the target.

The opportunity costs of deadlock have a more consistent effect on the dynamics of economic coercion. *Ceteris paribus*, as the sender's opportunity costs of deadlock increase, the sender is less likely to satisfy the coercion condition. If it does choose to threaten sanctions, it will obtain less significant concessions. An increase in the sender's costs makes economic sanctions less viable and less profitable. An increase in the target's costs makes economic sanctions more viable and more profitable.

Table 2.1 reproduces the 2×2 schema of how the cost and alignment variables interact. As can be seen in the table, the gap in costs has a consistent effect on the outcome, while alignment has a contradictory effect.

Relaxing some technical assumptions leads to several corollaries. If the target country tries to engage in balancing behavior at any point during the coercion attempt, the basic model's predictions are intensified. Balancing against a threat will increase conflict expectations on both sides; this will encourage the coercion attempt, but also reduce the expected concession. If for normative reasons the demand has an all-or-nothing character, one would expect to see sustained deadlock between adversaries more often than between allies. Finally, the introduction of a carrot option to the coercion game does not seriously affect the use of economic coercion. Economic inducements will be used primarily when the sender is unable to threaten sanctions. When both options are available, the carrot will be chosen only if a narrow set of conditions are met.

Theories need to be intellectually compelling and empirically plausible. This chapter has dealt with the first task; the remainder of the book will tackle the second task. The next chapter looks at existing econometric analysis and well-known case studies to see if the conflict expectations model has any explanatory power.

Appendix
Proofs of lemmas

Lemma 1: In the simple coercion game, there exists a demand D such that Sender will always prefer acquiescence to deadlock.

Proof: Compare the utilities of acquiescence and deadlock for Sender:

$$U_S(AQ) = (1 + (1 - \beta))D^*$$

$$U_S(DL) = -c_S + (1 - \beta)c_T$$

$U_S(DL) > U_S(AQ)$ if and only if:

$$-c_S + (1 - \beta)c_T > (1 + (1 - \beta))D^*$$

$$\frac{-c_S + (1 - \beta)c_T}{2 - \beta} > D^*.$$

From Equation 2.4:

$$\frac{c_T - (1 - \beta)c_S}{2 - \beta} = D^*.$$

Substituting for D^*:

$$\frac{-c_S + (1 - \beta)c_T}{2 - \beta} > \frac{c_T - (1 - \beta)c_S}{2 - \beta}];$$

$$0 > \frac{c_S - (1 - \beta)c_T}{2 - \beta} + \frac{c_T - (1 - \beta)c_S}{2 - \beta}.$$

Normalizing, we get:

$$0 > [1 - (1 - \beta)^2][c_S + c_T].$$

We know that β is less than zero, so the coefficient is greater than zero. We also know that c_T is greater than zero, and that $c_T > c_S$ in order for acquiescence to be a possible outcome. The right-hand side can never be less than zero, which means $U_S(DL)$ can never be greater than $U_S(AQ)$. Thus, $U_S(AQ) > U_S(DL)$. QED.

Lemma 2: Unless $\alpha > D^*$, Sender will prefer acquiescence to status quo ante.

Proof: Compare the utilities of acquiescence and status quo ante for Sender:

$$U_S(AQ) = (2 - \beta)D^*;$$
$$U_S(SQA) = \beta(\alpha) - (1 - \beta)(\alpha - \alpha)$$
$$= \beta\alpha.$$

$U_S(SQA) > U_S(AQ)$ if and only if:

$$\beta\alpha > (2 - \beta)D^*$$

Since $\beta < 2 - \beta$, I can temporarily remove the coefficients without affecting the inequality. In order for $U_S(SQA)$ to be greater than $U_S(AQ)$, the benefit from not making a threat would have to exceed the optimum possible concession. In other words, α would have to be greater than D^*. QED.

Looking at the coefficients, unless $\beta = 1$, α must be significantly greater than D^* in order for SQA to be preferred. If $\beta = 0$, then Sender cares only about relative gains, and will always prefer acquiescence.

Lemma 3: The sender is more likely to prefer tradeoff over other options if the demand is non-negotiable, and as $(\tau - \sigma)$ increases.

Proof: Assume for now the coercion condition is not satisfied. Compare Sender's utility for status quo ante and tradeoff:

$$U_S(TO) = \beta(D - \sigma) + (1 - \beta)(D - \sigma + D - \tau)$$
$$= (2 - \beta)D - \sigma - (1 - \beta)\tau.$$

From equation 2.5:

$$D' = \frac{\tau + (1 - \beta)\sigma}{2 - \beta}.$$

Substituting:

$$U_S(TO) = \tau + (1 - \beta)\sigma - \sigma - (1 - \beta)\tau$$
$$= \beta(\tau - \sigma);$$

$$U_s(SQA) = \beta(\alpha) - (1 - \beta)(\alpha - \alpha)$$
$$= \beta\alpha.$$

$U_s(TO)$ is greater than $U_s(SQA)$ if and only if:

$$\beta(\tau - \sigma) > \beta\alpha, \text{ or } (\tau - \sigma) > \alpha.$$

If the coercion condition is not satisfied, the sender will offer the carrot if the gap between the target's reward and the sender's costs outweighs the benefit from doing nothing. Conflict expectations play no direct role in this decision, although they obviously affect whether the coercion condition is met or not.

Now assume the coercion condition is satisfied and the demand is negotiable. Sender's choice is between acquiescence and tradeoff. Comparing the utilities:

$$U_S(TO) = \beta(\tau - \sigma);$$
$$U_S(AQ) = (2 - \beta)D^*.$$

From Equation 2.4:

$$D^* < \frac{c_T - (1 - \beta)c_S}{2 - \beta}.$$

Substituting:

$$U_S(AQ) = c_T - (1 - \beta)c_S.$$

Sender prefers the carrot to the stick if and only if:

$$\beta(\tau - \sigma) > c_T - (1 - \beta)c_S.$$

Note that as $\beta \to 0$, the left-hand side of the equation goes to zero, while the right-hand side remains positive. Since both equations are linear, there exists some value β^* such that if $\beta < \beta^*$, Sender prefers acquiescence to tradeoff, i.e. the stick over the carrot. Note that even if $\beta = 1$, Sender may still prefer a stick strategy to the carrot.

Now assume the coercion condition is satisfied and the demand is non-negotiable. If the demand is less than the optimum possible concession, then Sender chooses between tradeoff and acquiescence. If the demand is greater than the optimum possible concession, then the comparison is between Sender's utility for tradeoff and deadlock:

$$U_S(TO) = \beta(\tau - \sigma)$$

$$U_S(DL) = -c_S + (1 - \beta)c_T.$$

When $\beta = 1$, $U_S(DL) < U_S(TO)$, but when $\beta = 0$, $U_S(DL) > U_S(SQ)$. Therefore, there exists a β' such that if $\beta < \beta'$ Sender will prefer deadlock, and if $\beta > \beta'$ Sender will prefer tradeoff. Comparative statics show that β' is clearly lower if $(\tau - \sigma)$ is bigger.

Thus, if the alternative equilibrium is acquiescence, Sender will be less likely to prefer the carrot when conflict expectations are high. If the alternative equilibrium is deadlock, then there exists a range of values of β, c_S, and c_T such that tradeoff is the preferred option. This range expands as τ increases and σ decreases.

3   Plausibility probes

In all scientific enterprises, the elegant theory must confront the somewhat inelegant facts. Facts in international relations can be slippery. Quantitative data are inexact at best. Qualitative data can be interpreted in multiple ways. This makes testing a difficult process.

This chapter conducts a plausibility probe to see how well the established theories of economic coercion, compared with the conflict expectations model, can explain variations in the initiation and outcome of economic coercion. A plausibility probe is like dipping the first toe in the water. Swimmers want to know if the water is temperate enough to go deeper. Researchers want to know if the empirical climate is friendly enough for more extensive forays. By looking at the existing research, it is possible to see if the evidence fits with existing explanations, or if the conflict expectations model can contribute a better and fuller understanding of economic statecraft.[1]

The first part of this chapter looks at the statistical data sets and studies to compare the conflict expectations model to the alternative set of explanations. The existing sanctions data sets show that the success rate of economic coercion attempts is higher than previously thought. Sanctions are not always fruitful, but there is significant variation in the outcome. The evidence from previous statistical analyses rejects the alternative hypotheses that sanctions are caused by either domestic pressures or the absence of feasible alternatives. It supports the model's prediction that the target's expected opportunity costs and conflict expectations play an important role. Previous

---

[1] One could argue that this burden is greater for rational choice theories that have been criticized for a failure to consider credible alternatives or subject hypotheses to empirical tests. See Green and Shapiro (1994), chapter 2.

large-*N* efforts to explain sanction outcomes categorically reject the claim that sanctions success can be explained by variables such as aggregate power, the threat of military force, or the presence of multilateral cooperation. Domestic forces within the target country appear to have some effect. The evidence lends support to the conflict expectations model.

The second part of this chapter focuses on three prominent cases of US economic sanctions. The evidence shows that even where the alternative explanations would be expected to have some validity, they fail to explain significant facts within the case. The logic of conflict expectations can credibly explain important parts of the story. This part of the chapter looks at: US sanctions against the Soviet Union following the invasion of Afghanistan in 1979, US attempts to prevent its European allies from completing a pipeline deal with the Soviet Union in 1982, and the American linkage of economic statecraft to human rights improvements during the 1970s.

First impressions

It is one thing to argue that economic coercion is an ineffective policy tool after analyzing one or two cases. It is another to reach the same conclusion after analyzing fifty. The conventional wisdom about sanctions crystallized when Klaus Knorr dismissed the utility of economic diplomacy in *The Power of Nations*. The large number of cases that he reviewed made this assertion all the more powerful. He based his analysis on twenty-two cases of economic sanctions and twenty-five cases of foreign aid suspension. Classifying more than 75 percent of the events as policy failures, he attributed the few successes to implicit military pressure or other extenuating circumstances.[2]

In 1975, Knorr's analysis contained the greatest number of economic coercion events. Since then, other researchers have generated larger and more detailed events data on various aspects of economic coercion. These data sets contain situations in which the sender country threatened to interrupt economic exchange with the target country unless the target acquiesced to political demands. They generally omit cases of sanctions used to extract purely economic concessions, such as trade or tariff disputes.

Three collections of data merit examination. Richard Ellings as-

[2] Knorr (1975), chapter 6, n. 30, and chapter 7, n. 31.

sembled information on 107 instances of economic sanctions between 1945 and 1981.[3] Ellings's research focuses on the correlation between aggregate power and the use of embargoes as a foreign policy tool. To examine the cause of sanctions initiation, Ellings gathers data on structural variables such as military power, aggregate economic power, and international stability. He also considers domestic causes such as changes in presidential administration and business cycles. These tests represent a good first step in determining whether states choose to initiate economic coercion as a result of domestic pressures or for other reasons.

James Blessing collected data on 126 coercion attempts between 1948 and 1972 where the United States disrupted aid flows to coerce a target country.[4] Blessing's research deals with both the initiation and outcome of economic coercion attempts. To test the determinants of outcomes, he codes the events as discrete successes or failures.[5] To test alternative hypotheses, he collected a plethora of dichotomous variables for each coercion event. The independent variables include whether the target country received significant amounts of aid; whether the country was allied with the United States; the regime type of the target country; and the target's geographic location. Blessing's results represent a good check to see how the conflict expectations model stacks up against other theories.

Gary Hufbauer, Jeffrey Schott, and Kimberly Elliott (HSE) gathered evidence for 116 cases of trade or aid sanctions from 1914 to 1990.[6] They attempt to isolate the determinants of coercion outcomes. They code the relative success of the episode on a four-point scale. As with Blessing's work, the event is judged to have been successful if the target country met all of the sender's stated demands. Unlike Blessing, they allow for partial concessions and disputed outcomes. To determine the causes of sanctions success, they collect an impressive number of independent variables. These include the cost to the target country as a percentage of GNP; the degree of international cooperation in the sanctions effort; the cost to the sender country of imposing sanctions; the prior relationship between sender and target; the size ratio of the two actors; and the "economic health and political

---

[3] Ellings (1985).   [4] Blessing (1975, 1981).

[5] There are some ambiguous cases. For example, the United States suspended aid transfers to all of the combatants in the 1967 Six Day war. The war did end, but the role of aid suspension in this outcome is questionable. See Blessing (1981), p. 532.

[6] HSE (1990a, 1990b).

stability" of the target nation. An additional set of dummy variables includes whether companion policies such as covert action or military maneuvers were used; whether the target country received assistance from other countries; and the type of sanctions used (export sanctions, import sanctions, or finance sanctions). A number of econometric studies rely on the HSE data. The results can be used to sift through competing explanations.

The HSE outcome codings reveal that the conventional wisdom is overly pessimistic in its assessment of economic statecraft. Both HSE and Blessing refute the blanket assertion that economic coercion is rarely successful. The most conservative evaluations of their data sets reveal that sanctions were completely successful in at least a third of the attempts. A more generous estimate would place the success rate at 50 percent. These results contrast sharply with Knorr's pessimistic conclusion.

Why do Knorr's and the other data sets have such disparate results? To be sure, there are differences of opinion in the cases that are common to all of the data sets.[7] More important, however, is that the Blessing and HSE sets include far more observations. Knorr admits that his case selection is unscientific, and his events chosen because they "came to the author's attention with sufficient detail for analytic purposes."[8] As noted previously, because sanctions against adversaries are far more likely to capture public attention, such an approach would lead to the conclusion that economic coercion is rarely effective. A more comprehensive approach can reveal lesser-known successes between states with low conflict expectations. Neither Blessing nor HSE believe that economic sanctions are a cure-all, but they do show a fair number of cases where economic sanctions can force countries to agree to political concessions. In other words, there is variation that needs to be explained.

Statistical studies of sanctions initiation

To determine the cause of aid suspensions, James Blessing compares the set of 59 countries that had their aid suspended between 1948 and 1972 against a null set of 59 countries that received US foreign aid but did not have it suspended. He first examines the cases of suspension to see if domestic forces such as public opinion, congressional

[7] See Baldwin (1985), pp. 311–18.   [8] Knorr (1975), p. 337, n. 31.

pressure, or business interests can explain US economic pressure. He finds that none of these factors influenced US decision-making. Domestic pressure played a minimal role in motivating the coercion events. He concludes, "there have been few cases where aid was suspended primarily in response to either domestic pressure in the United States or congressional pressure ... In the vast majority of the 126 cases, however, aid was suspended by the executive branch more directly in response to recipient behavior, rather than in response to overt congressional pressure."[9] He also finds that economic interests play a minimal role in the initiation of economic coercion. Of the 126 cases, the issue is "political-military" in more than three-quarters. Protecting American economic interests from expropriation or nationalization is a factor in only 7 percent of the cases. This fact is somewhat at odds with the notion prevalent in the dependency literature that the "typical" case of US economic coercion involves guaranteeing US foreign investments.[10]

Rejecting domestic-level explanations, Blessing moves on to test various international factors that could determine the cause of initiation. He does this by comparing the countries that had their aid suspended with the set of countries that received US aid but did not face any economic coercion. He collects information on the target's regime type, geographic location, level of American economic investment, level of United States aid, and alliance type. The model developed here predicts that coercion is more likely in instances of high aid levels and no alliance. The size of US aid represents the target's opportunity costs of deadlock. A defense alliance indicates that conflict expectations should not be significant.

Blessing uses chi square tests to test his independent variables. His results weakly support the conflict expectations model. His only significant result is that coercion is likelier if aid levels are high; the result is significant at the 1 percent level. Contrary to the conflict expectations model, there is no significant correlation between the existence of a defense alliance and a coercion attempt. However, this is due in part to the fact that most of the high aid states were allies of the United States (twenty-two out of twenty-seven), whereas most low aid states were not.[11] If allies receive higher levels of aid, then

[9] Blessing (1981), p. 330.
[10] Ibid., pp. 330–1. See Olson (1979) for a review of the dependency literature with regard to economic coercion.
[11] Blessing (1975), p. 131.

they face a bigger gap in opportunity costs, and therefore are just as likely to satisfy the coercion condition as adversaries. Since Blessing does not control for aid levels when testing the role of alliance type, it is impossible to determine whether conflict expectations have any independent effect. No other variable registered as significant. Blessing's overall conclusion: "The United States has been more apt to suspend aid to those countries in which it had a high interest and was less apt to suspend aid to those states in which it had low interest."[12] Economic coercion was attempted in situations where the United States cared about the outcome; sanctions were not used as symbols.

To determine why states initiate attempts at economic coercion, Richard Ellings examines the incidence of economic sanctions between 1945 and 1981, with an emphasis on the cases where the United States is the primary sender. In looking at the data, Ellings comes to many of the same conclusions as Blessing. For example, he finds that of the 107 sanctions disputes, only 14 percent are associated with economic interests; the bulk of the cases deal with political/ military disputes. Furthermore, he also finds that domestic political variables had little influence on sanctions initiation. Ellings concludes, "Economic booms or recessions, American troops at war or at peace, a Republican or Democrat in the White House, an election year or not, and a strong or weak Congress all seem to have mattered little in comparison with considerations of international structure and conflict."[13] An additional result is that sanctions are used in concert with military statecraft in only 20 percent of the observations. In most situations, the threat or use of economic coercion is the only tool of pressure in a coercion event.

Ellings also tests to see whether sanctions initiation is correlated with the change of system-level neorealist variables over time. To measure the aggregate power of the United States, he uses the US share of global national product, exports, military expenditures, and military exports. Other explanatory variables include turbulence in the international system and geographic location. The conflict expectations model of economic coercion does not include any of these explanatory variables, so Ellings's tests represent a check on whether alternative systemic explanations can account for the variation in

---

[12] Blessing (1981), pp. 528–9.

[13] Ellings (1985), p. 135. He does find sanctions a more popular policy tool during the Carter administration, owing to the sudden emphasis on human rights issues; beyond that, there is no consistent link between sanctions and presidential administrations.

coercion attempts. Both military expenditures and geographic location can act as proxies for the feasibility of more forceful measures. One would expect to see more cases of sanctions when military spending is low, because it makes that option less feasible. One would also expect to see more attempts when the target is in a less accessible part of the globe.

Ellings's results suggest that none of the alternative explanations can fully explain when a sender country will threaten economic coercion. As with Blessing's results, there is no correlation between the location of the target country and the likelihood of sanctions initiation. The results, combined with Blessing's, reject the idea that economic sanctions are symbolic actions used when the sender has little interest or ability to affect the outcome.

Another variable, turbulence in the international system, shows a strong positive correlation with the incidence of sanctions. In the cold war era this means that the United States used economic coercion at times when other states in the international system took actions that threatened American hegemony. In other words, the United States practiced economic coercion when its interests were threatened. This is further evidence against either a domestic politics explanation or a theory of sanctions as purely symbolic action, but in itself is not a particularly startling result.

Finally, Ellings gets results that support his causal argument, but fail to explain much of the variation. As the concentration of power in the hands of the United States wanes during the postwar era, sanctions are used more often. However, Ellings also acknowledges that this relationship is not strong. At most, the measures of aggregate power account for a "humble" 14 percent of the variance in sanctions initiation.[14] Military expenditures have a weaker relationship, explaining only 10 percent of the variation. When non-American sanctions are included in the analysis, this correlation is further weakened. His results suggest that alternative explanations are needed to explain the initiation of economic coercion attempts.

A. Cooper Drury uses the HSE data to explain the initiation and maintenance of US economic sanctions between 1948 and 1978.[15] He tests three candidate explanations. First, he uses the Conflict and Peace Data Bank to measure the "present and expected future relations," between the United States and the possible target.[16] This

[14] Ibid., p. 131.   [15] Drury (1997).   [16] Ibid., p. 61.

measure closely matches the description of conflict expectations presented in chapter 2. Measures are also developed for the speed with which the crisis occurs and the extent of target's provocative behavior. In addition, Drury also tests to see whether the president incorporates domestic pressures into his decision-making calculus. The hypothesis is that sanctions induce a "rally-round-the-flag" effect. Presidents will be more willing to sanction if public approval is low, or an election creates the need for decisive action, or both. He therefore includes a dummy variable for election years, and a measure of presidential approval. Drury tests his hypotheses using binary time-series, cross-sectional analysis on dyad-years. He then retests the competing models using a fixed-effects approach, controlling for each dyad to assess the generalizability of the contending explanations.

The conflict expectations approach and the domestic politics approach make contrasting predictions for Drury's results. The model developed here would predict that the conflict expectations measure should be strongly correlated with the decision to initiate and maintain sanctions, and significant across all of the tests. The other variables measure the domestic political environment; the conflict expectations model would not predict them to be significant or generalizable. A domestic politics approach would predict that sanctions are much more likely when the conflict escalates quickly and the target engages in provocative behavior. This is consistent with the claim that sanctions are enacted in response to public pressures to 'do something' in a crisis. A domestic politics approach would also expect these sort of pressures to be most acute during an election year, or when presidential approval is low. The domestic variables should therefore be significant.

Drury's results provide extremely strong support for the model presented here.[17] The measure for conflict expectations is positively correlated with the decision to employ economic coercion, and significant at the 1 percent level. Changes in conflict expectations also correspond to US decisions to lift or strengthen economic sanctions. When more bilateral conflict is anticipated, sanctions are strengthened. The fixed-effects estimation shows that conflict expectations are not sensitive to any particular dyad; the effect is constant across the entire set of countries. In all of Drury's estimates, this measure is

[17] The results described in the next two paragraphs are from Drury (1997), chapters 5 and 6.

significant at the 1 percent level. Furthermore, it is the only variable to retain significance in all of the testing procedures. Drury concludes that, "this finding shows that the president is acting 'rationally'; that his actions are based primarily on his interaction with the target and not domestic or personal factors."[18]

The domestic politics approach does not fare as well. Presidential approval is negatively correlated with the decision to sanction, with significance levels close to 5 percent, but Drury concludes that: "while significant, this effect is not very strong."[19] The electoral variable trends in the opposite direction; presidents are less likely to impose sanctions in an election year. Finally, both of the domestic political measures lose their statistical significance in the fixed-effects estimation. Although domestic politics appears to be marginally significant when the target is a Latin American country, it is insignificant in explaining US sanctioning behavior towards the rest of the world. Drury concludes that these variables affect the US decision to sanction only at the margins.

In conclusion, the econometric evidence suggests that the conventional wisdom does a poor job of explaining when economic coercion will be attempted. None of the existing explanations fared well. Blessing and Ellings categorically reject the hypothesis that domestic forces are the cause. Neither study finds that economic coercion is used to sate public opinion or to take symbolic action because there are no other feasible actions. Drury's results provide only marginal support for a domestic explanation. All three researchers agree that sanctions are a purposive tool of foreign policy, to be employed in situations where the United States has a significant interest in the outcome. Overall, the empirical support for the existing theories of sanctions initiation is weak at best and insignificant at worst.

The support for the conflict expectations model is reasonably strong. All three studies find that sanctions are more likely when target nations act in ways contrary to the sender's interests. These results are consistent with the basic assumptions made in the model. Blessing finds that economic coercion is more likely to be threatened if the target's opportunity costs of deadlock are high, but the alliance variable was found to have no significant effect. This may have been a result of the correlation between high aid levels and alignment. Drury's results strongly support the hypothesis that senders are more

---

[18] Ibid., p. 126.   [19] Ibid., p. 110.

likely to sanction targets when conflict expectations are high. Further testing is needed, but these results are encouraging.

Statistical studies of sanctions outcomes

In a recent paper on sanctions, Jaleh Dashti-Gibson, Patricia Davis, and Benjamin Radcliff complain, "there is a virtual absence of systematic empirical studies of the conditions that render sanctions likely to succeed."[20] These authors exaggerate. There have been at least ten statistical analyses of sanctions outcomes. Whether these studies are all useful is another question entirely.

For the purposes of the conflict expectations model, Blessing and HSE's coding of the outcome variable is problematic. Both data sets define a success as the extent to which the target agreed to the sender's original demand.[21] A dependent variable of "success" or "failure" does not jibe perfectly with the theory of economic coercion developed here. The proper dependent variable for this model is the size of the agreed concessions relative to the status quo, and not the size of the concessions relative to the sender's original demand. For example, if the demand is some form of economic compensation, agreeing completely to a $10 million reparation demand should count less than an agreement to provide 20 percent of a $100 million demand for reparations. The Blessing and HSE codings are biased in favor of complete acquiescence to a small demand over partial acquiescence to a large demand. Furthermore, all of the econometric investigations in this chapter include the size of the demand in their set of explanatory variables, making the results even less useful as a check on the conflict expectations model.

There is a further problem in the HSE data set with case selection.

---

[20] Dashti-Gibson, Davis, and Radcliff (1997), p. 608.

[21] HSE have a second dimension of success that is even more problematic. They code the contribution that economic sanctions made to the outcome. In their own work, they multiply this coding with the success coding to create their dependent variable.

This methodology is flawed; using a dependent variable that consists partially of whether sanctions contributed to the outcome is tautological in the extreme. The goal of the research effort is to determine if the independent variables have an effect on the policy outcome. Their contribution is determined by the sign and significance of their coefficients in a multivariate regression. Including the contribution part of the dependent variable distorts the results.

Because of this, I omit discussion of the papers using HSE's original dependent variable. This includes van Bergeijk (1989, 1994), Li (1993), and Simon (1997).

Some of their observations would not fit under the definition of economic coercion presented here. For example, they include the strategic embargoes of the Soviet Union and China, which were long-term containment strategies with no clearly associated demand. They also include several instances of wartime embargoes, such as the Allied blockade of the Central Powers during the First World War. These cases also do not fit, and including them may skew the statistical results.[22]

Despite the differences in the dependent variable and case selection, the previous empirical investigations of these studies can provide information on whether the alternative theories of economic coercion have any explanatory power. These theories claim to predict when sanctions will succeed or fail; on their own terms, using only the success variable is appropriate. Because of the problems with the dependent variable, any support for the conflict expectations model should be muted. If there are significant results, so much the better.

Blessing performs separate chi square tests on the data to examine which independent variables have significant explanatory power. His factors include the target's regime type, the cost of the aid disruption, the alliance relationship between the target and sender, the level of private American investment in the target country, and issue type. If the target's response to economic coercion is driven by domestic weakness, then one would expect to see authoritarian governments being less likely to concede. If conflict expectations drive the target's response, then the target's costs and the presence of an alliance should be positively correlated with a successful outcome.

Blessing's results provide mild support for the conflict expectations model and a mild rebuke for the domestic politics argument. He concludes, "aid suspension by the United States tends to be more successful in dealing with countries with one or more of the following characteristics: an Authoritarian Conservative or Traditional Conservative government, a formal alliance with the United States, the receipt of relatively large gross amounts of American aid, and relatively little direct private American economic investment."[23] None of these variables is statistically significant in the pairwise tests, but the coefficients trend in the direction predicted by the conflict expectations model, and against the direction predicted by the domestic

[22] On case selection, see Pape (1997). On strategic embargoes, see Mastanduno (1992).
[23] Blessing (1975), p. 144.

politics school. The only variable Blessing finds to be significant is the issue type, but his definition of this issue makes any interpretation of this result problematic.[24]

There are at least six econometric studies that test the HSE data with a rigorous methodology and generate significant results. Two studies, one by San Ling Lam and the other by Kimberly Elliott and Peter Uimonen, use probit techniques to test which independent variables collected by HSE are significant.[25] Two more studies, one by A. Cooper Drury and the other by Dashti-Gibson et al. at Notre Dame, use logistic regressions to analyze the data.[26] They differ somewhat in their sample size and the choice of independent variables. Two other research efforts use the HSE data to test their own theories. T. Clifford Morgan and Valerie Schwebach examine whether military threats and military power influence sanctions outcomes.[27] Lisa Martin is concerned with the causes of multilateral cooperation in sanctions implementation, but her results have some bearing on the utility of economic coercion.[28]

Unfortunately, HSE include only one domestic-level variable in their study, an ordinal measure of the target country's overall economic health and political stability. One would expect that the target's "health" should be negatively correlated with sanctions success, but the variable, as coded, is too much of a catch-all. The measure includes systemic as well as domestic-level factors, political as well as economic factors. It can be thought of as a control variable for domestic forces within the target country, but the measure is too broad to confirm any specific hypothesis.

The signaling school would expect several variables to be significant. The sender's costs, because they show credible commitment, should be positively correlated with a successful outcome. Multilateral cooperation should be positively correlated with a successful outcome. Cases where the aggregate power of the sender is much larger than the target, or where companion policies of covert, quasi-military, or regular military force are observed, are also expected to be more successful.

The conflict expectations model makes several predictions of the

---

[24] See ibid., p. 144, n. 9, for his definition.
[25] Lam (1990); Elliott and Uimonen (1993).
[26] Drury (1997); Dashti-Gibson, Davis, and Radcliff (1997).
[27] Morgan and Schwebach (1997).
[28] Martin (1992).

statistical results. As noted earlier, the cost figures correspond closely to the model's notion of opportunity costs. The target's costs should be positively correlated with sanctions success and the sender's costs should be negatively correlated with sanctions success. The prior relationship variable is the best measure of conflict expectations. Since it takes a higher value if the two countries are close allies and a lower value if they are adversaries, it should be positively correlated with a successful outcome.

A review of the evidence rejects the alternative explanations and provides some support for the conflict expectations model. The prior relationship variable produces mixed results. Only Lam and Drury include the measure of prior relations. Lam finds the variable to trend in the predicted direction; consistent with the conflict expectations model, the closer the prior relationship, the more likely that the outcome was a success. The result is significant at the 10 percent level, but given the problems with the dependent variable as coded, it is an encouraging sign. Drury, on the other hand, does not get a significant result, and the trend is in the other direction. Drury's results are somewhat disconcerting, but are mitigated by the fact that none of his alternative explanatory variables (costs to sender, the target's domestic health, cooperation with the sender, third-party assistance to the target, the type of sanction employed) are significant either.

Four of the studies incorporate a direct measure of the target's opportunity costs of sanctions, and with one partial exception the variable was found to be positively correlated with a successful outcome, and statistically significant. Lam finds the target's costs to be significant at the 5 percent level; Drury also finds a positive correlation, significant at the 10 percent level. Using a probit regression, the Elliott and Uimonen study finds significance at the 1 percent level; using logistic regressions, Morgan and Schwebach also find the target's costs to be significant at 1 percent. The Notre Dame study divided the cases into two groups. The target's costs were significant at the 10 percent level in cases involving the destabilization of the target regime, but the measure was insignificant with the other set of observations. This could be because the second set of observations includes all of the inappropriate cases mentioned earlier. On the whole, these results suggest a clear link between the target's opportunity costs and the outcome of a coercion event.

Lam, Martin, and Morgan and Schwebach include a measure of the sender's opportunity costs. At first glance, the results appear to be contradictory. Lam finds the sender's costs to be negatively correlated with sanctions success and significant at the 5 percent level. Morgan and Schwebach find the same correlation at a 1 percent level of significance. These results support the conflict expectations model and reject the hypothesis that the sender's costs are a signal for stronger measures. However, Martin provides compelling statistical evidence that the greater the sender's costs of coercion, the more international cooperation the sender obtains in sanctioning the target.[29] The evidence indicates that although higher costs to the sender lead to enhanced multilateral cooperation, they are negatively correlated with a successful outcome.

How can both claims be correct? The way out of the conundrum is to examine the effect international cooperation has on the outcome. Only Lam and Drury include HSE's measure of international cooperation as an independent variable. They find that cooperation has an insignificant but *negative* effect on the outcome. Martin may be correct in finding that the primary sender's costs can act as a signal to attract multilateral cooperation, but that this does not lead to a greater number of concessions.[30]

The argument that sanctions success can be explained by military force or relative capabilities has absolutely no empirical support. Lam, as well as Elliott and Uimonen, include dummy variables indicating the use of covert or military action. Lam finds no statistically significant effect on the outcome. Elliott and Uimonen find that, if anything, the use of quasi-military force has a *negative* effect on the chances of success. Broader measures of power also produce disconfirming results. Morgan and Schwebach test to see if the military balance of power influences the sanctions outcome. Their argument is that sanctions are merely a stalking horse for the threat of military force. They find that the military balance of power trends in the predicted direction but has no significant effect on the outcome of economic coercion. Looking at ratios of gross national product, both Lam and Elliott and Uimonen show that economic coercion is less likely to succeed if the sender is significantly more powerful than the target. This result is significant at the 1 percent level in Elliott and Uimonen's

---

[29] Using two-tailed tests, Martin finds the cost to the sender to be positively correlated and significant at the 5 percent level using both ordered probit and event count analysis.

[30] See Drezner (1997a) and Drury (1997, chapter 3) for more on the relationship between multilateral cooperation and sanctions success.

study, and at the 5 percent level in Lam's. Summed up, these results provide no support for the signaling approach.

Of the other independent variables, two appear to have some significance. According to Lam, if the target receives third-party support, then sanctions success is less likely. This result is significant at the 5 percent level. The measure of the target country's overall economic health and political stability also appears to be significant. Lam, and Elliott and Uimonen, find that sanctions are more likely to succeed if the target country is in a "distressed" situation. Elliott and Uimonen find this to be significant at the 1 percent level; Lam's study shows it to be significant at the 10 percent level. The Notre Dame study finds it to be significant in the destabilization cases, but insignificant for the rest of the observations. Drury does not get a statistically significant result. Overall, these results suggest that third-party assistance to the target and the effect of domestic politics within the target country merit further examination. The statistical tests in the next chapter will include these measures as control variables.

In conclusion, the statistical studies of sanctions outcomes support the conflict expectations model and reject other system-level explanations. The target's opportunity costs of deadlock, the sender's opportunity costs of deadlock, and the prior relationship between the two countries trend in the predicted directions and in all but two instances are statistically significant. These results are particularly encouraging given the coding problems mentioned above. On the other hand, variables that measure the aggregate balance of power, the use of companion military policies, and the presence of multilateral cooperation perform badly. They are either statistically insignificant or trend away from the predicted direction. This suggests that economic coercion is not a stalking horse for military threats or relative capabilities. Of the control variables, only the target's domestic stability and third-party assistance to the target appear to have any explanatory power.

This section suggests that the alternative hypotheses cannot explain much variation in the initiation and outcome of attempts at economic coercion. The rest of the chapter looks at three well-known cases of economic sanctions to see if the conflict expectations model can contribute a better understanding to the causal story. Each case is broken down into the parts of the case consistent with the conventional wisdom, and those that fit the conflict expectations model.

Case study 1: the grain embargo

What the conventional wisdom tells us

In late December of 1979, the Soviet Union invaded Afghanistan to ensure the loyalty of its unstable ally. In response, the Carter administration enacted a series of economically coercive measures. These included restriction of Soviet fishing rights in US waters, a curtailment of Aeroflot services to the United States, and a stoppage of high-technology exports. The most costly step, however, was the decision to halt the export of 17 million metric tons of grain to the USSR.[31]

The costs of the embargo to the United States were significant. Presidential candidate Ronald Reagan claimed that the price of the sanctions to the federal government was 1 billion dollars. Daoudi and Dajani estimate the price to the US economy as follows:

> Government purchases of grain originally intended for the Soviet Union at a cost of $2.5 billion.
>
> Restrictions on this year's production, with the government required to pay farmers more than $2 billion to induce them to divert cropland from cultivation of grain crops.
>
> A loss of about $2.5 billion in returns on foreign trade, in addition to whatever reduction may result from lower prices that other overseas customers may pay."[32]

The costs to the agricultural sector seemed particularly devastating. The US Department of Agriculture estimated that farm incomes dropped forty percent in 1980. Carter's opponent in the Democratic party primary, Senator Edward Kennedy, claimed the sanctions were "going to hurt the American farmer and taxpayer more than the Soviet aggressor."

The Soviet Union's opportunity costs of sanctions turned out to be minimal. The other grain exporters – Australia, Canada, the European Community, and Argentina – pledged not to take advantage of the US embargo, but over time did just that. Argentina was the most egregious violator. Two weeks after the US decision, the Argentine Minister of Agriculture declared that Argentina would not participate in the embargo. In April of 1980 it signed a long-term grain deal with the Soviet Union, guaranteeing exports for five years. Once Argentina

---

[31] Another 8 million tons were shipped under a 1975 grain agreement that Carter decided not to abrogate.
[32] Daoudi and Dajani (1983), p. 141.

stopped cooperating, the other countries also defected and began selling increased amounts of grain to the Soviet Union. In 1980, the USSR was able to import a record amount of 31 million metric tons.[33] This shows how difficult it is to apply unilateral sanctions on an easily substitutable commodity. Naturally, the Soviets refused to leave Afghanistan. Fulfilling his campaign pledge, President Reagan lifted the embargo three months after taking office.

The consensus on this episode is that the grain embargo is an example of how sanctions can hurt the sender more than the target. A 1996 *Foreign Policy* article argues: "Economically, sanctions can hurt the target country less than the implementing country. When the United States imposed a grain embargo on the Soviet Union in 1980, the Soviets easily found other suppliers, but the United States found no alternative buyers."[34] Indeed, the costs to the United States were so significant that after the declaration of martial law in Poland the Reagan administration refrained from implementing the embargo again because of the prohibitive costs to the US government.[35] This case is frequently cited as evidence that in responding to crisis situations in the public glare, policy-makers take impulsive and costly actions that fail to work.[36]

---

[33] Paarlberg (1980, 1987).

[34] Lavin (1996), p. 145.

[35] Haig (1984), p. 251.

[36] David Baldwin has a different take on this episode. He agrees that the costs to the United States were significant, but argues that this enhanced US diplomacy. On p. 264 of *Economic Statecraft*, he comments, "the most important costs were not those imposed on the Soviet Union but rather those the United States was willing to impose on itself, for it is those costs that bolster the credibility of the message." He goes on to argue that in sending a clear signal, the Soviets refrained from further expansion into South Asia, and were stopped from using military force in Poland, because they were concerned about the prospect of a strong western response.
There are two replies to this argument. First, although it is true that the Soviets failed to take further aggressive action in South Asia or the Middle East, ascribing this action to the grain embargo would be foolhardy. The military quagmire in Afghanistan was more than enough to deter further aggressive action; indeed, the war was so costly to the Soviets that it prevented them from taking forceful action in the region when it was approved by the United Nations, such as the Gulf war. Sanctions played a limited role in deterring aggression. Second, there is no evidence to suggest that the Soviets were intimidated by the prospect of sanctions in their policies towards Poland. In their memoirs, both Alexander Haig and Ronald Reagan note that Soviet leaders asserted the right to take whatever action was necessary. In the end, although there were military exercises on the Polish border, Soviet economic pressure was sufficient to extract the necessary concessions from Poland. See Haig (1984), pp. 242–3, 250.

What the conflict expectations model tells us

According to the model presented here, the United States was willing to incur significant costs to employ economic coercion because it faced its greatest adversary, and was therefore thinking in terms of relative gains. Still, even a sender concerned only with relative gains should not knowingly incur the greater costs. If this case is consistent with the conflict expectations model, then American policy-makers must have believed they could hurt the Soviet Union more than they hurt the US economy, although they would have been willing to incur significant costs because of the adversarial relationship between the two countries.

The US decision to implement the grain embargo was framed in terms of the concern for relative gains and reputation. The quote from Senator Kennedy in the preceding section shows that the chief domestic criticism of the sanctions was not the absolute costs to the United States, but rather that those costs were relatively greater than those incurred by the Soviet Union. This criticism displays the twin facts that American policy-makers were extremely concerned with relative gains in this interaction with the USSR, and that they incorporated this concern into rational calculations of the costs and benefits of sanctions.

The foreign policy leaders within the Carter administration were clearly willing to bear significant costs if they believed that the Soviets would be hurt even more. Carter's Secretary of State Cyrus Vance and his National Security Advisor Zbigniew Brzezinski agree that the embargo was imposed because it hurt the Soviets the most. Vance comments, "No other measure was as costly to the Soviet Union or as clear a demonstration that the United States was prepared to accept significant sacrifices to impose a price for aggression." Carter notes in his memoirs: "Other economic steps would have some effect, but an analysis of possible sanctions revealed that this was the only one which would significantly affect the Soviet economy."[37]

US policy-makers were also concerned about their reputation for toughness because they anticipated future conflicts with the Soviets. In his testimony to Congress, Vance noted: "We confront a serious and sustained Soviet challenge, which is both military and political ... In that sense, Afghanistan is a manifestation of a larger problem, evident

---

[37] Vance (1983), p. 389; Carter (1982), p. 474. See also Brzezinski (1983), pp. 431–3.

also in Ethiopia, South Yemen, Southeast Asia and elsewhere." Brzezinski urged President Carter to develop a reputation for toughness in dealing with the Soviets, arguing that only then could negotiations not be seen as a sign of weakness. Carter, in his diary entry for January 3, 1980, underscored his concern about US reputation: "This is the most serious international development that has occurred since I have been President, and unless the Soviets recognize that it has been counterproductive for them, we will face additional serious problems with invasions or subversion in the future."[38] In deciding among its options, the Carter administration was concerned with both relative gains and reputational effects because it anticipated frequent conflicts with the Soviet Union.

Washington wanted Moscow to suffer more than itself. How can this be reconciled with the common perception that the grain embargo accomplished the reverse? There are three parts to the answer. First, in their decision to use economic coercion, Carter and his advisors were misinformed about the costs to Moscow. Second, the Soviets incurred damage from the sanctions that the accepted narrative overlooks. Third, the estimates of US costs have been grossly exaggerated.

When the National Security Council met to determine the extent of the sanctions, Carter was told that the Soviets were more vulnerable to a grain embargo than was actually the case. There was evidence to support this belief. The Soviet grain harvest was abysmal, and immediate imports were needed to ensure the size of its livestock herds. Robert Paarlberg notes, "In most respects, circumstances in January 1980 seemed tailor-made for a high degree of success ... If the Soviet Union would ever be vulnerable to US food power, this seemed the time."[39] Most important, it was generally believed that other suppliers would be unable to substitute for the United States. Both Brzezinski and Carter note in their memoirs that they did not think Argentina would be capable of replacing the US supply. Brzezinski comments, "The President was also influenced by the Agriculture Department's firm opinion that no other country could replace the United States as a major seller to the Soviet Union – a conclusion which within days was shaken by Argentina's announcement that it would partially replace American grain shipments." This assessment is confirmed by an entry in Carter's diary a few days after the key

[38] Vance (1983), p. 396; Brzezinski (1983), p. 432; Carter (1982), p. 473.
[39] Paarlberg (1980), pp. 144–5.

National Security Council meeting: "We're asking Australia and Canada not to replace the grain we might withhold. Argentina doesn't have any on hand in addition to what they've already sold."[40] The Department of Agriculture estimate was not completely incorrect; Argentine grain exports fell by roughly 50 percent in 1980.[41] The mistake was in not believing that Buenos Aires would redirect their exports in response to higher Soviet prices. The Carter administration misperceived the extent to which the grain embargo could damage the Soviet Union. When the decision was made, Carter expected the Soviets to suffer more than they actually did.

The actual costs to Moscow were nevertheless significant. To acquire grain from Argentina, the Soviet Union was forced to pay a 25 percent premium on immediate grain and feed imports. It had to pay $23 million in trans-shipment costs to circumvent the embargo. It is true that the Soviet government was able to import a record tonnage of grain, but this overlooks the fact that this was still 4 million tons less than planned, a 12 percent shortfall; 600,000 metric tons of meat were lost as a result of the feed shortage. Had the embargo been maintained, meat production would have fallen even further. All told, the yearly damage to the Soviet Union from all of the US economic sanctions was estimated at more than half a billion dollars.[42]

Just as the costs to Moscow have been minimized, the costs to the United States have been exaggerated. Daoudi and Dajani divide the costs into government purchases, government subsidies to farmers, and lost export opportunities. They assess the cost of each of these actions in the billions. Each of the estimates is overstated or wrong. First, although the US government did accumulate significant costs in purchasing the grain intended for the Soviet Union, it was able to sell off significant amounts of this purchase on the world market by midsummer.[43] Thus, the federal government was able to recoup most of its $2 billion. Second, Daoudi and Dajani are incorrect about the subsidies to farmers. The Carter administration declined to pay for any diversion of acres for either corn or wheat. Finally, there were no costs to the agricultural sector from lost export opportunities. By volume, wheat exports increased by 26 percent, and corn exports rose by 37 percent during the first six months of the embargo. In the first

---

[40] Brzezinski (1983), p. 431; Carter (1982), p. 476.
[41] Paarlberg (1987), pp. 188–9.
[42] Paarlberg (1980), HSE (1990a), pp. 163–74.
[43] Paarlberg (1980), p. 147.

fiscal year after the embargo was in place, exports increased from 89.2 to 108.8 million metric tons. The American share of total grain exports increased by 3 percent between June 1979 and June 1980. This was possible because of aggressive expansion into the Mexican and Chinese markets.[44] Thus, two of the three claimed costs were non-existent, and the third was far less than the original outlay.

Overall, it would be fair to say that in dollar terms, US costs were still larger than Soviet costs.[45] This is the assessment of economists and political scientists that have looked at the case in depth. However, because Soviet gross national product was roughly half the American GNP, the Soviets still suffered heavier economic losses than the United States. Although the grain embargo was one of the costliest sanctions episodes in American history, the target still incurred greater proportional costs than the sender. Thus, even if the Carter administration had not overestimated the costs to Moscow, the decision to embargo was consistent with the conflict expectations model.

In a situation where the sender and target anticipate frequent conflicts in the future, and the costs to the sender are almost as great as the costs to the target, the model predicts that the predicted concessions should be minor at best. This is consistent with the Soviet response to the sanctions. The Soviet ambassador to the United States, Anatoly Dobrynin, note that the Soviet Politburo interpreted the US sanctions as the start of a more confrontational American strategy.[46] The only proposed concessions were extremely minor. At an informal meeting between Brzezinski and Dobrynin in March 1980, the Soviets offered to replace the president of the new Afghan government, or make a tentative date for a Soviet pullout. Total withdrawal was never directly discussed, and the discussions never got off the ground.[47]

In conclusion, a closer look at the post-Afghanistan sanctions reveals that the Carter administration was willing to incur significant costs when it believed the Soviets would suffer more, and because of the heightened expectations of future conflict. Also consistent with the model, the Soviets offered only token concessions in response.

---

[44] Paarlberg (1987), pp. 198–200. See also Gardner (1984).

[45] HSE estimate the costs to the United States at $750 million, and to the USSR at $525 million. The Soviet estimate, however, fails to include revenue lost from the Olympic boycott. HSE (1990a), pp. 79, 171.

[46] Dobrynin (1995), p. 448.

[47] Ibid., pp. 450–1, and Brzezinski (1983), p. 435.

Case study 2: the pipeline sanctions

What the conventional wisdom tells us

In the late 1970s, in an effort to diversify their energy imports away from OPEC countries, Western European nations began negotiations with the Soviet Union to secure natural gas imports from Siberia. The Soviets proposed to build a 5,000-kilometer pipeline with an annual transit capacity of 40 billion cubic meters of natural gas.[48] To the countries of Western Europe, this meant two things: a guaranteed source of energy free from OPEC, and the prize of lucrative pipeline contracts to generate jobs during a crippling recession.

Washington was not keen on this arrangement. According to the contracts signed, West Germany, Italy, and France would all depend on the USSR for more than 30 percent of their total gas supply. To the United States, this dependency on Soviet energy left its NATO allies vulnerable to communist economic coercion. At the July 1981 Ottawa summit, President Reagan tried to dissuade the European states from exporting pipeline compressors, arguing that they gave the Soviets a boost in high-technology goods. If the allies had cooperated, the construction of the pipeline would have been disrupted.

The European response was tepid. Within the next month, West Germany had signed an outline agreement for financing the pipeline. In September, construction contracts worth $3.47 billion were signed between European firms and the Soviet government. During the fall, Italy and West Germany signed contracts for gas purchases.

The declaration of martial law in Poland gave the United States an excuse to exhort the allies to sanction the Soviet Union. In response to the situation, the United States and its European allies enacted a number of sanctions against Poland. The United States also wished to punish the Soviets, and announced in late December 1981 a series of economic sanctions, including a ban on oil and gas equipment exports. The Western European allies refrained from those sanctions, because they would have affected the pipeline.

For the next six months, the United States put diplomatic pressure on its allies to participate in the sanctions against the Soviet Union. This pressure yielded nothing beyond a NATO declaration condemning the situation in Poland. The plans for the pipeline con-

---

[48] Jentleson (1986), p. 172, and chapter 6, *passim.*

tinued. In January, France signed a gas purchase deal. At the Versailles economic summit in June, Reagan again prevailed upon the allies to join the pipeline embargo, with little success. In response, Reagan announced on June 18 that the United States was extending the ban on oil and gas equipment sales to foreign subsidiaries of US firms, and foreign firms that were using US technology. The ban was retroactive, applying to technology licenses that were already granted. Penalties included ten-year prison sentences for executives, a fine of $100,000 for each infraction, and the denial of trading privileges with the United States. In essence, these measures threatened European firms with heavy sanctions unless the American demands were met.

In response, all of the allies rejected the extraterritorial and retroactive nature of the sanctions. The dispute led to deep fissures in the NATO alliance. The European Community issued a formal protest against the sanctions. West German chancellor Helmut Schmidt affirmed: "The pipeline will be built." The French Foreign Minister described relations with the United States as a "progressive divorce." He went on to observe, "we no longer speak the same language." Even the UK, Washington's closest ally, invoked the Protection of Trading Interests Act to ensure that the embargo would be overridden.

Matters came to a head in late August. France ordered Dresser-France, the French subsidiary of Dresser Industries, to fulfill its contract and ship its compressors to the USSR. The firm complied, and the United States barred the firm from importing US goods or services until further notice. Over the next six weeks, the United States imposed penalties against firms in Italy, the UK, and West Germany for delivering on their contracts. All of the states refused to concede. At the same time as the Reagan administration was applying pressure against its allies, Washington refused to impose another grain embargo. There is considerable evidence that because the United States was reluctant to take action costly to itself, it undercut its credibility with Western Europe.[49] As the fall progressed, the United States found itself increasingly isolated on the issue. David Baldwin notes, "By the fall of 1982, the relationship between Polish martial law and the embargo became increasingly obscure, as the

[49] See Martin (1992), chapter 8.

preexisting differences of opinion ... among NATO members became ever more apparent."[50]

In the end, Washington backed down. On November 13, Reagan announced that all sanctions against Western Europe would be lifted because an agreement had been reached on exports to the Soviet Union. The United States claimed that the Europeans had compromised their positions. Empirically, this is a dubious proposition. In the six months after the incident, European firms signed more than $1.5 billion in new contracts with the Soviets. Gas imports from Siberia were curtailed, but this was mostly because of a slackening of demand and a drop in oil prices. One assessment concluded, "it is not too harsh to characterize the pipeline controls as the least effective and most costly controls in US history."[51] There is no doubt that the United States acquiesced completely on this issue.

The economic and political fallout from the episode was considerable. Economically, the sanctions made US firms appear to be unsafe trading partners. A German official from AEG-Kanis commented: "There is a doubt, a lack of trust, a feeling against the United States, that is the worst thing to come out of this affair."[52] After the episode, US firms encountered greater difficulties trying to export to European companies fearful of a future embargo. Foreign direct investment in the European Community also became a sensitive issue. The strains on the NATO alliance were also considerable.

This episode would seem to completely falsify the conflict expectations model. First, the United States decided to coerce its allies despite the lack of conflict expectations and the high cost of sanctions to itself. Second, the Western European countries refused to acquiesce despite the significant opportunity costs of deadlock and minimal expectations of future conflict with the United States.

What the conflict expectations model tells us

In game theory, a complete strategy must provide instructions for a player at each of its decision nodes. A subgame perfect equilibrium strategy must provide the player with an incentive-compatible decision at every choice node, even if that choice is off the equilibrium

---

[50] Baldwin (1985), p. 289.

[51] Henry Moyer and Linda Mabry, quoted in HSE (1990a), p. 217. See also Jentleson (1986) and Wolf (1987).

[52] Quoted in HSE (1990a), p. 214.

path. In other words, if one of the players makes a mistake, and both players find themselves at a point in the game that is unexpected, the players still pursue a rational course of action. The pipeline sanctions case is an example of off-the-equilibrium behavior. The problematic part of this case for the model is the US decision to apply sanctions against Western Europe. According to the model, that option should not have been taken. *After* that mistake was made, however, the choices of the sender and targets were rational. The allies correctly perceived that the United States preferred the status quo to a stale-mate. The United States compared the possible outcomes and ration-ally chose to back down.

Why did the United States decide to apply the sanctions in the first place? There are two reasons, both of which violate the assumption of the foreign policy leader as a rational unitary actor. First, it needs to be remembered that the US sanctions were directed against firms, not countries. The coercion of firms is usually easier than the coercion of nation-states.[53] CEOs do not care about relative gains or political reputation; they care about profits. If the sanctions had stayed at the firm level, there is every reason to believe that they would have been successful. Martin documents that the key European firms were prepared to accede to US demands until their governments inter-vened. Dresser-France, for example, only agreed to ship equipment to the USSR after the French government threatened to requisition the firm's facilities and carry out the order anyway. John Brown Ltd of Great Britain indicated that it would go bankrupt if the sanctions were implemented indefinitely. Martin concludes, "It appeared that Euro-pean firms would comply with the sanctions unless their governments prohibited them from doing so. Faced with the choice of the Soviet market or US technology, they would give in to American demands in spite of the sales and jobs they would lose."[54] By originally targeting firms rather than countries, US policy-makers believed they had circumvented the coercion condition. The Reagan administration did not err in thinking that the firms preferred to acquiesce; it erred in believing that the allied governments would not transform the situa-tion into an interstate dispute.

The second reason for the decision was the lack of unity within the US foreign policy regime. The Reagan administration was divided

[53] See Shambaugh (1999).
[54] Martin (1992), p. 219.

into two camps on the pipeline issue. The hardliners, led by Secretary of Defense Caspar Weinberger, were extremely concerned about relative gains *vis-à-vis* the Soviet Union. Weinberger said at one point during the crisis: "Without constant infusions of high technology from the West, the Soviet industrial base would experience a cumulative obsolescence which would eventually also constrain the military industries."[55] This faction believed that any friction within NATO was worth the benefit of reduced commerce with the USSR. In other words, Weinberger thought of the Soviet Union and not Western Europe as the target, and was willing to incur significant political costs to employ sanctions.[56] The other faction, led by Secretary of State Alexander Haig, agreed with Weinberger's basic premise but differed over tactics. Haig also believed the pipeline was a bad idea, but that the time for stopping it had long since passed. Any sanctions against Western Europe would produce nothing but discord between the allies. Haig correctly perceived that the NATO allies disagreed with the United States on this issue. He did not prefer deadlock to the status quo.

US policy in June 1982 is best explained by the schism within the Reagan administration on this subject. At the beginning of the month, it seemed that Haig's approach would prevail. At the Versailles summit in early June, Haig had negotiated a tentative agreement not to sanction Western European firms, and to bolster the exchange rate value of the French franc. In exchange, the allies would have agreed to restrict export credits to the Soviet Union. That deal fell apart as a result of its inadvertent public rejection by Treasury Secretary Donald Regan, and then France's repudiation of the tacit agreement. Following this, National Security Advisor William Clark, a Weinberger ally, scheduled the critical National Security Council meeting to discuss the pipeline issue on a day when Haig was not in Washington. At that meeting, a majority of the participants opposed the sanctions option. Clark, however, presented only the hardline option to Reagan, and it

---

[55] Quoted in Jentleson (1986), pp. 177–8. There was considerable merit for this approach. Oil and gas exports were responsible for 62.3 percent of the Soviet Union's hard currency earnings in 1980. This revenue increased by only 2.4 percent in 1981, while grain imports were surging.

[56] Instinctively, Reagan viewed the matter this way as well, although this was in part due to his focus on the Soviet Union and ignorance about Western Europe. See Reagan (1990), pp. 306, 320; Cannon (1991), p. 203.

was quickly approved. Partially in response to this action, Haig resigned as Secretary of State later in the month.[57]

The initiation decision is not a particularly good fit with the assumptions of the conflict expectations model. The US foreign policy regime in June 1982 bears no resemblance to a unitary actor. However, this case does not provide much support for the other explanations in the literature. The US decision was not made in reaction to domestic pressures. Following the June 18 decision, polling data showed that only 48 percent of Americans supported these sanctions, as opposed to the 70 percent that favored the grain embargo after its announcement. The act of coercion threatened to be exceedingly costly to US firms doing business in the European Community, yet this cost did not seem to signal resolve to the targeted countries.[58] None of the arguments credibly explains the June 18 decision. It appears to be a genuine outlier for any theory.

Once the decision to coerce was made, however, the conflict expectations model correctly predicts the outcome to be the status quo. The allies had every reason to believe that the United States did not want to go to deadlock. Washington had a reputation for backing down from sanctioning its NATO allies. In the early 1950s, the United States was able to use economic statecraft to force European concessions on the strategic embargo. Once aid levels to Europe declined, however, Washington failed to satisfy the coercion condition with its closest allies, and switched to a carrot strategy on this issue.[59] For example, when the issue of European energy dependency on the USSR came up in the early 1960s, the United States responded by subsidizing allied restrictions on Soviet imports.[60] In the build up to the pipeline dispute, the United States tried the same approach, offering American coal as a substitute for Soviet energy, but the carrot was not substantial enough. Furthermore, previous attempts to use extraterritorial sanctions to enforce an American embargo had failed. In 1965, a French subsidiary of a US company had been sanctioned for

---

[57] Haig (1984), pp. 306–16. There is evidence that Reagan's decision at the NSC meeting was due to his growing disenchantment with Haig. According to Robert McFarlane, Reagan had decided for the hard-line option prior to the NSC meeting because he wanted to force Haig to resign: "It seemed to me one of the very few times when the president really asserted himself for reasons other than what he thought about policy." See Cannon (1991), p. 203.

[58] On the costs to the United States, see Wolf (1987).

[59] Mastanduno (1992); Leigh-Phippard (1995).

[60] Jentleson (1986), chapter 6.

shipping goods to the People's Republic of China. The French government resisted the extraterritorial sanctions, and the United States eventually backed down and accepted the status quo.[61]

Even after the June 18 announcement, the Europeans had every reason to believe the United States would back down. There was tremendous domestic pressure on Reagan to reverse his decision. After the announcement, as Bruce Jentleson notes, "The only question was whether the immediate outcry was louder in Washington or in Europe."[62] Haig's resignation demonstrated the split within the administration. As the summer progressed, Congress attempted to reverse US policy. The House Foreign Affairs Committee voted 22–12 to repeal the sanctions; seven of seventeen Republicans voted against Reagan. On the key floor vote, the measure was defeated by a vote of 206 to 203, but the close vote was an effective signal of Reagan's weakness. Diplomatically, every US action indicated an eventual retreat. Immediately after the sanctions were first invoked in August, the United States communicated a willingness to start exploratory talks on settling the issue. Sanctions against the firms were scaled back when it seemed they would cause real damage. As early as the first weekend in October, the allies learned from the new Secretary of State, George Shultz, that Washington was going to back down.[63]

Once US policy-makers realized that the Europeans would not acquiesce, the only option was to back down. A week after the NSC decision, Commerce Secretary Malcolm Baldridge warned about the high cost of implementing the sanctions. Shultz's chief concern was the high cost to US businesses. Apparently by November, even Weinberger realized that the Europeans would not budge, and preferred backing down to the costs of sustained deadlock. Conflict expectations with the allies were extremely low. At this juncture, the United States and its European allies were in agreement on a host of issues ranging from exchange rates to the deployment of intermediate nuclear forces. Even on this issue, there was significant agreement on stopping Soviet industrial espionage and restricting high-technology exports. As Jentleson points out, "while European governments were still somewhat uncomfortable with the United States' broad interpret-

---

[61] Wolf (1987), p. 217.
[62] Jentleson (1986), pp. 194–5.
[63] Ibid., pp. 203–7; Shultz (1993), pp. 137–43.

ation of what constituted military significance, they had less dispute with the basic economic defense objective of limiting Soviet military capabilities, or at least not enhancing them with Western technology."[64] The United States derived no utility from inflicting damage on Western Europe. Even though it found itself off the equilibrium path, it followed its equilibrium strategy and backed down.

Contrary to the conventional wisdom, the pipeline sanctions failed to lead to a significant rift between the United States and Europe. During the disagreement, the German chancellor took pains to point out that this was an isolated dispute. Immediately after the incident, the Foreign Ministers of Denmark, France, the UK, Italy, and West Germany met to discuss the long-run implications of the dispute. The Danish Foreign Minister's notes about the meeting concluded: "the majority felt that what ought to count was that sanctions had in fact now been lifted. A positive outcome had been obtained, and a trade war had been avoided. In the light of this, one ought not to think too much of the events preceding the result. In other words: let bygones be bygones." All of the countries agreed with this summary, and transmitted the message to the United States.[65] In 1982, these governments agreed to increase the interest rate on export credits to the Soviet Union. In 1983, they permitted the installation of Pershing II nuclear missiles on their soil despite massive public demonstrations. In the long run, the NATO alliance was unaffected by the pipeline issue.

In conclusion, the conflict expectations model would not have predicted that the United States would have attempted economic coercion against its European allies. However, no other theory of economic statecraft seems capable of explaining it either. The model does predict that the European states would stand firm on the issue, because they had every reason to believe that the United States preferred the status quo and would quickly back down. Once the Reagan administration realized that the allies were standing firm, the high costs of coercion and minimal expectations of future conflict made the status quo preferable to a stalemate. This case represents an outcome that is off the equilibrium path, but nonetheless consistent with the conflict expectations model.

---

[64] Jentleson (1986), p. 181.
[65] Shultz (1993), p. 143.

Case study 3: economic sanctions and human rights

How the case fits the conventional wisdom

The emergence of human rights as an element of American foreign policy had many causes. The quagmire in Southeast Asia and the US-supported coup in Chile that overthrew an elected government left many Americans disillusioned by Washington's amoral foreign policy.[66] Congress, reacting to public pressure, began attaching amendments to trade legislation linking tariff rates and foreign aid to human rights. Thus, from the beginning the ends of human rights were tied to the means of economic statecraft. The first example of this was a nonbinding section of the 1973 Foreign Assistance Act, stating: "It is the sense of the Congress that the President should deny any ... military assistance to the government of any foreign country which practices the internment or imprisonment of that country's citizens for political purposes." The sense of the Congress was ignored by both the Nixon and Ford administrations. Over the next three years, the legislative branch reacted by passing more restrictive and binding legislation, mandating the executive branch to respond to a growing tide of public opinion.[67]

The priority for human rights found renewed strength with Jimmy Carter's 1976 election victory. His focus on human rights was partly in response to survey data showing that the issue appealed to both liberal and conservative voters. One campaign official confirmed, "it was a beautiful campaign issue, an issue on which there was a real degree of public opinion hostile to the (Ford) Administration. That's actually how it started for Carter." Administration officials later concurred that a key benefit of the policy was the strong public support it received. Polling data from the campaign confirmed the resonance of the issue with voters. Carter announced in his inaugural address: "Our commitment to human rights must be absolute."[68]

Carter's words were backed up in both staffing decisions and policy outcomes. A Bureau of Human Rights and Humanitarian Affairs was created within the State Department, its head appointed at the

---

[66] Sikkink (1993).
[67] The quote is from HSE (1990b), p. 336. On the origins of the human rights policy, see Schoultz (1980), Drew (1977), and Congressional Research Service (1979), pp. 16–30.
[68] Both quotations from Drew (1977), p. 38.

assistant secretary level. Most of the officials appointed came from human rights and civil rights backgrounds. The first assistant secretary of state for human rights and humanitarian affairs, Patricia Derian, was the founder of the Mississippi Civil Liberties Union. Howard Wiarda argues that this bureau overwhelmed the rest of the State Department bureaucracy: "When there were conflicts between the regional bureau (such as for Latin America) and the human rights bureau, the dispute was settled by a special committee led by then-Deputy Secretary of State Warren Christopher. Invariably, the Christopher committee sided with the human rights bureau and against the regional bureaus."[69]

The expression of this policy was the public use of economic coercion. Joshua Muravchik notes, "The heart and soul of the Carter human rights policy was the application of punishments to governments found to be violating human rights." A report for the Senate Foreign Relations Committee agreed: "Though no conventional instrument of US foreign policy will be excluded as a potential tool in efforts to strengthen human rights conditions, primary focus will be on the use of military sales, bilateral aid, multilateral project assistance, and diplomatic entreaties."[70] Within a month of taking office, Carter suspended grant military assistance to Ethiopia, Uruguay, and Argentina. According to one estimate, diplomatic action was taken against twenty-eight other countries between 1977 and 1981.[71] By December 1978 the issue was embedded in US foreign policy. In that month, Carter proclaimed, "Human rights is the soul of our foreign policy."[72]

What was the effect of this policy? According to the conventional wisdom, the policy produced, at best, marginal results. A Congressional Research Service report surveyed fifteen countries and found significant change in the human rights situations in only five or six. Muravchik compared the Freedom House scores for the targeted countries before and after the policy and found that there was, if anything, a weak trend towards more authoritarian regimes.[73] Two separate studies of the Latin American cases conclude that any

---

[69] Wiarda (1995), p. 71.
[70] Muravchik (1986), p. 161; Congressional Research Service (1979), p. 54.
[71] Muravchik (1986), p. 176.
[72] Carter quoted in HSE (1990b), p. 338.
[73] Muravchik (1986), p. 176; Congressional Research Service (1979), pp. 68–84.

observed success can be explained by the variation in domestic support within the target countries for human rights reform.[74]

Many blamed the policy failures on Washington's highly public approach. One advisor's statement summarized both the naiveté and condescension of the Carter administration's approach: "I think that the mulish world has noticed the two-by-four." Wiarda writes, "Derian's approach in dealing with these critical countries was to rant and rave and condemn the entire nation or its armed forces as 'fascist' ... thus forcing the rest of the population to defend the regime or the rest of the officers to defend the military institution on nationalistic grounds." Lars Schoultz concurs, noting that Derian "was willing to push the issue beyond the bounds of normal diplomatic discourse."[75] Latin American countries such as Brazil or Argentina strongly resisted the sanctions; Brazil threatened to sever diplomatic relations. Not surprisingly, all of the targeted states had authoritarian regimes, and were well equipped to withstand the costs of US economic diplomacy.

Given this record of public failure, it is not surprising that when Ronald Reagan took office, the human rights issue was de-emphasized. By 1983, the political climate had changed enough for Reagan to successfully veto legislation tying foreign aid to progress on human rights.

A brief glance at this narrative suggests that domestic politics heavily influenced the use of economic statecraft to obtain human rights concessions. Sanctions were initiated in response to strong public pressure and applied indiscriminately to friends and foes alike. Economic coercion was used by authoritarian elites to rally public support behind the existing target regime, preventing the sanctions from working. Once the issue died down in the United States, so did the attempts at economic coercion. It would appear that domestic political pressures can explain the entire case.

How the case fits the conflict expectations model

The model makes three predictions for this case. First, it assumes that any demand is viewed by both actors as a transfer of political assets that can affect future conflicts. Human rights are usually debated on moral terms, but for the conflict expectations model to be a causal

---

[74] Martin and Sikkink (1993); Morgan and Schwebach (1996).
[75] Carter advisor quote from Drew (1977), p. 62; Wiarda (1995), pp. 71–2; Schoultz (1981), p. 127.

mechanism, the sender and target should view the issue as inherently political. Second, despite domestic political pressures, US policy-makers should be governed by conflict expectations and opportunity costs in their decisions to use sanctions. Third, the target countries should vary their response because they anticipate a different number of future conflicts with the United States. Allies should concede more than adversaries.

An assumption of the conflict expectations model is that the sender and target countries view the demand as a transfer of political assets. Human rights would seem to be an idealistic and normative issue that would not intrude into other arenas of policy. However, consistent with the assumption, both the sender and the target viewed the issue as directly related to their national interests. US policy-makers believed that human rights concessions would expand American influence over the targeted countries. There was a consensus in Washington that states with greater domestic freedoms would pursue less aggressive foreign policies and be more amenable to American influence. W. David Clinton observes, "The debate over human rights in American foreign policy also witnessed a determined effort to prove that the vigorous advocacy of human rights would advance the national interest defined in terms of power – the power of the United States to influence others and to avoid being threatened by others."[76]

The Carter administration certainly adhered to the link between human rights and expanded influence. In reviewing the policy, Derian noted, "Human rights is an area where our ideals and our self-interest strongly coincide," since progress on human rights "strengthens our position and influence in the world." Brzezinski concurred, describing the policy as "politically useful." In his memoirs, Carter observed, "The respect for human rights is one of the most significant advantages of a free and democratic nation in the peaceful struggle for influence, and we should use this good weapon as effectively as possible." Even Caspar Weinberger, hardly a friend of the Carter administration, adopts a similar line on this issue, "If the Soviet Union were less totalitarian, it would also be less of a military threat, since a less controlled and more liberalized regime could not possibly allocate so much of a nation's resources to military expenditures."[77] In

---

[76] Clinton (1994), p. 216.

[77] Derian and Brzezinski quoted in ibid., p. 246; Carter (1982), pp. 149–150; Weinberger quoted in Jentleson (1986), p. 178.

pushing the issue, the United States believed that states respecting human rights would be more constrained in other international disputes. Human rights progress made US diplomacy easier in the long run, and increased US influence on other issues.

The target states also viewed human rights concessions to the United States as a political transfer. This was more obvious in the reaction of adversaries. Andrei Gromyko, the Soviet Foreign Minister, was convinced that the United States was taking advantage of small Soviet concessions on emigration in 1974 to make larger demands now, and that conceding again would lead to increased US leverage in the future. Anatoly Dobrynin notes, "Moscow believed Carter was deliberately interfering in the Soviet Union's internal affairs in order to undermine the existing regimes in the Soviet Union and Eastern Europe." The congressional policy review concurred in this assessment: "The Soviet Union, most analysts agree, treats as extremely serious any threat to its control over internal dissension, and consequently reacted very strongly to what seemed to be a gratuitous challenge implicit in the President's early statements and actions relating to human rights conditions in the Soviet Union."[78] Soviet allies reacted in a similar fashion. The Marxist regime in Ethiopia, a state that was in the process of realignment when it was sanctioned, was suspicious of the human rights accusations. They noted that the United States had failed to reproach the previous regime, which was more closely allied to Washington.

Even the Latin American regimes viewed the human rights demands as affecting their national interest. At this point, the militaries in the region believed strongly in the notion of a "national security state." This ideology held that the military was the sole national institution in the country. Without authoritarian rule, it was feared the state would be engulfed in societal conflicts. According to this logic, acquiescing on the human rights issue would have weakened the national security of the state by giving more power to narrow-minded interests.[79] This explains the target regime's own disutility of conceding. The Latin American regimes were also automatically suspicious of Washington using any concessions to expand its influence in the region. These countries believed that the United

---

[78] Dobrynin (1995), p. 388; Gromyko (1989), pp. 293–4; Congressional Research Service (1979), p. 52.
[79] See Crahan (1982) and Alves (1985), pp. 1–28.

States strengthened or weakened different sectors of society to achieve its own less altruistic ends.[80] The 1970s were the high point of the dependency thesis; conceding on this issue was perceived by some to reinforce US hegemony in the region. In conclusion, the sender and all of the targets viewed the human rights demands as a transfer of political power affecting future conflicts.

Because the human rights issue was viewed as a political dispute, one would expect to see the United States behave in a manner consistent with the coercion condition in using economic statecraft. The executive branch's reaction under Nixon and Ford provides the first piece of evidence that the sender regime was reluctant to coerce allies and able to withstand public pressure on the matter. Henry Kissinger, the paramount foreign policy leader between 1973 and 1976, took a clear position on the subject. He did not oppose the goals of human rights policies, but he was extremely wary of the means to achieve them, particularly economic coercion. His objections correspond to the conflict expectations model; he was particularly concerned that allies as well as adversaries would be punished. In 1976 he observed:

> Our alliances ... serve the cause of peace by strengthening regional and world security. If well-conceived, they are not favors to others but a recognition of common interests. They should be withdrawn when those interests change; they should not, as a general rule, be used as levers to extort a standard of conduct or to punish acts with which we do not agree.

The concern in this statement was that human rights issues would become a policy that would be uniformly and consistently applied, regardless of the bilateral areas of common interest. Kissinger feared that because aid suspensions were the chief tool of this policy, the United States would threaten allies even though it preferred the status quo to a deadlock situation over human rights.[81]

Kissinger's statements were backed up by action, or rather, nonaction. Prior to Carter's election, the big target of congressional ire was Chile's military government. Yet despite increasingly restrictive legislation, the Ford administration found ways around the law and continued the flow of aid to its perceived ally. Despite public opinion, the sender's foreign policy regime was unwilling to threaten coercion.

---

[80] Wesson (1981), p. 6.
[81] Kissinger quote from Schoultz (1982), p. 305.

Schoultz observes: "The case of economic aid to Chile demonstrates that an administration with a will can find a way to circumvent congressional limitations."[82]

The folk wisdom is correct about the change in policy once the Carter administration took office. As many commentators have observed, human rights was a rare issue where Carter's foreign policy team was in agreement. They are incorrect, however, about the use of economic coercion to obtain human rights concessions. Among US aid recipients during the Carter administration, there is no statistical correlation between the amounts of US aid and their human rights record.[83] If domestic political factors explain the incidence of sanctions, then one would expect to see the Carter administration ignore conflict expectations and be as willing to sanction allies as adversaries. Despite the rhetoric, this was not the case. Carter's chief foreign policy criticism during the presidential campaign was that human rights had not been sufficiently stressed in US policy towards the Soviet bloc. When he took office, his first foreign policy action on human rights was to raise the issue of Soviet and Czech dissidents.[84] Carter's first public actions were directed against cold war adversaries, not third world allies.

There was little problem with rhetorically bashing the Soviets over human rights; as pointed out earlier, this was popular across the political spectrum. Lars Schoultz observes that once the question of aid suspension came up, Carter's position shifted to a "relative rather than absolute commitment to human rights."[85] Decision-making within the Christopher committee incorporated conflict expectations into its choice between the status quo and a possible stalemate. Contrary to Wiarda's claim, most observers agree that the Christopher committee erred on the side of not sanctioning. One State Department official described the decision-making process as follows: "What happened was that if anyone, including one of the regional Assistant Secretaries ... put up a strong argument against zapping any of these countries, he won."[86] By 1978, after reviewing the countries receiving US security assistance, the committee agreed that twelve countries qualified as "gross violators" of human rights, mandating economic

---

[82] Schoultz (1980), p. 329; on Chile, see also Martin (1992), pp. 124–8.
[83] Stohl, Carleton, and Johnson (1984).
[84] Drew (1977), p. 38.
[85] Schoultz (1982), p. 308.
[86] Drew (1977), p. 43.

sanctions.[87] None of the countries were ever officially classified as such, however; such a charge would have mandated the suspension of all foreign aid. Carter feared that such a public act would bind the administration's hands. The Christopher committee used this flexibility to exempt four countries from any sanctions because of "extraordinary circumstances": South Korea, Iran, Zaire, and the Philippines. One of the participants in the meetings attributes this decision to their close alignment and the opportunity costs of coercion:

> Iran was judged critical because it shared a long border with the Soviet Union, was a major supplier of oil to the West, and defended our strategic interests in the Persian Gulf. Military ties with South Korea were deemed essential to deterring the threat of an invasion from the north. Military bases in the Philippines were judged critical to the United States and a security assistance relationship essential to keeping the base. Finally, Zaire, the third largest country in area in Africa, was the source of nearly all the West's cobalt, a material crucial to the performance of high performance jet engines."[88]

In these cases, the United States was unwilling to bear the costs of deadlock. Because of political alliances, the United States did not anticipate any future conflicts with these countries. Washington did not need to establish a tough bargaining position, and there was no expectation that there would be significant future disputes where human rights concessions could be used as leverage. On the other hand, the United States could have incurred costs from a stalemate either from a loss of strategic imports or the reduced effectiveness of its military bases.

There appear to be three categories of countries that the United States either imposed or maintained human rights sanctions during the Carter administration. The first consists of clear adversaries: the Soviet Union, its Warsaw Pact allies, and its third world allies such as Ethiopia, Vietnam, Cambodia, Laos, Angola, Mozambique, and Cuba. The second group consisted of significant allies like Brazil or Argentina where the United States anticipated other conflicts, in areas such as nuclear proliferation and commodities trade. The final group consisted of small Latin American nations: El Salvador, Haiti,

---

[87] Conflict expectations also affected which countries were even considered for sanctions. Indonesia, for example, was kept off the gross violators list because it was classified as a vital ally. Cohen (1982), p. 269.

[88] Ibid., p. 270. See also Drew (1977), pp. 57–8.

Guatemala, Nicaragua, Paraguay, and Uruguay. All of these countries were allies, but their economies were small enough for economic coercion to have an appreciable impact, and the coercion condition could be satisfied.

It is also clear that the United States adjusted its demands to whether the target was an ally or an adversary. For example, the Carter administration's expectations of Soviet concessions were minimal. One foreign policy advisor stated that US demands consisted mostly of the reunification of families and the right to marry foreign nationals. By contrast, the demands on the Latin American countries were more ambitious.[89] US policy-makers knew the limits of economic statecraft in producing concessions. This led some human rights supporters to grow suspicious of Carter's public proclamations. One activist said, "With regard to giving military aid to repressive regimes, I see little difference between this administration and the Nixon–Ford approach."[90]

Contrary to the accepted wisdom, the United States placed strategic calculation ahead of domestic political pressures. Although the Carter administration believed the issue to be important, sanctions were only threatened when the coercion condition was satisfied. There was no blanket or uniform policy; human rights was merely one of several issues considered in crafting foreign policy. This is also the rueful conclusion of a participant in the Christopher committee: "the charge that its pursuit of human rights was "single-minded" and to the exclusion of other interests was far wide of the mark."[91] A congressional review of the policy concurred: "In executing its human rights policies, the administration has avoided designing a comprehensive system of guidelines or principles. Rather, the structure of the administration's overall human rights policy has evolved from a series of decisions based on individual cases in which the particular needs of US foreign policy and capabilities of US influence are both considered."[92] Sanctions were only employed in situations where the opportunity costs of stalemate and the expectations of future conflict meant that deadlock was preferable to the status quo.

---

[89] On demands made of the Soviets, see Drew (1977), p. 57; for Latin American demands, see Pastor (1988).
[90] Quoted in Schoultz (1982), p. 322.
[91] Cohen (1982), p. 270.
[92] Congressional Research Service (1979), p. iii.

The final step for the conflict expectations model is to show that the target countries determined the magnitude of their concessions based on their concern for relative gains and reputational effects. This would appear to have been the case. In the aggregate, economic sanctions were rather successful in Latin America.[93] Even policy skeptics like Muravchik concede that human rights abuses in Argentina, Chile, and El Salvador declined quickly after the Carter administration came to power.[94] The "disappearances" of opposition leaders in Argentina fell from 500 in 1978 to less than a tenth of that figure in 1979. After 1978, there were no political disappearances in either Chile or Uruguay. Haiti's leaders began releasing political prisoners on the day of Carter's inauguration. The progress on human rights in the late 1970s paved the way for the wave of democratization over the next decade. By contrast, Carter administration officials conceded that the Soviet Union and its allies made few concessions.

Consider the different responses of Ethiopia and Brazil to the human rights sanctions. Three weeks before the sanctions decision, Colonel Mengitsu Haile Mariam had become the undisputed leader through the execution of seven colleagues, including the titular head of state. The domestic situation was far from stable. The previous fall, Mengitsu had been shot in the leg, probably by a member of the radical civilian opposition. The new regime also faced several secessionist threats. The United States was unsympathetic to these challenges: previous requests for military aid in defeating rebels in Eritrea had been denied. By 1977 these rebels controlled a significant percentage of Ethiopia's coastline. Mengitsu believed that only the continuation of terror would permit the implementation of radical land reform and the suppression of rebels in Eritrea. He viewed the human rights sanctions as a direct attack on his regime.[95]

---

[93] Martin and Sikkink (1993) argue that domestic constraints explain why Guatemala did not concede as much as Argentina. Their case is persuasive, but it contradicts the claim that weaker polities are more likely to concede. By 1978, the Argentinian military had largely eliminated leftist insurgents within its country. The regime's domestic strength permitted its leaders to acquiesce to US pressure. In contrast, leftist rebels in Guatemala were having more success in the countryside in the late 1970s. The regime's declining power induced its leaders to adopt a hard-line position and reject any concessions to the United States. This example shows how the domestic politics argument can lead to contradictory predictions.

[94] On successes in Latin America, see Muravchik (1986), pp. 175–6; HSE (1990b), pp. 417–67; and Wesson (1981), pp. 96–7.

[95] David (1991), pp. 106–13. See also Nelson and Kaplan (1981), pp. 222–5.

Two months later, the United States informed Mengitsu of its intention to close down its communication base at Kagnew within six months. Given those policies, the regime must have anticipated future conflicts.[96] Given those conflict expectations, and the promise of significant military and economic aid from the Soviet Union, Ethiopia felt no need to make concessions. In April 1977, Ethiopia abrogated the 1953 defense agreement, and kicked out a US military advisor group. The order stated, "The existence of an American Military Assistance Advisory Group is useless at a time when the American government takes every opportunity to create hatred against revolutionary Ethiopia by depicting her as a country in which human rights are violated."[97] Not surprisingly, there were no concessions; Soviet aid more than compensated for the loss of American support, and the Ethiopians believed that any concessions would be used as leverage in future conflicts.

Brazil's reaction to the economic pressure on human rights is a study in contrasts. Contrary to Wiarda's claim, the military regime did not use the sanctions to rally popular support behind the regime. The reaction was very mild; ironically, the Brazilian government restricted the media from commenting on any friction over human rights with the United States. Robert Wesson comments: "Foreign interference in this regard does not seem to have been widely resented." The Foreign Minister, rather than scolding Washington, agreed with the aims of the policy in an interview with the *New York Times*. The resistance to acquiescence came from certain sectors of the military. Their concern was that Carter was using the human rights campaign as a means for extracting concessions on Brazil's nuclear weapons program in the future.[98] Thus, the objection to human rights concessions arose from concern that acquiescence on this issue would be translated into leverage on other issue areas.

---

[96] Within two years, Ethiopia accused the United States of siding with Somalia during the dispute over the Ogaden and refused to compensate the United States for expropriated property; the United States responded by raising tariffs for Ethiopian imports.

[97] Nelson and Kaplan (1981), p. 222.

[98] Wesson (1981), pp. 94–8; the quote is from p. 98. Parenthetically, Brazil was clearly concerned about relative gains on the nuclear issue as well. The US demand was to cancel a contract for a West German reprocessing plant. Brazilian officials were suspicious that the real goal was to keep the country dependent upon US enriched uranium, enhancing US commercial dominance over Brazil's nuclear industry.

Brazil's conflict expectations with the United States were still lower than Ethiopia's. As the model predicts, the Brazilian regime was prepared to make greater concessions. By 1980, all political prisoners had been released. As Brazil demonstrated a willingness to acquiesce, there were frequent consultations with US officials to maintain the overall bilateral relationship. In the two years after sanctions were initiated, the first lady, the Secretary of State, and Carter himself visited the country. Contrary to the conventional wisdom, bilateral relations were on solid footing by 1978, and the United States could claim that significant concessions had been made.

In conclusion, the conventional wisdom is correct that public pressure led to the addition of human rights as a relevant issue of foreign policy. However, in deciding which countries to coerce, the United States, even during the Carter administration, incorporated issues of opportunity costs and conflict expectations into its decision-making calculus. It refrained from sanctioning allies where no other conflicts were expected. There was a greater willingness to threaten sanctions against troublesome allies and adversaries. All of the states involved believed the human rights issue had a political as well as a moral dimension. The extent of the concessions varied with the expectation of future conflict. Allies that anticipated fewer conflicts were more willing to concede than adversaries. Furthermore, contrary to the conventional wisdom, allied targets generally did not use the sanctions as an excuse for rallying public support. There is no question that domestic politics within the United States can explain the prominence of the human rights issue, but the evidence indicates that the conflict expectations model can explain the overall pattern of economic statecraft.

Summary

This chapter's plausibility probe of economic coercion reveals that the conventional wisdom's assertions about sanctions are false. Economic coercion is no panacea, but the variation in the outcomes is sufficient to falsify the blanket claim of ineffectiveness. A review of the statistical evidence calls into question alternative explanations about economic sanctions, and demonstrates clear support for the conflict expectations model, although this support is at best preliminary. In all but one of the tests, the variables representing the best proxies for the target's opportunity cost, the sender's opportunity costs, and the expectations of future conflict trend in the predicted direction, and with two exceptions were statistically significant. In testing the outcome of coercion events, several of the econometric results are flawed by misspecification and endogeneity. Further statistical testing is needed to confirm the correlation among the variables.

The conventional wisdom about economic sanctions fares extremely poorly. Previous statistical studies conclude that domestic political forces do not play a significant role in influencing US decisions to threaten economic coercion. Given the reputation of the United States as a "weak" policy-making state, the conclusions represent a strong rejection of the domestic politics argument. International factors extraneous to the conflict expectations model find little resonance with the data. Multiple tests confirm that neither military power nor military threats affect the outcome of a sanctions attempt. The level of cooperation is not correlated with either the rate of success or the significance of the demand. Finally, the statistical evidence categorically rejects the argument that high sender costs can effectively signal resolve and thus lead to a successful outcome. High sender costs are found to be negatively correlated with sanctions success. These traditional explanations cannot be completely discounted, but they no longer have any privileged status.

Three cases of economic sanctions were examined because they were expected to fit the alternative hypotheses better than the conflict expectations model. Indeed, the broad outlines of each case revealed that cost and alignment cannot explain all the variation in this phenomena. However, a closer look reveals that the conflict expectations model is consistent with the details in each case. In the case of the grain embargo, US policy-makers believed that the sanctions would impose greater costs on the Soviet Union than the United States. Because of the heightened conflict expectations, there was a willingness to incur considerable costs provided the target incurred even greater costs. The pipeline sanctions reveal that if one side makes a strategic miscalculation, the conflict expectations model can still predict each side's behavior. The human rights sanctions show that although public opinion can bring issues to the forefront of the foreign policy arena, opportunity costs and conflict expectations govern the implementation and outcome of economic statecraft. The model generates a clearer understanding of each of these cases, even though they were chosen because of their suitability to alternative explanations.

At the beginning of this chapter, I compared a plausibility probe to dipping a toe into water of uncertain temperature. It has been found that the water is not ice cold. More rigorous testing is needed. The next chapter proceeds with new statistical tests of the conflict expectations model.

4   Statistical tests

Chapter 3 provided a plausibility probe of existing statistical analysis and well-known case studies. It found the existing literature on economic sanctions inadequate to the task, while the conflict expectations model received qualified support. A second cut is warranted. This chapter uses events data from Hufbauer, Schott, and Elliott (HSE) to explicitly test the hypotheses developed in chapter 2. It starts by describing the criteria used to include or exclude observations. It then details how the dependent and independent variables are operationalized, using data from HSE and other sources. Finally, the hypotheses predicting the causes and outcomes of coercion attempts are evaluated.

Selecting the appropriate sample

HSE's events data will be used for testing the model's hypotheses. The HSE database has the advantage of a relatively large sample size and an impressive inventory of recorded independent variables. The drawback is that this data set has been criticized for controversial codings and questionable methodology.[1] In addition, the selection of cases could be open to bias. HSE admit that their sample, "probably omits many uses of sanctions imposed between powers of the second and third rank ... also, we have overlooked instances in which sanctions were imposed by major powers in comparative secrecy to achieve relatively modest goals. To the extent of these omissions, our

---

[1] See Morgan and Schwebach (1997), Pape (1997).

generalizations do not adequately reflect the sanctions experience of the twentieth century."[2]

Despite these misgivings, the HSE study provides the most comprehensive data about sanctions. No other data set contains as many documented cases of economic coercion. Richard Ellings observes that the HSE effort "is very likely the best sanctions policy analysis yet to be published. Its data base is the largest of this genre of research." In a review article, Edward Mansfield notes that the HSE data "are widely recognized as the best of their kind."[3] In one sense, relying on the HSE coding lessens the question of bias. By using their codings, as opposed to generating my own, more objectivity is injected into the research effort. Finally, it should be kept in mind that the goal of the statistical tests is not to estimate coefficient sizes or calculate precise effects. The use of statistics is merely to confirm central tendency and significance. Until superior methods of measurement can be developed, that is all that can and should be asked from statistical results in international relations.

Some of the criticisms leveled against HSE can be muted through more meticulous case selection. The HSE database contains 115 cases between 1914 and 1990 that range from economic coercion as it is understood here to sanctions against firms, from strategic embargoes to all-out economic warfare during armed conflict. A number of cases are beyond the scope of this study. The conflict expectations model addresses situations where a sender country uses economic diplomacy to coerce a target country into a policy concession. Including observations that do not fit that description will add more noise to the data and potentially introduce bias into the results. For this reason, two categories of events are excluded.

Embargoes designed to impair war-fighting ability are not included. This includes cases like the Allied embargo of the Central Powers during World War I, or the efforts of CoCom to prevent sensitive technology exports to the Soviet Union. CoCom is often cited as an exemplar of economic statecraft, but it does not fit the description of economic coercion.[4] Strategic embargoes or wartime embargoes do not fit the conflict expectations model because there is no attached demand to the sanctions. They are not efforts at coercion, they are

---

[2] HSE (1990a), p. 4.
[3] Ellings (1985), p. xvi; Mansfield (1995), p. 579.
[4] Mastanduno (1992).

efforts at limiting a rival's power. They meet the textbook definition of "embargo," but do not qualify as coercion events. This criterion eliminates seven cases.[5]

Sanctions with no clearly identifiable primary sender or target are also eliminated. This criterion excludes situations where the sender or target is an international organization such as the Organization of African Unity or the Arab League and an initial sender country cannot be identified from the case history.[6] These sorts of cases are outside the domain of the model because they are not really bilateral disputes, and thus the actors are not clearly defined. Coding conflict expectations is difficult without a well-defined bilateral relationship. This step removes an additional nine cases.[7]

Excluding the cases outside the model's purview reduces the sample size from 115 to 99 observations. It is telling that these criteria remove only sixteen observations, yet they include several cases that have been subjected to intense scrutiny, such as the League of Nations sanctions, the Arab boycott of Israel, the Western allies' strategic embargo of the Soviet Union, and the United Nations sanctions imposed against South Africa. It suggests that the typical sanctions episode is markedly different from the characterization produced in previous studies, and demonstrates the potential bias of previous efforts to explain sanctions.[8]

One other set of observations is problematic and will be partially excluded. In eleven of the sanctions episodes, the sender used regular

---

[5] They are: 14–1, UK vs. Germany (World War I); 39–1, Allied powers vs. Axis (World War II); 46–1, Arab League vs. Israel (Israeli independence); 48–5, CoCom vs. USSR, COMECON (containment); 49–1, ChinCom vs. China (communist takeover of mainland); 50–1, UN vs. North Korea (Korean war); 54–4, US vs. North Vietnam (Vietnam war). Including these cases only strengthens the statistical results.

[6] For example, case number 73–1, the Arab League versus the United States, can be included because it is clear that Saudi Arabia was the primary sender (Lindsay, 1986). However, case number 63–5, the United Nations and the Organization of African Unity versus Portugal, is eliminated, because no single country initiated the call for sanctions.

[7] They are: 21–1, League of Nations vs. Yugoslavia (border dispute with Albania); 25–1, League of Nations vs. Greece (border dispute with Bulgaria); 32–1, League of Nations vs. Paraguay and Bolivia (ending the Chaco War); 62–1, UN vs. South Africa (apartheid); 63–5, UN, OAU vs. Portugal (decolonization); 65–4, US vs. Arab League (Arab boycott of Israel); 77–4, Canada vs. the European Community (nuclear safeguards); 78–6, Arab League vs. Egypt (Camp David accords); 79–3, Arab League vs. Canada (move of Israeli embassy to Jerusalem).

[8] See Galtung (1967), Doxey (1987), Renwick (1981), Baldwin (1985), Martin (1992), and the discussion in chapter 1, pp. 20–1.

military force after sanctions were imposed. It could be argued that including these cases would taint the results. This is certainly not true of any tests about the initiation of economic coercion, since in all of the cases sanctions were attempted prior to the use of force and were given some chance of succeeding. Including these observations in tests on the outcome is more problematic, since the military contribution would be expected to overwhelm the sanctions contribution.[9] In some of these instances, economic coercion played an important supporting role in obtaining concessions, but overall, it is somewhat far-fetched to claim that anything other than the use of force caused the outcome. I will therefore include these cases when testing the coercion condition, but exclude them when testing the concession function.[10]

The number of usable observations can be increased for two reasons. While the HSE study has an impressive number of cases, in one sense the authors have self-censored the number of data points, by making a distinction between cases and observations.[11] For the purposes of this study, the unit of observation is an event where a sender country threatens economic coercion unless a target country acquiesces to its demands. It is possible, however, that coercion might be used repeatedly against a single target in order to obtain different concessions in the same issue area. It is also possible that the sender might coerce multiple targets over the same issue. In either of these instances, HSE group a number of coercion events as part of one case. Their cases need to be parsed into observations.

Most of HSE's cases contain only one observation, but several contain multiple events. For example, the coercion efforts by the United States to liberalize emigration in Eastern Europe are grouped into one case. This case really contains five different coercion events; the United States failed to coerce Czechoslovakia, East Germany, and Bulgaria in 1975, successfully coerced Hungary in 1978, and success-fully coerced Romania in 1983.[12] Another example is the American

[9] Pape (1997).
[10] These cases are: 18–1, UK vs. Russia (anti-Bolshevism); 48–2, India vs. Hyderabad (assimilation into India); 54–2, India vs. Portugal (control of Goa); 56–2, UK vs. Egypt (control of the Suez canal); 57–1, Indonesia vs. Netherlands (control of West Irian); 57–2, France vs. Tunisia (support for Algerian rebels); 67–1, Nigeria vs. Biafra (ending civil war); 78–7, China vs. Vietnam (Vietnamese invasion of Cambodia); 82–1, UK vs. Argentina (control of the Falkland Islands); 83–4, US vs. Grenada (destabilization of Bishop regime); 87–1, US vs. Panama (destabilization of Noriega regime).
[11] See King, Keohane, and Verba (1994) for more on this distinction.
[12] HSE (1990b), pp. 397–405.

economic pressure on Israel. HSE code these events as a single case from 1956 onward. In fact, this case masks six distinct and identifiable coercion attempts.[13] From the data and commentary on the outcomes provided in HSE, each of these observations can be given a straightforward individual coding. This generates an additional fourteen observations.[14] By increasing the number of observations in this fashion, more leverage can be applied to the testing procedures.

Another way of adding observations is to flesh out the data in the cases where sanctions were threatened but not implemented. For example, in late 1975 the United States threatened the suspension of economic and military aid to South Korea if that country persisted in acquiring nuclear weapons technology. Because South Korea acquiesced before the sanctions were imposed, HSE do not estimate the target's opportunity costs of coercion. Additional research into these cases, however, reveals a clear dollar value for the expected costs of coercion.[15]

Parsing out the cases with multiple observations and assigning cost figures to the sanctions cases that did not go past the threat stage increases the number of observations from 99 to 114. In testing the causes of sanctions outcomes, the cases of regular military force are excluded, reducing the number of observations to 103. These events range from 1917 to 1989, and represent a sufficiently large sample for statistical testing.

Operationalizing the variables

Concession size

As noted in chapter 3, one of the coding problems in HSE and other studies is that the dependent variable is defined as sanctions success. HSE code success on a four-point scale, with four a success and one a

---

[13] Ibid., pp. 142–8, and Blessing (1975), pp. 201–2.

[14] The cases parsed into individual observations are: 48–3, US vs. Western allies (creation of West Germany and control of West Berlin); 56–1, US vs. Israel (Sinai withdrawal, implementing UN resolutions, Palestinian autonomy talks); 71–1, US vs. India and Pakistan (halt war); 73–3, US vs. Chile (improving human rights); 75–3, US vs. Eastern Europe (liberalizing Jewish emigration).

[15] There are four relevant cases where the sanctions did not go beyond the threat stage: 61–3, West Germany vs. East Germany (the Berlin Wall); 62–3, USSR vs. Romania (limiting political and economic independence); 75–1, US vs. South Korea (acquisition of nuclear reprocessing technology); and 87–3, US vs. El Salvador (amnesty for rebels).

complete failure. The definition of success is narrowly defined as "the extent to which the policy outcome sought by the sender country was in fact achieved."[16] This is only a partial measure of concession magnitude, because it omits the relative significance of the original demand. A partial concession to a large demand (halting an invasion) might be more beneficial to the sender than a complete concession to a smaller demand (a diplomatic note of apology). A proper measure of concession magnitude should take into account both the size of the demand and the degree to which target met the demand. HSE's success coding adequately covers the latter part.

To determine demand size, one can still rely on HSE. They divide the cases into four relevant categories based on the sender's demand: modest changes in the target's foreign policy, a change in the target country's regime, disruption of military activity, and major changes in the target's foreign policy.[17] It is straightforward to rank these categories in order of importance to the target. Modest changes represent smaller demands. Episodes involving major changes in foreign policy, a change of government, or a change in military behavior represent larger demands. Therefore, all cases in the first category will be given a coding of 1 for demand size; all cases in the second, third, and fourth categories will be assigned a coding of 2. In cases where HSE assign multiple goals to the same event, the demand size takes the larger value.

Concession size can be calculated by multiplying HSE's success coding with the demand size. For example, if the demand size equals 2 and HSE's success coding equals 1, then the concession size would equal $2 \times 1 = 2$. By this logic, a large concession to a minor demand is equal to a minor concession to a large demand. This prevents an undervaluing of small concessions made on large demands.

A few adjustments need to be made. First, HSE's success coding is rescaled to range from 0 to 3 rather than 1 to 4. In this way, any coercion attempt that has no appreciable success will be coded as a zero, regardless of the original demand. Second, numerical gaps in the final coding are eliminated. Concession size is an ordinal measure. Rather than have categories in the coding with no observation (i.e. 5) it is rescaled to an ordinal rank from 0 (no concession) to 5 (largest

---

[16] HSE (1990a), p. 41.

[17] There is a fifth category, impairment of military potential. Most of these cases have been removed from the sample for reasons given in the previous few pages.

concession). Finally, a preliminary inspection of the data reveals that the concession size takes on a value of 4 only five times. Ordered probit techniques have difficulty converging in situations where one category has significantly fewer events. To correct for this, two categories (3 and 4) are combined. Thus, the final coding of concession size takes on values ranging from 0 to 4.[18]

Table 4.1 shows the new distributions of concession size with and without the events including the use of military force. A quick glance at the table shows that the modal outcome for concession size is zero. This helps to explain the belief that economic coercion does not work. Still, a zero outcome represents less than 30 percent of the outcomes. In more than 70 percent of the observations, the target made some concessions. In more than 20 percent of the cases significant concessions were made. The mean for the sample is 1.83 and the median is a 2, indicating a rather even distribution of outcomes. Excluding the military cases, the average falls to 1.71, but the median value stays the same. A blanket statement asserting that sanctions do not work is clearly incorrect.

Duration of the sanctions episode

The model hypothesizes that coercion events will remain in deadlock if the target and sender anticipate frequent conflicts. The proxy variable for sustained deadlock will be the length of the sanctions episode. Sanctions duration measures the number of years sanctions were maintained. The figures come originally from HSE, but have been updated to 1996. The cases involving military intervention are not included, since the lifespan of these events were cut short by the use of military force. The modal outcome was an episode of less than a year, and the mean was roughly five years. The fact that 70 percent of the episodes lasted less than five years indicated that sustained deadlock was not a common occurrence.

Opportunity costs of deadlock

One of the admirable qualities of the HSE research effort is the care taken to estimate the cost to target of sanctions. Rather than using gross trade figures, they estimate the price elasticities of demand and supply of the disrupted trade in order to determine the true economic cost. This represents a good approximation of the cost of asset-specific

---

[18] This does not alter the statistical results presented in this chapter.

Table 4.1. *Frequency distribution of concession size*

Coding	Coding description	Number of observations	Number of observations excluding cases of military force
0	No concessions	32	30
1	Minor concessions to a minor demand	19	19
2	Minor concessions to a major demand, or major concessions to a minor demand	24	23
3	Full concessions to a minor demand, or major concessions to a major demand	14	13
4	Full concessions to a major demand	25	18
Total		114	103

investment to the target. HSE then divides this number by the target's gross national product to compute cost.

One modification is made to the target's opportunity costs of sanctions. HSE incorporated third country assistance into their cost calculation. For example, if Yugoslavia suffered costs of $100 million from a Soviet coercion effort, but received $75 million in American aid as a substitute, HSE set the target costs at $25 million. This combines two effects that usually occur at different points in the coercion process. To better distinguish between the two effects, the cost variables are calculated excluding third country assistance. The target's costs of coercion range in value from 0 to 16 percent of GNP. More than a third of the coercion episodes involved costs of greater than 1 percent of GNP; the mean value is 1.8 percent.[19]

HSE do not provide comparable cost figures for the sender country. Instead, they use an ordinal measure ranging from 1 if the sender suffered no costs whatsoever to 4 if the sender suffered significant

---

[19] The UN sanctions against Iraq for its invasion of Kuwait are excluded from this calculation and all statistical tests of the coercion condition, because of its outlier status. Iraq's costs as estimated by HSE (48 percent of GNP) were three times the size of the next largest case.

economic losses. It is possible, using the information in the case histories, to develop a cardinal measure of the costs incurred.[20] The ordinal measure better reflects the costs as estimated by HSE, but the cardinal measure can be used to measure the actual gap in opportunity costs.[21] Therefore, both measures will be used. A glance at the ordinal figures reveals that in 44.7 percent of the cases, the sender incurred no costs from the coercion episode; in an additional 40 percent of the cases, the sender suffered minimal costs. This is because a large number of cases involve the disruption of aid rather than trade flows. This lends greater support to the hypothesis that regardless of conflict expectations, senders will never sanction unless the target country suffers greater costs.

Expectation of future bilateral conflict

As argued in chapter 3, a suitable proxy for the concern for the distribution of payoffs is the alignment between the two countries prior to the sanctions event. HSE use an ordinal coding of the prior relationship. It ranges from 1 (hostile) to 3 (amicable). This measure is useful because it incorporates intangible elements of the bilateral relationship that other possible measures lack. In roughly half of the cases the relationship was coded as neutral. One-sixth of the cases involved countries in an adversarial relationship, and the remaining third involved allies.

As a check on the HSE measure, I have constructed another variable to measure conflict expectations. This measure is also trichotomous. It takes on a value of 1 if the two countries shared an enduring rivalry during the sanctions episode.[22] It takes on a value of 3 if the target and sender share a formal security alliance.[23] If neither of these conditions are present, it takes on a value of two.[24]

---

[20] This assumes that the price elasticities of supply and demand are comparable. Because of the large number of cases involving aid suspension, however, this assumption does not come into play very often.

[21] For reasons of functional form, tests of the concession function will use the natural log of difference between the target's and sender's costs rather than both cost measures.

[22] The dyad is classified as an enduring rivalry if it meets the criteria specified in Diehl (1985).

[23] Data on alliances come from Small and Singer (1969), and Rengger (1990).

[24] A value of two was also given to two observations in 1968 involving the United States and Peru, when both a security alliance and an enduring rivalry were present.

Realignment

The expectation of future conflict will change considerably if the target decides to engage in balancing behavior. The model postulates that balancing behavior should raise conflict expectations, increasing the concern for relative gains and reputation, and thus lead to a reduced number of concessions. If the target realigns, the prior relationship does not affect the outcome; the post-balancing alignment is the important term.

HSE do not code whether the target country balances against the sender. Reviewing the cases, the target country realigned immediately before the coercion event on twelve occasions. They include two sorts of cases. In the first group of cases, the target state clearly switched their allegiance away from one of the cold war blocs. For example, Yugoslavia reacted to Soviet efforts at hegemony within the communist bloc by moving closer to Western Europe and the United States. Cuba reacted to US economic pressure by strengthening its alignment with the Soviet Union. The second group of cases involve internal revolutions that triggered drastic changes in foreign policy. The Iranian revolution of 1979 radically altered the country's foreign policy, rendering its previously close relationship with the United States null and void.

A dummy variable would be insufficient, because it would fail to register the *degree* of realignment. Iran's revolution, for example, meant a greater change in its prior relationship with the United States than the communist takeover of Ethiopia in 1976. Before the realignment, Iran was a close ally, while Ethiopia had a more distant relationship with the United States. Therefore, the realignment term will take a larger value if the target was previously a close ally. For example, if the target realigns from a neutral to an antagonistic relationship, the realignment term takes a value of 1; if the target realigns from a cordial to an antagonistic relationship, then the realignment term takes a value of 2. In this way, the balancing term accounts for the extent of the realignment.

Table 4.2 provides a concise description of the explanatory and dependent variables. Table 4.3 lists the control and alternative explanatory variables that will also be used. To test the signaling approach, a dummy variable is created that takes a value of 1 if the sender threatened to use more forceful measures during the sanctions episode. A measure of aggregate power equals the natural log of the

Table 4.2. *Dependent and explanatory variables used in statistical tests*

Name	Description
Concession size	Ordinal measure of the significance of the concession: 0 = no concession 1 = minor concessions to a minor demand 2 = minor concessions to a major demand, or major concessions to a minor demand 3 = full concessions to a minor demand, or major concessions to a major demand 4 = full concessions to a major demand
Sanctions length	Duration, in years, that the sender imposed sanctions on the target
Expectation of future conflict	*HSE measure* The prior relationship between the sender and target: 1 = antagonistic relationship 2 = neutral relationship 3 = cordial relationship *Alternative measure* 1 = enduring rivals 2 = neutral relationship 3 = formal allies
Target realignment	Measurement of target realignment immediately before or during the coercion event: 0 = no realignment 1 = moderate realignment 2 = significant realignment
Target's opportunity cost of sanctions imposition	The cost of sanctions to the target as a percentage of its gross national product
Sender's opportunity cost of sanctions imposition	*Cardinal measure* The cost of sanctions to the sender as a percentage of its gross national product *Ordinal measure* HSE's coding of the costs to the sender: 1 = net benefit 2 = minimal or no costs 3 = minor costs 4 = significant costs
Gap in opportunity costs	Natural log of the difference between the target and sender costs

Table 4.3. *Control variables used in statistical tests*

Name	Description
Target's regime type	Dummy variable = 1 if the target regime is a democracy
Target assistance	Dummy variable = 1 if the target received international assistance during the coercion event
Threat of military force or covert action	Dummy variable = 1 if the sender used threats of force during the coercion event
Target regime's domestic stability	*HSE measure* The target regime's overall economic health and political stability prior to the coercion attempt: 1 = Distressed political economy 2 = Political economy with significant problems 3 = Strong and stable political economy *Alternative measure* Frequency of contested domestic institutions in the previous decade
Aggregate power	Natural log of the ratio of the sender's GNP to the target's GNP
Cooperation with the sender	Measurement of international cooperation garnered by the sender in implementing sanctions: 1 = No cooperation 2 = Minor cooperation 3 = Modest cooperation 4 = Significant cooperation

ratio of the two countries' size as measured by gross national product. A higher number increases the sender's size relative to the target. The signaling approach makes three predictions. First, senders should incur greater costs when threatening or using force in addition to sanctions; by doing this, the sender communicates a more credible signal to the target. Second, the threat of military statecraft, or the differences in aggregate power, should be positively correlated with concession size. According to this approach, the causal mechanism that determines sanctions success is the prospect of military conflict, not the use of economic coercion. The third hypothesis is that the difference in opportunity costs should have an insignificant or negative effect on the outcome. If the signaling hypothesis is correct, then the target's costs of coercion are irrelevant, and the sender's costs should be positively correlated with concession size. As a test of a domestic politics approach, HSE's measure of the target country's political stability and economic health is included. This trichotomous measure takes on a value of 1 if the target regime is distressed, a value of 2 if the regime faces significant problems, and a value of 3 if the regime is strong and stable. As noted in chapter 3, this measure is somewhat problematic because of its catch-all nature. Therefore, as an additional check, another measure of the target regime's stability will be used. This measure is a ten-year average of occasions when the target country's governing institutions are contested, as coded by Kurt Dassel and Eric Reinhardt from the Polity II data set.[25] A domestic politics approach would predict that if the target regime's governing institutions have suffered from recent instability, it would be more vulnerable to collapse in the presence of sanctions. The weaker the target regime's hold on power, the greater the expected concessions. For a domestic politics approach of the causes of economic sanctions, a dummy measure of the sender's democracy is used.[26]

Two other control measures are included. HSE use a four-category measure of the international cooperation the sender received in its coercion attempt, with a higher number reflecting greater cooperation. This variable is expected to be positively correlated with concession size. Finally, a dummy variable measures whether the target country received third-party assistance during the sanctions episode. It is expected that if the target received assistance, the expected concession size would be reduced.

Testing the causes of sanctions initiation

Sample bias makes it difficult to test the coercion condition. The ideal way is to compare the actual set of coercion events with episodes where the sender considered sanctions but elected to accept the status quo ante. While HSE collected data on cases involving sanctions, there is no companion data set where the sender considered economic coercion but then rejected that choice. Using random dyads that include events where sanctions were not imposed, as well as events

---

[25] Dassel and Reinhardt (1999). Their measure has been given a negative sign so that this measure corresponds to the HSE health measure; the higher the value, the more stable the target country.

[26] Data on the sender's regime type comes from Doyle (1986).

where sanctions were used, is problematic. There is no appropriate measure of expected costs that could be used for both sets of data.[27]

While comparing events with nonevents would be ideal, hypotheses about the coercion condition can also be tested by analyzing correlations within the set of coercion events. The model predicts that within the set of coercion events, there should be recognizable patterns in the data.

The first hypothesis derived from the coercion game is that the target's opportunity costs of sanctions imposition should always be greater than the sender's opportunity costs. If the HSE sample contains multiple cases where the sender's opportunity costs of deadlock are greater than target's costs, it would strongly repudiate the model presented here. Table 4.4 displays the distribution of the gap between the target's opportunity costs and the sender's opportunity costs. The results provide confirmation for the first hypothesis. In only one of the 114 cases is the cost to sender greater than the cost to target; Canada's sanctions against Japan in 1974 imposed a cost of 0.04 percent of Canada's GNP, but only a cost of 0.01 percent of Japan's GNP. In all of the other events, the target's opportunity costs of deadlock are greater than or equivalent to the sender's costs. In each of the cases where the target's opportunity costs are essentially zero, sender's costs are also equivalent to zero. This punctures a widely-held myth that sanctions are often as damaging to the sender as they are to the target.

The model also predicts that as conflict expectations diminish, the ratio of opportunity costs must improve for the sender to prefer initiating a coercion attempt. For example, the United States preferred incurring the costs of the 1979 grain embargo against the Soviet Union only because the expectations of future conflict were so prevalent in

---

[27] Richardson and Kegley (1980) and others use target's exports to sender as a percentage of GNP, or total exports, as a measure of the costs of severing economic relations. For this model, that measure would be inappropriate for several reasons. First, this excludes financial flows. Second, it does not include sender's reliance on target for an export market. This is assumed away in most of the models which use this measure, because the sender is perceived to be impervious to economic damage. Another possible reason for assuming this away is that when the trade ratios are divided, in order to obtain $c_{(S)}/c_{(T)}$, the trade figures fall out and one is left only with a ratio of target and sender's GNP or total trade. Finally, this sort of measure fails to distinguish between asset-specific trade flows and trade flows with high degrees of demand elasticity. One reason the HSE effort is so widely used is that it incorporates price elasticities in computing the costs to target and sender.

Table 4.4. *Distribution of the gap in opportunity costs*

Difference in opportunity costs[1]	Number of observations	Percent
<0.0	1	0.88
Between 0.0 and 0.5	59	51.75
Between 0.5 and 1.0	14	12.28
Between 1.0 and 5.0	29	25.44
Between 5.0 and 10.0	6	5.26
Greater than 10.0	5	4.39
Total	114	100.00

Note: [1] (Target's costs as a percentage of GNP) – (Sender's costs as a percentage of GNP)

that relationship. A similar scenario of costs and benefits with, say, the UK, would not have satisfied the coercion condition, because of the close alliance between the United States and the United Kingdom. If target and sender have minimal conflict expectations and a sanctions event is observed, the costs to target should be large and the costs to sender should be small.

The coercion condition is examined by using a difference of means test. This test was performed with the realignment cases excluded. If the target realigned itself away from the sender prior to the coercion event, then the codings for conflict expectations would be inaccurate and skew the results.[28] Table 4.5 shows the average costs to the sender and target countries at the three different levels of HSE's alignment measure. For the sender's costs, I use the ordinal measure from HSE as well as the cardinal measure developed here. The results support the model's hypotheses. As the bilateral relationship switches from antagonistic to neutral, the average of the target country's opportunity costs unambiguously increases, more than doubling in value. The *t*-test reveals statistical significance at the 10 percent level. The target's average costs increase more dramatically when the relationship switches from neutral to cordial; the mean increases by a factor of three. The difference is significant at the 1 percent level. This result confirms that the target's opportunity costs are negatively correlated with alignment. For the sender to prefer threatening economic sanc-

---

[28] Including the realignment cases slightly strengthens the statistical relationship between the HSE measure of alignment and the cost terms, and slightly weakens the statistical relationship between the alternative measure of conflict expectations and the cost variables.

Table 4.5. *Testing the coercion condition*

	Mean value with hostile alignment (standard error)	Mean value with neutral alignment (standard error)	Mean value with cordial alignment (standard error)
Ordinal measure of sender's opportunity costs	2.20 (0.172)	1.55 (0.092)	1.52 (0.112)
Cardinal measure of sender's opportunity costs	0.147 (0.140)	0.033 (0.18)	0.008 (0.009)
Target's opportunity costs	0.366 (0.207)	0.718 (0.130)	2.54 (0.648)
Number of observations	20	49	31

tions in a relationship with minimal expectation of future conflict, the target must suffer significantly greater costs.

Looking at the sender's opportunity costs, a weaker but contrasting pattern emerges that is consistent with the model's predictions. Using the ordinal measure, the sender's opportunity costs decrease unambiguously as the bilateral relationship switches from antagonistic to neutral. The *t*-test shows significance at the 1 percent level. This is consistent with tabular chi square tests that show a negative correlation between alignment and the sender's costs that is significant at the 1 percent level. These results lend support to the model's plausibility. The sender's costs decrease slightly as the bilateral relationship switches from neutral to cordial, but the change is not statistically significant. This suggests that the key empirical difference is the switch from antagonistic to neutral. The cardinal measure of the sender's costs displays a similar pattern, but there is no statistically significant difference of means between the different alignment categories.

As a further check on the validity of the results, table 4.6 shows the difference of means tests when the alternative measure for conflict expectations is used. These results also support the conflict expectations model. The same pattern is observed with the target's opportunity costs, although it does not acquire statistical significance. With the measures for the sender's costs, however, the relationship is stronger than with HSE's alignment measure. Using the ordinal

Table 4.6. *An alternative test of the coercion condition*

	Mean value with enduring rivalry (standard error)	Mean value with neutral alignment (standard error)	Mean value with formal alliance (standard error)
Ordinal measure of sender's opportunity costs	2.63 (0.183)	1.66 (0.092)	1.45 (0.098)
Cardinal measure of sender's opportunity costs	0.354 (0.351)	0.034 (0.016)	−0.002 (0.003)
Target's opportunity costs	0.548 (0.508)	1.32 (0.344)	1.18 (0.313)
Number of observations	8	59	33

measure, the sender's costs increase as the expectations of future conflict increase. The difference between the rival and neutral categories is significant at 1 percent for both tables; the difference between the neutral and allied categories is significant at 10 percent. Chi square tests on the tabular data confirm a positive correlation between conflict expectations and the sender's costs that is significant at 1 percent. The cardinal measure of the sender's costs shows a similar pattern; as conflict expectations increase, so do the sender's costs. The difference between the neutral and allied categories is significant at 5 percent.

Although these tests support the conflict expectations model, they do not address the alternative explanations for the initiation of economic sanctions. Consider the domestic politics argument first. The argument is that domestic public opinion in the sender country drives the sender regime to use sanctions as a symbolic tool. This logic is generally used to describe why democracies, particularly the United States, use economic coercion so frequently. In a democracy, public pressure has a better chance of forcing the regime to take at least symbolic action as a response.

A quick glance at the data provides some support for this hypothesis. The sender was a democracy in 84 percent of the observations. However, this fact is overdetermined. The United States was responsible for more than two-thirds of the sanctions attempts. It was also the economic hegemon between 1917 and 1989. It is unclear whether the United States was the primary sender because it was a democracy or because it was the hegemonic power.

Using the cost data, it is possible to construct a difference of means test for the democracy argument. If democracies are more prone to use sanctions to sate public opinion, then one would expect these sender regimes to use sanctions under less favorable cost conditions. In response to public pressure, a leader will care less about the national interest and more about shoring up domestic support. The regime would be willing to incur significant material costs in return for a boost in popularity. If this hypothesis is true, democratic senders should incur greater costs to themselves when sanctioning, and inflict fewer costs on the target. Nondemocratic senders, on the other hand, need not worry about public opinion. They are more likely to use sanctions when its costs are minimal and the target's costs are significant.

Table 4.7 displays the difference of means tests. The results do not provide strong support for the effect of public pressure within the sender country. Looking at the target's opportunity costs of deadlock, the average cost in the nondemocratic cases is higher, but the difference is not statistically significant. Furthermore, looking at the ordinal measure of the sender's costs, the results are the exact opposite of the predicted trend. Authoritarian senders incurred, on average, greater opportunity costs in their coercion attempts. The difference is significant at 5 percent. This result weakens the hypothesis that democracies are compelled to employ economic coercion in response to public pressure.

It is possible that democratic senders respond to public pressure by imposing only symbolic sanctions rather than costly ones. This would certainly fit the cost pattern. If this is true, then democratic senders, in imposing only symbolic sanctions, should win fewer concessions from the target state. If the sender government is only imposing sanctions because of domestic political concerns, it will care less about the target's response and more about soothing public opinion. Therefore, as a final test of the domestic politics hypothesis, the outcome of sanctions imposed by democratic senders is compared with authoritarian senders. Table 4.7 shows that the difference of means test does not support the domestic politics hypothesis. Democratic senders on average generate greater concessions, although the difference is not statistically significant. This result does not fit with the logic of democratic senders imposing half-hearted sanctions merely to sate public opinion.

Table 4.7. *Test of the domestic politics hypothesis of sanctions initiation*

	Mean value with democratic sender (standard error)	Mean value with authoritarian sender (standard error)
Ordinal measure of sender's opportunity costs	1.64 (0.070)	2.06 (0.189)
Cardinal measure of sender's opportunity costs	0.038 (0.029)	0.288 (0.216)
Target's opportunity costs	1.64 (0.303)	2.61 (0.922)
Concession size	1.88 (0.150)	1.61 (0.413)
Number of observations	96	18

Finally, the signaling hypothesis suggests that the costs incurred by the sender should be positively correlated with the scope of military force. In a world of imperfect information, greater costs can send a signal of intent that threats will be carried out. Table 4.8 provides a tabular comparison of HSE's ordinal measure of the sender's costs and its use of military statecraft. The results provide strong support for the signaling hypothesis. There is a positive correlation between the sender's costs and the escalation of military coercion. Chi square tests show this correlation to be significant at the 1 percent level. Difference-of-means tests reveal that the significant difference is between absence and presence of military statecraft; the difference between these two was significant at the 5 percent level. The difference between the threat and use of force was not statistically significant.

This test of the coercion condition provides strong support for the model. These results are particularly encouraging given the state of the literature on economic sanctions. As noted in chapter 1, although there has been some testing of when sanctions "work," there has been almost no serious analysis of the origins of a coercion event. In most narratives, sanctions are imposed either to placate domestic interests or to send a symbolic message.[29] Frequently the effort is described as an instinctive response to target behavior. It is true that states will

[29] See Barber (1979), Mayall (1984), Kaempfer and Lowenberg (1988), and Miyagawa (1992).

Table 4.8. *Test of the signaling hypothesis*

	No cost of sanctions to sender	Minimal cost of sanctions to sender	Moderate costs of sanctions to sender	Total
No threat or use of military force	40	34	4	78
Threat of military force	9	6	10	25
Use of regular military force	2	6	3	11
Total	51	46	17	114

Note: Pearson chi square = 22.001 ($P < 0.000$.); Gamma = 0.4683; Kendall's tau-b = 0.2801

consider the use of economic coercion in response to target provocations. The results in this section suggest, however, that sender governments engage in rational calculations prior to coercion attempts, and that these calculations are conditioned by the conflict expectations between the two countries. Sanctions are threatened or employed only when the state prefers deadlock to the status quo. Sanctions costly to the sender are likelier if the expectations of future conflict between the two countries are heightened.

The alternative explanations have a mixed record. No support was found for the domestic politics approach. The difference in the way that democratic states sanction as opposed to authoritarian states did not follow the predictions. On the other hand, the argument that sanctions act as signals did find empirical support; senders incurred greater costs when they threatened or used military force.

Testing the causes of sanctions outcomes

The previous section tested when the sender country would prefer to employ economic coercion. This section tests what causes the magnitude of the target's concessions. To measure the determinants of concession size, I will use ordered probit estimations. Ordered-probit models assume that there exists an underlying, continuous metric of concession size that can only be observed as an ordinal variable. The continuous measure is determined by the independent variables. An ordered-probit technique generates maximum likelihood estimates of two sets of parameters: the coefficients of the independent variables, and the threshold values of the unobserved measure that cause the observed dependent variable to jump from one category to the next. The coefficients and standard errors in an ordered-probit regression can be used for significance tests but otherwise are of limited use.[30]

The conflict expectations model makes straightforward predictions about the signs on the key independent variables. For reasons of functional form, the natural log of the difference in opportunity costs will be used rather than separate cost terms.[31] As the gap in opportunity costs increases, the target should be willing to concede more to avoid a deadlock outcome. Therefore, this term should be positively correlated with concession size. Both the HSE and alternative measures for conflict expectations should be positively correlated with the magnitude of the target's concessions; as bilateral relations are perceived to be more harmonious, the target should be willing to make greater concessions. If the target engages in realignment, the model predicts fewer significant concessions, since that increases conflict expectations. The realignment measure, therefore, should take a negative sign.

The domestic politics and signaling approaches also make straightforward predictions. In the domestic politics approach, the target should make greater concessions if the regime is less stable. Therefore, the measures for the target regime's political stability should be negatively correlated with concession size; the more stable the target country, the less likely it will make significant concessions. The signaling approach would predict that measures of military threat and aggregate power should be positively correlated with the size of concessions. As previously noted, this approach also argues that the difference in opportunity costs should not have a significant effect.

Table 4.9 shows two ordered-probit results using the HSE variables. The first set of estimates includes only the cost, alignment, and balancing terms; the second includes the set of control variables listed in table 4.3. The results provide strong support for the basic model. In

---

[30] In particular, the coefficient values do *not* represent the marginal contribution of the independent variables. In the linear regression model, an increase in variable X_1, *ceteris paribus*, should cause an increase in Y by $\beta_1(\Delta X_1)$. An increase of ΔX_1 in an ordered probit regression affects the estimated probability distribution of the underlying dependent variable. See McKelvey and Zavoina (1975) for the derivation of the ordered probit. King (1989, pp. 115–17) and Greene (1990, chapter 20) provide summaries.

[31] This is to better approximate the concession function developed in chapter 2.

Table 4.9. *Testing the concession function*

Independent variable	Model 1		Model 2	
	Estimated coefficient	*t*-statistic	Estimated coefficient	*t*-statistic
Gap in opportunity costs	0.159	2.909**	0.227	3.277**
Alignment	0.465	2.659**	0.441	2.340*
Realignment	−0.667	−2.610**	−0.598	−2.081*
Threat of military force			0.183	0.298
Aggregate power			−0.129	−2.020*
Assistance to the target			−0.475	−1.413
Health of the target regime			−0.445	−2.430*
Cooperation with the sender			−0.343	−2.393*
Log likelihood	−149.80		−142.31	
Number of observations	103		103	

Note: ** Significant at 1%; * significant at 5%.

both regressions, the gap in opportunity costs takes a positive sign; the greater the gap in opportunity costs, the more the target will concede. The cost term is significant at the 1 percent level. The alignment term also takes a positive sign. As the expectations of future conflict between the two countries declines, the target will make a larger concession. This means that if an ally and an adversary face the same opportunity costs of deadlock, the ally will still concede more. This result is significant at the 1 percent level in the first regression, and at the 5 percent level in the second. Realignment takes a negative sign; if the target balances against the sender's threat, conflict expectations increase, leading to fewer concessions. The realignment term is significant at 1 percent in the first regression, and at the 5 percent level in the second. Likelihood-ratio tests confirm that the entire model is significant at 1 percent for both regressions.

The alternative set of explanatory variables produced mixed results. The domestic politics approach does find statistical support. The target's economic health and political stability takes a negative coefficient as predicted; as the target's health improves, it makes fewer concessions. This result is significant at the 5 percent level. The signaling approach, however, gets no support. The military statecraft variable trends in the expected direction but is statistically insignificant. The aggregate power measure is significant at the 5 percent level, but it takes on a negative coefficient. *Ceteris paribus*, as the sender acquires more power, it is less likely to generate significant concessions. Although the signaling hypothesis appears to have some explanatory power for the causes of initiating a coercion attempt, it cannot explain the outcomes.

The biggest surprise is international cooperation. This variable is *negatively* correlated with concession size. The result is significant at the 5 percent level. *Ceteris paribus*, increasing the number of sanctioning states decreases the expected number of concessions. This result violates an assumption made by most policy analysts. International cooperation is far from a necessary prerequisite for a successful coercion episode. A partial explanation is that added costs to the target from enhanced cooperation are absorbed by the cost measure; the measurement for international cooperation does not take into account the increased damage to the target caused by the increased cooperation. Nevertheless, some policy analysts claim that international cooperation lends greater legitimacy and moral suasion to the sanctions effort. This statistical result shows that this argument lacks an empirical foundation.

Table 4.10 shows the statistical results with the alternative measures for conflict expectations and the target regime's political stability. These results support the conflict expectations model and cast greater doubt on the alternative explanations. The conflict expectations measure takes a positive coefficient and is significant at 1 percent for both regressions. The cost term maintains its positive coefficient and its statistical significance. The new measure for the target regime's political stability does not perform as well. Although it trends in the predicted direction, it does not acquire statistical significance. Neither the military statecraft nor the aggregate power hypotheses take on statistical significance in this estimation.

Another hypothesis developed in chapter 2 is that a sustained deadlock is more likely when conflict expectations are heightened. Because the dependent variable is a duration measure, ordinary least squares is inadequate. To test this hypothesis, the Weibull estimation technique is used. If the model's prediction is correct, then the alignment variable should be negatively correlated with the length of

Table 4.10. *Alternative test of the determinants of concession size*

Independent variable	Estimated coefficient	t-statistic	Estimated coefficient	t-statistic
Gap in opportunity costs	0.586	3.081**	0.649	2.932**
Absence of conflict expectations	0.152	3.170**	0.248	3.810**
Threat of military force			0.257	0.911
Aggregate power			−0.085	−1.459
Assistance to the target			−0.683	−2.074*
Target regime's political stability			1.914	1.260
Cooperation with the sender			−0.326	−2.250*
Log likelihood	−151.03		−140.84	
Number of observations	103		101	

Note: ** Significant at 1%; * Significant at 5%.

the sanctions episode; a non-negotiable demand is far more likely to lead to deadlock between adversaries than allies.

The results of the Weibull estimation can be seen in Table 4.11. The results confirm the model's predictions. Alignment has a negative effect on the duration of the sanctions episode. When the sender and target are close allies, the reduced conflict expectations are less likely to cause a sustained deadlock. The result is significant at 1 percent. The realignment term is positively correlated with the duration of the episode, as expected, and also significant at 1 percent. The duration of the sanctions episode decreases as the gap in opportunity costs increases; the result is significant at 5 percent. None of the alternative explanatory or control variables attains statistical significance.

Table 4.12 shows the statistical results when the alternative measures for conflict expectations and the target regime's political stability are used. The results provide further support for the conflict expectations model. The alternative measure for conflict expectations performs as well as the HSE measure. The cost term's statistical significance increases to 1 percent. The control variables produce some genuinely odd results. The aggregate power measure takes a positive and significant sign. This implies that as the sender's power increases *vis-à-vis* the target, the sanctions episode will last longer.

Table 4.11. *The determinants of sanctions length*

Independent variable	Estimated coefficient	*t*-statistic
Constant	2.251	2.411*
Alignment	−0.530	−2.904**
Realignment	0.888	3.302**
Difference in opportunity costs	−0.154	−2.059*
Threat of military force	−0.265	−0.918
Aggregate power	0.110	1.665
Assistance to the target	0.256	0.758
Target regime's political stability	−0.251	−1.359
Cooperation with the sender	0.184	1.346
Sigma	1.053	
Number of observations	103	
Log likelihood	−147.95	

Note: ** Significant at 1%; * significant at 5%.

Similarly, the target regime's institutional stability takes a negative sign and a significance level of 1 percent. This implies that as the target regime becomes less stable, the sanctions episode will last longer. These results do not fit well with either a domestic politics explanation or one based on aggregate power.

The statistical results from this section provide solid empirical support for the conflict expectations model. The greater the gap between the target and sender's opportunity costs, the greater the target's concessions. As the target and sender anticipate fewer political conflicts in the future, the magnitude of the target's concessions will increase. Cases where the target engages in realigning behavior produce smaller concessions. All of these results are extremely robust to the variation in the set of control variables.

The other possible explanatory variables do not perform as well. The signaling explanation of economic sanctions performs dismally. Neither the threats of military statecraft nor the measure of the aggregate power balance performed as predicted. The military statecraft variable was statistically insignificant in all of the tests performed. The measure of aggregate power was intermittently significant, but not in the direction predicted by its proponents. It is possible that senders will use costly sanctions to signal military action, but the signal apparently fails to register with the target country. Military statecraft is irrelevant to sanctions outcomes, unless

Table 4.12. *Alternative test of the determinants of sanctions length*

Independent variable	Estimated coefficient	*t*-statistic
Constant	1.399	2.329*
Absence of conflict expectations	−0.544	−2.835**
Difference in opportunity costs	−0.241	−3.772**
Threat of military force	0.128	0.504
Aggregate power	0.180	3.447**
Assistance to the target	0.320	1.147
Target regime's political stability	−5.358	−3.658**
Cooperation with the sender	0.047	0.376
Sigma	1.107	
Number of observations	101	
Log likelihood	−142.93	

Note: ** Significant at 1%; * significant at 5%.

regular military force is used. The domestic politics explanation fares a little better. The HSE measure of the target regime's economic health and political stability is statistically significant: the less healthy the target regime, the greater the concessions. This hypothesis, however, is robust only to the HSE measure; alternative measures of the target regime's institutional stability lose their statistical significance.

Given the admittedly small sample size, as well as the inherent noise in international relations data, these results provide powerful confirmation for the conflict expectations model of economic coercion. The results are even more robust when one considers the problem of multicollinearity. The coercion condition implies that there is a significant correlation between the expectation of future conflict and the gap in opportunity costs. Placing the alignment and cost terms on the right-hand side introduces multicollinearity, depressing the statistical significance of the correlated variables. Despite this effect, the individual variables still demonstrated considerable explanatory power.

Summary

The methodology described in this chapter is not perfect. Regression estimates are only as good as the data involved, and there are controversies surrounding some of the HSE codings. Creating the measure of concession size involves the combination of ordinal variables. The excluded cases cover many of the more famous sanctions events. These criticisms have merit, but do not compromise this chapter's results.

The conflict expectations model performed well in the statistical tests executed in this chapter. In only one of the 114 observations is the sender's costs of deadlock greater than target's costs. Difference-of-means tests revealed that within the sample of coercion events, conflict expectations were positively correlated with the costs to sender, but negatively correlated with the costs to target. This is consistent with the coercion condition. For the sender to initiate sanctions, it must be willing to accept deadlock rather than backing down and continuing the status quo. With minimal conflict expectations, the sender does not prefer deadlock unless the costs to the target are very high and the costs to itself are very low. These tests are robust to alternative measures of conflict expectations.

The tests of the concession function also provide significant empirical support for the conflict expectations model. As the cost differential between target and sender increases, so do the target's concessions. As the alignment between the target and sender grows closer, concession size increases. Heightened conflict expectations increase the likelihood of a sustained deadlock. The effect of conflict expectations is particularly robust. These results are also robust to alternative measures for conflict expectations.

The alternative approaches do not fare as well. Both the domestic politics and signaling explanations produce sporadic results. The domestic politics approach does not explain the initiation of sanctions attempts; senders do not initiate coercion attempts in response to domestic pressure, but rather from a rational calculation of the sender's interests in the international system. This approach does contribute to explaining the magnitude of the target's concessions, but is not robust to alternative measures. The signaling approach has the reverse problem. It does explain why the sender's costs are positively correlated with the use of military statecraft. It does not, however, explain the outcome of sanctions events; none of this approach's predicted effects occurred. The conflict expectations model does a better job explaining both the initiation and outcome of economic coercion.

The statistical tests support the model. This ends part I. The rest of the book will use comparative case studies to examine the validity of these hypotheses further.

II Economic coercion in the former Soviet Union

5 Russian power and preferences

The motivation

Part II of this book examines Russia's use of economic coercion among the newly independent states (NIS) of the former Soviet Union between 1992 and 1997.[1] When the Soviet Union collapsed in December 1991, fifteen newly sovereign states were created, including the Russian Federation (see figure 5.1 and table 5.1). In the five years after the breakup of the USSR, Russia repeatedly used its economic leverage to extract concessions from the other fourteen newly independent states. While the Russians had considerable economic power over most of the NIS, there was significant variation in Moscow's use of economic diplomacy and in the magnitude of concessions granted to Moscow. This variation provides an excellent opportunity to test whether the statistical significance of conflict expectations is the result of genuine causality or spurious correlation. Comparative methodologies can test whether the conflict expectations approach is the only causal explanation for successful economic coercion, or whether there exist alternative paths to the same outcome.

The cases of Russian foreign economic policy have been selected for several reasons. First, they provide an ideal "natural experiment." Because economic coercion is a possibility in the international system,

---

[1] The NIS include the Baltic countries of Estonia, Latvia, and Lithuania, and the eleven non-Russian members of the Commonwealth of Independent States (CIS). The European members are Belarus, Ukraine, and Moldova. The Transcaucasian members, located between Russia and the Middle East, are Georgia, Armenia, and Azerbaijan. The Central Asian members, wedged between Russia, China, and South Asia, are Turkmenistan, Kazakhstan, Uzbekistan, Kyrgyzstan, and Tajikistan. For a general overview of these countries, see Dawisha and Parrott (1994).

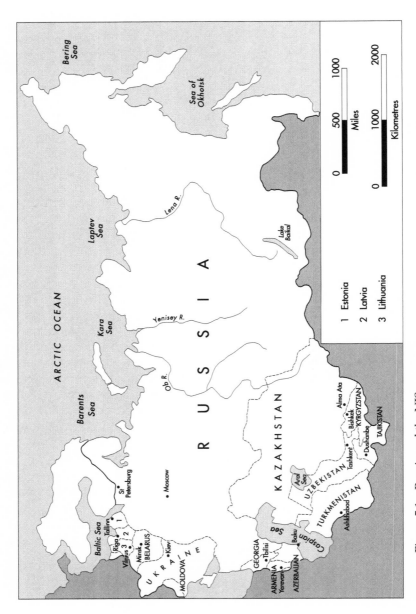

Figure 5.1   Russia and the NIS

Table 5.1. *An introduction to the NIS*

Country	Capital city	Population (million 1989)	Size (square miles)
Armenia	Yerevan	3.4	11,506
Azerbaijan	Baku	7.5	33,436
Belarus	Minsk	10.3	80,154
Estonia	Tallinn	1.6	17,413
Georgia	Tbilisi	5.5	26,911
Kazakhstan	Alma Ata/Astana[1]	17.1	1,048,000
Kyrgyzstan	Bishkek	4.4	76,641
Latvia	Riga	2.7	24,595
Lithuania	Vilnius	3.8	25,174
Moldova	Chisinau	4.5	13,012
Russia	Moscow	147.0	6,592,813
Tajikistan	Dushanbe	5.7	55,251
Turkmenistan	Ashkhabad	3.8	188,455
Ukraine	Kiev	51.4	233,089
Uzbekistan	Tashkent	19.8	173,591

Note: [1] Kazakhstan announced plans to move its capital from Alma Ata to Astana by the end of the millennium.
Source: Data from Twinning (1993).

nation-states will try to restrict the level of interdependence to avoid vulnerabilities.[2] Interdependence was not something to be feared within the former Soviet Union until after its disintegration. These newly sovereign states started their existence with greater asymmetric dependencies than normally exist among international actors, and they are therefore archetypal candidates for threats of economic coercion. Furthermore, their economies are less financially sophisticated than the advanced industrial states. This makes it easier to observe economic threats. It takes less effort to document a Russian threat to cut off gas supplies than a United States effort to manipulate a developing country's currency.

Second, an inherent weakness of large-N studies of economic sanctions is the difficulty of comparing demands and concessions across events. For example, it is problematic to compare El Salvador's 1987 concession to improve its human rights regime with Israel's 1982 agreement to halt its invasion of Lebanon. The advantage of studying these cases is that the Russian demands fall into a few narrow

[2] See Waltz (1979) and Gowa (1994).

categories. Moscow's priorities towards these countries have been consistent, despite the turbulence of its domestic politics and its erratic relationship with the NATO countries.

Third, examining Russian economic statecraft corrects an understandable bias in the literature towards cases where the United States is the primary sender. Of the 116 cases in the HSE data set, the United States was the primary sanctioner in two-thirds. By their own admission, however, HSE note that their collection techniques were biased towards the United States.[3] Examining only those cases can transform a study of economic statecraft into an analysis of US foreign policy. A general theory of economic coercion should explain all events, not just the subset of observations involving the United States.

This chapter looks at Russia's policy aims in its "near abroad," as well as the economic levers at its disposal. It examines Russia's policy preferences towards its near abroad, measures the NIS degree of economic vulnerability, analyzes the conflict expectations among them, and then predicts the extent of their concessions.

Russian policy preferences

Analysts have characterized Russian foreign policy since 1992 as chaotic and riven with domestic disputes.[4] This may have been true of its policy towards NATO and the United States, but Russian preferences and policies towards the post-Soviet states have been remarkably consistent.[5] After a brief period of confusion in early 1992, Russia

---

[3] HSE (1990a), pp. 4–9.

[4] A word about the sources for this chapter and chapter 6. Several of them are electronic newspapers and magazines, and therefore lack page numbers or titles. Archives for each of these can be found on the World Wide Web. The web address for *RFE/RL Daily Reports* and its successor, *OMRI Daily Digests*, is http://www.omri.cz. The web address for both the *Jamestown Monitor* and *Prism* is http://www.jamestown.org. Finally, press reports culled from the the Foreign Broadcast Information Service will be designated FBIS-SOV-year-number. A January 1, 1996 report, for example, would be written as FBIS-SOV-96–1.

[5] See Hanson (1996), and Scott Parrish, "Chaos in foreign-policy decision-making," *Transition*, May 17, 1996, pp. 30–3 on the incoherence of policy-making in Moscow. For Russian evidence of policy consistency towards the NIS, Sergei Karaganov's Foreign and Defense Policy Council (FDPC) published "A strategy for Russia," *Nezavisimaya Gazeta*, August 19, 1992, and "A strategy for Russia II," *Nezavisimaya Gazeta*, May 27, 1994. The FDPC includes influential Russian policy-makers that cover the spectrum of policy preferences. For western analyses, see Brzezinski (1994), McFaul (1995), Russell (1995), and Hill and Jewett (1994).

enunciated its goals towards other former Soviet states quite clearly. Moscow wanted the NIS to be subservient to Russia and to no other great power. Alexei Arbatov's summary statement puts it well: "Consistent policy-making should envision as the maximum desirable goal economic integration and close political cooperation with some of the principal republics. The minimal vital goal should be good-neighborly relations with them and the prevention of an emergence of a coalition of republics hostile to Russia, supported by major powers."[6]

Leading officials in the Russian government made repeated statements confirming this preference. Boris Yeltsin, in his September 1995 decree on "The Establishment of the Strategic Course of the Russian Federation with Member States of the CIS," instructed the Russian government to be "firmly guided by the principle of intolerance of damage to Russia's interests." These interests include Russia taking the mantle of "the leading power in the formation of a new system of inter-state political and economic relations over the territory of the post-Soviet expanse." Andrei Kozyrev, Russia's first Foreign Minister, stated in January 1994: "the CIS and the Baltics ... [constitute] a region where the vital interests of Russia are concentrated ... We should not withdraw from those regions which have been the sphere of Russia's interest for centuries." Ivan Rybkin, the first Speaker of the Russian Duma, argued that the Commonwealth of Independent States (CIS) is "the zone of Russia's interests ... where Russia must say: Gentlemen, keep out of here, it will be bad if you don't."[7]

Nominal independence of the NIS gave Russia the best of both worlds. It could scavenge these states for valuable assets and concessions, but avoid incurring any of the costs associated with subsidizing their regimes or economies.[8] To achieve this end, Russia had four specific demands: control over strategic Soviet assets, military basing rights in the NIS, autonomy for ethnic Russians living abroad, and

[6] Arbatov (1994), p. 14.

[7] Yeltsin quoted in Kathleen Mihalisko, "Yeltsin outlines strategy for a renewed superpower," *Prism*, October 6, 1995; Kozyrev quoted in Webber (1996), p. 100; Rybkin quoted in *Jamestown Monitor*, "Russian politicians glance at the 'Near Abroad,'" November 29, 1995.

[8] Contrary to the conventional wisdom in the United States, the vast majority of Russians did not wish to reabsorb the NIS during this period. Furthermore, the Russian citizenry has managed to carve out an identity distinct from *homo sovieticus*; there is little public demand for political reintegration. See *Segodnya*, "Concept of preserving national state, reviving empire examined," in FBIS-USR-94-087, August 11, 1994, pp. 7–12.

control over energy deposits and infrastructure. To achieve those ends, Moscow was willing to use its economic leverage to coerce these states into making concessions.

First, Russia wanted to be the sole inheritor of the USSR's great-power trappings. By taking over the Soviet Union's seat on the United Nations Security Council, the Russian Federation declared itself to be the legal successor to the USSR, and resisted efforts by other states to control any Soviet property.[9] To this end, Moscow asked the NIS for exclusive ownership of all former Soviet foreign assets and debts from the other republics. These debts were formidable. By 1992 the USSR was $77.7 billion in debt, and $11.8 billion in arrears to official and unofficial creditors.[10] On the asset side, the Soviet Union owned a considerable array of hard-currency properties, such as embassies, hard-currency reserves, gold, and outstanding loans. The nominal value of the loans was estimated at $162 billion. Given the debtor countries, however, the odds of collecting the money were not good.[11] Moscow wanted all of the other post-Soviet states to renounce their claims to both the assets and debts, in an effort to make debt collection and payment easier and become the USSR's true successor. Some of the states, however, were convinced that this move would profit Russia in the end.

The most important Soviet assets were the nuclear warheads on NIS soil. When the USSR disintegrated, Belarus, Ukraine, and Kazakhstan inherited considerable nuclear stockpiles, as table 5.2 shows. Ukraine became the world's third-largest nuclear power overnight. To prevent a proliferation of nuclear-armed states, both the United States and Russia wanted the weapons and warheads transferred to Russian soil.

Second, Moscow needed to maintain control over strategic bases and borders in the NIS countries. Table 5.3 provides a partial listing of the strategic bases in the target states. Securing basing rights served the triple purpose of maintaining the old Soviet military infrastructure in intelligence-gathering and logistics, keeping troops in the NIS as foreign policy levers, and deferring the cost of housing these troops in Russia. The border patrol was also significant; Russia wanted to use

---

[9] For example, despite repeated Ukrainian requests, Russia refused to transfer any of the Soviet stations in Antarctica. See *OMRI Daily Digest*, "Ukrainian Roundup," February 8, 1996.

[10] International Monetary Fund (1994), section IV.

[11] The principal debtors were Cuba, Mongolia, Vietnam, Afghanistan, Ethiopia, India, Iraq, Nicaragua, and Syria.

Table 5.2. *Distribribution of land-based nuclear weapons in the former Soviet Union*

Country	Weapon type	No. of weapons	No. of warheads
Russia	ICBMs[1]	1,003	5,800
	Bombers	100	1,300
Belarus	ICBMs	81	81
	Bombers	0	0
Kazakhstan	ICBMs	104	1,040
	Bombers	40	320
Ukraine	ICBMs	176	1,240
	Bombers	41	667

Note: [1] Intercontinental ballistic missiles.
Source: Dawisha and Parrott (1994), p. 261.

the old Soviet border as its first line of defense rather than paying an estimated billion rubles per kilometer to regulate its new and somewhat undefined border.[12] Moscow was clear in its desire to keep troops in the NIS. In Yeltsin's September 1995 decree on the CIS, he pushed for the establishment of a unified border-defense system and sustaining the Soviet military infrastructure. The document constantly blurs the difference between Russia's security interests and the security interests of the CIS as a whole.[13] In its communiqués and statements, the Russian Foreign Ministry made clear distinctions between the "internal borders" of the CIS countries and the "external borders" between the CIS and the rest of Eurasia.

Third, Russia has pressured the NIS to award greater autonomy to ethnic Russians. As early as March 1992, the first Russian official to draft a policy towards the CIS, Fedor Shelov-Kovedyaev, asserted in *Izvestiya*: "With or without documents, Russians (outside the Russian Federation) are under the protection of Russia." In early 1993, Boris Yeltsin commented: "I believe the time has come for authoritative international organizations, including the United Nations, to grant Russia special powers as guarantor of peace and stability in this region (the former Soviet Union)." In 1994, Sergei Shakrai, then vice-Premier, stated: "We believe that Russia bears international legal

---

[12] The billion ruble per kilometer estimate was made by the commander-in-chief of the Russian border guard in 1995: Brzezinski and Sullivan (1997), p. 189.
[13] Mihalisko, "Yeltsin outlines strategy for a renewed superpower."

Table 5.3. *Strategic military bases in the former Soviet Union*

Target state	Size of national armed forces	Russian troops based there as of July 1993	Strategic military assets
Armenia	25,000	5,000	Army base, Gyumri Army group headquarters, Yerevan Border with Iran, Turkey
Azerbaijan	20,000	0	Early warning radar station, Mingechaur Border with Iran
Belarus	125,000	25,000	Early warning radar station, Baranovichi Naval communications station, Veleika Border with Poland, Slovakia
Estonia	2,000	7,000	Submarine base, Paldiski
Georgia	10,000	10,000	Seismic laboratory, Eshera Naval ports, Vatumi and Poti Air bases, Vaziani and Akhalkalaki
Kazakhstan	120,000	63,000	Space cosmodrome, Baikonur Nuclear testing facilities, Semipalatinsk Early warning radar station, Saryshagan Border with China
Kyrgyzstan	15,000	8,000	Seismic stations Border with China
Latvia	4,500	23,000	Early warning radar station, Skrunda Space communications station, Ventspils Naval port, Liepaya
Lithuania	11,000	12,000	Transit corridor to Kaliningrad
Moldova	10,000	8,000	Army group headquarters, Tiraspol
Tajikistan	14,000	24,000	Space control station, Nurek Border with Afghanistan
Turkmenistan	34,000	15,000	Border with Afghanistan, Iran
Ukraine	500,000	60,000	Black Sea port, Sevastopol Black Sea fleet headquarters, Donuzlav Strategic bomber airfields, Priluki and Uzin
Uzbekistan	40,000	20,000	Space tracking station, Mount Maidanak

Source: "Soviet army all in pieces," *Los Angeles Times*, July 20, 1993, p. A1; "Russia's military presence in the near abroad," *Transition*, October 20, 1995, pp. 8–9; *Economist*, "Touchy bears," May 21, 1994, p. 61.

responsibility for citizens of the former USSR who have not gotten equal and proper status in the new states." Russian military doctrine explicitly states that it has the right to intervene in the CIS to protect minority interests.[14] Moscow has demanded regional autonomy for regions in other countries with a Russian plurality, such as the Transdniestr region in Moldova, the Crimean peninsula in Ukraine, and *oblasts* in northern Kazakhstan. It also demanded that ethnic Russians in the NIS be granted dual citizenship. According to this proposal, these individuals would have been citizens of their resident country and the Russian Federation.

Finally, Russia wanted to be first among equals in exploiting the energy resources of the former Soviet Union. This was consistent with its goal of minimizing Western foreign direct investment in the CIS. Moscow viewed investment in the NIS as a zero-sum game between Russia and the West; American or European inflows meant a loss of Russian influence.[15] Deputy Prime Minister Alexei Bolshakov, while chairing a Russian commission on CIS cooperation, publicly stated that, "The USA and its allies are achieving more and more new positions in CIS countries, which often harms Russian interests." Russian demands in this area meant different things to different republics. For the European post-Soviet states, it meant control over pipelines and state utilities. For the southern republics, particularly the Caspian littoral states, it meant a stake in their energy extraction sectors. The Russian government has made repeated statements demanding "priority rights" to oil and mineral deposits in Kazakhstan, Turkmenistan, Uzbekistan, and Azerbaijan. One official in Moscow stated his country's preferences as follows: "The proposed agreements would exempt Russian companies from taxes or royalties, and would give Russia priority in choosing export routes for Caspian oil and gas. As part of Russia's special position, the Caspian states would form joint ventures with Russian companies."[16]

[14] Shelov-Kovedyaev quoted in John Lough, "Defining Russia's relations with neighboring states," *RFE/RL Research Report*, May 14, 1993, p. 56; Yeltsin quoted in Suzanne Crow, "Russia asserts its strategic agenda," *RFE/RL Research Report*, December 17, 1993, p. 2; Shakrai quoted in *TRUD*, "Plight of Russians in 'near abroad' debated," in FBIS-SOV-94–135, July 14, 1994, p. 10; Martin Klatt, "Russians in the 'near abroad,'" *RFE/RL Research Report*, August 19, 1994, p. 43.

[15] Brzezinski and Sullivan (1997), pp. 188–9.

[16] Bolshakov quoted in *OMRI Daily Digest*, "Bolshakov on Russian CIS policy," January 11, 1996; anonymous quote in *Jamestown Monitor*, "Moscow Ministry pursuing preemptive mineral rights in Caspian Sea," December 6, 1995.

Moscow had considerable energy resources of its own, but it also wanted to strengthen its financial-industrial groups. These corporations, such as the energy giants Gazprom and LUKoil, are plurality-owned by the Russian government. Several high-ranking officials in the Yeltsin administration came from these firms and maintain ownership stakes. This makes it hard to say where these companies end and the Russian state begins.[17] Moscow preferred for these firms to own all stages of production, from the deposits of oil and natural gas, to the pipelines that ferry the unrefined products, to the refineries that process the fuel, to the utilities that distribute the energy. Gazprom and LUKoil were aggressive in carrying out Moscow's wish to convert NIS energy debts into legal control over their oil deposits, natural gas deposits, pipelines, and energy utilities. The Russian government designated LUKoil as its official agent for exploiting hydrocarbon deposits in the Caspian states, drawing comparisons with the British chartered trading companies of the eighteenth century. Russia's motivation on this issue was also political. One observer noted, "Russia does not seem so interested in making money as in keeping all of these countries under its thumb."[18]

In conclusion, the Russian Federation made several demands of the near abroad. To ensure that the NIS maintained only nominal independence, Moscow wanted these countries to cede control of strategic Soviet assets to Russia, permit Russian troops to patrol their borders and occupy strategic bases, ensure the autonomy of ethnic Russians, and grant Russian companies stakes in their energy sectors. The ends have been well defined. The next section examines the means of Russian economic influence.

Russia's ability to coerce

Russia's demands of the NIS were clearly articulated. Just as clear was its preferred policy of using economic coercion to extract concessions. As early as May 1993, Russian deputy Prime Minister Alexander Shokhin observed about the benefits of closer CIS integration: "It appears that so far everyone is willing to gain advantages from the economic alliance while preserving full political sovereignty. This

---

[17] Peter Rutland, "Russia's natural gas leviathan," *Transition*, May 3, 1996, p. 12. When the pro-government party, Our Home is Russia, was created, a popular joke in Moscow was that the party's real name was Our Home is Gazprom.
[18] Hunter (1996), p. 118.

won't work." The *Economist* concurred, noting that Russia's policy, "stresses economic pressure rather than military intervention, trade rather than destabilization."[19]

Russian policy-makers were candid about the use of economic coercion. The Foreign and Defense Policy Council (FDPC), an influential group of Russian academics, businessmen, and politicians across the political spectrum, published a series of documents outlining the substance of Russia's foreign policy. They stated:

> Russia may suggest a model for cooperation with neighboring countries but should not try to impose them by force or fiat. The people and leaders of the neighboring countries should make their choice. In doing so, they should take note that the refusal to cooperate would ensure less economic, political, and military support from Russia.

Yeltsin's September 1995 decree on the CIS parroted this report, arguing that failure to adhere to "the model proposed by Russia" would affect, "the scale of economic, political, and military support from Russia." The Russian Foreign Ministry made similar statements, as did the legislative branch. In late 1995, Alexei Manannikov, the vice-chairman of the Federation Council's International Affairs Committee, called for using "pressure instruments," such as economic sanctions, to bring recalcitrant republics into line. Sergei Karaganov, head of the FDPC, articulated Russian policy this way: "Russia is becoming an imperial power of the 20th century; we no longer need physical control over territory, we can have economic influence."[20]

It is extremely odd, at first glance, to think of the Russian Federation as a country capable of economic coercion. Almost any analysis of the Soviet Union/Russia in the late 1980s and early 1990s described the country as a formidable military power with no corresponding economic strength.[21] Economic indicators would seem to confirm this summary. Russia's gross domestic product shrank by a third between 1991 and 1994. Inflation eroded the worth of the ruble, depreciating its

---

[19] Shokhin quoted in Morrison (1993), p. 691; *Economist,* "A teddy bear, after all?" December 10, 1994, p. 49.

[20] FDPC quote from "A strategy for Russia II"; decree quoted in Mihalisko, "Yeltsin outlines strategy for a renewed superpower"; on Kozyrev and the Foreign Ministry, see Vladimir Socor, "Kozyrev signals harder line on CIS Policy," *Prism,* July 14, 1995. Manannikov quoted in *Jamestown Monitor,* "Russian politicians glance at the 'near abroad,'" November 29, 1995; Karaganov quoted in Chrystia Freeland, "From empire to nation state," *Financial Times,* July 10, 1997, p. 11.

[21] See Kennedy (1987) and Brzezinski (1994).

value from 35 rubles to the dollar in January 1991 to roughly 5,000 by June 1995.[22] This does not sound like a country capable of threatening economic sanctions.

Yet despite the upheaval, the Russian Federation had three significant economic levers at its disposal to coerce the NIS. First, the NIS needed Russia as a market for exports and strategic inputs. Second, several of the republics relied almost exclusively on oil and natural gas imports from Russia. Third, the energy-exporting countries needed Russian pipelines to transport their oil and natural gas to importers with hard currency. In combination, most of the NIS faced moderate to high opportunity costs of being sanctioned. Russia, by contrast, had few vulnerabilities.

Table 5.4 shows the importance of the Russian market to each of the target states during 1994. Russia was the most important export market for all potential targets except Turkmenistan. In ten of the fourteen republics, it was also the most significant source of imports. There is no questioning Moscow's importance to these states. The degree of importance, however, varied by country.[23] A glance at the figures shows that Kazakhstan, Moldova, Ukraine, and Belarus were extremely dependent on Russia. They relied on Russia for more than half of their entire trade. Armenia and Georgia sent more than half of their exports to Russia, and Tajikistan depended on Russia for more than half of its imports. Because these countries needed the Russian market, they were vulnerable to the manipulation of tariff rates, custom duties, or trade laws.

In both absolute and proportional terms, Russia was likely to suffer far less than most of the near abroad. Ukraine remained Russia's most important trade partner, but this masked the degree of asymmetric

---

[22] *Economist*, "Comrade bean-counter," October 7, 1995, p. 83.

[23] The pace of economic reform is a secondary factor affecting the costs of coercion. Countries that had yet to initiate serious reforms tried to hold on to the status quo in their trading patterns. This meant a greater dependence on Russia for credits, inputs, and export contracts. If Russia chose to coerce, these economies faced much higher costs in trying to substitute to other markets. Privatized firms respond more quickly to exogenous shocks than state-owned companies. Furthermore, macroeconomic stability, an essential part of the transition from plan to market, makes it easier to trade with market economies. Low inflation reduces the risks associated with foreign exchange. An economy in hyperinflation finds it much more difficult to deal with convertible currencies. Finally, a market economy can make quick and efficient adjustments to price fluctuations in energy resources. If Russia chose to halt the flow of oil and natural gas to a market economy, the costs to the target country would be less than if the flow was halted to an unreformed economy.

Table 5.4. *NIS trade dependence on Russia, 1994*

Target country	Imports from Russia (percentage of total)	Exports to Russia (percentage of total)	Trade with Russia (percentage of total)
Armenia	48.8	52.7	49.7
Azerbaijan	15.2	22.0	18.2
Belarus	71.0	65.9	69.1
Estonia	17.6	21.5	19.3
Georgia	14.9	58.0	22.0
Kazakhstan	59.4	67.6	62.6
Kyrgyzstan	48.0	47.3	47.6
Latvia	23.5	28.1	25.5
Lithuania	39.3	28.2	34.4
Moldova	67.2	61.9	64.9
Tajikistan	57.4	26.4	41.0
Turkmenistan	22.1	10.1	17.1
Ukraine	63.0	43.4	54.2
Uzbekistan	47.5	45.7	46.6

Source: International Monetary Fund, *Direction of Trade Annual*, 1994.

dependence. In 1994, Ukraine accounted for 11 percent of all Russian trade; Russia accounted for 54 percent of all Ukrainian trade. Belarus and Kazakhstan were also significant trade partners with Russia, ranking among its top ten importers and exporters. Russia conducted moderate amounts of trade with Moldova and Uzbekistan; the rest of the NIS barely registered on the balance of payments.

Another source of CIS trade dependency on Russia was that trade deficits were financed with Russian credits. In 1992, it was estimated that by the end of 1993, Moscow would have subsidized the rest of the CIS to the tune of $17 billion.[24] At a December 1995 meeting of the CIS Interstate Economic Committee, Russian Prime Minister Viktor Chernomyrdin proposed that CIS debts to Russia be repaid in the form of equity swaps in national utilities.[25] As Table 5.5 shows, these debts were mounting only six months after independence. That Russia wanted its debts repaid was certainly not a form of economic coercion. What was coercive was the attempt to force the NIS to repay in the form of ownership stakes in strategic utilities and industries.

The industrial organization of the former Soviet Union enhanced

[24] *Transition,* "Slow progress for CIS economies," February 15, 1995, p. 19.
[25] *Jamestown Monitor,* "Russia seeks debt-for-equity swap," December 27, 1995. See also Rossen Vassilev, "Oil diplomacy in the near abroad," *Prism,* May 3, 1996.

Table 5.5. *NIS debt to Russia, June 1992*

Country	Indebtedness to Russia (billions of rubles)
Armenia	2.3
Azerbaijan	15.9
Belarus	22.0
Estonia	3.7
Georgia	11.3
Kazakhstan	46.7
Kyrgyzstan	4.5
Latvia	1.4
Lithuania	9.0
Moldova	4.6
Tajikistan	3.7
Turkmenistan	18.1
Ukraine	159.3
Uzbekistan	13.9

Source: Dawisha and Parrott (1994).

these vulnerabilities. The Soviet economy was designed to have single factories monopolize the production of key intermediate goods. For example, only one plant in the USSR made sewing machines; for goods such as diesel locomotives, tram rails, and oil drilling equipment, the biggest plant was responsible for more than 95 percent of production. Any restriction of trade between states disrupted these production processes.[26] Because Russia had the lion's share of these monopoly plants, it had the fewest production processes disrupted by the breakup. As one Kazakhstani national security official noted: "Russia is the main producer of everything in the former Soviet Union."[27] Of the NIS, it was the least vulnerable to a trade disruption. The asset-specific nature of Soviet industry increased the NIS opportunity costs of switching trade partners.

Although Russia was the least dependent economy among the NIS, it had some sectoral vulnerabilities. For example, energy exports were a primary source of hard currency earnings for Russia. This energy was shipped to European markets through pipelines that run through Ukraine, Belarus, and Latvia; 90 percent of all Russian gas exports were shipped through Ukraine. If these republics had blocked access

[26] *Economist*, "The best of all monopoly profits ... ," August 11, 1990, p. 67.
[27] Dostan Eleukenov, "Central Asian security," Presentation at the Center for International Security and Arms Control, Stanford, California, October 5, 1995.

to the pipelines, Russia would have been stripped of an important share of its hard-currency earnings. In other sectors, Moscow needed strategic inputs from the NIS. Russian textile mills depended almost exclusively on Uzbek cotton; the oil industry relied on extraction equipment from Azerbaijan and Ukraine; automobile manufacturers needed tires from Armenia. Russia relied on Kazakhstan for many of the inputs for its nuclear power industry. One Kazakhstani plant produced nearly all of Russia's uranium dioxide powder, and made approximately 80 percent of the nuclear fuel used by the CIS. It would have been difficult for Moscow to find another source.[28] Still, given Russia's large energy reserves, these are examples of trade sensitivities, not acute vulnerabilities.

Energy represents another dimension of dependence. Tables 5.6 and 5.7 show that some of the target states were more vulnerable than others. The European republics and Georgia depended primarily on Russia for oil and natural gas. These countries imported at least 90 percent of their oil and/or natural gas from the Russian Federation. Armenia imported its energy through Russian pipelines, so it was also dependent on Moscow. Azerbaijan and the Central Asian republics appeared less vulnerable, because they had their own hydrocarbon deposits. Tajikistan, Uzbekistan, and Kyrgyzstan did not need Russia for their energy needs. Azerbaijan, Kazakhstan, and Turkmenistan were energy exporters.

The energy-exporting states still faced extraordinary high costs if Russia used economic coercion. As one Russian official put it, "we have them by their pipelines."[29] Given their landlocked status, these countries needed a pipeline system to deliver their exports to accessible seaports. From 1992 to 1996, the only pipelines linking these countries to any importer with hard currency ran through Russia. If Moscow denied them access to Russian pipelines, it would deny these countries vital export revenues with no cost to itself. If anything, Russia would benefit slightly by restricting competition with its own hydrocarbon exports.

Table 5.8 summarizes the vulnerability of the NIS by the three dimensions described above. Only two countries escaped any significant vulnerability: Kyrgyzstan and Uzbekistan. Seven other countries

---

[28] Sagers (1993), p. 389; Porter and Saivetz (1994), p. 78; Office of Technology Assessment (1994), p. 52.
[29] Quoted in J. Robinson West, "Pipelines to power; Russia's grip on the oil and gas from its former colonies," *The Washington Post*, June 8, 1994, p. A23.

Table 5.6. *Energy production in the former Soviet Union*

Country	Natural gas output, 1992 (billion cubic meters)	Crude oil output, 1992 (million metric tons)	Petroleum refining, 1991 (million metric tons)	Nuclear power capability
Armenia	0.0	0.0	0.0	Yes
Azerbaijan	7.8	11.0	15.8	No
Belarus	0.2	2.0	35.8	No
Estonia	0.0	0.0	0.0	No
Georgia	0.0	0.1	1.8	No
Kazakhstan	8.8	27.5	18.0	Yes
Kyrgyzstan	0.1	0.1	0.0	No
Latvia	0.0	0.0	0.0	No
Lithuania	0.0	0.0	11.5	Yes
Moldova	0.0	0.0	0.0	No
Russia	640.4	395.8	286.5	Yes
Tajikistan	0.1	0.1	0.0	No
Turkmenistan	60.1	5.3	7.1	No
Ukraine	20.9	4.4	54.6	Yes
Uzbekistan	42.8	3.1	7.9	No

Source: Dawisha and Parrott (1994).

Table 5.7. *NIS energy dependence on Russia*

Country	Ratio of energy production to consumption	Crude oil imported from Russia as a percentage of consumption	Gas imported from Russia as a percentage of consumption
Armenia	3	–	0
Azerbaijan	110	14	0
Belarus	5	91	100
Estonia	–	–	100
Georgia	20	82	27
Kazakhstan	120	–	–
Kyrgyzstan	45	–	0
Latvia	–	–	100
Lithuania	–	94	100
Moldova	1	–	100
Tajikistan	55	–	0
Turkmenistan	555	16	0
Ukraine	60	89	56
Uzbekistan	80	55	0

Source: Schneider (1993) and Dawisha and Parrott (1994).

Table 5.8. *NIS vulnerability to Russian economic coercion*

Target country	Trade dependency[1]	Energy dependency[2]	Pipeline dependency
Armenia	X		
Azerbaijan			X
Belarus	X	X	
Estonia		X	
Georgia	X	X	
Kazakhstan	X		X
Kyrgyzstan			
Latvia		X	
Lithuania		X	
Moldova	X	X	
Tajikistan	X		
Turkmenistan			X
Ukraine	X	X	
Uzbekistan			

Notes: [1] Trade dependence defined as relying on Russia for over 50 percent of imports or exports.
[2] Energy dependence defined as relying on Russia for over 80 percent of oil or natural gas consumption.

(Armenia, Azerbaijan, Estonia, Latvia, Lithuania, Tajikistan and Turkmenistan) were only vulnerable in one dimension. Five other countries, Ukraine, Moldova, Belarus, Georgia, and Kazakhstan, were vulnerable in two dimensions. By contrast, Russia lacked any broad-based vulnerability in its dealings with the NIS.

Conflict expectations with Russia

The theory of economic coercion developed here argues that the opportunity costs of deadlock tell only part of the story in explaining economic coercion. The expectations of future conflict also need to be measured. One way this can be inferred is by examining the NIS alliance policies with Russia and other countries. This section examines the degree to which the NIS aligned themselves with Russia.

Although nearly all of the NIS made some sort of official declaration of neutrality, in practice these countries varied somewhat in their bilateral relations with Russia. The seriousness of non-Russian threats and the history of relations with Russia helped to determine the alignment of these states. For example, Kazakhstan perceived serious security threats from both China and Iran that threatened its borders and internal stability. These threats, combined with a history of Russian benevolence, led Altma Ata to ally with Moscow.[30] Ukraine, by contrast, saw Russia as its greatest threat. Kiev viewed its three hundred-year union with Moscow as a period of subjugation. Lacking other serious threats, Ukraine chose to pursue a more independent foreign policy. Kiev crafted a defense doctrine recognizing the threat from Russia.[31]

Some of the NIS had additional disputes with Russia. These included the demarcation of new borders, relations with NATO countries, and the organizational structure of the CIS. Moscow refrained from threatening to use economic coercion on these matters. Nevertheless, those states in disagreement with Russia would have elevated conflict expectations. Concessions on other issues such as basing rights could have led to increased leverage on border disputes or relations with the United States. The Baltic republics, Azerbaijan, Kazakhstan, and Ukraine faced difficult negotiations in demarcating their border with Russia.

One group of states – Armenia, Belarus, Kazakhstan, Kyrgyzstan, Tajikistan, and Uzbekistan– easily qualify as Russia's allies. These states, plus Russia, were the only countries to have signed and ratified the CIS charter by the January 1994 deadline. All of these states are members of the CIS Collective Security Treaty, which pledges member countries to assist each other in case of external attack. These were also the last group of states to join NATO's Partnership for Peace, which Russia had been reluctant to join.[32] Finally, each of these states signed wide-ranging friendship and cooperation treaties with Russia.[33] With the exception of Kazakhstan, none of the states had border disputes with Russia. Although minor frictions occasionally crept into their bilateral relations with Russia, this group had minimal conflict expectations. These countries chose to voluntarily align themselves closely with Russia through security pacts and integration agreements.

Another group of countries – Estonia, Latvia, Lithuania, Moldova, and Ukraine – just as clearly qualify as Russia's adversaries. None of

---

[30] Schmiedeler (1995). On the perceived fear of China, see Lamulin (1995).

[31] Morrison (1993).

[32] Tajikistan has yet to join the Partnership for Peace, in part because of its domestic turmoil. For dates on entry, see the NATO web site at http://www.nato.int/pfp.

[33] Webber (1996), pp. 104–5, n. 47.

these countries are members of the CIS Collective Security Treaty. The Baltic states are not CIS members. Ukraine joined the CIS as an associate member, actively resisted all Russian overtures and consistently rejected any strong institutional role for the CIS. It was the main brake in any move towards closer CIS integration, particularly military cooperation. Only Moldova is a full member of the CIS, and as will be seen in the next chapter, that was mostly the result of Russian coercion. These were the first NIS to apply for NATO's Partnership for Peace program in the face of Russian qualms about it. In their first five years of existence, none of these countries signed friendship treaties with Russia. Moldova and Lithuania tried brief periods of conciliation, as will be noted in chapter 6. Overall, however, each of these countries viewed Russia as its greatest security threat and the most likely source of future international conflict.

At first glance, the three remaining countries – Azerbaijan, Georgia, and Turkmenistan – seem more difficult to code, but a closer look reveals their preferences. Turkmenistan refused to sign the CIS Collective Security Treaty and refrained from joining other CIS organs, and applied to join the Non-Aligned Movement. However, while this country resisted multilateral cooperation with Russia, it has been a keen advocate of close bilateral ties. In July 1992 a friendship and cooperation treaty was signed, including a military agreement creating a national defense force under joint Turkmen–Russian command. The Turkmen Foreign Minister commented at the time, "I believe that we should have special relations with Russia. They can be counted on in troubled days." By 1995, an agreement established the two countries as "strategic partners" through the year 2000. No other CIS country has signed a similar agreement with Russia.[34] This country had few expectations of future conflict with Russia, and counts as an ally.

Georgia and Azerbaijan, on the other hand, signed the CIS Collective Security Treaty only in response to Russian economic and military pressure, as will be seen in chapter 6. Consider the case of Azerbaijan. At the time of independence, its parliament rejected CIS membership, and its president was an ardent nationalist who pursued close relations with Turkey. Following a coup in June 1993, the new president talked of closer ties with Russia. He persuaded the parlia-

---

[34] Foreign Minister quoted in Dawisha and Parrott (1994), p. 220; Lowell Bezanis, "Joining forces with Iran and Russia," *Transition*, May 11, 1995, pp. 70–87.

ment to approve membership in the CIS and the Collective Security Treaty. He hoped that this would alter Moscow's position on Azerbaijan's conflict with Armenia over the disputed region of Nagorno-Karabakh. Since late 1993, however, Azeri–Russian relations could be described as adversarial. In 1995, an Azerbaijani foreign policy advisor stated: "Russia ... is Azerbaijan's greatest enemy and the most substantive obstacle on its road to independence." Azerbaijan refused to sign any additional security agreement with Russia. In 1996 it threatened to quit the CIS altogether.[35] The history of Russian–Georgian relations tells a similar story.[36] Georgia refused to sign the Collective Security Treaty until its ruling regime faced civil war. It refused to ratify the agreement for several years afterwards. It resisted further security accords with Russia. Both Georgia and Azerbaijan applied to join the Partnership for Peace program ahead of the Russian Federation, and both had border disputes with Russia as well. Although they hoped that entering the Collective Security Treaty would ease tensions with Russia, both of these states anticipated frequent conflicts.

Predicting the outcomes

This classification enables the conflict expectations model to predict how much each country is likely to concede. Table 5.9 displays the model's predictions.

Belarus and Kazakhstan, because of their minimal expectations of future conflict and large costs of being coerced, are predicted to make the most significant concessions. Moldova, Georgia, and Ukraine faced greater expectations of future conflict but also faced significant opportunity costs of deadlock; they are expected to make moderate concessions. Turkmenistan, Tajikistan, Armenia, Kyrgyzstan, and Uzbekistan were all close allies with Russia and faced only moderate costs of coercion relative to the other NIS. The model would predict fewer sanctions attempts because it would be more difficult to satisfy the coercion condition. Because Russia faced minimal costs in sanctioning most of these countries, however, one would still expect to see some cases of sanctions. The model predicts moderate concessions

---

[35] *OMRI Daily Digest*, "Azerbaijan's Parliament threatens to quit CIS," March 20, 1996; Azeri offical quoted in Schmidt (1995), p. 266.
[36] Webber (1996), p. 273, n. 19.

Table 5.9. *Predicting the pattern of economic coercion in the NIS*

	Low expectations of future conflict	High expectations of future conflict
Large gap in opportunity costs of coercion	Significant concessions Belarus Kazakhstan	Moderate concessions Georgia Moldova Ukraine
Moderate gap in opportunity costs of coercion	Few coercion attempts Armenia Kyrgyzstan Tajikistan Turkmenistan Uzbekistan	Minor concessions Azerbaijan Estonia Latvia Lithuania

from these countries because of the reduced expectations of future conflict. Finally, Azerbaijan, Lithuania, Latvia, and Estonia anticipated numerous future conflicts and faced moderate costs of coercion. According to the conflict expectations model, Russia would have been able to extract only minor concessions from these countries.

It should be noted that no other systemic explanation generates the same set of predictions as the conflict expectations model.[37] Any measure of aggregate power or military power would predict that all of these countries except Ukraine would make generous concessions. A geopolitical explanation would predict distinctions between the European, Transcaucasian, and Central Asian NIS, but would be hard pressed to explain any variation within those groups such as Belarus and Ukraine or Kazakhstan and Uzbekistan. Finally, NIS relations with the United States do not match the model's predictions. The United States sided with Russia on several demands, such as nuclear nonproliferation and the treatment of ethnic Russians. In addition, between 1992 and 1994 Russia received almost all US aid apportioned to the former Soviet Union.[38] Furthermore, the United States strongly supported Armenia and spurned Azerbaijan during most of the

---

[37] See Drezner (1997b) for a fuller explanation.
[38] Brzezinski (1994).

period in question. The conflict expectations model predicts that Armenia would concede more than Azerbaijan. The model generates a unique set of predictions.

With the predictions in place, the next chapter will examine the episodes of Russian economic coercion.

6   The extent of NIS concessions

Introduction

This chapter chronicles Russia's use of economic statecraft towards
the post-Soviet states from mid-1992 to mid-1997. For each event, it is
necessary to determine the precise Russian demand, demonstrate the
calculated use of Russian economic diplomacy as a policy tool, and
ascertain the extent of the target state's concessions. For each coercion
attempt, the salience of conflict expectations, opportunity costs, the
threat of military force, and the strength of the target regime is also
evaluated.

Because of the recent nature of these coercion attempts, I have relied
primarily on press accounts as the primary source of information.[1]
Because media attention has varied across republics, some of the
coercion attempts are easier to document than others. In most
instances, Russian policy elites were publicly candid about threatening economic disruption to procure concessions. In a few cases, the
linkage was only implied. In most of these events, the press assumed
that Russia's chief diplomatic tool was the unspoken threat of
economic or military coercion. To avoid overinterpretation, I have
tried to keep the journalistic speculations to a minimum, relying
instead on actions and comments from foreign policy elites and
regional experts.

---

[1] These include area publications such as the *RFE/RL Daily Report*, *OMRI Daily Digest*,
Jamestown Monitor, *RFE/RL Research Report*, *Transition*, *Prism*, Foreign Broadcast Information Service daily reports of Central Eurasia, and Economist Intelligence Unit
quarterly reports of the target countries. These reports have been supplemented by
broader news sources, particularly the *New York Times*, *Economist*, *Washington Post*, *Los
Angeles Times*, *Financial Times*, and the *Financial Times Energy Economist*.

According to some Russian officials and scholars, economic state-craft was not a credible policy tool. In 1995 the Russian Minister for CIS Affairs claimed, "We can't even put effective economic pressure on Tajikistan." One Russian academic analysis concluded: "Sanctions should not be regarded as an instrument of routine political inter-action between nations."[2] Despite these protestations, Moscow used its economic levers of diplomacy on more than thirty-five occasions between 1992 and 1997. These efforts have not gone unnoticed by Western analysts.[3] There have been several notable successes at securing concessions after threatening to disrupt economic exchange, but the record is not one of universal success. The following sections review each of the targeted countries in turn, from Belarus, the country predicted to make the greatest number of concessions, to Estonia, the country predicted to make the fewest.

Belarus

Russia had four demands of this country: (1) a return of all nuclear weapons to Russian soil; (2) basing rights for its armed forces and border patrol; (3) control of the Belarusian energy sector, particularly its oil refineries, gas pipelines, and utilities. At the same time, Moscow wanted to avoid any costly subsidies of the Belarusian economy.

To Western observers, the Belarusians appeared at first to be remarkably docile on the nuclear weapons issue. A US Office of Technology Assessment finding concluded: "Belarus has been the most forthcoming of the three non-Russian nuclear inheritor states of the FSU [former Soviet Union] in terms of fulfilling its commitments to the international community in arms control and nonprolifera-tion."[4] Minsk ratified both the START-I and Non-Proliferation Treaties within two years of independence. Because of these early confidence-building measures, the issue garnered little attention after 1994. The last warheads were removed from Belarusian soil in November 1996.

Minsk's docility on the nuclear weapons issue was the result of several factors, not all of them related to the possibility of coercion. It

---

[2] Ministerial quote from *BBC Summary of World Broadcasts*, "Minister warns against economic pressure on CIS states," September 25, 1995. Sanctions quotation from Konovalov, Oznobistchev, and Evstafiev (1995).

[3] See Blank (1995), Porter and Saivetz (1994), Hill and Jewett (1994), and Harris (1994).

[4] Office of Technology Assessment (1994), p. 42.

would have been difficult to maintain the weapons, given the absence of a nuclear infrastructure. The human costs of the Chernobyl accident had also turned Belarusian public opinion against anything nuclear.[5] However, the threat of economic coercion prevented Belarus from using the weapons as a bargaining chip. In its first few months of independence, the Belarusian leadership did make noises about keeping the missiles. In January 1992, the Belarusian Defense Minister Piotr Chaus declared: "so long as the property of the former Soviet Union has not been apportioned, (nuclear) weapons must stay in the territory of Belarus." The head of state resisted signing an agreement transferring legal ownership of the missiles to Russia, noting that he felt more confident in international negotiations with nuclear weapons behind his back.[6] Chaus was removed from his position, and the ownership agreement was signed, but these actions show that the Belarusians were tempted to use the weapons as bargaining chips.

Given the prospect of Russian economic coercion, such a strategy would have been costly. A Belarusian expert on nonproliferation observed: "Belarus depends strongly on economic and military-logistical support from Russia, and the decision to go nuclear would have been regarded as anti-Russian, in turn provoking Russia to inflict economic sanctions on Belarus ... clearly, given Belarus's overwhelming dependence on Russia, nuclear independence is a pipe dream." One Western ambassador agreed that the Belarusians had transferred the weapons "because the Russians told them to." On this issue, Belarus met all of Russia's demands without Russia resorting to any overt threat of coercion, but an implicit threat was widely acknowledged.[7]

Belarus's attitude towards the transfer of weapons indicates that it did not perceive acquiescence on this issue leading to significant concessions in the future. The close relationship between Minsk and Moscow was reflected in the evolution of the Belarusian military doctrine in late 1992. It was implicitly assumed that any enemy of Belarus would be an enemy of Russia. The Belarusian national interest was defined in lock-step with Russia's preferences. The Belarusian Prime Minister acknowledged in 1993, "it is not Russia that needs

---

[5] Paznyak (1995). See also Reiss (1995), pp. 133–9. This explanation is weakened, however, by a 1996 Belarusian announcement that it would build a nuclear reactor to reduce its energy dependency on Russia.

[6] Paznyak (1995), p. 159; Sokov (1997), p. 22.

[7] Paznyak (1995), pp. 166, 172; Reiss (1995), p. 136.

Belarus ... it is we who need Russia." This close identification of interests grew with the election of Alexander Lukashenka to the presidency in the summer of 1994, and was responsible, ironically, for Belarus being the *last* NIS to relinquish all of its nuclear warheads. In January 1996, Lukashenka proposed that the weapons stay in Belarus, in order to protect both Minsk *and* Moscow against NATO expansion.[8] Only after Russia insisted on the transfer of the warheads did Lukashenka acquiesce. This convergence of interests reduced, in Minsk's eyes, the significance of transferring the nuclear warheads to Russian soil.

Russia also had remarkable success in gaining control over strategic military and energy assets. Its main lever was Belarus's rapidly increasing energy debt. Belarus imports over 90 percent of its energy from Russia. Between March 1992 and March 1993, Russia increased its quoted price for a metric ton of oil from $4 to $50. By 1994, Belarus was paying $75 per ton, and was told to expect a price rise to $95 in the following year. Belarusian debts quickly mounted, reaching $420 million by January 1995. By the second quarter of 1995, Russia was charging $112 per ton, and refusing to accept Belarusian products as barter.[9]

Belarus lacked the economic wherewithal to pay any of the debts, and could not risk a cutoff of energy supplies. Guided by Russian suggestions, it agreed to political concessions as a way to reduce its debt load. In 1992, Minsk quickly agreed to the "zero option" proposed by Russia, renouncing all claims to Soviet assets held abroad. This covered energy debts in 1992. By September 1993, it had racked up $333 million in new debt to Russia. Moscow's response was to slash its oil exports to Belarus to roughly 30 percent of previous levels, and threaten to cut the flow of oil again by half if some compensation was not forthcoming. An agreement was reached whereby Minsk waived all customs fees for oil.

These concessions failed to significantly reduce Belarus's debt, so in December 1994 the Belarusians acquiesced to additional Russian demands. In return for 4 million tons of oil, the government agreed to ship MTZ tractors to Russia. As an indication of the extent of

[8] Prime Minister quoted in Dawisha and Parrott (1994), p. 183; on Lukashenka, see *Jamestown Monitor*, "Belarus threatens to redeploy nuclear weapons," January 19, 1996; on the Belarusian defense doctrine, see Paznyak (1995), pp. 156–7.

[9] Ustina Markus, "Heading off an energy disaster," *Transition*, April 14, 1995, pp. 10–13; Economist Intelligence Unit, *Country Report: Belarus and Moldova*, 3rd quarter 1995, p. 13.

Belarusian concessions, each tractor paid off only $9,000 in debt to Russia even though Belarus had sold the same tractors to China for $15,000 per unit. In addition, Belarus agreed to provide LUKoil and YuKOS (another Russian oil firm) with shares in Belarusian oil refineries and petrochemical plants. In January 1996, another agreement was struck between the two countries to transfer 51 percent of the Mazyr oil refinery and 74 percent of the Novopolotsk refinery to a Russian-dominated joint venture. It was also agreed that the joint venture would receive 51 percent of any future public offerings in the Belarusian oil sector. In October Lukashenka stated that he would privatize the Naftan refinery by decree and provide the requisite 51 percent share to LUKoil and YuKOS. These concessions were considerable, and attracted some criticisms in Parliament. Belarus had little choice but to barter because Russia had demonstrated that it would otherwise cut supplies.[10]

All of these concessions were made to keep the oil flowing; Belarus still had to pay its debts for receiving natural gas. In August 1993, Gazprom cut daily shipments to a third of their previous levels. Belarusian officials confirmed that the Russians were using pressure tactics to secure agreement on transferring control of the state gas monopoly Beltranshaz to Gazprom. Minsk continued to acquiesce. Following the August cuts, the Belarusian leadership agreed to lease Beltranshaz to Gazprom for ninety-nine years, and waived all gas transit fees. This agreement fell apart, however, because conservatives in the Belarusian Parliament were reluctant to privatize any firms. In March 1994, Gazprom cut its gas supplies even further. Belarus responded by stripping debtor enterprises of their shares in joint-stock companies and transferring the equity to Gazprom. This did not halt the wave of concessions, however. In early 1996, Belarus agreed to waive all transit fees for oil and natural gas shipped from Russia to Europe in exchange for forgiving further natural gas debts.[11]

Finally, Russia secured control of key military bases. In April 1994, a monetary union was announced between the two countries. The

---

[10] Quote from Ustina Markus, "Heading off an energy disaster," *Transition*, April 14, 1995, pp. 10–13; *OMRI Daily Digest*, January 26, 1996; *Segodnya*, "Belarus strengthens cooperation with LUKoil and YuKOS companies," in FBIS-SOV-96-075, April 17, 1996, p. 47; *OMRI Daily Digest*, "Russian oil firms in Belarus," October 1, 1996.

[11] Markus, "Heading off an energy disaster"; Economist Intelligence Unit, *Country Report: Ukraine, Belarus, and Moldova*, 3rd quarter, 1993, pp. 29–30; *Jamestown Monitor*, "Minsk announces debt deal with Russia," January 4, 1996.

agreement included a major political concession; Belarus agreed to allow Russian armed forces and border guards to use its military bases free of charge. This included the early warning station at Baranovichi, the naval communications station in Veleika, and air force bases for 130 strike aircraft. The accord represented a reversal in Belarusian policy; in 1992, Minsk preferred a withdrawal in Russian troops, and complained of the ecological damage caused by the bases. In 1994, Belarusian authorities claimed that the concession on bases cost it $900 million per year. The actual monetary union was called off by the Russians. Russian Prime Minister Viktor Chernomyrdin refused to further subsidize Minsk and said that no monetary union could occur until Belarusian reforms reached Russian levels.[12]

The Belarusians had two reasons for making all of their concessions. First, the costs of stalemate were considerable. As previously noted, Belarus was extremely dependent on Russia for its energy and electricity needs. Its percentage of trade conducted with Russia actually increased after independence, from 61.4 percent in 1992 to 69.1 percent in 1994. In addition, its lack of reform meant that more than half of the gross national product was devoted to the military–industrial complex; losing Russian contracts would have thoroughly crippled the country. Second, the Belarusians had no expectations of future conflict with Russia. When asked about security implications of the Russian takeover of oil refineries, the head of the Belarusian state oil monopoly commented: "The merging of Russian oil companies with enterprises of the Belarusian oil sector has only one primary objective – an increase in the welfare of Belarusian and Russian peoples. In my opinion, in this case our security will not suffer." This has been echoed by statements from higher levels. In December 1995, President Lukashenka said that his regime's foreign policies were "ninety percent similar" to Russia's.[13]

Neither of the alternative explanations – the threat of military force or the domestic vulnerability of the target regime – appear to be

---

[12] Douglas Clarke, "Russia's presence in the 'near abroad,'" *Transition*, October 4, 1995; Dawisha and Parrott (1994), p. 251; Economist Intelligence Unit, *Country Report: Ukraine, Belarus, and Moldova*, 4th quarter, 1994, p. 27; *RFE/RL Daily Report*, "Chernomyrdin rules out monetary union with Belarus," September 12, 1994.

[13] Oil president quoted in *Vo Slavu Rodiny*, "The integration of Russian and Belarusian oil companies – for the benefit of the people," in FBIS-SOV-96–095, May 15, 1996, p. 60. Lukashenka quote from *Jamestown Monitor*, "Belarus leaders disappointed with Russian policies," December 5, 1995; see also Ustina Markus, "Belarus: missed opportunities in foreign policy," *Transition*, August 25, 1995, p. 64.

salient in explaining the Belarusian concessions. Although there is always the possibility that Russia used covert threats of military force, none were reported. The target regime did not suffer from serious ethnic cleavages or institutional weakness. The country underwent an orderly, democratic transfer of power in 1994. In the fall of 1996, Lukashenka did usurp Parliament through legally questionable referenda, but Belarus had already made most of its concessions by this juncture. The significant costs of coercion and close relationship with Russia appear to explain why Minsk was willing to make any concessions asked by Russia. The Belarusian regime preferred the meager rewards of acquiescence to the greater costs of deadlock.

By 1998, Belarus had agreed to hand over all nuclear weapons, waive all fees for the trans-shipment of energy to Europe, granted Russian troops full basing rights rent-free, and handed over significant equity shares of Belarusian oil refineries and other firms to Russia. In return, Russia continued to raise its energy price, albeit to a level still below market prices, stalled an attempt at monetary reform, repeatedly threatened to halt energy shipments, and generally ignored Belarusian preferences. The repeated threats and cutoffs from Russia and its suppliers raised some hackles in Minsk. Several officials complained about the increase of energy prices to market levels. Lukashenka threatened to impose excise duties on Russian alcohol and tobacco.[14]

The predominant Belarusian reaction, however, was to bind itself even more tightly to Moscow. The Belarusian Parliament officially ratified the CIS Collective Security Treaty in April 1993; in 1994, it agreed to the abortive monetary union. A customs union was formed in 1995. In 1996, President Lukashenka went one step further, signing a treaty with Yeltsin creating a "Community of Sovereign Republics." The treaty stipulated that the two countries would coordinate their foreign policies, military policies, and border patrols, set up a common market, and synchronize reforms. Three supranational organs were set up to administer the treaty. One interpretation of this union is that Lukashenka hoped to escape future coercion attempts, but still retain the benefits of its close relationship with Russia through the creation of binding institutions.

At first, the steps towards confederation reaped some benefits.

---

[14] *Jamestown Monitor*, "Belarus leaders disappointed with Russian policies," December 5, 1995.

Russia charged less than world prices to Minsk, and theoretically waived all import duties as part of the customs union. It agreed to write off an additional $1.4 billion in debt in February 1996 when the treaty was first announced. Lukashenka announced that Russia had agreed to finance the Belarusian air force. Within a few months, however, Moscow backtracked. Lukashenka complained in July 1996 that Russian tariffs were still in place and that Moscow had not forgiven $600 million in Belarusian gas debts. In December 1996, Gazprom cut gas supplies by 15 percent for three days to force Minsk into paying off some of its debt. Russian air defense officials repudiated Lukashenka's statement about financing the Belarusian air force. In October 1996, Chernomyrdin publicly described the two-nation community as only "ink on paper."[15]

Kazakhstan

The Russians had five demands of the Kazakhstanis: (1) the return of nuclear weapons; (2) the securing of strategic bases and borders; (3) equity stakes in joint ventures to exploit Kazakhstan's large reserves of oil and natural gas; (4) preventing western control over strategic mineral deposits; (5) autonomy for ethnic Russians in northern Kazakhstan.

Alma Ata's response to the nonproliferation demand says much about the reduced conflict expectations between Kazakhstan and Russia. The Kazakhstani government initially used its nuclear weapons as bargaining chips to raise its international profile. As early as September 1991, Kazakhstani president Nursultan Nazarbayev suggested that his country could legally join the Nuclear Non-Proliferation Treaty as a nuclear state, since weapons had been tested on Kazakhstani soil prior to 1967.[16] In April 1992, the Kazakhstani vice president reiterated the intent to join the NPT as a nuclear state. In May, Nazarbayev noted, "Some Russian politicians have territorial

---

[15] Chernomydrin quoted in *OMRI Daily Digest*, "Chernomyrdin: Belarus must reform to integrate," October 21, 1996; *OMRI Daily Digest*, "Belarusian–Russian relations," September 26, 1996; *Jamestown Monitor*, "Belarus leaders discover Moscow doesn't deliver," July 23, 1996; *OMRI Daily Digest*, "Gazprom threatens Belarus with gas cuts," January 6, 1997. Economist Intelligence Unit, *Country Report: Belarus and Moldova*, 3rd quarter 1996, p. 16.

[16] The Non-Proliferation Treaty permits states that tested weapons prior to 1967 to join the agreement as nuclear states. See John W. R. Lepingwell, "Kazakhstan and nuclear weapons," *RFE/RL Research Report*, February 19, 1993, p. 59.

claims to Kazakhstan. There are Chinese textbooks that claim that parts of Siberia and Kazakhstan belong to China. Under these circumstances, how do you expect Kazakhstan to react?"[17]

In the end, Kazakhstan acquiesced to Russian and American pressure. Nazarbayev was satisfied with a limited amount of US aid, and a ceremonial visit from US Vice-President Gore to celebrate the passage of the NPT. The Parliament quickly ratified both START-I and the Non-Proliferation Treaty. On May 31, 1995, Kazakhstan announced itself to be nuclear free. Kazakhstan conceded for two reasons. First, as with Belarus, if it had proven more recalcitrant, it is likely that the counterfactual would have been a threat of economic coercion. Nazarbayev handed over the tactical nuclear weapons without a word of protest for fear of creating tensions with Moscow. Second, Nazarbayev perceived that the greater threat to Kazakhstan's sovereignty was from China, and wanted security assurances that his country would be protected from that threat. With regard to Russia, Nazarbayev publicly stated that Alma Ata's security concerns with China were eliminated with the signing of the CIS Collective Security Treaty in May 1992.[18] By placing such importance on the security treaty, Alma Ata demonstrated that it did not think of Russia as the most serious threat to its sovereignty. This explains its reaction to Russian economic coercion on other issues.

Moscow was able to secure basing rights to all of the sites it has requested on favorable terms. The negotiations over the Baikonur cosmodrome were typical. Baikonur was the Soviet equivalent of Cape Canaveral. It was the launch sight of all manned Soviet flights; in 1994, 63 percent of all Russian spacecraft blasted off from Baikonur. With the breakup, Kazakhstan claimed ownership of the base, and demanded $7 billion from Russia for its use for the next ten years.[19] Given that Baikonur was the only place where Russia could launch its Proton rocket, and given its desire to remain competitive in the commercial space market, the costs of deadlock for Moscow could have been significant.

The Russian response was to use its own economic leverage. On a visit to Kazakhstan in mid-1993, Russian Defense Minister Pavel

---

[17] Sokov (1997), p. 28.

[18] Reiss (1995), pp. 139–49.

[19] Sonni Efron, "Next step: Russia launches hope for revived space program," *Los Angeles Times*, March 21, 1995, p. 1; Fred Hiatt, "Russia leases back cosmodrome," *Washington Post*, March 29, 1994, p. A14.

Grachev warned, "without Russian specialists none of the CIS states is able to use on its own any strategic facility." In March 1994, the commander of Russia's military space program announced plans to build a new cosmodrome on a strategic missile base near Blagovesh-chenk in the far east. Plans were also made to upgrade Russia's other launching pad, Plesetsk, to cosmodrome status.[20]

Three days after this announcement, the Kazakhstanis agreed to lease Baikonur to Russia for $115 million annually for the next twenty years, with an option for an additional ten years. This represented a significant climbdown for Alma Ata. The Russians, in the same announcement, said that the actual rent would be based on usage, and budgeted only $82 million for 1994. Since the agreement, Russia has failed to make any payments for use of the base. In addition, Kazakhstan allowed Russia to turn the adjacent city of Leninsk into a Russian federal district.[21]

In the case of Baikonur, Russia knew that the costs of disagreement for Alma Ata were far greater than Russia's. Prior to the March 1994 agreement, President Nazarbayev had tried to shop the cosmodrome to other countries, including the United States.[22] There was little interest. Defense Secretary William Perry, on a visit to Baikonur, said that the base was far too big for anyone's needs. Alma Ata, left with little choice, settled for the best deal Russia would offer. A similar outcome occurred in other dimensions of military cooperation. By 1995, Kazakhstan had agreed to the creation of "joint armed forces" with Russia; Nazarbayev compared the agreement with the Soviet Union's relationship with its Warsaw Pact allies. As part of the agreement, Russia was able to deploy its forces near the Kazakhstani border with China.[23]

The Russians were also vigorous in their use of economic coercion with regard to energy concerns. As noted earlier, Russia wanted first access to these assets. Kazakhstan was the most aggressive among the NIS in pursuing Western multinational investment. The prototype of this sort of investment was the April 1993 deal between Chevron and

---

[20] Grachev quoted in Hunter (1996), p. 121; Carey Goldberg, "Russia space program hopes to regain its old 'Canaveral,'" *Los Angeles Times*, March 26, 1994, p. A2.

[21] Hiatt, "Russia leases back cosmodrome," A14; Effron, "Next step: Russia launches hope for revived space program," p. 1; *OMRI Daily Digest*, "Russia debt to Kazakhstan for Baikonur grows," October 2, 1996.

[22] Hiatt, "Russia eases back cosmodrome," p. A14.

[23] Olcott (1997), pp. 92–3.

Kazakhstan setting up a joint venture (Tengizchevroil) to explore the largest oil deposit in Kazakhstan. Chevron committed itself to investing over $20 billion into the Tengiz field over the next forty years, and at least $1.5 billion in the first three years. For its significant natural gas deposits in Karachagansk, Alma Ata awarded a contract to British Gas and Italy's Agip to develop the field. These firms pledged at least $5 billion in investment. This sort of foreign direct investment was by no means limited to those projects. Deals were also signed with Western firms to develop the smaller Kumkol oil field, as well as offshore sites on the Caspian shelf. When these contracts were signed, President Nazarbayev bluntly stated: "Russia will not get an equity share in Tengiz or Karachagansk." He later warned, "Kazakhstan is ready for wide-ranging cooperation with Russia, but if the vital supply routes including oil and gas pipelines are closed, we will have to turn southward."[24]

The Russian response was a series of economically coercive steps to get access to the most lucrative hydrocarbon deposits. First, Moscow consistently refused Kazakhstani requests to increase the transit quota for Tengiz oil to be processed to Russian refineries. As a result, in 1995, Tengizchevroil produced only 60,000 barrels per day even though its operating capacity was more than twice that amount. In reaction, Chevron announced a reduction of its planned annual investment from $500 million to $50 million in 1995, due to "political uncertainty." Stripped of its ability to export directly, the Kazakhstani state oil company was forced to sell its oil to Russia for ridiculously low prices. Russian gas plants refused to increase the amount of gas Russia imported from Karachagansk, and also limited the amount Kazakhstan could export to other countries. Russia further threatened to purchase its output at only 15 percent of world prices unless Gazprom was given a stake in the field. These actions forced British Gas to reconsider its planned investment in the region. Finally, Russia halted payments for Kazakhstani coal imports and reduced its supply of fuel.[25] In September 1994, Russian Prime Minister Chernomyrdin

---

[24] Nazarbayev quoted in Hunter (1996), p. 118, and Brzezinski and Sullivan (1997), p. 179; Dorian, Zhanseitov, and Indriyanto (1994), pp. 413–18; Sagers (1994), pp. 271–83.

[25] *OMRI Daily Digest*, "Kazakhstan asks Russia to raise oil transit quota," September 28, 1995; Economist Intelligence Unit, *Country Report: Kazakhstan, Turkmenistan, Kyrgyzstan, Tajikistan, Uzbekistan*, 1st quarter 1995, pp. 14–15, and 2nd quarter 1995, p. 16; Blank (1995), p. 384; John Lloyd and Steve LeVine, "British Gas rethinks 6bn dollar investment

held talks with the Kazakhstani Prime Minister on both the Tengiz and Karachagansk developments. The link between the pipelines and Russian involvement in the Kazakhstani energy sector was transparent. The director of the Kazakhstan Institute for Strategic Studies observed: "It is clear enough that Russia is holding Kazakhstan hostage, using its monopoly on the pipelines to control the gas and oil from the Caspian region, including western Kazakhstan."[26]

Kazakhstan's response was to make substantial concessions. In early 1995, Kazakhstan granted Gazprom a 15 percent stake in the Karachagansk project. An earlier deal with British Gas and Agip was reduced to a maintenance contract, and their equity stakes were reduced accordingly. Alma Ata nullified its contract with a Canadian firm to explore the Kumkol field. Instead, Yuzhneftgaz signed a joint venture deal with LUKoil with a 50/50 split in ownership. Later in the year, less than six weeks after the Kazakhstani quota request was denied, it was announced that LUKoil would gain a 20 percent ownership stake in Tengizchevroil. Kazakhstan and Chevron would give LUKoil 10 percent each. This was later scaled back; LUKoil received only 5 percent of the Tengiz project. The purpose of the concession from the Kazakhstani perspective was clear. One Russian newspaper, *Kommersant-Daily*, observed, "Obviously... in the case of LUKoil, Kazakhstan is going after the good graces of the Russian government." After the Russians were cut in on the Tengiz deal, Kazakhstan's transit quota through the Russian pipeline system was quadrupled.[27]

Kazakhstan also agreed to a redistribution of shares in the Caspian Pipeline Consortium (CPC) in the spring of 1996. When the original agreement was inked in 1992, Russia and Kazakhstan each owned 25 percent of the venture, and an Omani investment company owned the rest. As a result of that firm's insolvency, the deal stalled. Russia resisted Chevron's request to acquire the Omani stake without a quid pro quo stake in the Tengiz development. In the final agreement

in Kazakhstan," *Financial Times*, September 8, 1994; *Petroleum Economist*, "The gas industry in the former Soviet Union," September 1995, p. S36; Forsythe (1996), p. 42; LeVine, "Moscow pressures its neighbors to share their oil, gas revenues," p. A24.

[26] Kasenov (1995), pp. 274–5.

[27] LeVine, "Way sought for pipeline to bypass Russia," p. 5; *OMRI Daily Digest*, "LUKoil joins the Chevron–Tengiz deal," November 3, 1995; *Kommersant-Daily*, "US Mobil, LUKoil to join Tengiz oil project," in FBIS-SOV-95–204, October 19, 1995, p. 67; *OMRI Daily Digest*, "Kazakhstan to increase oil exports," April 18, 1996.

Russia owned 44 percent of the pipeline and Kazakhstan's share declined to 20.75 percent.[28] The agreement specifies that the first part of the pipeline construction will be completely within Russia proper, and complement Russian efforts to transport oil from Azerbaijan. Only after that phase is completed will the Tengiz field have its own route. In agreeing to this deal, Kazakhstan also reversed itself on the exploration of the Caspian shelf. Presidents Nazarbayev and Yeltsin agreed that the reserves would be jointly developed.[29]

By December 1996, Russia controlled every transit option and had a hand in every major energy project in Kazakhstan. Since then, it has been willing to use concessions in one project to gain concessions from another project. In early 1998, Russia used its plurality of ownership in the CPC to slow pipeline construction so that it would not start until the turn of the century. At the same time, LUKoil's chairman met with Nazarbayev and indicated an interest in acquiring another 5 percent of the Tengiz project.[30]

Given Russian success at earlier coercion attempts, it is not surprising that Moscow continued to use the stick to wring further concessions from Alma Ata. Kazakhstan had been actively privatizing its metallurgical and mining interests. In early 1995, Kazakhstan leased fourteen large oil and metallurgical companies to Western firms. In November of that year, Alma Ata announced plans to sell shares in fifty-three other metallurgical plants. In response to the auction, Moscow threatened to cut off electricity to northern Kazakhstan if certain mines were leased to a Western company. As a further hint, Russian deputy Prime Minister Oleg Soskovets proposed in the same month that the Kazakhstanis hand over the management of several mining enterprises to Russia in lieu of Kazakhstani debts. The Kazakhstani Prime Minister had made a similar suggestion earlier, but the timing of the Soskovets statement was certainly serendipitous. By January 1996, there was a perceptible shift in Alma Ata's policy; the government cut the Russians in on several deals. Alma Ata was also more lax in enforcing the contracts with Russian firms. The

---

[28] This calculation includes the shares allotted to state-owned firms in both countries.

[29] See Michael Gordon, "New pact for Kazak–Russian oil pipeline," *New York Times*, April 29, 1996, p. A7; *Economist*, "Pipe dreams in Central Asia," May 4, 1996, pp. 37–8; *Financial Times Energy Economist*, "Meanwhile in Kazakhstan," April 1996, pp. 4–6.

[30] Economist Intelligence Unit, *Country Report: Kazakhstan*, 4th quarter 1997, p. 16.

favoritism to Russian firms continued throughout that year.[31] The country was still able to auction off significant stakes to Western multinationals, but in the areas where it cared, Moscow got its way.

Russia was able to extract these concessions because its costs of coercion were minimal while Kazakhstan's were overwhelming. If anything, Russia may have benefited from restricting the Tengiz output and cutting off electricity. Cutting off the oil also kept the world price higher, giving Russia additional monopoly rents. The same was true of the electricity cutoff; it was cut off again in April 1996 because Alma Ata was $160 million in arrears. Russia did not suffer significant costs, while Kazakhstan's foreign exchange earnings were held hostage.[32]

In addition, Alma Ata did not believe that conceding in the present would lead to a deteriorating security position in the future. The Kazakhstani leadership did not think that dealing the Russians in on its hydrocarbon revenues would jeopardize its security, because it anticipated minimal conflict with the Russian Federation. Nazarbayev commented in 1991, "If two Kazakhs in a village get carried away by an argument, you need to call a Russian friend and let him arbitrate. I witnessed it myself. That is how we lived and grew up. The development of virgin lands, the creation of industry in the republic, and the associated influx of people from other parts of the country."[33] Alma Ata did not wish to lose its oil revenues, but it did not perceive the issue in terms of relative gains. It was therefore willing to concede and avoid the immediate costs of deadlock.

An alternative explanation for Kazakhstani acquiescence is the weakness of the target regime. Although the government's legitimacy was never questioned, and Nazarbayev's grip on power strengthened between 1992 and 1997, ethnic cleavages were an issue of paramount importance. In 1991, 37 percent of the Kazakhstani population were

[31] *OMRI Economic Digest*, "Controversy over privatization plans," November 2, 1995; *OMRI Daily Digest*, "Russia proposes takeover of several Kazakh enterprises," September 15, 1995; *OMRI Daily Digest*, "Russian government debates economic policy towards CIS," September 27, 1995; *Financial Times Energy Economist*, "Kazakhstan sells its silver," June 1995, pp. 12–17; "West benefits from Kazakhstan sell-off," *Financial Times*, June 3, 1996, p. 5; Economist Intelligence Unit, *Country Report: Kazakhstan*, 1st quarter 1996, p. 7, and 2nd quarter 1996, p. 18; *OMRI Daily Digest*, "Russian Ownership of Kazakhstan industries," December 13, 1996.
[32] Ibid. See also *OMRI Daily Digest*, "Russia cuts electricity supply to Kazakhstan," April 9, 1996.
[33] Quoted in Schmiedeler (1995), n. 54.

ethnic Russians, geographically concentrated in the northern regions of the country. One of the reasons given for moving the capital from the southern city of Alma Ata to the more centrally located town of Astana was to keep a closer eye on the ethnic Russians. Several commentators have speculated that the Kazakhstani leadership needed to pander to the Russians or their country would be divided.[34]

If this were true, then one would expect Alma Ata to be even more accommodating on Russian demands for greater autonomy for ethnic Russians, since that issue was the most likely to attract Russian attention. Yet Nazarbayev's policies on this issue contradicted this prediction. Instead, he pursued a policy designed to enhance the political power of the ethnic Kazaks in this region through ethnic patronage, changes in language laws, the repression of ethnic Russian organizations, and the jailing of Russian nationalists.[35]

As with other issues, Moscow demanded more autonomy for ethnic Russians in northern Kazakhstan, pushing very hard for dual citizenship and greater privileges for ethnic Russians. In November 1993, Alexander Shokhin, the Russian Minister for External Economic Relations, threatened economic sanctions and the denial of trade credits unless Kazakhstan agreed on dual citizenship. In that same month Russian Foreign Minister Andrei Kozyrev, while visiting Central Asia, commented, "Russia is ready to defend its citizens and in this purpose will use all its power, including economic sanctions and credit and financial policy."[36]

Kazakhstan conceded the least on this issue because on this matter, compromises in the present could have been translated into greater concessions in the future. Nazarbayev was most sensitive to concessions in this area, because Russia could have used these concessions to threaten Kazakhstan's sovereignty. Russian nationalists who spoke of a single Slavic state inherently included northern Kazakhstan, slicing the republic in half. Acquiescence in this arena could be exploited in the future to subvert Kazakhstan's autonomy. Nazarbayev knew this when he responded to Kozyrev's statement by drawing a comparison to the Nazis: "Whenever one starts talking about the protection of Russians in Kazakhstan, not Russia, I recall Hitler who began to 'support' the Sudeten Germans at one time." Less

---

[34] See, for example, Hunter (1996), p. 91.
[35] See Rubinstein (1994) and Bremmer (1994).
[36] Quoted in Hill and Jewett (1994), pp. 35–6.

artfully, he commented to a reporter in 1994: "Just imagine if the Russians ... had two passports in their pockets. They would have one foot in Russia and the other here. That would destabilize the situation in Kazakhstan."[37]

Moderate concessions were made on this issue. Nazarbayev issued a decree that greatly liberalized the system granting citizenship, a step the Russians acknowledged as significant. In 1996, a bilateral agreement granted Russian citizens special rights in Kazakhstan, including the ability to work for the government and to buy and sell property. Nevertheless, Alma Ata consistently rejected the dual citizenship option, and continued to harass Russian organizations. Moscow's continued dissatisfaction with Kazakhstan on this issue is further evidence for the paucity of the concessions. Moscow demanded bilateral negotiations at the ministerial level on the issue of the Cossacks living in northern regions, calling it "an issue of state importance." Alma Ata rejected these demands. By 1997, due in part to Nazarbayev's policies, the Russian percentage of the population had fallen from 37.7 percent to 32 percent, while the Kazakh share increased dramatically from 39.5 percent to 51 percent. In 1997, the Parliament made Kazakh the state language, with all civil servants required to be fluent by the year 2006.[38]

In summary, the Russians adroitly used economic coercion to obtain most of their objectives. This prompted some resentment in Alma Ata; in December 1995 Nazarbayev noted: "It is time the Russian government thought about the reasons why Uzbekistan, Azerbaijan, and Kazakhstan are seeking new partners and alternative paths of development."[39] Between 1992 and 1997, however, Nazarbayev pushed for closer integration with Russia and stronger multilateral institutions. In 1994 he suggested a "Eurasian Union" that even Moscow rejected as too constricting. In 1995 Kazakhstan joined Belarus and Russia in a customs union. In 1996, those three countries and Kyrgyzstan formed a "group of four" to better integrate their economies. As with Belarus,

[37] Ibid., p. 37; Brzezinski and Sullivan (1997), p. 185.
[38] Quoted in *Jamestown Monitor*, "Moscow/Kazakhstan," November 6, 1995. See also Economist Intelligence Unit, *Country Report: Kazakhstan*, 2nd quarter 1996, pp. 9–11; interview with Alexander Shokhin, *BBC Summary of World Broadcasts*, February 9, 1994; ITAR-TASS, "Treaty ratified on political status of Russians, Kazakhs" in FBIS-SOV-96–105, May 30, 1996, p. 56; Heleniak (1997), pp. 368–70; *Economist*, "Speaking of camels," February 15, 1997, p. 34.
[39] *Jamestown Monitor*, "Kazakh President objects to Russian policies," December 28, 1995.

Kazakhstan's strategy was to bind Russia to enough institutions so as to constrain its power. This strategy has had a mixed record. Despite the customs union, Russia maintained high barriers to trade with its southern neighbor. Moscow also continueed to restrict the country's exports through Russian pipelines. The Kazakhstani official in charge of the oil transport quota insisted that, "there is plenty of capacity, but they don't listen to us. They (the Russians) are keeping us in a bind." She went on to observe, "With gas, the situation is even worse. They just don't want to let us export at all."[40] The ability of these institutions to constrain Russian coercion attempts is uncertain at best.

Turkmenistan

Russia had three objectives in this country: (1) protection of Russian minorities; (2) basing rights and the ability to deploy its border guard; (3) control over the Turkmen hydrocarbon reserves.

Turkmenistan's president, Saparmurad Niyazov, was originally hostile to all of these demands. The first Foreign Minister of Turkmenistan, Avdy Kuliev, observed: "At first, Niyazov wanted to do without Russia and play the anti-Russian card." Soon after independence, Turkmenistan initiated a series of discriminatory policies towards the Russian minority. Niyazov's policy on defense cooperation was similar. Although he officially welcomed defense cooperation with Moscow, he also resisted the extent to which Russia wanted command and control over the troops.[41]

The Russian reaction was to use economic coercion to extract concessions. According to Kuliev: "after Niyazov quarreled with Moscow, Russia stopped providing food supplies. Bilateral trade was reduced to a minimum, and that had an effect on the people ... there's no meat, there's no flour, and there hasn't been milk for a long time." Turkmen concessions to the assorted Russian demands were forthcoming. In the summer of 1992, a defense accord was signed between

---

[40] *Financial Times Energy Economist*, "Meanwhile in Kazakhstan ..." April 1996, pp. 4–6; *Jamestown Monitor*, "Kazakh–Russian summit prepared," March 21, 1996. On Nazarbayev's call for a Eurasian Union, see Economist Intelligence Unit, *Country Report: Georgia, Armenia, Azerbaijan, Kazakhstan, and the Central Asian States*, 2nd quarter 1994, p. 36.

[41] Kuliev quote from Lowell Bezanis and Elizabeth Fuller, "There is only one way out – by getting rid of this leader and this government," *Transition*, May 17, 1996, p. 37. See also Dawisha and Parrott (1994), p. 253.

the two countries to allow Turkmen armed forces to be under joint Russian–Turkmen command. Russia was granted complete control over air defense and air control units in the country. In late 1993, Turkmenistan granted its ethnic Russians dual citizenship.[42]

Turkmenistan agreed to Russia's demands for several reasons. Ethnic Russians held most of the high-skilled positions in both industry and government. The exodus of these skilled workers would have caused a serious "brain drain" on the economy. Most of the NIS faced this conundrum, but Turkmenistan's situation was particularly acute, because of its sparse population and permeable borders. By agreeing to dual citizenship and Russian control of its military, Turkmenistan benefited by keeping its skilled personnel in the country, as well as having its border patrolled. It did not view acquiescence as too costly.

Despite the benefits, it is also clear that the outcomes were not the country's first choice. Russia successfully coerced Turkmenistan because of the opportunity costs of no agreement and because Turkmenistan did not view the concessions in terms of future disputes. Ashkhabad needed to trade with Moscow in order to procure equipment for its energy industry, as well as vital foodstuffs. Furthermore, Niyazov viewed Russia as less serious a threat than other neighbors such as Iran and Uzbekistan. There was little concern for relative gains. Kuliev notes, "In the end, Niyazov realized that he couldn't survive without Russia, and now he's prepared to sign any treaty, any agreement."[43] Precisely because Niyazov did not fear future conflicts with Russia, and because the immediate costs of deadlock were significant, he was willing to make generous concessions in the present.

The extent of Turkmenistan's acquiescence can be seen in how it reacted to Russian pressure for a slice of its gas reserves. Any concessions on this front would have been significant. It is estimated that the fuel and energy industries are responsible for 80 percent of Turkmenistan's national income. President Niyazov's priority in foreign policy was to translate Turkmen energy reserves into hard currency, boosting the national income of the country. Kuliev commented: "Niyazov was counting on the country being able to survive

[42] Ibid.
[43] Bezanis and Fuller, "There is only one way out – by getting rid of this leader and this government," p. 37.

on the proceeds of our oil and gas, which would generate enough wealth that everyone would have a Mercedes." As early as 1991, the republic was trying to woo Western investors for development of the South Caspian and Amu Dar'ya basins. Yet between 1992 and 1994, Niyazov's efforts at luring foreign investment proved frustrating. In total, the contracts with foreign multinationals produced only $300 million in promised investments, far less than the sums generated by Kazakhstan or Azerbaijan.[44]

One of the reasons why Turkmenistan had difficulties attracting Western investment was the lack of an export route for its hydrocarbons. During this time, Turkmenistan was completely dependent on pipelines running through Russia to get its energy to market. This route greatly constrained the growth of Ashkhabad's energy sector. In 1992, for example, the country produced 83 billion cubic meters (bcm) of natural gas, but Russia limited its export quota to 11.3 bcm. In 1993, Russia restricted Turkmenistan's export quota further, allowing Turkmenistan to ship only 8.2 bcm to hard-currency buyers instead of the agreed 11.3 bcm. In November 1993, Russia barred all Turkmen gas deliveries to nations outside the CIS through its pipelines, and refused to hand over $185 million in revenue from its sales to Europe. The export ban cost Ashkhabad $2 billion annually. Gas production fell to 60 bcm in 1993, and to 33.4 bcm for the first eleven months of 1994. Moscow only permitted Turkmen exports to other CIS countries that were incapable of paying their bills. Ukraine owed Turkmenistan $700 million by spring of 1994; Georgia owed $394 million for gas shipments in 1993 and 1994. Russia also purchased Turkmen gas on the cheap and resold it to Turkey at a 300 percent markup.[45]

In response, Niyazov first tried to defray the costs of stalemate by finding an alternative export route. However, none of these alternatives panned out because of a lack of financing. Ashkhabad acquiesced in November 1995. Russia and Turkmenistan agreed to set up a joint venture, Turkmenrosgaz, to exploit the resources in the

---

[44] Ibid, p. 35; Sagers (1994), pp. 291–3.

[45] Lowell Bezanis, "Joining forces with Iran and Russia," *Transition*, August 11, 1995, pp. 71–2; Steve LeVine, "Way sought for pipeline to bypass Russia," *New York Times*, September 9, 1995, p. A5; Blank (1995), pp. 383–4; Dorian, Rosi, and Indriyanto (1994), p. 417; *Financial Times Energy Economist*, "Here come the Turkmenis ... ?" January 1995, pp. 20–1; *Petroleum Economist*, "The gas industry of the former Soviet Union," September 1995, p. S36; Steve LeVine, "Moscow pressures its neighbors to share their oil, gas revenues," *Washington Post*, March 18, 1994, p. A24.

Caspian shelf and the right bank of the Amu Dar'ya river. The firm was granted complete control over natural gas exports from Turkmenistan to the CIS. Gazprom was given 46 percent of the joint venture. The agreement also stated that Turkmenistan would sell Russia 10 bcm of natural gas at prices below the world market rate. With the deal, Ashkhabad announced plans to increase gas production to 48 bcm. Russian and Western observers agreed that the deal left Turkmenistan at the mercy of Russian preferences, and ensured that Turkmen gas will not be exported to Western Europe.[46]

Following the agreement, Turkmen officials still complained about being shut out from the European market. In June 1997, Niyazov suspended the joint venture. Russia responded by cutting off Turkmenistan's pipelines to Ukraine and the Transcaucasus. As a result, Turmenistan's gas output fell by half in 1997. As of early 1998, negotiations between the two countries hinged on the gas price Turkmenistan would receive from exports. Niyazov wanted the price per thousand cubic meters raised from $36 to $42. Given that Russia has sold the same gas for $83 in Europe, even a settlement at $42 amounts to a very sizeable concession on Turkmenistan's part.[47]

Russia successfully used its control over the pipelines to get significant concessions from Turkmenistan. It was able to coerce its close ally because of the high costs of deadlock that Turkmenistan faced, coupled with Russia's nonexistent costs. Indeed, Moscow may have benefited from the coercion attempt. Restricting Turkmen exports allowed Russia to sell its own natural gas to the Europeans. By forcing Turkmenistan to export its gas only to the CIS, Russia was able to substitute its less creditworthy buyers with guaranteed hard-currency payments.

For Turkmenistan, the short-term costs of substituting away from the Russian pipelines were considerable. Given the options of remaining stalemated or conceding to an ally, it appears to be choosing the latter. The decision allowed it to increase its natural gas pro-

---

[46] *Jamestown Monitor*, "Turkmenistan's balancing act," November 20, 1995; *Finansovyye Izvestiya*, "Ashgabat has coordinated future gas export prospects with Russian interests," in FBIS-SOV-96-043, March 4, 1996, 59; Economist Intelligence Unit, *Country Report: Georgia, Armenia, Azerbaijan, and the Central Asian States*, 1st quarter 1996, pp. 20–34, and 2nd quarter 1996, pp. 37–9.

[47] *Financial Times Energy Economist*, "Lines to Turkmenistan," April 1996, pp. 2–3; John Thornhill and Charles Clover, "Russia raises Turkmen hackles," *Financial Times*, January 21, 1998, p. 4; Economist Intelligence Unit, *Country Report: Georgia, Armenia, Azerbaijan, and the Central Asian States*, 1st quarter 1998.

duction, easing economic pressure. Despite the obvious use of economic coercion, the government in Ashkhabad did not complain about its treatment. In fact, Niyazov attempted to move closer to Moscow so as to prevent further coercion attempts. In May 1995, Niyazov and Yeltsin signed an agreement establishing the two countries as "strategic partners" through the year 2000, although Turkmenistan has yet to sign the CIS Collective Security Treaty. In July 1996 he stated that the two countries "don't have a single disputed or vague issue." The closer relationship to Russia produced some benefits. Unlike other NIS, Turkmenistan was able to trade in barter and rubles with Russia. It was also able to coordinate policies on energy reserves in the Caspian Sea.[48] For the first five years of its independence, however, Turkmenistan repeatedly acquiesced in the face of Russian economic coercion.

Kyrgyzstan

Russia had three objectives in this republic: (1) minority rights for ethnic Russians; (2) access to military bases; (3) control over key industrial sectors. Kyrgyzstan was quickly forthcoming on the bases issue. In April 1993, Bishkek signed an agreement with the Russians permitting them to man a key communications station on Kyrgyz territory.[49] There was no evidence of economic coercion behind this decision.

The Kyrgyz leadership was also quick to accede to Russian preferences on the minorities issue, although on this issue economic pressure did play an implicit role. In early 1994, as a signal of Bishkek's desire to maintain good bilateral relations, Kyrgyz President Askar Akaev announced that he would agree to "temporary" dual citizenship status in order to prevent a continued exodus of Russian technocrats. Russia did not make a specific threat of economic coercion, but Akaev's melodramatic statement indicated his concern about the costs of noncompliance: "If we break these relations, there is a risk that the Kyrgyz will return to their traditional nomadic life as cattle breeders." Akaev linked the decision on dual citizenship to the

---

[48] Niyazov quoted in *OMRI Daily Digest*, "Niyazov on Russian elections, state orders," July 2, 1996; Economist Intelligence Unit, *Country Report: Georgia, Armenia, Azerbaijan, Kazakhstan, and the Central Asian States*, 2nd quarter 1995, p. 37.

[49] Bess Brown, "Central Asian states seek Russian help," *RFE/RL Research Report*, June 18, 1993, p. 85.

effect a refusal would have on the Kyrgyz economy. The absence of conflict expectations also affected Kyrgyz strategy. Akaev noted in March 1994 that the dual citizenship option would not be granted to Tajiks. This was because Tajikistan had made territorial claims on his country, and such a concession would lead to an inevitable loss of territory.[50]

Given the small size of the Kyrgyz republic, and its cooperation on the military issue, one would have expected Moscow to leave it alone. The absence of conflict expectations and Kyrgyzstan's energy independence did not make it a ripe candidate for economic pressure. On the whole Bishkek was able to woo Western investment without Russian interference. Between 1993 and 1996, Kyrgyzstan took in the highest level of foreign investment per capita of all the NIS. The country signed a joint venture with a Canadian company involving rights to mine Kumtor, estimated to be the eighth largest gold field in the world.[51] Moscow made no attempt to acquire a share in that joint venture.

Moscow did, however, exploit Kyrgyz financial difficulties to extract concessions. When Bishkek decided to issue its own currency in July 1993, Russia responded by proposing that Bishkek's 110 billion ruble trade debt be converted into dollars at an unfavorable exchange rate, vastly increasing Kyrgyzstan's debt burden. The Kyrgyz government protested, and Moscow backed down on this issue, agreeing to the more realistic exchange rate. Nevertheless, the arrears to Russia accumulated. In early 1996, the Kyrgyz government acquiesced to a Russian proposal; Moscow would be compensated by choosing among equity stakes in thirty-nine different state enterprises. Russia was given the right to decide which plants it wanted to control. As a result of this deal, Russia's State Property Committee acquired a 51 percent stake of the Kyrgyz electricity monopoly, a 70 percent stake of a metallurgical plant, more than 65 percent of two tobacco companies, stakes in several mining and chemical firms. An additional agreement established a joint venture to develop Kyrgyzstan's hydroelectric potential; Russia will be able to purchase Kyrgyz electrical output at less than market rates.[52]

[50] Akaev quoted in Brzezinski and Sullivan (1997), pp. 192–4.
[51] *OMRI Daily Digest*, "Cameco will invest $160 million in Kyrgyzstan this year," January 31, 1996; Bruce Pannier, "In the land of Manas," *Transition*, December 27, 1996, pp. 32–8.
[52] Economist Intelligence Unit, *Country Report: Georgia, Armenia, Azerbaijan, Kazakhstan,*

Russia also used some carrots to extract concessions. Moscow agreed to defer the repayment of Bishkek's debt until the year 2000. It also granted Kyrgyzstan more than $20 million in credits. These carrots have come with additional demands, however. For example, all aid has been tied to the purchase of Russian-made goods.[53]

The lack of conflict expectations is particularly salient in explaining Kyrgyzstan's concessions. As noted previously, both countries were in agreement on defense and minority issues. There were no other disputes between them. The costs of any trade disruption with Russia were significant enough for the leadership to prefer acquiescence to a sustained deadlock. It is also noteworthy that Russia backed down on its more aggressive attempt to coerce Kyrgyzstan, and has refrained from using economic pressure on any other issue. There was no apparent threat of military force, and the Kyrgyz regime was not prone to institutional instability or ethnic disputes. Neither of these alternative explanations appears to be important.

The concessions on economic issues gave Bishkek pause about its close relationship with Moscow. There was one statement from the Kyrgyz Foreign Minister indicating that the government was seeking stronger ties with China to maintain a "balance of interests" between Beijing and Moscow.[54] As with Kazakhstan and Belarus, however, the predominant Kyrgyz response was to enter into stronger institutional arrangements with Moscow. In March 1996, Kyrgyzstan joined the CIS customs union and signed an integration agreement with the other three countries in the organization, Russia, Belarus, and Kazakhstan. President Akaev argued that despite some objections the country had no choice; its dependence on the Russian market made it necessary to join the institution.[55] This statement shows that Kyrgyzstan's opportunity costs were greater than previously thought. The integration

and the Central Asian States, 2nd quarter, 1993, p. 68; *OMRI Daily Digest*, "Uzbekistan cuts off gas supplies to Kyrgyzstan," January 26, 1996; Peter Rutland, "Russia's energy empire under strain," *Transition*, May 3, 1996, pp. 6–11; *Jamestown Monitor*, "Kyrgyzstan to combine hydropower system with Russia's," March 22, 1996; *OMRI Daily Digest*, "Russia gains Kyrgyz assets in return for debts," April 16, 1996.

[53] *Jamestown Monitor*, "Old debts postponed and new credits granted for Kyrgyzstan," November 22, 1996.

[54] *Jamestown Monitor*, "Kyrgyz Foreign Minister seeks alternatives to Russian-led CIS security arrangements," February 21, 1996.

[55] *Jamestown Monitor*, "Kyrgyz Prime Minister critical of Russian protectionism," March 8, 1996; *Jamestown Monitor*, "Kyrgyzstan forced by weakness into economic unions," May 8, 1996.

decision is consistent with Belarusian and Kazakhstani behavior. All three states found the cost of a deadlocked situation too great. Because they did not perceive Russia as their most serious security threat, they were not as concerned with relative gains. In response to Russian coercion attempts, they have tried to create institutions that strengthen ties with Moscow while constraining its ability to act unilaterally.

Armenia

The Armenian–Russia relationship between 1992 and 1997 was characterized more by harmony than conflict. This was partly due to Armenia's low costs of coercion. Unlike most of the other NIS, Russia did not have an energy lever over the Armenians. This was not because Yerevan had ample energy resources. The December 1988 earthquake forced the shutdown of the Medzamor nuclear reactor, which had supplied the republic with 36 percent of its power needs. Following that decision, the country relied on natural gas from Turkmenistan shipped through Azerbaijan and Georgia. With the outbreak of hostilities between Armenia and Azerbaijan, the Azeris sabotaged their pipeline. Using indigenous resources, the Armenian government was capable of producing only 12–15 percent of its energy needs. The energy blockade proved crippling; electric power was rationed to just one hour a day. The economy collapsed. In 1992, GDP shrank by 52 percent; in 1993 it dropped an additional 15 percent.[56]

The imposed autarky reduced Russia's willingness to coerce its sole ally in the Transcaucasus. Armenia's costs of deadlock were not great, while the geopolitical costs to Russia would have been significant. This does not mean Russia has not tried to advance its interests in the country. When the Armenian government decided to restart its nuclear reactor, it turned to Russia as its sole source of support for technical assistance and nuclear fuel. Russia agreed to provide a 110 billion ruble credit line to start up the reactor. As collateral, Yerevan agreed to hand over 15 percent of the equity shares in Medzamor, as

---

[56] *Los Angeles Times*, "Gas line explosion severs Armenia's energy supply," January 24, 1993, p. A6; *Washington Post*, "Armenia's nuclear risk," May 28, 1995, p. A35; Chrystia Freeland, "Survey of Armenia," *Financial Times*, June 7, 1995, p. 35; Ara Tatevosyan, "Living dangerously with nuclear power in Armenia," *Transition*, May 3, 1996, pp. 23–5.

well as several of the country's most profitable state enterprises. The Russian Duma approved the deal, noting that it meant Armenia would be dependent on Russian technology.[57]

Russia only threatened economic coercion against Armenia once, but the timing of the incident and magnitude of the concession is important. In 1992 the Russians had tacitly sided with Armenia in its conflict with Azerbaijan, despite its official status as a neutral mediator. To that end, it covertly supplied Armenia with more than a billion dollars worth of arms, including T-72 battle tanks and Scud missiles.[58] Russia had strategic interests in the Caucasus, and the nationalist Azeri leadership proved itself unwilling to cooperate with Moscow. In June 1993, however, the Azeri nationalists were replaced by a more accommodating set of leaders. In the next few months, Azerbaijan took several steps to align itself closer to Russia, such as signing the CIS charter and the Collective Security Treaty.[59] During this time, the Armenians experienced great success on the battlefield. Separatists seized complete control over the disputed enclave of Nagorno-Karabakh, and regular Armenian forces conquered roughly a quarter of Azerbaijan's territory.

As Baku inched towards Moscow, Russia responded with a more belligerent attitude towards Armenia. First, in July 1993, the Russian central bank took steps to eject all of the NIS from the ruble zone. Armenia indicated a willingness to continue using the ruble, but Russia demanded deposits of gold or precious metals in exchange for maintaining a single currency. Armenia decided to issue its own currency. Because of its ill-preparedness, the new currency, the dram, quickly plummeted in value.

That incident was targeted at all of the NIS still using the ruble. In November 1993, Russia took more coercive action against Yerevan. A Russian envoy, traveling from Azerbaijan to Armenia to consult about the peace negotiations, was fired upon in the Karabakh region by Armenian forces. Despite Yerevan's claim that the fault lay with the Azeris, Russia seized upon the incident to apply pressure. Foreign Minister Andrei Kozyrev threatened Armenia with a cutoff of aid if the Armenians did not apologize for the incident and curtail

---

[57] Elizabeth Fuller, "No confederation on the horizon," *Transition*, July 14, 1995, p. 58; Tatevosyan, "Living dangerously with nuclear power in Armenia," pp. 23–5.
[58] Martin Sheff, "Armenia armed by Russia for battles with Azerbaijan," *Washington Times*, April 10, 1997, p. 11.
[59] See the section on Azerbaijan.

assistance to the Nagorno-Karabakh separatists. The next day, during the Armenian Prime Minister's visit to Moscow, Kozyrev again threatened sanctions if the Armenians did not acquiesce. Immediately afterwards, the Armenians apologized for the incident.[60] Yerevan also continued to insist that Russia remain the sole mediator, blocking the Organization for Security and Cooperation in Europe (OSCE) from further efforts to intervene.

Russia continued to put the squeeze on Armenia to stabilize the conflict. In March 1994, the Russians held up the shipment of more than a thousand tons of wheat seed to Armenia. US relief agencies had purchased the seeds from Russia, but Moscow insisted on the payment of an export duty. Moscow halted the delivery even though the Armenians were close to famine, and even though goods shipped to another country in the CIS Economic Union were legally exempt from export duties.[61] It was around this time that the front lines in the Nagorno-Karabakh stabilized, despite the Armenian preponderance of power. Russian pressure was acknowledged to be a factor in Armenia's decision to acquiesce.[62] As of July 1998, the ceasefire has remained in place.

Moscow's chief lever of economic coercion during these episodes was the curtailment of economic and military aid, which would have been economically costless to Russia. It was when Azerbaijan took a more accommodating stance that Russia felt it could coerce Armenia. The Armenians were willing to acquiesce because they did not perceive Moscow as a threat. In 1995, the two countries signed a defense treaty establishing Russian bases on Armenian soil. Government officials in Yerevan welcomed the agreement, arguing that a Russian presence enhanced its security. In 1996, the two countries agreed on the construction of a pipeline to run from Russia to Turkey through Armenia. Armenia's first deputy Prime Minister wrote in 1997: "Cooperation with Russia is the critical direction for our security

[60] Interfax, "Kozyrev demands Armenia apologize for attack," in FBIS-SOV-93–224, November 23, 1993, p. 19; "Kozyrev warns Armenia over aid," *Financial Times*, November 23, 1993, p. 2; *Kommersant-Daily*, "Kozyrev suggests economic sanctions against Armenia," in FBIS-SOV-93–227, November 29, 1993, p. 9; Interfax, "Kozyrev reaction viewed," in FBIS-SOV-93–226, November 26, 1993, p. 66.
[61] Raymond Bonner, "Russia is holding up seed bought by US," *New York Times*, March 22, 1994, p. A11.
[62] Emil Danielyan, "No war, no peace in Nagorno-Karabakh," *Transitions*, August 1997, pp. 46–7.

policy."[63] The near-total absence of conflict expectations and Armenia's moderate opportunity costs of coercion make it an unlikely candidate for future coercion attempts. With one exception, this country failed to satisfy Russia's coercion condition.

Tajikistan

Russia had two goals in this country: (1) Acquiring control of strategic industries; (2) securing a ceasefire between the neocommunist regime and the armed opposition, thus permitting Russian peacekeeping troops to withdraw.

Scholars who claim that any success with economic coercion is really the result of military pressure or a weak target regime would expect sanctions to be a roaring success in this country. Embroiled in a civil war since independence, Tajikistan's neocommunist regime relied on Moscow for financial and military support. Approximately 24,000 Russian peacekeepers have been stationed in the country, and elements of the Russian border patrol have guarded its frontier with Afghanistan. With its military dependence upon Moscow, one would expect that even the slightest hint from Moscow would lead to substantial concessions from Dushanbe. A conflict expectations model would predict more reluctance on Moscow's part. With its economy shattered by the war, Russia could do little more to damage the country's economy.

Russia's first use of economic pressure was largely accidental. In the first eighteen months after the Soviet break-up, most of the republics were using a mixture of Russian and Soviet rubles for currency. This proved to be a drain on the Russian Treasury. Because the NIS central banks were more willing to issue credit than Moscow, these republics were essentially exporting inflation to Russia. Such implicit subsidies were too costly, and in July 1993 the Russian government announced harsh new conditions. To stay in the ruble zone, states would be required to deposit gold and other valuable metals in the Russian central bank in exchange for rubles. All of the CIS countries, except

---

[63] Douglas Clarke, "Russia's military presence in the 'near abroad,'" *Transition*, October 20, 1995, p. 9; *Jamestown Monitor*, "Will Armenia join Russian-led customs union?" April 22, 1996; *OMRI Daily Digest*, "Armenian Prime Minister on relations with Russia," December 31, 1996; Vartan Oskanian, "A new security agenda for Armenia," *Transitions*, September 1997, p. 59.

Tajikistan, rejected the conditions, which served Russian interests by reducing the generation of ruble credits.

Dushanbe agreed to Moscow's terms. In July 1994, the head of the National Bank of Tajikistan announced that the country had agreed to place one ton of gold in Moscow, as well as recognize Russia as the joint owner of the country's two hydroelectric stations, and the Regar aluminum smelter. This smelter was the prime earner of Tajik hard currency, and this was therefore a significant concession. After the offer, Russian Foreign Minister Andrei Kozyrev announced that the Russian army "would guard important economic facilities," and seized control of the plant from the local strongman. The Tajik leadership made further concessions to appease Moscow. It acceded to Russian requests and granted dual citizenship to its ethnic Russian population. The government also gave LUKoil and Gazprom equity stakes in its joint ventures with Western multinationals to ensure a steady supply of energy.[64]

Despite these extremely generous terms, however, Moscow was reluctant to maintain the monetary union, calculating that deadlock was less costly than the status quo. The Russian central bank was miserly in its transfer of rubles to Dushanbe, constantly delaying shipment. Finally, in February 1995, Moscow announced that the currency union would only last until the end of the year. Even that agreement had its associated demands. The deputy chairman of the Russian central bank demanded that Russia have complete access to the Tajik cotton crop. The Russian Duma granted aid to Dushanbe conditional on the Tajik government using the money to purchase Russian-made equipment for its heavy industries.[65]

Moscow's ability to pressure Dushanbe using monetary policy provides an intriguing comparison to its more problematic attempt to use overt threats of military withdrawal to alter Tajik positions. In 1992, Moscow covertly supported the neocommunist side during a six-month civil war. This use of military assistance was successful, and guaranteed a loyalist Tajik regime. The military dependency was so great that between 1993 and 1995, a Russian general was named the

[64] Economist Intelligence Unit, *Country Report: Georgia, Armenia, Azerbaijan, and the Central Asian States,* 3rd quarter, 1994, p. 63; Porter and Saivetz (1994), p. 87; Igor Rotar, "Inter-clan fighting again threatens to split the republic," *Prism,* March 8, 1996; McFaul (1995), p. 42; *Economist,* "This way, the Hitlerites," March 28, 1998, p. 42.
[65] Economist Intelligence Unit, *Country Report: Georgia, Armenia, Azerbaijan, and the Central Asian States,* 1st quarter, 1995, p. 34; Brzezinski and Sullivan (1997), pp. 209–10.

Tajik Minister of Defense in the government of Emomali Rakhmonov. By the middle of 1993, most commentators assumed that the Tajik government would have to kowtow to any Russian demand. Alexander Shokhin spelled out Russian expectations in November 1993:

> This is a kind of protectorate. But for Russia this is a burden economically ... and to take them under financial protectorate means to assume political responsibility for whatever is going on there. This means wasting money on military operations on financing, say, the Tajik government's reluctance or inability to negotiate with the opposition ... There is a need for some compromises, and first and foremost, financial support on Russia's part must be made contingent upon demands for political negotiations and a settlement of conflicts.[66]

Despite this expectation, however, Russia found it difficult to convert its combined economic and military leverage into substantial changes in the Rakhmonov government's policy. In 1995 and early 1996, Moscow attempted to pressure the Rakhmonov regime to negotiate a permanent ceasefire with the various opposition clans. The government in Dushanbe resisted such a move. Russia responded with military pressure. At the January 1996 CIS summit, a resolution was passed stating that peacekeeping troops would be withdrawn by July 1996 unless a ceasefire halted the conflict. Russian President Yeltsin declared, "It is necessary to push President Emomali Rakhmonov into a dialogue with the opposition." Russian Foreign Ministry officials expected that this diplomatic nudge and military threat would be sufficient, noting that, "as far as one can judge, Dushanbe listens attentively to our opinion."[67]

Despite these diplomatic hints, the Tajik government held fast to its position. No substantial progress was made in the talks. In mid-February, Russian Foreign Minister Yevgeny Primakov backed down from the CIS resolution, stating that there was no timetable for the withdrawal of CIS troops. Starting in March 1996, the Dushanbe regime initiated a series of offensives against the opposition forces. The Economist Intelligence Unit concluded: "Outside observers have been able to exert only limited pressure on the various protagonists to reach agreement ... Russian officials have privately expressed their

---

[66] Hill and Jewett (1994), p. 44. See also Shahrbanou Tadjbakhsh, "Tajikistan: from freedom to war," *Current History*, April 1994, pp. 173–7.

[67] Quoted by Interfax, "Military 'will not interfere' in Tajik affairs," in FBIS-SOV-96–023, February 2, 1996, pp. 11–12.

frustration with his [Rakhmonov's] political inflexibility. Yet, despite this, Russia still appears to be committed to maintaining a military presence, albeit limited, in the country."[68]

Why was the overt military pressure an insufficient threat? This case is particularly puzzling because of the weakness of the Rakhmonov regime. One Western diplomat observed, "You still don't have a real state here. It is a collection of various forces fighting for power."[69] Rakhmonov's power base rested on a fragile coalition between his own base of supporters from Kulyab and clans from the city of Khojent.[70] A domestic politics approach would predict that Rakhmonov's domestic weaknesses would enhance Dushanbe's vulnerability to Russian pressure.

In this instance, the weakness of the target regime may have increased its inflexibility. The Khojent clans that supported the government did not want an accord with the Islamic opposition. Rakhmonov lacked the autonomy to make any agreement stick. At the time when Russia put pressure on Rakhmonov to cut a deal with the opposition, two government brigades mutinied and threatened to take Dushanbe. Given a choice between alienating his domestic or foreign supporters, he chose the latter option. This is also the conclusion of Russian analysts. One Russian newspaper observed, "The Rakhmonov government that is remaining in place only with the use of Russian bayonets is too weak to guarantee independent Russian interests in Tajikistan."[71]

In 1997, Russia's continued economic and diplomatic pressure did succeed in forcing Rakhmonov to sign a peace accord that gave the opposition 30 percent of the parliamentary seats, and included opposition brigades in the army. Why was Russian pressure successful in 1997 but not 1996? For two reasons: first, the success of the Taliban in Afghanistan raised fears that their brand of Islam would spread to Tajikistan and the rest of Central Asia. This increased Russia's desire for a settlement; it increased its pressure on the Tajik government.

---

[68] Economist Intelligence Unit, *Country Report: Georgia, Armenia, Azerbaijan, and the Central Asian States*, 1st quarter, 1996, p. 20.
[69] Steve LeVine, "Tajiks talk of peace between battles," *New York Times*, January 6, 1997, p. A8; *Economist*, "Tajikistan: hold your breath," March 15, 1997, p. 35.
[70] Muriel Atkin, "Tajikistan's civil war," *Current History*, October 1997, pp. 336–40.
[71] *Novaya Yezhhednevnaya Gazeta*, "Drug business in the Pamir is being run by CIA and KGB associates," in FBIS-SOV-96–070–S, April 10, 1996, p. 107; *OMRI Daily Digest*, "Trouble in Tajikistan's 'Wild West,'" January 8, 1997.

Second, Rakhmonov made the decision to ally with the Islam opposition against the Khojent clans; he was therefore prepared to give the opposition more power at the expense of his erstwhile allies.[72] An April 1997 assassination attempt of Rakhmonov, in Khojent, helped to seal the deal. In this case, the combination of economic pressure, military threats, and the target regime's domestic instability produced a potential diplomatic success for Russia. This success is far from guaranteed, however; in 1996, the regime's weakness reduced the possibility of concessions, and there were signs in 1998 that the peace agreement would not hold.[73]

Uzbekistan

Russian–Uzbek relations are unusual, compared with Russia's relationships with its other allies, in the complete absence of economic coercion. Like all of the other republics, Uzbekistan suffered costs when it was ejected from Russia's ruble zone in 1993. Beyond that episode, however, there is no evidence of any threat of economic or military coercion. Surveys of Central Asia focus on Kazakhstan, Tajikistan, or Turkmenistan as the objects of Russian coercion; Uzbekistan is rarely mentioned.[74]

Minor policy differences between the two countries on energy investment, the treatment of ethnic Russians, the pace of CIS integration, and relations with Russia's other Central Asian allies shows Moscow's reticence to use economic pressure on its ally. Russian involvement in the development of Uzbek hydrocarbon deposits was welcomed, but so were Western investors. The Russians had a hand in the development of Uzbek natural gas. A joint venture between Uzbekneftgaz and LUKoil was scheduled to tap four new fields in southern Uzbekistan by 1996. Early in 1995, Gazprom, Uzbekneftgaz, and the US firm Enron signed a protocol to develop up to fifteen fields with more than 500 bcm of gas in reserves. Uzbekistan also permitted Western investment in the oil sector. A joint venture between Uzbekneft and the American Cornelius Consortium was arranged to

---

[72] Charles Clover, "Tajikistan peace agreement leaves unanswered questions," *Financial Times*, July 1, 1997, p. 9; *Economist*, "Tajikistan: a sort of peace," September 20, 1997, p. 36.

[73] Hugh Pope, "New fighting in Tajikistan could derail peace process," *Wall Street Journal*, March 26, 1998, p. A16.

[74] Blank (1995); Sagers (1994); Porter and Saivetz (1994); Hill and Jewett (1994).

explore the Fergana basin, with reserves estimated to be at least 300 million tons. Uzbekistan strongly encouraged US and British investment in its mining sector. Western investment in manufacturing was brisk, while Russian efforts to create new trading structures have failed. Russia did not use any economic pressure to acquire a stake in any of these joint ventures.[75]

Uzbekistan's policy on minority rights was also indicative of Moscow's reluctance to coerce. Tashkent gave ethnic Russians enough cultural autonomy to earn praise from the Russian government. However, Uzbek President Islam Karimov rejected requests for dual citizenship. Furthermore, rather than encouraging its ethnic Russian population to stay in the country, the government sent ethnic Uzbeks to study in Turkey, compensating for the loss of Russian specialists.[76] As in other issues, Moscow refrained from any economic coercion on this issue.

Uzbekistan took some actions that directly contravened Russian preferences without triggering any reaction. In early 1996, Uzbekistan voiced qualms about the pace of CIS integration. It refused to send a delegation to the Interparliamentary Assembly to protest recent Russian steps to deepen integration. Tashkent also refused to permit CIS troops to patrol its border with Afghanistan. In the latter half of 1996, Karimov took some steps to improve relations with the United States and increased contacts with NATO.[77]

In its regional policy, Uzbekistan developed the reputation of bullying Russia's other Central Asian allies. Because the other countries were unable to consistently pay for their energy, Tashkent threatened to turn off the spigot without significant concessions. Tashkent periodically interrupted gas supplies to Kyrgyzstan, Kazakhstan, and Tajikistan. When the Kyrgyz government introduced its own currency in May 1993, the Uzbeks cut travel, telephone, and gas

---

[75] *Petroleum Economist*, "The gas industry of the former Soviet Union," September 1995, p. S36; Sagers (1994), pp. 295–6; "Uzbekistan: economic overview," *Bisnus On-Line*, (http://www.itaiep.doc.gov/bisnus), June 1996 ; *Financial Times Energy Economist*, "Into the Fergana: only the brave ... " November 1993, p. 12; Arkady Dubnov, "A portrait of power," *New Times*, May 1996, p. 42.

[76] Interview with Alexander Shokhin, *BBC Summary of World Broadcasts*, February 9, 1994; Constantine Dmitriev, "Hostages of the (former) Soviet Empire," *Transition*, January 12, 1996, p. 21.

[77] *OMRI Analytic Brief*, "Primakov in Central Asia: a view from the South," February 26, 1996; *Jamestown Monitor*, "Uzbekistan developing links with NATO," November 15, 1996.

links in retaliation for the lack of policy coordination. At the same time, President Karimov made nationalist speeches proclaiming the idea of a new Turkestan. With significant Uzbek minorities in all of the other central Asian republics, these statements generated anxiety in Uzbekistan's neighbors.[78]

An examination of the bilateral relationship reveals that Russia refrained from coercing Uzbekistan for three reasons. First, Tashkent's costs of deadlock were much lower than the other countries in the allied category. Unlike most of the other NIS, Uzbekistan had built up little to no debt to Russia. The energy reserves and refining complexes made Tashkent self-sufficient in fuels. Of all the post-Soviet states, Uzbekistan experienced the smallest decline in energy consumption between 1988 and 1993. In fall 1994, President Karimov declared that his country would be self-sufficient in oil within the year. Addressing the Parliament, he said, "We speak little of it in the press because there are too many envious people who realize that the country's oil independence will help it head off any external pressure." Karimov was clearly wary of the possibility of Russian economic coercion. Furthermore, unlike Turkmenistan or Kazakhstan, Uzbekistan was not a significant exporter of oil. Moscow could not use its control of pipelines to coerce Tashkent.[79]

Second, Russia would have incurred significant economic costs if it had imposed economic sanctions. The Russian textile industry relied on Uzbek cotton. In 1992, Tashkent was the second largest exporter of cotton in the world, behind the United States, and Russia was the largest importer. Russian mills nearly ground to a halt when Uzbekistan sold its 1992 crop on the world market. Economic coercion would have either increased Moscow's dependence on the United States as a source of cotton or have imposed significant sectoral costs.[80]

Third, the close alignment between the two countries greatly lowered any expectations of future conflict. On most issues, Uzbekistan demonstrated a willingness to cooperate with Russia. Both

---

[78] Reported in Economist Intelligence Unit, *Country Report: Georgia, Armenia, Azerbaijan, Kazakhstan, and the Central Asian States*, 2nd quarter, 1993, p. 87; 3rd quarter, 1994, p. 64; 3rd quarter 1995, p. 58; *OMRI Daily Digest*, May 2, 1996; Hunter (1996), chapter 5.

[79] *Financial Times Energy Economist*, "A few useful figures etc.," May 1994, pp. 21–4; Karimov quoted in Interfax, "Self-sufficiency in oil in 1 year predicted," in FBIS-SOV-94–185, September 23, 1994, p. 67.

[80] "Economic and trade overview of Uzbekistan"; Ann Sheehy, "The CIS: a shaky edifice," *RFE/RL Research Report*, January 1, 1993, pp. 37–40.

countries were more concerned with the threat of Islamic fundamentalism from the south than with the threat from each other. Karimov
was particularly concerned about such a threat, since a domestic
Islamic movement could have subverted his regime. Tashkent made
repeated statements welcoming a Russian presence in the region. In
March 1994 Karimov told Russian TV, "Russia is a great superpower
and as a great superpower has interests beyond its territory." In
February 1996 he put it more bluntly: "Russia has been and will
remain Uzbekistan's strategic partner. This hinges on the commonality
of approaches to the assessment of the danger of fundamentalism's
onslaught from the south." These statements have been backed up
with the CIS Collective Security Treaty and a bilateral treaty on
military cooperation signed in February 1994 permitting Russian
troops on Uzbek soil. The Tajik civil war strengthened bilateral
relations; each country viewed the other as a source of stability in the
conflict. Given the agreement of interests and the unfavorable ratio of
opportunity costs, Russia's expected utility from a deadlock outcome
was less than the status quo. Russia could not satisfy the coercion
condition in this relationship.[81]

Moscow understood that so long as Uzbekistan cooperated on
important issues, coercing Tashkent was not an option.[82] *Moskovskie
Novosti* commented in March 1996, "Uzbekistan's leaders seem to
have developed confidence in their country's stability and in the
ability of their economy to survive, if not on its own, then at least
without Russia." Karimov has made similar statements about the
bilateral relationship: "If Russia always remembers that [Uzbekistan is
an equal partner], we are prepared to cooperate."[83] Even as Karimov
criticized Russia's conception of the CIS, he stated that he wanted
closer relations with Moscow, pledged cooperation on ending the
Tajik civil war, and granted Russia observer status in the Central
Asian economic union.

In conclusion, Russia did not use economic coercion against Uzbeki-

---

[81] Economist Intelligence Unit, *Country Report: Georgia, Armenia, Azerbaijan, Kazakhstan,
and the Central Asian States*, 2nd quarter, 1994, p. 70; Roger Kangas, "Taking the lead in
Central Asian security," *Transition*, May 3, 1996, pp. 52–5; Sodyq Safaev, "Challenges
facing Uzbekistan in a changing international environment," presented at the Center for
International Affairs, Harvard University, May 15, 1997.
[82] One possible reaction, although no linkage was officially implied, was the decision
by the Russian Duma in March 1996 to lift the tariff on non-CIS cotton imports.
[83] Kangas, "Taking the lead in Central Asian security," p. 55.

stan. This country was perhaps the least vulnerable of its allies to economic pressure, and any economic disruption would have imposed costs on Russia as well. The close alignment between the two countries reduced conflict expectations considerably. As a result, Russia was unwilling to threaten economic sanctions because it preferred the status quo to a potential deadlock scenario. The close alliance between the two countries encouraged some economic cooperation and the partial coordination of their foreign policies. On other issues, however, Uzbekistan acted in ways that did not perfectly jibe with Russia's interests. Because of the costs of deadlock, Moscow chose not to respond.

Moldova

Russia had four demands of this country: (1) joining the CIS; (2) ownership stakes in Moldova's energy infrastructure; (3) legal autonomy for the ethnic Russians living in the Transdniestr region; (4) basing rights for the Russian Fourteenth Army.

Russia was successful in using economic coercion to force Moldova into the CIS. Although Moldova participated in its founding meeting of the CIS in Alma Ata in December 1991, its Parliament never ratified membership. In August 1993, Russia imposed prohibitive excise taxes and custom duties on Moldovan imports, in response to Chisinau's refusal to fully join the CIS. Six weeks later, Moldovan President Mircea Snegur agreed to join the CIS Economic Union, but declined to sign the CIS Collective Security Treaty. One observer commented: "Snegur's retreat from his former, strongly held position clearly represented a political concession to economic pressure."[84] Despite this concession, Moscow refused to remove the tariffs for another six weeks, until December 1. This delay contributed to a disastrous balance of trade with Russia. Moldova was unable to pay for its energy imports, and quickly accumulated debt. Had Russia lifted the tariffs earlier, before the onset of winter, this would have reduced its leverage in future coercion attempts.

Moldovan attitudes towards the Commonwealth of Independent States reflect the country's concern for relative gains in its relationship

---

[84] Vladimir Socor, "Isolated Moldova being pulled into Russian orbit," *RFE/RL Research Report*, December 17, 1993, pp. 14–15. See also "Economic difficulties blunt nationalist drive in Moldova," *New York Times*, December 27, 1993, p. A8.

with Russia. Official Moldovan statements about joining the CIS in early 1992 made it clear that its primary usefulness was "making possible a civilized divorce from the defunct USSR and its successors," and "precluding the emergence of a new center or any structure above this commonwealth." As Russia began to conceive of the CIS as a mechanism for reintegration, Moldova's leadership backed away from the organization.[85] Moldova knew that it had disagreements with Moscow on basing rights and the Transdniestr issue. Joining the CIS was viewed as providing Russia with an additional diplomatic lever. Only the high costs of staying outside the economic union made Chisinau back down and acquiesce. Even though the concession was relatively minor, Moldova was concerned about granting Russia additional leverage in future disputes.

Moldovan foreign policy became somewhat less anti-Russian after the ouster of the pro-Romanian Prime Minister in June 1992. Parliamentary elections in February 1994 gave the ex-communists more power and produced a stronger pro-Moscow tilt. One analyst described the dynamic as follows: "Moldovan leaders have lately shown a tendency to react to Moscow's pressure or snubs by becoming ever more accommodating, sometimes at the cost of narrowing their room for maneuver, in the hope of earning Russia's goodwill."[86] The conflict expectations model predicts that as Chisinau adopted a more accommodationist stance towards Moscow, it would acquiesce to more substantial Russian demands. This is because it would have a reduced fear that present concessions would be translated into future weakness. At the same time, Moldova refused to join the Collective Security Treaty or other political organs of the CIS.[87] Moscow's ability to coerce would still be constrained by some Moldovan expectations of future conflict.

Prior to mid-1994, Moldova refused to make concessions on the Russian ownership of Moldovan energy enterprises. Following the shift in Moldova's foreign policy, Russia's economic diplomacy became more profitable. In late 1993, Gazprom halted gas deliveries to convince the Moldovan government to acquiesce and swap debt for equity in its energy complex. In July 1994, after the tilt towards Moscow, Gazprom announced that it would acquire shares in the state

---

[85] Vladimir Socor, "Moldova," *RFE/RL Research Report*, February 14, 1992, pp. 11–13.
[86] Ibid., p. 9.
[87] Brzezinski and Sullivan (1997), pp. 251–2.

utility Moldovagaz. A joint venture, Gazosnabtranzit, was set up to manage the gas export pipelines that run to Romania, Bulgaria, and Turkey. Gazprom was given majority ownership of the joint venture. This did not stop the increase in Moldovan energy debts. In November 1994, Gazprom again shut down all gas supplies. Chisinau, in response, agreed to transfer ownership stakes in Moldova's largest cement plant and electrical power station.[88]

In November 1995 it was announced that LUKoil would set up a joint stock company, LUKoil-Moldova. The joint venture planned businesses in several economic sectors, including petroleum products, gasoline stations, insurance, and investment funds for joint ventures. LUKoil's presence was given the personal endorsement of President Snegur. The nationalist press was highly critical of these concessions. One newspaper wrote in early 1996, "Moldova is financially subdued by the former metropolis which brutally punishes any attempt to diversify the sources of energy ... Day by day Bessarabia is becoming more dependent upon the Slavonic states."[89]

Three factors explain Moldovan concessions. First, as already noted, in 1994 the target state was attempting to bandwagon closer to Russia. Conflict expectations were therefore reduced, making larger concessions a possibility. Second, the opportunity costs of deadlock were considerable. Over 90 percent of Moldova's fuel came from Russia; only Belarus was as dependent. Third, ironically, Moldova increased its own costs of stalemate by insisting on exercising its sovereignty over the breakaway Transdniestr region. This region was dominated by ethnic Russians fearful of Moldovan rule. In early 1992, armed insurrection prevented Chisinau from controlling that territory. Its Soviet-style economy proved to be so inefficient that it was responsible for more than half the Moldovan debt. Despite the fact that Chisinau had only *de jure* control over the area, the government was compelled to pay the debt to reinforce its sovereignty claim.[90]

To obtain autonomy for the Transdniestr region, Russia used both

[88] *RFE/RL Daily Report*, "Russia acquiring ownership rights in Moldova," July 11, 1994; Economist Intelligence Unit, *Country Report: Belarus and Moldova.* 4th quarter 1994, p. 46, 1st quarter 1995, p. 26, 2nd quarter 1995, p. 25, and 3rd quarter 1995, p. 25.
[89] Quote from *BASAPRESS*, "Weekly sees growing economic dependence on Russia," in FBIS-SOV-96–078, April 22, 1996, p. 52; *Jamestown Monitor*, "Moldova's President approves deal with Russia's LUKoil," November 23, 1995.
[90] *Economist*, "Bessarabian homesick blues," October 30, 1993, p. 38; *RFE/RL Daily Report*, "Russia seizes Transdniestr businesses," July 11, 1994.

economic and military diplomacy. The military diplomacy came in the form of the Fourteenth Army. In late 1991 and early 1992 it assisted ethnic Russians living in Transdniestr to arm themselves and take control of all organs of power in the region. Following a brief war in the first half of 1992, both sides agreed to have the Russian army participate in a joint peacekeeping force with Moldovan and Transdniestr troops. Since that agreement, the Russians have used the presence of the Fourteenth Army as a lever to get Moldova to agree to a federal structure for the country. The economic diplomacy came in the form of encouraging Transdniestr dependence on Russia and choking off Moldovan efforts to control the region. When Moldovan government officials attempted to arrest the secessionist leaders, railway traffic with the former Soviet Union was blockaded. Russian officials acknowledged that in the first nine months of 1993, the Transdniestr region received $30 million in cheap energy and raw materials. In July 1994, the Russians shipped old Soviet rubles to the region so that the secessionists could issue their own currency and not be forced to rely on the Moldovan leu.[91]

Russian pressure did succeed in softening up Chisinau's position at first. Moldova agreed to Russian and Ukrainian participation in the implementation of any agreement on Transdniestr. In 1996, the Moldovan leadership appeared willing to consider a federal structure for the state as a way of giving the breakaway region more autonomy. Arrangements were made for President Snegur to sign an agreement with Transdniestr authorities that would have normalized relations and recognize the breakaway region as a "state-territorial formation."

At the last minute, however, conflict expectations and domestic politics prevented Snegur from signing it. The deal triggered strong nationalist opposition within Moldova; there were fears that Russia would use its influence over the Transdniestr region to wring even larger concessions in future conflicts. Domestic politics also played a role. With a presidential election a few months away, Snegur could not afford to acquiesce. Instead, the Moldovan regime used its own economic pressure to raise the Transdniestr region's costs of deadlock.

---

[91] Ibid.; see also *BASAPRESS*, "Dniester accuses Chisinau of provoking 'cash shortage,'" in FBIS-SOV-96–013, January 19, 1996, p. 62; Vladimir Socor, "Creeping putsch in eastern Moldova," *RFE/RL Research Report*, January 17, 1992, pp. 8–13; Steven Erlanger, "Tiraspol journal; the Russians have come! When will they go?" *New York Times*, May 21, 1993, p. A4; Igor Rotar, "Transdniester: the last days of the unrecognized republic?" *Prism*, September 1996.

For example, Chisinau stopped shipments of a German-minted currency to Transdniestr in order to increase the region's dependence on the Moldovan leu. This policy worked very well; Transdniestr authorities accused Chisinau of waging an "economic cold war." By December 1996 there was speculation about when the breakaway region would collapse from hyperinflation and a stagnating economy. Russia backed down on its demands, pressuring Transdniestr to sign an agreement in May 1997 that recognized Moldova as a "common state."[92]

Ironically, even if Transdniestr collapsed, moderate concessions on this issue were still likely. This is the result of Russia's use of economic diplomacy to keep the breakaway region isolated from Moldova. Because of thorough economic reforms, the Moldovan economy has very low inflation and a privatized economy. It is in much better shape than Transdniestr. A political and economic reunification would impose significant costs on the rest of the country. Any political reconciliation would give Transdniestr greater autonomy in return for not bailing out its economy. Thus, Russian economic and military coercion achieved its desired result, but not because of economic pressure.

Moldova has also resisted both military and economic pressure to acquiesce on the issue of basing rights. As early as June 1993, Russia had requested basing rights in Moldova. Russian Foreign Minister Andrei Kozyrev compared the Moldovan situation to the Russian role in Georgia, implying that military force would be used unless concessions were made. Chisinau responded that the request was "unacceptable under any circumstances." Moldova did not sign the collective security treaty when it joined the CIS. In July 1994 the government announced that its new constitution declared a state of "permanent neutrality" and forbade the stationing of foreign troops. It also rejected Moscow's repeated *quid pro quo* offer of basing rights for eliminating the secessionist leadership in Transdniestr. It consistently refused to allow Russian military bases on its soil, claiming it violated the constitution and its proclamations of neutrality.[93]

---

[92] Economist Intelligence Unit, *Country Report: Belarus and Moldova*, 4th quarter, 1995, pp. 20–3; Dan Ionescu, "Playing the 'Dniester card' in and after the Russian election," *Transition*, August 23, 1996, pp. 26–8; Dan Ionescu, "Life in the Dniester 'black hole,'" *Transition*, October 4, 1996, pp. 12–14; Gottfried Hanne, "Playing two different tunes, as usual, in Moldova," *Transitions*, December 1997, pp. 68–71.

[93] Socor, "Isolated Moldova being pulled into Russian orbit," p. 11; Mihai Gribincea,

Officially, Russia seemed to back down in its demands. In October 1994, the Moldovan and Russian Prime Ministers signed an agreement ensuring the departure of the Fourteenth Army within three years. Military equipment was steadily transferred to Russian soil. However, in June 1995, Russian Defense Minister Pavel Grachev publicly repeated the Russian request for military bases. The Fourteenth Army commanders were even more belligerent, insisting that their presence was necessary for the protection of Russian nationals.[94] Chisinau had refused to meet these demands. The Russian response to this was mixed. Russia took actions indicating that it may simply ignore Moldovan preferences, and unilaterally declare that the troops will remain as peacekeepers. At the same time, President Yeltsin indicated to the Organization for Security and Cooperation in Europe that Russia would reduce its forces in Moldova by half by the end of 1997.[95]

To what extent did Moldova's domestic politics affect its behavior? The Moldovan government was relatively weak; it faced two secessionist movements and strong pressure from some segments of the population to merge with Romania. To a certain extent, this weakness played a role in Snegur's willingness to cut a deal with Russia. Several analysts agree that Snegur's domestic weakness prompted him to look to Moscow as a way to boost his personal popularity. However, the target regime's domestic vulnerability cut both ways in dealing with Russia. Towards the end of 1996, Snegur took a much harder line in responding to Russian pressure. His motive was to win the nationalist vote in the November presidential election. Although the target regime's weakness contributed to some concessions, domestic politics were also partly responsible for Moldova's resistance to Russian pressure in 1996.

On review, Moldovan concessions to Russia were mixed. Russia was successful in manipulating its tariff rates to coerce Moldova into the CIS. The Snegur administration also acceded to Russian ownership of industrial assets. Snegur's willingness to agree to Moscow's

---

"Challenging Moscow's doctrine on military bases," *Transition*, October 4, 1995, p. 8; Gribincea, "Rejecting a new role for the former 14th Russian Army," *Transition*, March 22, 1996, pp. 38–40; Hill and Jewett (1994), pp. 61–5.

[94] "Challenging Moscow's doctrine on military bases," p. 8.

[95] Ibid. See also *Jamestown Monitor*, "Russian troops in Moldova attempting *fait accompli*," June 6, 1996; *Jamestown Monitor*, "Russian military presence in Moldova to be legalized in Duma," October 22, 1996; Hanne, "Playing two different tunes," p. 71.

terms increased as the Moldovan government realigned itself closer to Moscow. This realignment was not complete; Moldova refused to sign the CIS Collective Security Treaty. The country repeatedly tried to use the OSCE as an institutional brake on Russian pressure. It also took steps to avoid further trade dependence on Russia by holding talks with Ukraine on forming their own free trade area.[96] Chisinau maintained some expectation of future conflict with Moscow. It held firm on both the Transdniestr and basing rights issues. Russian economic pressure, by itself, was capable of generating only minor concessions. The conflict expectations model provides an incomplete explanation of these coercion events. The target regime's domestic politics, as well as the use of military pressure, also influenced the outcome. Moldova compromised on Transdniestr autonomy because of the military balance of power. Military pressure will also be necessary to alter Chisinau's position on basing rights.

Georgia

Russia had two goals in this country: (1) Georgian membership in the CIS and the Collective Security Treaty; (2) basing rights for the Russian armed forces.

In the first five years of independence, Georgia rivaled Tajikistan as the most unstable of the NIS. Georgia's first president, Zviad Gamsakurdia, was stridently anti-Russian. Georgia was the only non-Baltic republic that refused to attend the founding meeting of the CIS in Alma Ata. As Gamsakurdia's rule became more autocratic, a civil war broke out, driving him out of power. The last Soviet Foreign Minister, Eduard Shevardnadze, became head of state in February 1992. Although Gamsakurdia fled the capital, his supporters continued to fight against the regular Georgian military. In addition to the ongoing civil war, Shevardnadze's government also faced two groups of separatists. In south Ossetia, the local leadership insisted on greater autonomy, as well as closer links with the north Ossetians, who lived across the border in Russia. In Abkhazia, rebel forces were trying to eject Georgian troops.

---

[96] On the use of the OSCE, see Socor, "Creeping putsch in eastern Moldova," pp. 8–13, and Hill and Jewett (1994), pp. 61–5. On the customs union, see *Jamestown Monitor*, "Ukraine, Moldova eye customs union," January 12, 1996.

Despite the target state's incredible weakness, it acted as a coherent actor, acquiescing to Russian pressure only when threatened with disintegration. There were few policy changes; Shevardnadze maintained Gamsakurdia's positions on the CIS and basing rights, and made repeated requests for Russian troops to withdraw and to transfer their heavy equipment to Georgian forces. Georgian preferences did not change as a result of the transfer of power. Furthermore, the collapse of the Georgian state was caused by the failure of economic coercion to generate the concessions. When the Russian military realized that sanctions would not work by themselves, they ratcheted up the pressure, aiding the secessionist movements. Once it became clear that the new Georgian leadership was not willing to join the CIS or grant basing rights, Russia disrupted almost all bilateral exchange. Fiona Hill and Pamela Jewett note:[97]

> Seeking to preserve its leverage in the region, Russia initially responded to Georgia's efforts for independence by denying Georgia the credits it provided to other former republics, and launching an economic blockade. Trade between the two countries ground to a halt and telephone service and gas pipelines were repeatedly severed. Russia also imposed an embargo on key medical supplies including insulin. As a result, the country's GNP declined, inflation soared and consumer goods and medication became scarce.

Despite the economic pressure, Tbilisi refused to acquiesce. Shevardnadze repeated his demand to have the military equipment transferred to Georgian forces. Russia ignored this request, but appeared to comply with Georgian demands on the withdrawal of troops. By April 1993, the Russians announced that of the 150,000 troops on Georgian soil in 1991, the number had been reduced to approximately 19,000.[98]

Economic coercion failed because the Georgian leadership anticipated repeated conflicts with Russia. Hill and Jewett described Georgia as "the most staunchly anti-Russian republic of the former Soviet Union."[99] Georgian nationalism was predicated on the notion of complete autonomy from Moscow. Any concession had the poten-

[97] Hill and Jewett (1994), p. 47.
[98] Economist Intelligence Unit, *Country Report: Georgia, Armenia, Azerbaijan, Kazakhstan, and the Central Asian States*, 1st quarter, 1994, p. 23.
[99] Hill and Jewett (1994), p. 46.

tial of encouraging future Russian demands, which could have threatened Georgian sovereignty. Certainly, the establishment of Russian bases would have given Moscow additional leverage in future disputes. These sovereignty concerns made Georgia prefer an economic embargo to acquiescence. Conceding to the Russian demands would have transferred too much leverage over Georgia's sovereignty into Moscow's hands.

Russia also anticipated numerous future conflicts, which explains the severity of the economic sanctions. In contrast to the steps taken to coerce its allies, Russia was willing to disrupt all of its bilateral trade with Georgia. This imposed significant costs on the border regions in the northern Caucasus, a region where Moscow had difficulty exerting its control. Nevertheless, Russia preferred incurring some losses and imposing greater costs on a stridently nationalist adversary in a strategic border region to the status quo.

When economic coercion failed to work, the Russian military applied indirect military pressure as well. Local commanders supplied the Abkhaz with military hardware and air support. The Abkhaz represented less than 25 percent of the population in Abkhazia; only outside support could have given them a chance against the Georgian army. Russian Defense Minister Pavel Grachev visited Russian troops in Abkhazia in February 1993 without stopping in Tbilisi, a diplomatic snub to Georgia. While there, he announced that the removal of Russian troops from the region would weaken Moscow's control over the Black Sea, and therefore "every measure to ensure that our troops remain there" would be taken. In that same month, a Russian plane was shot down while bombing the provincial capital, Sukhumi, a clear indication of the extent of Russian support. Thomas Goltz observes, "without the active assistance of the Russian military, it is impossible to imagine that the separatists could have pushed the conflict out of control."[100]

Despite Russian assistance, Georgian troops successfully resisted two Abkhaz assaults on Sukhumi in early 1993. However, in response to Russian pressure, Shevardnadze agreed to a ceasefire in July 1993. In accordance with Moscow's terms, Tbilisi withdrew its heavy equipment from the province. In September, Abkhaz forces launched a surprise third attack with covert Russian assistance. Georgian troops were quickly overwhelmed. Shevardnadze made repeated pleas to

---

[100] Ibid., pp. 47, 51–2; Goltz (1993), p. 104.

Yeltsin and Grachev for assistance, but their terms for intervention were tantamount to giving Russia total military control of the coastal province. Shevardnadze refused, and Georgian troops were ejected from all of Abkhazia within the month.

Following the fall of the province, Georgia looked ready to disintegrate. Gamsakurdia's forces took advantage of the government's disarray and marched towards Tbilisi. The Georgian Defense Minister defected and joined the opposition forces. Shevardnadze dismissed the head of Parliament, accusing him of sabotage. At this juncture, the Russians made it clear to Shevardnadze that he could not expect any economic or military support unless he agreed to join the CIS and allowed the Russian military bases in the country. Bruce Porter and Carol Saivetz comment, "Russia's military operations in Georgia during the latter months of 1993 are best described as a form of overt military blackmail." On October 22, 1993, less than a month after the fall of Sukhumi, Shevardnadze issued a decree announcing Georgia's accession to the CIS. Soon after this, Russian paratroopers landed in the country. With Russian assistance, Tbilisi was able to rout Gamsakurdia's forces and impose a stable ceasefire with Abkhazia.[101]

As the Georgian state continued to depend on Russian troops for its very survival, it also continued to make concessions to Moscow. In February 1994, the two countries signed a protocol of intent concerning military bases. Shevardnadze was clear about the source of Georgian concessions: "We are forced to take this step because we have to think about the future ... The only force that can help us and guarantee the restoration of Georgia's territorial integrity is Russia. If Russia decides that is not in its interest, it will never happen."[102] Over the next year, the Georgians retreated from their positions involving the rental fees and duration of the arrangement, and agreed to allow Russia to run four military bases for the next twenty-five years.

By 1996, however, the threat of Georgia's collapse had subsided. The Georgian state had successfully eliminated all of its paramilitary threats. A new constitution was written. Elections were held that gave Shevardnadze's party an overwhelming majority in the Parliament. Georgia's trade patterns had changed to the point where Russia was

---

[101] Economist Intelligence Unit, *Country Report: Georgia, Armenia, Azerbaijan, Kazakhstan, and the Central Asian States*, 2nd quarter, 1993, p. 24, and 1st quarter, 1994, p. 25; Porter and Saivetz (1994), p. 85.
[102] Quoted in Gribincea, "Challenging Moscow's doctrine on military bases," p. 5.

only its seventh largest trading partner.[103] As Georgia's regime strengthened its hold on power, and its economic dependence on Russia waned, Shevardnadze began to resist Russian pressure.

The Georgian Parliament had yet to ratify the basing agreement, and Shevardnadze insisted that it would not take place unless Russia took more active steps to reunite Abkhazia with Georgia. Russia responded to this recalcitrance by withholding all military aid to Tbilisi in the summer of 1996. By November, however, Russia backed down, agreeing to transfer military hardware, including armored personnel carriers and naval vessels. Moscow also agreed to grant Shevardnadze more influence over the regulation of Russian peace-keeping forces. The Russian Defense Ministry described these steps as carrots to ensure the ratification of the basing treaty.[104] In the end, Russia had to offer some carrots in addition to the stick in order to soften Georgia's position. These carrots have not been completely successful; although Russia has its bases, the Parliament had yet to ratify the agreement in 1998.[105]

The sanctions episodes against Georgia would appear to fit both the existing explanations and the conflict expectations approach. On the one hand, while Russia did extract significant concessions from Georgia, this cannot be attributed to economic coercion; Russian military statecraft, combined with the weakness of Shevardnadze's regime, combined to produce the outcome. As the Georgian state recovered from the events of 1993–94, it was able to resist further Russian pressure. This story fits perfectly with the conventional wisdom about economic sanctions.

Nevertheless, the conflict expectations approach can also explain the episode in part. First, because Russia anticipated frequent conflicts from the recalcitrant Georgian regime, it was willing to incur greater costs and use more extreme measures of economic coercion against

---

[103] *Jamestown Monitor*, "Georgian–Russian economic relations also in crisis," December 11, 1996; see also Stephen Jones, "Georgia's return from chaos," *Current History*, October 1996, pp. 340–5.

[104] *Jamestown Monitor*, "Moscow holds out carrot to Georgia for military bases," November 1, 1996.

[105] At the same time Russia was proffering the carrot, there were signs that it was also ratcheting up its threats. In February 1998, Shevardnadze survived his second assassination attempt, rumored to be sponsored by Russian elements. Furthermore, on a recent trip from Turkey, Georgian fighters were unable to escort the presidential plane because those fighters had been sabotaged while parked on a Russian base. Stephen Kinzer, "A defiant satellite nation finds Russia's orbit inescapable," *New York Times*, May 2, 1998, p. 12.

Georgia than any of its allies. The model developed here also explains why economic diplomacy was insufficient to make Tbilisi acquiesce. Because of its expectations of future conflict, Georgia viewed its relations with Russia in strictly relative terms. Given those preferences, its leadership preferred a costly deadlock to making significant concessions. Shevardnadze backed down only when, as a result of Russia's actions, his state verged on total collapse; once that threat passed, he was able to wring additional concessions from Moscow. This episode also suggests why the conventional wisdom about sanctions has persisted. Senders are more likely to apply military pressure and destabilize a target regime when economic coercion fails, i.e., when conflict expectations are high. Since military statecraft carries a higher profile than economic statecraft, the most visible sanctions episodes are also those where purely economic coercion is not likely to generate significant concessions.

Ukraine

Russia had several demands of its neighbor: (1) an agreement to renounce its claims to all Soviet assets abroad, in return for obviating its share of Soviet debts; (2) the transfer of all nuclear weapons to Russian soil; (3) Russian control of the Black Sea fleet; (4) exclusive basing rights in the port of Sevastopol; (5) control of both the energy industry and pipeline infrastructure.

Ukraine has a special place in the Russian consciousness. According to Russian historians, their national origins began in Kiev over a millennium ago. With the countries fused together for three hundred years, most Russians have great difficulty thinking of Ukraine as an independent country. Mikhail Gorbachev acknowledged that it was ridiculous to think of the Soviet Union without Ukraine. Zbigniew Brzezinski, in a telling statement, observes, "It cannot be stressed enough that without Ukraine, Russia ceases to be an empire, but with Ukraine suborned and then subordinated, Russia automatically becomes an empire."[106] Given Ukraine's extreme energy dependence, one would expect it to be a primary candidate for Russian economic coercion.

Ukraine proved recalcitrant to Russian demands. In 1992, it refused to accept the zero option for Soviet debts and assets. It signed the

---

[106] Brzezinski (1994), p. 80.

Lisbon Protocol, in which it promised to ratify the START-I and Non-Proliferation treaties and return all weapons to Russia. However, to the annoyance of both Russia and the United States, Kiev started to waver. Ukraine temporarily halted the transfer of tactical nuclear weapons to Russia in March 1992 before agreeing to their shipment to Russia. Ukrainian forces seized control of an airfield where some of the weapons were stored. Even then, Ukrainian President Leonid Kravchuk reaffirmed his security concerns, noting, "this problem is especially acute in situations when our neighbors such as Russia present territorial claims." One Ukrainian general said in June 1993, "only idiots give up nuclear weapons."[107] Kiev insisted that it would not return the weapons to Russia unless it received compensation for the enriched uranium contained in the warheads, as well as security guarantees from Russia and the United States. The Ukrainian Parliament passed a resolution declaring the weapons to be the property of Ukraine. On the Black Sea fleet issue, Kravchuk insisted that Ukraine had sovereignty over half the fleet, as well as the bases in Sevastopol, contrary to Russia's position that the fleet and base were part of the CIS military structure.

The Russian response to Ukrainian statements was to use economic pressure in an attempt to gain concessions. Viktor Shokin, a Russian deputy Prime Minister, warned Ukraine that Moscow would raise its energy prices to world levels without concessions. In a February 1993 news conference, he said, "If Russia is going to give subsidies, then there should be some weighty reason for doing this, in particular, possible concessions on other issues." Russia quickly raised the price from 1,600 rubles (four dollars) per 1,000 cubic meters to $40 in hard currency, and pledged to increase the price further to $80 by January 1994. Ukraine soon racked up a considerable energy debt. By September 1993, it was estimated at $2.5 billion. Furthermore, Russia halted all trade in nuclear materials with Ukraine. This meant that Kiev could not get nuclear fuel for its reactors, and was forced to keep its spent fuel, even though it was limited in its ability to properly store or reprocess the radioactive material.[108]

[107] Kravchuk quoted in "Four former Soviet republics agree on nuclear arms," *New York Times*, April 29, 1992, p. A9; General quoted in Steve Call and R. Jeffrey Smith, "Ukraine could seize control over nuclear arms," *Washington Post*, June 3, 1993, p. A1.
[108] Eric Whitlock, "Russian–Ukrainian trade: the economics of dependency," *RFE/RL Research Report*, October 29, 1993, pp. 38–42; Reiss (1995), p. 111; Shokin quoted in Hill and Jewett (1994), pp. 74–5.

Economically, these sanctions were severe. Ukraine was one of the least energy-efficient republics in the former Soviet Union. If economic motivations were the only criteria, Kiev would have acquiesced. Instead, Ukraine refused to concede. The Ukrainian Prime Minister, Leonid Kuchma, responded to Shokin's statements by observing, "Russia is trying to bring about a full paralysis of the Ukrainian economy ... I cannot understand the Russian position. It is not motivated by economics. It can only be seen as some sort of pressure on Ukraine." The chief political advisor to President Kravchuk stated, "Ukraine will never recognize that Ukrainian territory is a sphere of special Russian interest ... we want relations of equality."[109] In contrast to Turkmenistan or Kazakhstan, the Ukrainian government viewed the situation in relative terms. Kiev did not want to make concessions that would undermine its bargaining position in future conflicts.

In the fall of 1993, Russia became even more explicit in its use of economic coercion. Four days before a September 1993 summit meeting between Presidents Yeltsin and Kravchuk at Massandra, Moscow cut gas supplies to Ukraine by 25 percent as a hint of its position. At the summit, the Russian negotiators proposed that in exchange for forgiving the gas debt, Kiev should hand over the entire Black Sea fleet, including basing rights in Sevastopol, *and* agree to the immediate transfer of all nuclear weapons to Russian soil. Yeltsin recounted later on Russian television that he had said, "Why don't you give up your part of the Black Sea Fleet, and we will cancel your debts?" He threatened to withhold further oil and gas shipments if Ukraine failed to acquiesce on both issues.[110]

It is safe to describe the Ukrainian response at Massandra as muddled. Yeltsin's initial reaction to the summit was that Kravchuk and the Ukrainians had agreed to all of Moscow's terms. In a televised address, he claimed that the agreement had been a "forced, but inevitable" step for Ukraine, and that, "neither Russia nor the world community could permit (Ukraine) becoming a nuclear power." After a confusing delay, however, the Ukrainian leadership stated that they had never agreed to Moscow's terms, and accused the Russians of using "economic *diktat*" in their negotiations. Soon afterward, the

---

[109] Hill and Jewett (1994), p. 75.
[110] Reiss (1995), p. 108; Bohdan Nahaylo, "The Massandra summit and Ukraine," *RFE/RL Research Report*, September 17, 1993, pp. 1–6.

Russians backed down from their initial claims of victory. The Russian misperception of what precisely was agreed to at Massandra may have been purposeful, so that Yeltsin could boast of his negotiating prowess just before his October 1993 confrontation with the old Supreme Soviet.[111]

This is one instance where domestic constraints probably affected Ukrainian decision-making. At first, Kravchuk indicated he was inclined to accept the Russian proposal. In a press conference on September 6, he justified his decision, noting: "we had to act on the basis of realism. Suppose we had slammed the door and left. The gas would have been turned off and there would have been nothing left to do."[112] At the same time, Kravchuk took considerable heat for this position. Nationalists called for his impeachment. Protests in the Western city of Lviv attracted several thousand demonstrators. Kravchuk's own Defense Minister indicated his strong opposition to the Russian proposal. Faced with these costs of agreement, Kravchuk backed down from his earlier position, tabling the proposal and taking no further action, thus preserving the status quo ante.

Another explanation for the Ukrainian preference for deadlock on these issues was its expectations of future conflict with Russia. Kiev was troubled by the security implications of any concessions. In early 1992, commenting on the transfer of tactical nuclear weapons to Russia, Ukrainian president Leonid Kravchuk said explicitly, "I don't want to make anyone stronger." Western observers also noted this concern. John Morrison notes: "Relations with Moscow are perceived as a zero-sum game in which any sign of military weakness or the slightest false diplomatic move, could put Ukraine's hard-won independent state-hood at risk." Mitchell Reiss concurs: "Kiev began to realize that Moscow was the true beneficiary of Ukraine's denuclearization, both in terms of receiving the withdrawn weapons and their nuclear material and in terms of collecting its dismantlement assistance."[113]

Kiev's expectations were predicated on their perception of the Russian threat. Moscow took a number of diplomatic steps suggesting that it did not take Ukrainian independence seriously. Russian officials warned European countries not to build embassies in Kiev because they would soon be downgraded to consulates. Moscow's

---

[111] Ibid., pp. 2–4.

[112] Quote in Morrison (1993), p. 695.

[113] Ibid., p. 680; Kravchuk quoted in Eleanor Randolph, "Kiev halts a-weapons transfers," *Washington Post*, March 13, 1992, p. A1; Reiss (1995), p. 95.

ambassador to Ukraine told Western diplomats that independence was only a "transitory" phenomenon.[114] With this attitude, Kiev was understandably worried that any concession would be perceived as a loss of sovereignty. The distribution of benefits mattered in this relationship because Russia would exploit any concession as a sign of Ukrainian integration with Russia. This expectation of future conflict blunted Russia's ability to convert its economic leverage into significant concessions.

The nuclear issue was eventually settled in a tripartite agreement among the United States, Russia, and Ukraine in January 1994. In the final agreement, Ukraine agreed to transfer all nuclear weapons to Russia within the next seven years. In return, Russia agreed to provide Ukraine with enriched uranium worth approximately $1 billion for its nuclear reactors. All three countries pledged "respect for the independence, sovereignty, and territorial integrity of each nation."[115] These commitments and the hefty economic inducement satisfied Kiev's concerns. On June 1, 1996, Ukraine was pronounced a nuclear-free state.[116]

On the Black Sea fleet issue, Russia had limited success using economic statecraft. The threat to disrupt natural gas led to some concessions, but not enough to increase Russia's leverage for future conflicts. In another summit meeting at Sochi in April 1994, Yeltsin and Kravchuk agreed that Ukraine would sell part of its half of the fleet in exchange for debt relief. In the final distribution, Ukraine kept 164 ships, and Russia 669 ships. The division of the fleet started in March 1996.[117] Ukrainian recalcitrance on this issue was the result of the long-run implications of complete acquiescence. A transfer of all of the ships to Russia would have given Moscow additional leverage in maintaining its base in Sevastopol. In the more distant future, a strong Russian military presence in the Crimea could have undercut Ukraine's jurisdiction in the region. Ukraine's concern with the relative distribution of gains forced Moscow to settle for fewer concessions rather than accept a stalemate.

---

[114] Hill and Jewett (1994), p. 76.

[115] Quoted in John W. R. Lepingwell, "The trilateral agreement on nuclear weapons," *RFE/RL Research Report*, January 28, 1994, p. 14.

[116] *OMRI Daily Digest*, "Last nuclear warheads removed from Ukraine," June 3, 1996.

[117] *RFE/RL Daily Report*, "Black Sea fleet negotiations," August 17, 1994; *OMRI Daily Digest*, "Ukraine receives 27 Black Sea fleet vessels," March 28, 1996; Ustina Markus, "Black Sea fleet dispute apparently over," *Transition*, July 28, 1995, pp. 31–5

Economic coercion generated only minor concessions on basing rights. From 1992 to 1995, the two sides' bargaining positions were fixed. Moscow insisted on exclusive rights to Sevastopol, and access to other coastal assets. The Ukrainians continued to insist on basing part of their fleet in Sevastopol and denying Russia the use of ports beyond the Crimea. The prospect of Russian economic coercion was ever present. In May 1995, a deputy commander of the Russian navy reminded Ukrainian negotiators of their energy debts to Russia, and stated that they should not expect Moscow to make all the concessions. In January 1996, Moscow halted all payments to Ukraine with regard to the Black Sea fleet. Ukraine refused to back down. It decided to place its naval command headquarters in Sevastopol, and asserted control over most of the other ports in Ukraine, including the most modern base at Donuzlav. In July 1996, the Ukrainian Parliament approved a new constitution that barred foreign troops from being permanently stationed in the country. The Black Sea fleet could only stay on a temporary basis, although the definition of "temporary" was flexible. In mid-1996, Russia took steps indicating that it would back down. The Russian navy made preparations to base the fleet in Russian ports such as Novorossisk and Sochi.[118]

In the fall, however, Moscow renewed its efforts to kick the Ukrainians out of Sevastopol. National Security Advisor Alexander Lebed and Moscow Mayor Yuri Luzhkov both stated publicly that Sevastopol was a Russian city and Ukraine had no rights to it. The Duma passed a nonbinding resolution that echoed Lebed and Luzhkov. The Yeltsin administration and the Foreign Ministry rejected these claims, but Russian naval commanders based in Sevastopol supported the resolution, and even Yeltsin's foreign policy aide argued that Ukraine would eventually be reintegrated into Russia. Russian negotiators rejected Ukraine's terms for dividing the base at Sevastopol and insisted on having monopoly basing rights in the city, as well as outright ownership of the bases and coastal infrastructure.[119]

---

[118] Ibid.; *Jamestown Monitor*, "Progress on Black Sea fleet bases," December 6, 1995; *Jamestown Monitor*, "Admiral Baltin sinks," February 2, 1996; *OMRI Daily Digest*, "Bases for Black Sea fleet sought in Russia," March 20, 1996; *Jamestown Monitor*, "Black Sea fleet: differences now focus on coastal assets," March 7, 1996; *OMRI Daily Digest*, "Update on Ukraine's new Constitution," July 1, 1996.

[119] *Jamestown Monitor*, "Lebed demands Sevastopol from Ukraine," October 14, 1996; *Jamestown Monitor*, "Luzhkov reiterates Russia's claim to Sevastopol," October 22, 1996;

The renewed demands came with added economic and diplomatic pressure. Russia violated a bilateral free-trade agreement and slapped a 20 percent value-added tax on all goods imported from Ukraine in early October. The volume of trade between the two countries declined by 20 percent in the first quarter of 1997.[120] Ukraine's negotiations with Gazprom over its gas supplies were occurring at the same time as its negotiations with Moscow over Sevastopol. Chernomyrdin delayed a scheduled visit to Kiev and put off signing a bilateral treaty on cooperation until the issue was resolved. One newspaper noted:

> Kiev is anxious to discuss with Chernomyrdin reliable Russian gas supplies, removal of Russian trade barriers on Ukrainian goods, official recognition of existing borders, and the interstate political treaty. But Moscow continues to hold these issues, as well as Chernomyrdin's visit, hostage to an agreement on the fleet and its bases.[121]

A Ukrainian newspaper published an October 1996 memorandum that allegedly came from the Yeltsin administration, stating that because of now-President Kuchma's intransigence, Moscow should take steps to subvert his regime.[122]

The dispute was finally resolved in May 1997, with the signing of three intergovernmental agreements. On the basing issue, the two sides agreed to a twenty-year lease that could be renewed for another five years. The annual rent was set at $97.75 million. Ukraine agreed to give Russia control over three of the five bays in Sevastopol. There were some concessions on the Ukrainian side; the rent figure was substantially less than the original Ukrainian proposal of $423 million. Ukraine's original position also gave Russia control over only two of Sevastopol's bays. Russia also made concessions, however. First, Russia legally recognized Crimea and Sevastopol as Ukrainian territory. As opposed to the Russian preference for kicking Kiev out of Sevastopol, Ukraine was recognized as "master of the waterway."

OMRI Daily Digest, "Duma warns Ukraine on Sevastopol," October 25, 1996; *Jamestown Monitor*, "Black Sea fleet talks adjourn in disagreement," November 7, 1996; *Jamestown Monitor*, "Russia turns up pressure on Sevastopol," November 21, 1996.

[120] Sherr (1997), p. 43.

[121] *Jamestown Monitor*, "Russia–Ukraine: visit off, pressure on," November 13, 1996; see also *OMRI Daily Digest*, "Ukrainians worried about Russian pressure over Sevastopol," October 2, 1996.

[122] *Jamestown Monitor*, "Ukrainian newspaper publishes controversial letter from Russian official," January 15, 1997.

Moscow further agreed to make an additional payment of $200 million to compensate for Ukraine's loss of tactical nuclear weapons. The debt and trade levers were lifted. Russia agreed to give Ukraine ten years to pay off its energy debts, and lifted the trade restrictions placed on Ukrainian products. One analysis concluded of the agreement: "If Kuchma has cut corners to secure an agreement, they have been comparatively small."[123]

Russia's eagerness to coerce, and Ukraine's reluctance to acquiesce are both explained by the conflict expectations model. As with the fleet issue, Kiev was wary that Russia could exploit the relative distribution of payoffs in the future. Concessions on Sevastopol would enhance Russian leverage on the status of Crimea, as well as other conflicts. President Kuchma was quoted in a Ukrainian paper arguing that if he acquiesced on Sevastopol, Ukraine would lose its independence. The Ukrainian Rada responded by mirroring the Duma's harder line, proposing legislation that would eject the Russians sooner rather than later. It also passed a law barring dual citizenship, a move designed to limit Russian influence in Crimea.[124] Kiev's expectations of future conflict made it unwilling to make significant concessions despite the significant opportunity costs of not conceding. The reaction within Russia also indicated the concern that leverage was lost for future disputes. A former commander of the Black Sea fleet condemned the deal, claiming it would prevent Russia from using its fleet in the future.[125]

Despite Russia's failure to exploit its energy lever to get significant concessions on security issues, it still hoped to acquire Ukrainian utilities. The energy lever was a powerful one. By February 1994, Ukraine owed Russia $3.4 billion; an immediate halt to all energy subsidies would have cut Ukraine's GNP by 3.5 percent.[126] Moscow switched tactics, asking for ownership stakes in energy enterprises and other firms instead of more overt security concessions. Gazprom was particularly interested in acquiring the pipeline infrastructure and gas monopoly, Ukrhazprom. Kravchuk seriously considered the demands, but the Rada rejected the terms because it viewed the

---

[123] Sherr (1997), p. 38.

[124] *OMRI Daily Digest*, "Black Sea fleet update," December 30, 1996; *Jamestown Fortnight in Review*, "Struggle for the heart of Europe," November 1, 1996; *OMRI Daily Digest*, "Ukraine tightens citizenship requirements," November 4, 1996.

[125] *RFE/RL Newsline*, "Mixed Russian reaction to Black Sea fleet deal," May 30, 1997.

[126] *Economist*, "Out of gas," March 12, 1994, p. 55; Krasnov and Brada (1997), p. 825.

energy infrastructure as a strategic asset. Instead, Kiev bartered less vital property to Russia. These assets included specialized drilling equipment, $60 million in fishing trawlers, a guarantee to build 145,000 square meters of housing for Russian gas-industry workers, and up to 30 percent of the Odessa port facility. Russia did have one notable success: Ukraine agreed to waive its claim to all Soviet assets abroad in exchange for further debt relief in early 1995. It steadfastly refused, however, to transfer control over its energy utilities, refineries, or pipelines to Russia.

Russia continued to apply economic pressure. In October 1995, Russia withdrew 200 categories of goods from the bilateral free trade arrangement, making them subject to tariffs. This move was estimated to cost Ukraine $1.5 billion annually. In January 1996, a Russian presidential decree expanded the range of goods subject to excise taxes to include Ukrainian tobacco, alcohol, and automobiles. It took actions on alcohol imports that specifically targeted Ukrainian producers. Moscow also halted supplies to the Drohobych oil refinery in Ukraine. Finally, in response to a surge in demand, Russia removed Ukraine from their joint electricity grid, forcing the closure of several industrial plants.[127]

Despite the increased pressure, Kiev gave no signs that it intended to acquiesce. Rather than pay in the form of ownership stakes, Ukrhazprom cracked down on its customers, cutting power to 7,000 delinquent enterprises. Kiev also tried to diversify its energy sources. The government halted plans to shut down Chernobyl, and reactivated one of its reactors. These measures seemed to have some effect. Following the debt rescheduling in early 1995, Ukraine was able to meet its payments, reducing Moscow's future ability to use its energy lever. In late 1996, discussions were held with Uzbekistan to diversify Ukraine's reliance upon Russian energy.[128]

---

[127] *OMRI Daily Digest*, "Ukraine criticizes Russia over trade, borders," October 26, 1995; *Jamestown Monitor*, "Russia tightens control over imported alcohol and tobacco," February 12, 1996; *OMRI Daily Digest*, "Russian–Ukrainian oil talks suspended," January 24, 1996; *Jamestown Monitor*, "Hit by Russian excise taxes, Ukraine seeks other trading partners," January 26, 1996; *Krasnaya Zvezda*, "Disconnection of energy system threatens Ukraine and Crimea with collapse," in FBIS-SOV-96–038, February 21, 1996, p. 43.

[128] *OMRI Daily Digest*, "Ukraine cut power to 7,000 enterprises," March 13, 1996; Economist Intelligence Unit, *Country Report: Ukraine*, 4th quarter 1993, p. 27; Intelnews, "Settlement of gas debt reached with Russia," in FBIS-SOV-96–043, March 4, 1996, p. 42; Uniar, "Kuchma meets with Russian Gazprom chairman," in FBIS-SOV-96–099, May 21,

Despite the seemingly large debt, Russia was unable to extract significant concessions. There were three reasons for this. First, Russia incurred moderate costs of coercion, raising Ukraine's utility from a deadlock outcome. Moscow sends 95 percent of its gas exports to Western Europe through Ukrainian pipes. Every time Russia cut back gas supplies to Ukraine, Kiev would respond by siphoning off the gas intended for Europe. Gazprom claimed that the first ten months of 1993, Ukrhazprom diverted 10 bcm of gas, or approximately 10 percent of its shipments to Europe.[129] It was forced to pay $4.7 million in fines to its European clients because of Ukrainian actions. Second, the International Monetary Fund made it clear to Russia that unless it rescheduled part of Ukraine's debt, it would not receive any funds.[130] This raised the Russian costs of coercion even more.

Third, Ukraine viewed any transfer to Moscow in relative terms. In a 1995 memo to Kuchma, the Ukrainian Foreign Minister cautioned that Russia intended to use the energy debts to seize strategic assets. He cautioned against any concessions, noting, "Russia does not intend to develop its relations with CIS countries on the basis of international law."[131] The Rada shared this apprehension; it decided not to privatize any energy facilities because it regarded them as strategic assets and did not want them to be acquired by Gazprom. Paul D'Anieri notes, "Overall, Ukraine has taken the extreme position ... in favor of preserving sovereignty at the expense of the economic efficiency which could be pursued through integration."[132] Kiev was wary that Russian control over its energy industry would leave it vulnerable to future attempts at economic coercion. As with the other points of dispute, the concern for the distribution of payoffs reduced Russian concessions. Because Ukraine derived some utility from Russia's opportunity costs of deadlock, it was unwilling to make significant concessions on this issue.

Russia's attempts at economic coercion in Ukraine bore limited fruit. Moscow was able to get Kiev to agree to the zero option. It was

1996, p. 39; Ustina Markus, "Energy crisis spurs Ukraine and Belarus to seek help abroad," *Transition*, May 3, 1996, pp. 14–18; *Jamestown Monitor*, "Agreement reached on gas supplies to Ukraine," December 9, 1996.

[129] Whitlock, "Ukrainian–Russian trade: the economics of dependency," p. 40.

[130] *Economist*, "Nicer and nicer," April 8, 1995, p. 45.

[131] Quoted in Brzezinski and Sullivan (1997), p. 292.

[132] D'Anieri (1995), p. 5. See also *OMRI Daily Digest*, "Ukrainian negotiations with Gazprom," October 31, 1996.

also able to procure an additional 30 percent of the Black Sea fleet. Russian attempts to coerce Kiev into handing over its nuclear weapons failed, however, and it was forced to extend security guarantees and subsidized nuclear fuel as sweeteners. Gazprom was frustrated in its attempt to gain equity stakes in Ukrainian enterprises. Russia was forced to share the Sevastopol base with the Ukrainian navy and pay rent for the use of the base; and it cannot count on keeping it beyond the twenty-year agreement. Because Ukraine antici-pated future disputes with Russia, it perceived bilateral relations in relative terms. This made it more reluctant to concede than Russia's allies.

Azerbaijan

Russia had five demands: (1) membership in the CIS; (2) ownership stakes in Azeri oil and gas deposits; (3) common control over the Caspian seabed; (4) the export route for those resources; (5) basing rights for the Russian military.

With independence, Azerbaijan courted Western oil companies to develop its oil fields. Amoco, British Petroleum, Statoil, Penzoil, and Turkish Petroleum all held negotiations with the State Oil Company of Azerbaijan (SOCAR). The first set of negotiations was over three offshore fields estimated to contain at least 4.5 billion barrels of oil. In May 1993, SOCAR announced what the Russian government referred to as "the deal of the century," allowing a Western consortium to invest $7.4 billion to exploit all three offshore sites. Profits from these fields were estimated at up to $48 billion over the next three years.[133]

Russia's response to its lack of participation in the project was to use its tariff rates to coerce Baku. One analyst commented, "Moscow has pursued a policy of frozen instability in the Caucasus and Central Asia, a policy of keeping instability at a level that frightens off Western investors while allowing Moscow to reclaim its positions of influence in the area." By the spring of 1993, Russia's tariff rates on Azeri products were higher than those placed on any other NIS. Not surprisingly, trade between the two states declined.[134]

The Azeri president during these negotiations, Abulfez Elchibey,

[133] Sagers (1994), pp. 283–8; Rossen Vassilev, "Oil diplomacy in the near abroad," *Prism*, May 3, 1996.
[134] Quote from Paul Goble, "Light at the end of the tunnel? Pipeline politics in the former Soviet Union," *Prism*, November 4, 1995; see also Alieva (1995), p. 301.

was an ardent nationalist. His foreign policy consisted primarily of pursuing a "special relationship" with Turkey and accusing Russia of siding with Armenia in the war over Nagorno-Karabakh. Under Elchibey, Baku refused to make any concessions, despite the economic costs of stalemate. He viewed any concession to Moscow as a loss of Azeri sovereignty, including membership in the CIS. Russia, discovering that economic coercion was unable to generate any concessions, used military statecraft to force Baku's hand. Moscow provided covert assistance to Elchibey's enemies in the spring and summer of 1993. Russia withdrew its troops from Azerbaijan ahead of schedule, permitting Armenian forces to seize additional territory during a May offensive. These actions encouraged the overthrow of Elchibey two weeks before he was to sign the agreement with the Western consortium. He was replaced by Heydar Aliyev, a former KGB general, who was thought to prefer stronger ties to Moscow.[135]

Russian pressure in this case succeeded in generating initial concessions. Aliyev first postponed and then restructured the "deal of the century." During this time, Azerbaijan seemed to ally itself with Russia. Aliyev convinced the Azeri Parliament to join the CIS in September 1993. Before the new arrangement was signed in September 1994, SOCAR sold one-third of its shares, or 10 percent of the consortium, to LUKoil for $15 million. The transfer of this percentage was equal to $5 billion over the life of the project, a significant financial windfall.[136] LUKoil was also given a 32.5 percent ownership stake in developing the Karabakh fields in 1994.

As Aliyev consolidated his control over Azerbaijan, however, he halted the realignment towards Moscow and resisted making further concessions. In early 1996, it was announced that SOCAR would transfer 10 percent of its stake in the Shah-Deniz oil and gas ventures to LUKoil. This agreement was delayed for several months because LUKoil had originally demanded at least a 25 percent stake, but Azerbaijan was only willing to make a 10 percent concession. In late 1996, Aliyev responded to continuing pressure from the Russian Foreign Ministry by cutting LUKoil out of a contract to develop the Ashrafi and Dan Uluzu oil fields. In announcing the agreement, Aliyev stated that he would resist "foreign forces" from "seeking to

---

[135] See Goltz (1993) and Sagers (1994).
[136] Alieva (1995), p. 302; Rossen Vassilev, "Oil diplomacy in the near abroad," *Prism*, May 3, 1996.

jeopardize Azerbaijan's international oil contracts."[137] A month later, Aliyev signed Baku's fifth large-scale oil contract, for the Lenkoran-Deniz and Talysh-Deniz fields, with two French firms, again cutting out Russia.[138] With regard to control over its hydrocarbon deposits, the new Azeri leadership has been willing to make some concessions to Moscow as a way of ensuring the uninterrupted development of its energy sector. These concessions, however, have been consistently less than Russia originally wanted, and have declined as Aliyev backed away from Moscow.

Russia was also frustrated in its attempt to change Azerbaijan's position on the Caspian seabed. Russia first used diplomatic pressure to challenge Azeri claims to offshore deposits in the Caspian Sea. Azerbaijan wanted the sea carved up among the five littoral states. This was because a large share of the oil deposits were thought to be within the Azeri slice of the sea. Because Russia had minimal deposits off its shore, its negotiators proposed that each country have exclusive rights within forty-five miles of its coastline, but that the rest of the Caspian be jointly developed.[139] Although the other littoral states were affected by the legal wrangling, Russia and Azerbaijan were furthest apart in their bargaining positions.

Baku ignored Moscow's wishes on this matter and, as previously noted, initiated joint ventures with Western multinationals to develop areas of the Caspian considered by Russia to be joint property. As Azerbaijan was negotiating these deals, Russia applied diplomatic pressure. The Russian Foreign Ministry sent a *démarche* to Great Britain (British Petroleum was a principal investor in Azerbaijan), warning that any project could not be recognized by Russia, and that, "any unilateral actions are devoid of a legal basis."[140] In November 1994, a memorandum from Russian Foreign Minister Kozyrev to Prime Minister Chernomyrdin recommended implementing an economic blockade on Azerbaijan unless it backed down on the Western multinational presence in the Caspian shelf. Less than six

---

[137] Aliyev quote from *Jamestown Monitor*, "Azerbaijan's fourth big oil contract signed," December 16, 1996; *OMRI Daily Digest*, "Shah–Deniz contract finalized," June 5, 1996; Ian Bremmer and Anthony Richter, "The perils of 'sustainable empire,'" *Transition*, March 5, 1995, pp. 14–15.

[138] *Jamestown Monitor*, "Azerbaijani–French summit yields big oil contract," January 15, 1997.

[139] *Economist* survey, "Caspian gamble," February 7, 1998, p. 7.

[140] Quoted in Blank (1995), p. 376.

weeks later, starting with the Chechen war, Moscow sealed off the Russian–Azeri border, including railway traffic, through which 70 percent of Azeri foreign trade passed. The Azeri costs from this blockade were estimated at $250 million.[141]

Despite this sustained economic pressure, Azerbaijan made no legal concessions. Because most of Azerbaijan's oil was in the disputed part of the Caspian, it knew that any concession on this matter would lead to a transfer of revenue from Baku to Moscow. The amount of money involved was considerable. Azerbaijan's oil sector claimed a growing percentage of its gross domestic product; 30 percent by 1997 and growing. In this case, ironically, Azerbaijan's prior concessions to Moscow *strengthened* its bargaining position on the Caspian. By cutting in LUKoil on some of the oil deals, that firm also suffered costs from Russia's policy. This pressure on the Yeltisn administration had some effect. In January 1998, Russia agreed that the seabed could be divided into national sectors, consistent with Azerbaijan's position.[142]

The Russians also pressured Baku to commit its oil exports to the Russian route. The renewed economic coercion was also costly for Russia. Azerbaijan produced up to 80 percent of the Soviet oil field and drilling equipment. By imposing these trade sanctions, the sender country incurs moderate costs for its own oil sector as well. Russia was willing to incur these costs because it viewed a deadlock outcome, where Azerbaijan suffered for defying Moscow, as preferable to the status quo, where Azerbaijan prospered from additional Western investment while diluting Russia's influence. One petroleum analyst observed: "The Russians want to keep Azerbaijan in the Russian fold. There will be no exports from that region without the Russians sanctioning them."[143]

Azerbaijan was unwilling to make significant concessions on the pipeline issue. In the fall of 1995, when the decision was made, the only export route for Central Asian oil and natural gas was through Russian pipelines that ran from Baku to the Russian Black Sea port of Novorossisk. If that pipeline complex had remained the primary route, Russia would have reaped lucrative transit fees and maintained its influence over its southern neighbors. The decision affected not

---

[141] *RFE/RL Daily Report*, November 9, 1994; analyst quoted in *Business Week*, "The great game comes to Baku," July 17, 1995, p. 48.
[142] *Economist*, "Caspian carve-up," March 7, 1998, p. 66.
[143] Rossen Vassilev, "The politics of Caspian oil," in *Prism*, January 12, 1996; *OMRI Daily Digest*, February 22, 1996.

only Azeri oil, but the oil produced from the rest of the Caspian shelf and Central Asia. Several alternative routes were proposed, however. Turkey suggested routing the gas through Georgia to the Turkish port of Ceyhan as a way of circumventing both Russian influence and the Bosphorus. Iran and Pakistan also offered to build transit routes. Exxon even commissioned a report to study the feasibility of shipping the oil through China to Japan. Baku's first decision, however, was how to export the oil it was already extracting. The choice was between a northern route through Chechnya to the Russian port of Novorossisk or a southern route through Georgia to the Turkish port of Ceyhan. Moscow's preference was clear, as was its willingness to disrupt the deal if its interests were not met. One of Yeltsin's foreign policy advisors stated after the September 1994 consortium deal, "(there is) no chance that the deal will stick if the pipeline goes south ... Russia is interested that we control the pipeline."[144]

By itself, the pipeline decision on early oil was not a significant Russian demand. If the Azeri government cared only about minimizing costs and maximizing revenue, the northern route would have been the winner. Most of the pipeline was already in place, and the consortium estimated that only an additional 27 kilometers of pipe – approximately $55 million – was needed to bring it up to specifications. By contrast, the southern route was largely hypothetical in 1994; 117 kilometers of pipe, priced somewhere between $150 million and $250 million, needed to be laid before that route was operational. Furthermore, the pipeline ran through politically unstable regions in Georgia and Turkey. From a purely economic outlook, the northern route was not a hard sell for the Russians, and Azerbaijan had no choice but to ship some early oil via Novorossisk.[145] If the Azeris cared only about the issue at hand, they would have chosen the northern route because of the cost–benefit analysis and the threat of Russian economic pressure.

Despite the threat of coercion and the economic logic of the Russian demand, Baku's concessions were minor. In October 1995, the oil consortium announced that Azerbaijan would pump oil through both a northern route to Novorossisk and a southern route to a Georgian port on the Black Sea. The distribution of oil along these routes would

---

[144] Sergei Karaganov, quoted in Jim Hoagland, "Russia: still playing 'the Great Game,' " *The Washington Post*, September 27, 1994, p. A21.
[145] *Platt's Oilgram News*, "Winner in Azeri pipeline decision seen as US government," October 11, 1995, p. 1.

change with time. The first 5 million tons of early oil was to be shipped through the northern route. At the time of the decision, however, the president of the oil consortium asserted that by 2002, the main export route would be through Georgia and Turkey to Ceyhan. He reiterated those plans in October 1996, announcing that the Baku–Supsa pipeline would be operational within two years.[146] The willingness of the consortium to invest in a riskier alternative route demonstrated a considerable resistance to Russian preferences on the issue, and a preference to incur greater costs rather than grant Russia complete control over Baku's energy exports.[147]

Azerbaijan's expectations of future conflict caused the government to think of the pipeline concession in terms of its effect on future disputes. This magnified the size of the demand from the target's perspective. Acquiescence to Moscow on this issue would have given the Russians considerable leverage in future interactions. The two countries were deadlocked on a host of issues, including Russia's role in the Nagorno-Karabakh mediation, autonomy for Azerbaijan's ethnic minorities, and cooperation on defense matters. Permitting the Russians monopoly control over the shipment of Azeri oil would have been too great a transfer of power. The Azeri Prime Minister, Foreign Minister, and the consortium president all made public assertions that national security reasons governed the primacy of the southern route.[148]

The Russian reaction to the decision was schizophrenic. Russian

---

[146] Lowell Bezanis and Elizabeth Fuller, "Routing decision suggests wrangling to come," *Transition*, November 17, 1995, p. 72; *Meridiani*, "Terry Adams: Caspian oil has no future without Georgia," in FBIS-SOV-96-095, May 15, 1996, p. 74; *OMRI Daily Digest*, "Baku–Supsa pipeline to be operational by late 1998?" October 11, 1996.

[147] Azerbaijan has also maintained its distance from Turkey. In April 1996, the oil consortium turned down a Turkish offer to finance the southern route, preferring to offer the project in public tender. Economist Intelligence Unit, *Country Report: Armenia, Georgia, Azerbaijan*, 2nd quarter, 1996, p. 36.

[148] *Krasnaya Zvezda*, "Clinton backs supporters of 'compromise,'" in FBIS-SOV-95-194, October 6, 1995, p. 72; *Turan*, "Yilmaz–Aliyev news conference covers pipeline, Karabakh," in FBIS-SOV-96-074, April 16, 1996, p. 61. There was considerable speculation in both the Western and Russian press that the Azeris made their decision because of US pressure. The day before the pipeline decision, President Clinton called President Aliyev to encourage the Azeris to choose the southern route. While this may have influenced the decision, it is hard to see how it could have been the deciding factor. The United States had no way to influence Azerbaijan beyond moral suasion; at the time of the decision, Congress was providing aid to Armenia and had cut off all funding for Azerbaijan.

Fuel and Energy Minister Yuri Shafarnik reacted negatively at first, threatening further economic coercion:

> We will react in a tough manner to attempts to bring down the level of our participation or to exclude us from projects in which Russia is interested. [Using oil as a weapon] is justified only when the really vital interests of this country are affected ... If Russia loses something in the Caspian, somebody else could lose ... some of their access to export pipelines.

Two days later, however, Shafarnik backed down, claiming the decision was a win for Russia. In January 1996, at the signing of the "early oil" pipeline agreement, Prime Minister Chernomyrdin brushed aside questions about Russia's legal objections to the Caspian development, suggesting that Moscow has dropped the issue.[149] This change in Russian attitude suggests that Moscow understood the limited utility of economic coercion in Azerbaijan, and preferred limited acquiescence to none at all.

Russia had little success with the basing issue and cooperation on defense matters. In May 1993, Azerbaijan became the only country among the NIS to have no Russian troops on its soil. When the blockade was imposed during the Chechnya invasion, an additional demand was for the right to use the early-warning radar station at Mingechaur, as well as the stationing of elements of the Russian border patrol along the frontier with Iran. Azerbaijan consistently rejected those demands. When it became obvious that economic sanctions alone would not work, Moscow resorted to security carrots. It covertly offered to support Azerbaijan in its dispute with Armenia over the Nagorno-Karabakh region in return for leasing Mingechaur.

Despite the offer, Aliyev signed a decree making the station the property of Azerbaijan. Aliyev's Defense Minister said that it would "never be a Russian military base." The Azeri commander of the border troops declared the proposal in conflict with Azeri national interests. The speaker of the Azeri National Assembly spelled out Baku's concern that acquiescence on this issue would lead to greater concessions down the road: "Are they going to dictate their terms if they get a military base here?" Moscow gave up its use of economic

---

[149] Shafarnik quoted in Lowell Bezanis and Elizabeth Fuller, "Routing decision suggests wrangling to come," *Transition*, November 17, 1995, p. 45; Interfax, "Moscow, Baku sign early oil transportation agreement," in FBIS-SOV-96–013, January 11, 1996, p. 21.

pressure, partially reopening the border to traffic in October 1996.[150] This episode shows that Russia's ability to extract concessions was constrained when Baku perceived the concessions as compromising its sovereignty. Any concession that would translate into future Russian leverage was rejected.

On the whole, the Russian coercion efforts in Azerbaijan produced some concessions. Azerbaijan joined the CIS; Moscow was able to gain ownership stakes in certain development projects. It should be noted, however, that most of the Azeri concessions came about after Russia took additional steps to ensure that Aliyev would come into power. As with Georgia, it appears that military statecraft and Azerbaijan's domestic weakness contributed to Azerbaijan's decision to make concessions. Even though Aliyev headed a vulnerable target regime and faced military and economic pressure from Russia, conflict expectations limited Azerbaijan's concessions. Russia was denied equity stakes in some oil projects. Baku decided to develop the southern pipeline route, despite a near-total shutdown of economic exchange with Russia. The Azeri government held fast on the legal status of the Caspian Sea. Finally, Russia was unable to get a basing agreement or further cooperation on defense matters. These decisions meant a loss of Russian influence in the region. They were consistent with Azerbaijan's fears that acquiescing would transfer too much power to a sender country with divergent foreign policies.

Lithuania

Russia had two demands of Lithuania. The first was guaranteed transit access to Kaliningrad. This territory is part of the Russian Federation but geographically separated from the rest of the country by Lithuania and Belarus. Kaliningrad became militarily significant to Russia with the disintegration of the Warsaw Pact and the independence of the Baltic states, eliminating those ports and facilities from

---

[150] Speaker quoted in Vadim Dubnov, "'Stability in Azerbaijan cannot be maintained by force,'" *New Times*, September 1996, pp. 44–5; Defense Minister quoted in *Jamestown Monitor*, "Azeri President rules out Russian basing rights at Gabala," February 5, 1996; *Financial Times Energy Economist*, "A three pipe problem," October 1995, p. 168; *Jamestown Monitor*, "Moscow using Karabakh conflict to gain bases in Azerbaijan," November 29, 1995; *Jamestown Monitor*, "Azerbaijan sidesteps Russian call to join CIS border defense pact," May 16, 1996; *Jamestown Monitor*, "Azerbaijan–Russia railway reopened," October 7, 1996.

the old Soviet naval infrastructure. Russia needed to ship military troops and equipment through rail lines in Lithuania to improve Kaliningrad's military facilities. The second was ownership stakes in Lithuania's oil and gas sectors. Unlike the other Baltic states, there was no conflict over ethnic autonomy for the local Russians. Lithuania granted citizenship to all of its residents. Its leadership was more willing to do this than the other Baltic states because at the time of independence less than 10 percent of the Lithuanian population was Russian. The corresponding figures for Latvia and Estonia were much higher.

The absence of rancor over the minorities issue did not mean there were no conflict expectations between Vilnius and Moscow. Lithuania's attempt to secede from the Soviet Union during the Gorbachev era led to a number of conflicts with Moscow, and reinforced a wariness of Russian domination.[151] Lithuania was the first NIS to apply for NATO membership. It pursued nationalist policies, refused to sell its energy facilities to Russian firms, and insisted on a new law regulating the transport of Russian military goods to Kaliningrad. In response, Boris Yeltsin remarked in 1992 that countries pursuing economic and political policies that differed from the Russian Federation would be forced to pay for energy deliveries in hard currency at world market prices. He mentioned Ukraine and the Baltic republics as examples.[152] The implication was that if Lithuania changed its policies, the likelihood of economic pressure would be reduced.

Vilnius rejected the Russian threats and issued its own counter-threats. Kaliningrad was completely dependent on the Lithuania power grid for its electricity. In 1992, every time Russia threatened to cut off energy supplies to Lithuania, Lithuania threatened to cut electricity to Kaliningrad. In November 1992, after the Russians continued to raise gas prices, Lithuania demanded that Russia pay market prices in transit fees for natural gas shipped through Lithuania

---

[151] Lithuania was also the first NIS to encounter economic coercion from Moscow. In early 1990, when the republic declared independence, Gorbachev responded with a complete embargo of oil, natural gas, and raw materials exports. Five months later, the Lithuanians agreed to "suspend" their declaration of independence in return for an end to the embargo.

[152] John M. Kramer, "'Energy shock' from Russia jolts Baltic states," *RFE/RL Research Report*, April 23, 1993, p. 41.

to Kaliningrad. Vilnius continued to threaten the disruption of natural gas to Kaliningrad well into 1993.[153]

The constant threat of coercion became an election issue in the country, and in October 1992 the nationalist president, Vytautus Landsbergis, was replaced by an ex-communist, Algirdas Brazauskas. Landsbergis accused Russia of placing Lithuania under an "energy embargo" during the election. Fiona Hill and Pamela Jewett concur, noting, "Moscow certainly played a role in the fall of the republic's first post-Soviet president." Indeed, Brazauskas's assessment of bilateral relations with Russia was revealing: "We have to be clear about this: we continue to receive basic raw materials (including 100 percent of our energy resources) from Russia, and no real alternative has been prepared. Relations with Russia have to be put in order, and this has to be addressed seriously and systematically."[154] With the change in power, Lithuanian and Russian energy officials met to determine, "whether and how the recent political changes in both countries would affect the attitude of Russian structures in charge of fuel resources towards their future cooperation with Lithuania."[155]

As Lithuania considered realigning itself closer to Russia, the conflict expectations model would predict increased Russian demands, because of the reduced concern for relative gains. That was exactly what happened. One analyst concluded, "The conciliatory attitude of Lithuania in the first half of 1993 seems to have raised hopes in Moscow that further concessions can be wrung from it."[156] To get what it wanted, Russia used both economic and military pressure. In August 1993, Russia announced that it would halt the withdrawal of Russian troops from the country until a formal agreement on military transit was signed. This did not immediately deter the Lithuanian realignment. In November 1993, Russia and Lithuania signed a most-favored-nation trading agreement. Despite the signing, Russia indicated that it wanted to reach a separate accord on military transit between Russia and Kaliningrad. Lithuania passed legislation imposing severe restrictions on the transport of military goods and personnel through Lithuania. The Russian Duma, in response,

---

[153] Sabonis-Chafee (1995); Saulius Girnius, "Relations between the Baltic states and Russia," *RFE/RL Research Report*, August 26, 1994, p. 30.

[154] Hill and Jewett (1994), p. 20; Brazauskus quoted in Kramer, " 'Energy shock' from Russia jolts Baltic states," p. 43.

[155] Kramer, " 'Energy shock' from Russia jolts Baltic states," p. 46.

[156] Girnius, "Relations between the Baltic states and Russia," p. 30.

decided to place all the Baltic republics into the highest tariff category on agricultural products. It agreed to ratify the most-favored-nation accord with Lithuania only if Vilnius agreed to Russia's demands on transit to Kaliningrad. The higher tariff rate was estimated to cost Lithuania approximately $150 million in export revenue annually.[157]

The combined economic and military pressure produced limited concessions. In early 1995, Lithuania agreed to extend the old regulations on military transport to the end of the year. In response, Russia approved Lithuania's most-favored-nation status. Russia also agreed to the removal of troops without a formal agreement. However, Lithuania requested compensation for the ecological damage done by the Russian troops.[158]

Lithuania's behavior suggests that it made a partial concession because of Russia's linkage between the military withdrawal and the transit agreement, rather than Russia's attempts at economic coercion. Even under the Brazauskus regime, Vilnius was wary of Russian attempts to reduce its sovereignty. The concession allowed Russia to increase its military strength on both of Lithuania's flanks, increasing Moscow's leverage in future conflicts. Lithuania appeared willing to pay higher gas prices and go to deadlock rather than acquiesce. However, if the Russian troops had stayed, its sovereignty would have been compromised even further.

While Lithuania was willing to make minor concessions in the short run, it also halted its *rapprochement* with Russia, and took steps to reduce its vulnerability to Russian economic and military pressure. To enhance its security, it was the second NIS to join the Partnership for Peace, and it increased its security ties with Denmark and Poland. To reduce its reliance on Russian energy, the government adopted drastic measures. Vilnius invested considerable resources to bring the Ignalina nuclear power plant, with Chernobyl-type reactors, up to Western safety standards. This was an extraordinary reversal for the Lithuanian leadership, since during the Soviet era many nationalists had favored the shutdown of the plant for environmental reasons. By 1993, Lithuania was relying on Ignalina for more than 85 percent of its electricity needs.[159]

---

[157] Economist Intelligence Unit, *Country Report: The Baltic States*, 2nd quarter, 1995, pp. 33–4.
[158] Saulius Girnius, "Compromise at the crossroads," *Transition*, March 29, 1995, pp. 44–6, 63.
[159] Sabonis-Chafee (1995), table 1.

Lithuania's lowered opportunity costs enabled it to resist Russian efforts to acquire ownership of Lithuanian facilities. For example, in late 1994, LUKoil offered to take an equity stake in the oil terminal under construction at Butinge. This facility would have allowed offshore crude to be pumped via pipeline from Butinge to the only oil refinery in the region, in Latvia. Lithuania rejected LUKoil's bid, despite its ability to bring in a Western partner (Italy's Agip). Gazprom also cut gas supplies to the country, hinting that acquiring an ownership stake in the Lithuanian state utility would ensure gas supplies. Gazprom kept up the pressure on Vilnius, curtailing its shipments by 25 percent in early 1996. As of July 1998, the Lithuanians had resisted all overtures to hand over equity stakes in its energy facilities.[160]

Russia managed to secure some concessions through economic coercion. It received an extension on the transit agreement, and prevented a hike in the transit fee for shipping oil. On the other hand, it was unable to acquire ownership stakes in the Lithuanian energy sector. Furthermore, the transit concessions were made only after additional military pressure was applied. It is also telling that Russia's policies towards Lithuania changed after Brazauskas took office. Moscow ratcheted up its demands despite a more conciliatory attitude from Vilnius. It managed to extract some concessions, but after partially acquiescing on those issues, Lithuania re-evaluated its relationship with Russia, took political and economic steps to reduce its vulnerability to Russian economic pressure, and made no further concessions.

Latvia

Russia had three demands of this country. (1) It wanted to maintain its military presence in the country, in the form of basing agreements. Of particular interest was the Skrunda early-warning radar site, a crucial part of the system used by the Soviet military to detect a US nuclear attack. (2) Given the large minority of ethnic Russians living in Latvia, it wanted these residents to be granted full Latvian citizenship. (3)

---

[160] *OMRI Daily Digest*, "Gazprom threatens action against Baltic states," February 5, 1996; Economist Intelligence Unit, *Country Report: The Baltic States*, 1st quarter, 1995, p. 40.

Moscow wanted to convert Latvia's gas debt into ownership of utilities, pipelines, and port facilities.

Russia was ready to link its economic leverage to the protection of Russian minorities. In September 1992, as citizenship laws were being drafted by the Baltic states, oil deliveries to Latvia were reduced. A month later, the first deputy Foreign Minister confirmed that sanctions were being considered against all the Baltic states. A few weeks after that statement, President Yeltsin singled out the Baltic states and Ukraine as countries that should be forced to pay hard currency for their energy deliveries, as a result of their differing economic and political policies.[161]

The Latvian response was to raise Russia's costs of attempting coercion. When oil deliveries slowed, Riga seized control of the oil pipeline running from the Russian border to the port of Ventspils and shut down deliveries. Riga demanded an increased transit fee for the pipeline, from $3 to $7 per ton. The Latvian press made a clear link between these steps and Russian economic pressure.[162] This move cost the Russians $70 million a month in unfulfilled contracts, although it also cost the Latvians $10 million in lost transit and port fees.

Riga enacted a law denying ethnic Russians citizenship unless they or their families resided in the country before June 17, 1940. Ethnic Russians would face a difficult time in getting citizenship; they are last in the queue compared to other nationalities, dual citizenship will not be allowed, and after the year 2000, the quota of those to be granted citizenship cannot exceed 0.1 percent of the population. This law meant that out of 2 million residents, 700,000 were noncitizens. In August 1994, President Yeltsin condemned the law as "militant nationalism." In his 1995 New Year address, he said that the Russians living in Latvia were the most oppressed of those living in the near abroad. In early 1996, Moscow continued to insist that trade relations between the two countries would be tied to the treatment of the Russians living in Latvia. In October 1996, the Duma passed a resolution calling for economic sanctions if the situation for Russian speakers did not improve. Latvia refused to budge. [163]

[161] John H. Kramer, " 'Energy shock' from Russia jolts Baltic states," *RFE/RL Research Report*, April 23, 1993, pp. 41–9.
[162] Ibid., p. 47.
[163] Economist Intelligence Unit, *Country Report: The Baltic States*, 1st quarter 1995, p. 24; Radio Riga Network Report, in FBIS-SOV-96–027, February 8, 1996, pp. 66–7; Constan-

In March 1998, Russia renewed its threat of economic coercion. Comparing the Latvian treatment of ethnic Russians to Pol Pot's Cambodia, the Foreign Ministry threatened to halt oil shipments unless the citizenship law was changed. Latvia prepared minor concessions in response to this threat; a law was drafted granting citizenship to all children born in Latvia after independence. However, this concession was in response to US pressure as well. In January 1998, the Baltic states signed a "charter of partnership" with the United States, pledging political support for inclusion into NATO. By agreeing to minor concessions, Latvia cemented its relationship with the United States, limiting further coercion attempts.[164]

Latvia resisted economic sanctions because of its expectations of future conflict with Russia. In July 1993, the vice-chairman of the Latvian Supreme Council was quoted as saying, "I stress, only Russia and no other state is our potential enemy." Latvia viewed the ethnic Russians as a potential lever for future Russian efforts to subvert its autonomy. The Russians represented a potential fifth column. Riga did not wish to grant the concession because of the probability that Moscow would use its influence with the ethnic Russians in future conflicts. The efforts at Russification during the Soviet era did nothing to reassure the Latvian regime. Riga preferred a deadlock outcome that was costly to both sides over total acquiescence.[165] Indeed, Latvia instead pursued a strategy of strengthening institutional security ties with the United States, European Union, and Sweden.

On the basing issue, Russia was also less than successful. Soon after the Soviet breakup, Moscow agreed to withdraw most of its troops from Latvia. Originally, however, it wanted to keep the Skrunda base for ten years. In addition to the economic pressures mentioned above, Russia also used military statecraft. Both President Yeltsin and Defense Minister Pavel Grachev hinted that it would unilaterally cancel the withdrawal if its demands were not met. Riga remained firm, and in March 1994 an accord was signed that reflected Latvian

tine Dmitriev, "Hostages of the (former) Soviet empire," *Transition*, January 12, 1996, p. 20; *Jamestown Monitor*, "Latvia threatened by Russian Duma," October 7, 1996.
[164] Steven Erlanger, "Clinton and 3 Baltic leaders sign charter," *New York Times*, January 17, 1998, p. A4; *Washington Post*, "Russia threatens sanctions against Latvia," March 8, 1998, p. A23; Erlanger, "US tries to defuse Russia–Latvia dispute," *New York Times*, April 16, 1998, p. A9.
[165] Quote from Vares (1995), p. 168; Dmitriev, "Hostages of the (former) Soviet empire," p. 20.

preferences. Russia agreed to abandon the most modern facilities at Skrunda, and use the older facilities (built in the 1960s) for only five and a half years. Latvia gained control of 80 percent of the base. In addition, Russia handed over its other bases to the Latvian military, including the air fields at Lociki. Finally, Russia agreed to withdraw all its troops, except those at Skrunda, by August 31, 1994. In return, Latvia agreed to grant some 60,000 to 80,000 retired officers residency permits. This concession was clearly in response to the added military threats. The troop withdrawal was carried out as planned, and most of the troops left as scheduled.[166]

In early May of 1994, ignoring the protests of the Russian military and scientific community, the Latvians destroyed the modern facilities at Skrunda in a dynamite explosion accompanied by music and fireworks. Three weeks later, the Baltija Bank, one of Latvia's largest, collapsed. Baltija had sold 51 percent of its bank portfolio to the Moscow-based InterTEKbank in exchange for Russian ten-year treasury bills. Mysteriously, the bills failed to arrive in Riga. The collapse of Baltija led to a general financial panic that threatened Latvia's thriving bank sector, and spread to Lithuania as well. One Russian paper explicitly linked the collapse of Baltija to the destruction of Skrunda. Bank regulations in Latvia were extremely lax, inviting all sorts of illegal activity, so the question of Russian involvement is at best uncertain. However, Moscow took full advantage of the crisis to emphasize Riga's vulnerability to Russian financial pressure. As a result of the government bailout, Latvia doubled its budget deficit in 1995 to 4 percent of GDP.[167]

Finally, Russia was able to extract minor concessions from the Latvians on the question of utility ownership. From the moment

---

[166] Economist Intelligence Unit, *Country Report: The Baltic States*, 2nd quarter 1994, p. 20; Jackson (1994), p. 10.
[167] Radio Riga Network report, in FBIS-SOV-95-086, May 4, 1995, p. 89; Economist Intelligence Unit, *Country Report: The Baltic States*, 4th quarter 1995, p. 26; Paul Goble, "Moscow's new politics built on sand," *Prism*, July 14, 1995; *Financial Times*, "Latvia recovers from banking crisis," September 30, 1995, p. 2. Two facts suggest that InterTEKbank might have purposefully withheld the treasury bills. First, the bank was created with the assistance of the Russian Fuel and Oil Ministry, which had its own reasons for punishing Latvia. Second, InterTEKbank's president, Alexander Trif, in an interview two weeks after Baltija's collapse, stated that a bank partially owned by the state cannot act as a private company, but must be an instrument for state policy. See *Kommersant-Daily*, "Mintopenergo: a worldwide story: InterTEKbank," in FBIS-SOV-95-116-S, June 16, 1995, pp. 7–11.

Gazprom raised its prices, Latvijas Gaze responded with similar price hikes to its customers. In the first three quarters of 1992, gasoline prices increased by 270 percent, household heating went up by 125 percent, and fuel oil increased in price by 100 percent.[168] By raising its prices immediately, the utility was able to keep its debt down to a manageable amount. By February 1994, Latvian debt to Gazprom totaled only $23 million, much smaller than the debts in Belarus, Ukraine, or Moldova. It was able to pay them off without bartering any assets to Russia.

Russia imposed stiffer economic sanctions against the Baltic states in July 1994, placing all of them in the highest tariff category for agricultural imports. At the same time, Gazprom offered to reduce Latvia's gas bill in return for a 50 percent equity stake in Latvijas Gaze, and control of the gas storage unit at Incukalns. Not coincidentally, in 1994 Gazprom started charging Latvia a gas price that was $2.50 higher per ton than it charged to Estonia, because of Gazprom's partial ownership of Estonia's gas utility. Latvia initially rejected the offer, holding talks with the Abu Dhabi Investment Authority instead. Negotiations were also held with Norwegian officials in June 1995 on providing gas supplies to the Baltic republics. In April 1997, the Latvians agreed to sell Gazprom a 16.25 percent stake in the company. In announcing the deal, the head of the Latvian privatization agency explained the decision: "Our first concern was that the current supply arrangements for gas are not disturbed. So we wanted Gazprom involved." As a counterweight to Gazprom's influence, however, Latvia sold an equal percentage of the company to two German companies. Russia's influence was thus diluted and balanced by the presence of Western firms.[169] For the rest of the energy sector, the Economist Intelligence Unit notes that, "while the government is prepared to let the Russian gas company participate as a bidder, it seems intent on retaining a majority stake in state hands." This has not stopped Gazprom from threatening to reduce deliveries.[170]

---

[168] Kramer, " 'Energy shock' from Russia jolts Baltic states," p. 48.

[169] Economist Intelligence Unit, *Country Report: The Baltic States*, 2nd quarter 1994, p. 29; 1st quarter 1996; Matthew Kaminski, "Latvia sells stake in its gas company," *Financial Times*, April 3, 1997, p.4.

[170] Economist Intelligence Unit, *Country Report: The Baltic States*, 4th quarter 1996, p. 26. Russian frustration on the ownership issue also spread to other industries. In November 1996, the two countries suspended the flights of the other country's official air carrier. The dispute was initiated by Russia's claim that Latvia's airline merited different

Russia has been frustrated at the low yield of its economic coercion attempts in Latvia. Russia received only minor concessions on the issues of citizenship or basing rights, and those were in part the result of military statecraft. Moscow also failed to lever Latvia's gas debt into significant ownership stakes in the energy sector. Riga's concern about the distribution of gains greatly reduced Russia's bargaining leverage. At the same time, Russia was willing to repeatedly use economic coercion despite the costs associated to its own economy.

Estonia

Russia's policy demands in Estonia paralleled those towards Latvia: (1) secure control over key military installations, particularly the nuclear submarine base in Paldiski; (2) Estonian citizenship for the ethnic Russians living in the country, particularly the military pensioners; (3) ownership stakes in strategic Estonian industries, particularly the energy utilities.

The first issue to flare up was the citizenship question. As this law was being drafted in late 1992, the Russian government warned Estonia to grant the ethnic Russians citizenship or face the consequences. One Russian official stated: "The government and parliament of Russia have quite a few levers to make the Estonian authorities realize the impermissibility of violating the rights of the republic's nonindigenous population ... [including] suspending the interstate treaty and imposing economic sanctions on Estonia." One month later, first deputy Foreign Minister Vitaly Churkin confirmed that sanctions were a policy option depending on Estonian actions. In the same week, Vice-President Alexander Rutskoi predicted that if sanctions were imposed, Estonian industry would "grind to a halt within a week."[171] In early 1993, the Russian Congress of People's Deputies suspended the 1992 free trade agreement between Moscow and Tallinn because of the citizenship issue.

Despite the Russian pressure, in June 1993 the Estonian Parliament passed an Aliens Law similar in content to Latvia's. Citizenship was granted only to citizens of interwar Estonia and their descendants, excluding most of the Russian population. The law required indi-

treatment because of its close relationship with the Scandinavian airline SAS. *OMRI Daily Digest*, "Latvia suspends Aeroflot flights to Riga," November 4, 1996.
[171] Kramer, " 'Energy shock' from Russia jolts Baltic states," p. 44.

viduals seeking citizenship to reside in the country for at least two years, and have some grasp of the Estonian language. It stripped 500,000 ethnic Russians of citizenship, and gave them two years to apply for residency or citizenship, or else face deportation.[172]

Russia reacted to the passage of the law with diplomatic and economic pressure. Russian Foreign Minister Andrei Kozyrev denounced it as "apartheid and ethnic cleansing in kid gloves." On June 25, Gazprom announced a halt in gas supplies to Estonia for four days. This was part of an effort to collect $10 million in gas debts to Russia, but the timing of the cutoff also sent a political message. Kozyrev took advantage of the opportunity to threaten a cutoff of oil deliveries to Tallinn unless there was a change in the treatment of the Russian minority.[173]

Estonia had reacted to previous Russian threats and cutoffs by refusing to back down. Indeed, it often retaliated with its own coercion attempts. For example, Tallinn cut off food supplies to Russian military bases whenever Moscow halted its deliveries to Estonia.[174] After the Parliament passed the 1993 law, however, Estonia faced pressure from European countries as well. Both the Conference on Security and Cooperation in Europe (CSCE) and the Council of Europe urged the Estonian president, Lennart Mari, not to sign the law as it was. While the CSCE admitted that the letter of the law did not infringe on human rights, it did object to its ultimate effect on the Russian minority. The Council of Europe's reaction was a bit stronger; it reversed an earlier position and said that the law did not meet European standards, and protested the vague wording of several of the clauses.[175] That statement was particularly damning, as Estonia had joined the Council only a month earlier.

Estonia changed its position in response to Russian economic coercion combined with moral suasion from the regional organizations. On July 6, President Mari returned the law to Parliament, refusing to ratify the original version of the law. On July 12 a modified version was passed. The concessions to Russia were minor, however. The new law eliminated some of the vague wording regarding the

---

[172] Dmitriev, "Hostages of the (former) Soviet empire," p. 19.
[173] Economist Intelligence Unit, *Country Report: The Baltic States*, 3rd quarter, 1993, pp. 11–15.
[174] Russell (1995), n. 42.
[175] Economist Intelligence Unit, *Country Report: The Baltic States*, 3rd quarter, 1993, pp. 11–12, and *Economist*, "Russians abroad: pawns or knights?" July 10, 1993, p. 39.

appeals procedure for individuals denied residency. Greater compensation was granted those who were denied. In evaluating the success of Russian economic coercion, however, two things are noteworthy. First, the new law still denied citizenship to all retired Russian officers of the Soviet army, which was a major bone of contention between Moscow and Tallinn. Second, all of the changes in the law were designed to meet the Council of Europe's objections. Russia's objections overlapped with the Council's, but the concessions did not address Russian concerns; 500,000 ethnic Russians were still required to apply for citizenship; the amended law only streamlined the application process. There is no denying that Russian coercion influenced the outcome. Its effect, however, was minor at best. The Estonian concessions were minimal, and tailored more to European than Russian demands.

Estonia was unwilling to acquiesce to Moscow's demands because of its fear that the concession would benefit Russia. As in Latvia, ethnic Russians constituted a substantial minority of the population. If they had all been granted citizenship, the natural fear was that their political influence would keep Estonia closely bound to Russia, and scuttle plans to join either NATO or the European Union. This outcome would have been anathema to the Estonian regime. Furthermore, Russian claims of human rights concerns did not jibe with their other actions. If Moscow had been genuinely concerned about their status, it could have increased orders from the large factories in Estonia where most Russians work. Russia took no action to ensure the health of these plants. If anything, the trade sanctions hurt the ethnic Russians more than the Estonians.[176] The inconsistency between Moscow's stated concerns and its actions increased Tallinn's suspicion that acquiescence would be exploited in future conflicts with Moscow. Only after regional European institutions added their voice was Tallinn prepared to grant minor concessions.

Russian behavior after the coercion episode did nothing to calm Estonian fears. One Russian official argued that autonomous enclaves should be created in both Estonia and Latvia. A Russian Foreign Ministry spokesman asserted that "economic means of influence" and "economic leverage" would be used in the future to persuade Estonia to change its mind. There was still no change in the citizenship law.

---

[176] Saulius Girnius, "Relations between the Baltic states and Russia," *RFE/RL Research Report*, August 26, 1994, p. 33.

Furthermore, Estonia decided in June 1996 to invalidate all former Soviet passports and started to issue "resident alien" passports to noncitizens, making it difficult for these individuals to leave the country.[177]

The Russians had greater success in acquiring ownership stakes in Estonian industries. In 1993 the Estonian government privatized its gas distribution company into a joint venture called Eesti Gaas. The ownership split was 30 percent to Lentransgaz, a subsidiary of Gazprom, and 70 percent to the Estonian government. This moderate concession by the Estonians eliminated the dispute about gas debt. It also resulted in lower gas prices as compared with Latvia, which refused to cede any equity shares to Gazprom until late 1996. Still, in an effort to prevent the Russians from increasing their leverage, the Estonian government sold an additional 14.69 percent of Eesti Gaas to a German firm, Ruhrgas, and another 15 percent to private Estonian investors, balancing the Russian investment.[178]

On the basing issue, Russia's negotiations with Estonia were even more antagonistic than those with Latvia. The story is similar. An agreement was reached in principle between the two countries for Russian troops to withdraw by August 31, 1994. Also in parallel with the Latvian case, the Estonians were adamant about the complete withdrawal of troops, whereas Russia wanted additional time to dismantle the submarine base at Paldiski. The Latvians, however, were able to finish their negotiations about the Skrunda base by March. Estonia refused to sign anything during that spring. By summer , the Russian Parliament approved an additional 50 percent tariff on Estonian agricultural exports. This was particularly painful to the Estonian balance of trade. Agricultural goods accounted for 42 percent of all exports to Russia. As a result of the tariff, Estonia's bilateral trade with Russia went from surplus to deficit by April 1995.[179] As with Latvia, Russia added military pressure to the coercion effort, hinting that it was willing to let the troops stay in Estonia unless its demands were met.

Despite the economic and military pressure, the eventual agreement conceded even less than in the Latvian case. On July 26, barely a

---

[177] *Jamestown Monitor*, "Russian Duma urges sanctions on Estonia," March 28, 1996; *Jamestown Monitor*, "Estonia denounced in Moscow," July 1, 1996.

[178] Economist Intelligence Unit, *Country Report: The Baltic States*, 2nd quarter, 1993, p. 18, and 3rd quarter, 1995, p. 15; " 'Energy shock' from Russia jolts Baltic states," p. 46.

[179] Economist Intelligence Unit, *Country Report: The Baltic States*, 3rd quarter, 1995, p. 6.

month before the withdrawal was supposed to be completed, Presidents Yeltsin and Mari worked out an agreement in a five-hour meeting. Yeltsin later described those negotiations as the toughest he had ever held as President. The final agreement resembled Latvia's in that Estonia agreed to grant residency permits, but not citizenship, to most of the Russian military pensioners. It also agreed to allow Russian personnel to shut down the facilities at Paldiski, although the base would still be under Estonian control. Unlike Latvia, however, the timetable was shorter; the Russians were given only a year to leave.[180] The Russian Duma ratified the agreement and fulfilled its terms, evacuating Paldiski by the agreed date.

Estonia's intransigence on this issue can also be explained by its fear that any concessions would be exploited by Russia in the future. Statements by Estonian officials indicated that they viewed Russia as their primary security threat. Tallinn knew that Russia was implacably opposed to Estonian membership in NATO or any other Western defense organization. One Russian quasi-official defense policy institute argued that if Estonia were to join NATO, Russia should immediately invade.[181] The two countries had yet to reach agreement on their common border. Allowing Russian troops in Estonia for an extended time would have given Russia much more leverage on these issues, and weakened Estonia's bargaining position. Because it anticipated future conflicts, the relative gains and reputation effects magnified the cost of any concession. Estonia was only willing to make minor concessions to avoid deadlock.

In evaluating the success of Russian economic coercion, the conclusion is almost identical to the situation in Latvia. On the citizenship issue, Estonia made minor concessions in response to Russian pressure. Like Latvia, it allowed military pensioners to obtain residency to facilitate the withdrawal of troops. Estonia made more concessions on the ownership issue than Latvia. This is partly because the Latvians had more levers at their disposal to raise Russia's costs of coercion, particularly by shutting down the pipelines. On the other hand, the Estonians conceded less on the basing issue. Russian economic pressure produced minor concessions, but far fewer than in the other NIS. This is true despite the more public attempts at coercion.

---

[180] Economist Intelligence Unit, *Country Report: The Baltic States*, 4th quarter, 1994, p. 12.
[181] *Dagens Nyheter*, "Real threat of war against Estonia," in FBIS-SOV-96–101, May 23, 1996, p. 55.

Russian–Estonian relations in 1996 showed that there would be a plethora of future conflicts between these two countries beyond the border disagreement. Russia claimed that Estonia owed it money for pre-1992 rubles; in response, Estonia shut off water to Russian border cities because of unpaid bills. The latter incident, although minor, prompted a formal diplomatic protest. In November, the Russian Foreign Ministry official in charge of the near abroad stated: "Normalization of Russian–Estonian relations is impossible without cardinal changes in the Estonian authorities' discriminatory policy toward our compatriots in that country." He also affirmed that Russia "categorically rejects the Estonian leadership's attempts at joining NATO ... and will make clear what the consequences will be on all aspects of Russian–Estonian relations." Opinion polls in Moscow showed Estonia was "Russia's number-one enemy." When asked about this, the Estonian ambassador to Russia replied, "I think it is a very great honor for a country as tiny as Estonia."[182]

Conclusion

This chapter has surveyed Russia's use of economic statecraft in its relations with the NIS. The next chapter will evaluate these events more systematically, but a few observations can be made here. The cases in this chapter demonstrate that Russia used economic coercion as an integral part of its policy towards the NIS in their first five years of independence. Every newly independent state save Uzbekistan was a target of Russian economic pressure. The issues at stake, and the costs of coercion, were far from minor.

In some cases, the target country's domestic politics and Russia's use of military statecraft played an important role in extracting concessions. It is harder to claim that they had a persistent effect on the outcome, however. Domestic concerns strengthened the resistance of Ukraine and Tajikistan to Russian pressure, but encouraged Azerbaijan and Georgia to acquiesce. It is difficult to divine a consistent pattern of how domestic politics affected the target state's decision-making calculus. In the case of military statecraft, Russia was able to

---

[182] Estonian ambassador's quote from *Economist*, "Honoured enemy," May 4, 1996, pp. 46–7; Russian Foreign Ministry quotes from *Jamestown Monitor*, "Moscow not interested in normalization with Estonia," November 4, 1996; *OMRI Daily Digest*, "Russo–Estonian water dispute," April 16, 1996.

use force to get its way in Georgia, but had less success with the same approach in Moldova. The threat of force appeared to have no consistent effect on the target country's willingness to concede.

Finally, there appear to be two long-run effects of Russian economic pressure. First, vulnerable target states relied on international institutions as a shield against further coercive action. Belarus and Kazakhstan consistently advocated the formation of multilateral institutions that increased their ties to Russia. These agreements strengthened economic integration but also, in theory, placed legal constraints on Russia's ability to coerce. Other allies that avoided frequent coercion attempts, such as Armenia and Uzbekistan, resisted the idea of deeper integration. Russia's adversaries tried to enter international organizations that excluded or diluted Russia's influence, such as NATO, OSCE, the Council of Europe, or the European Union. This was seen as a way to constrain Russia's ability to use its economic leverage. This pattern suggests that vulnerable allies, rather than change their foreign policy preferences, may try to create institutional structures that entrench their close relationship with the sender, but impede the sender's ability to coerce at will. Adversaries, anticipating frequent conflict, will look for institutional structures that exclude the sender and blunt the threat of economic coercion.

Second, it would appear that the high-water mark of economic coercion in the former Soviet Union has passed. As the NIS have encouraged trade and investment with the rest of the world, Russia's ability to use economic pressure has declined. At the same time, Moscow has recognized that the gains from NIS concessions have come at the price of turning the CIS into a moribund institution. In the first half of 1998, Russia's rhetoric indicated that it preferred to see a functioning CIS than continue to employ its economic power at will.

7 Evaluating the evidence

Introduction

Chapter 6 chronicled Russia's coercive interactions with the fourteen NIS during their first five years of independence. The case histories reveal thirty-nine distinct attempts to use coercion to extract concessions. This chapter evaluates how well the conflict expectations model predicts the variation in the attempts and outcomes of economic coercion.

Multivariate statistical analysis of these results would be incomplete. A sample of thirty-nine observations is a small one to rely only on statistical inference. Furthermore, the results allow for an alternative methodology. Statistical inference assumes that explanatory variables have mutually independent effects on the dependent variable. This overlooks the possibility that different combinations of these variables affect the outcome. For example, the statistical evidence in chapter 4 shows that the associated threat of military force or covert action, by itself, is not a significant factor affecting coercion outcomes. However, it may be a necessary part of a more complex causal pathway; if the target state is small and vulnerable to domestic discord, the threat of force may be a critical variable. In a world of complex causation, with a small set of observations, statistical inference is limited in its ability to control for interaction effects. For this, more supple techniques are needed. This chapter will use descriptive statistics and Boolean analysis to analyze Russian economic coercion.

Table 7.1. *Coding NIS concessions*

Issue area	Significant concession	Moderate concession	Minor concession
Basing rights	Exclusive control over military bases	Partial control over military bases	Partial and temporary control over military bases
Soviet assets	Russian control with no specific compensation	Russian control with compensation	Partial Russian control
Treaty memberships	Member of CIS Collective Security Treaty	Member of CIS	Signed but not ratified CIS membership
Treatment of ethnic Russians	Dual citizenship	Special rights for ethnic Russians and Russian citizens	Special rights for ethnic Russians
Ownership stakes	Majority or plurality control	Control greater than other foreign investors	Some ownership stake

Coding the data

Most of Russia's demands fell under five categories: basing rights, claims on old Soviet assets, treaty membership, treatment of ethnic Russians, and ownership stakes in strategic industries. Table 7.1 shows how NIS concessions were coded along these demands.

In order to test the conflict expectations model against alternative hypotheses independent variables measuring conflict expectations, opportunity costs, the use or threat of military force, and the target regime's institutional stability need to be coded. Each coercion event generated from chapter 6 is coded on the following independent variables:

1. Did the target and sender expect to have repeated political conflicts? These codings were described in chapter 5. In fifteen of the thirty-nine cases, the target and sender were close allies.

2. Was the gap between the target's and sender's opportunity costs of deadlock significant? Russia's costs of coercion were minimal for most attempts, so the coding

corresponds to whether the target state faced significant or just moderate opportunity costs, which was described in chapter 5. In nineteen of the thirty-nine instances, the gap in costs was significant.

3. Did Russia threaten or use its military power during the sanctions episode? This variable was coded from the history of each case. The threat or use of force was observed in thirteen of the thirty-nine cases.

4. Was the target state vulnerable to domestic political instability? For the NIS, there are two ways in which the target regime could have been vulnerable. First, if the regime came to power through extra-legal means, it would be more vulnerable to another regime change. Azerbaijan, Georgia, and Tajikistan fall into this category. Second, if the regime faced significant regional or ethnic cleavages, it would be vulnerable to ethnic discord and a potential civil war. Kazakhstan, Moldova, and Ukraine fall into this category. The target regime was vulnerable in twenty-three of the thirty-nine observations.

Table 7.2 provides a list of all the coercion events, including all of the variable codings.

Predictions and outcomes

The conflict expectations model makes two predictions about the pattern of coercion attempts. First, the sender should be more reluctant to coerce allies than adversaries. In particular, there should be fewer cases of economic sanctions against allies that have relatively low opportunity costs of deadlock. Under these conditions, the coercion condition will be difficult to satisfy, and the sender should prefer the status quo to a deadlock of imposed sanctions. Second, the sender should be willing to incur greater costs when sanctioning adversaries. Heightened conflict expectations make the sender care more about relative gains and reputation effects; therefore, it will be prepared to suffer some pain if the sanctions hurt the target even more.

The overall pattern of Russian economic coercion provides robust support for the conflict expectations model. There were fifteen coercion attempts against allies, and twenty-four attempts against

Table 7.2. *Summary of coercion episodes in the former Soviet Union*

Target country	Demand	Low expectations of future conflict?	Large gap in costs of coercion?	Threat or use of military force?	Target regime unstable?	Magnitude of target's concession
Belarus	Return of nuclear weapons	Yes	Yes	No	No	Significant
Belarus	Basing rights	Yes	Yes	No	No	Significant
Belarus	Ownership of energy industries	Yes	Yes	No	No	Significant
Kazakhstan	Basing rights	Yes	Yes	No	Yes	Significant
Kazakhstan	Return of nuclear weapons	Yes	Yes	No	Yes	Significant
Kazakhstan	Treatment of Russian minority	Yes	Yes	No	Yes	Moderate
Kazakhstan	Stakes in oil/gas joint ventures	Yes	Yes	No	Yes	Moderate
Kazakhstan	Ownership of strategic industries	Yes	Yes	No	Yes	Significant
Armenia	Ceasefire with Azerbaijan	Yes	No	No	No	Significant
Kyrgyzstan	Ownership of strategic industries	Yes	No	No	No	Significant
Tajikistan	Ownership of strategic industries	Yes	No	No	Yes	Significant
Tajikistan	Ceasefire with opposition troops	Yes	No	Yes	Yes	Moderate
Turkmenistan	Dual citizenship	Yes	No	No	No	Significant
Turkmenistan	Basing rights	Yes	No	No	No	Significant
Turkmenistan	Stakes in oil/gas ventures	Yes	No	No	No	Moderate
Moldova	CIS membership	No	Yes	No	Yes	Moderate
Moldova	Autonomy for Transdniestr	No	Yes	Yes	Yes	Minor
Moldova	Ownership of strategic industries	No	Yes	No	Yes	Significant
Moldova	Basing rights	No	Yes	Yes	Yes	None

Azerbaijan	CIS membership	No	No	Yes	Yes	Significant
Azerbaijan	Basing rights	No	No	Yes	Yes	None
Azerbaijan	Stakes in oil/ gas ventures	No	No	Yes	Yes	Minor
Azerbaijan	Property rights of Caspian Sea	No	No	Yes	Yes	None
Azerbaijan	Routing of oil pipeline	No	No	No	Yes	Minor
Georgia	CIS membership	No	Yes	Yes	Yes	Significant
Georgia	Basing rights	No	Yes	Yes	Yes	Moderate
Lithuania	Ownership of strategic industries	No	No	No	No	None
Lithuania	Military transit to Kaliningrad	No	No	Yes	No	Moderate
Ukraine	Return of nuclear weapons	No	Yes	No	Yes	Minor
Ukraine	Renouncing claim to Soviet assets	No	Yes	No	Yes	Significant
Ukraine	Division of Black Sea fleet	No	Yes	No	Yes	Moderate
Ukraine	Basing rights	No	Yes	No	Yes	Minor
Ukraine	Ownership of strategic industries	No	Yes	No	Yes	Minor
Latvia	Basing rights	No	No	Yes	No	Minor
Latvia	Treatment of Russian minority	No	No	Yes	No	Minor
Latvia	Ownership of strategic industries	No	No	No	No	Minor
Estonia	Basing rights	No	No	Yes	No	Minor
Estonia	Treatment of Russian minority	No	No	Yes	No	Minor
Estonia	Ownership in strategic industries	No	No	No	No	Moderate

adversaries. Per country, Russia averaged 2.1 attempts for each ally, and 3.4 attempts for each adversary. Table 7.3, however, provides the strongest empirical support. As predicted, Russia was far more reluctant to threaten economic sanctions against allies that faced only moderate opportunity costs than any other category. The number of attempts per country is less than half the rate in the other three categories.

The pattern of Russia's opportunity costs of coercion further supports the model's predictions. One indicator of Russia's costs is the type of economic pressure used. Russia's levers can be divided into general trade sanctions, financial sanctions, and its use of pipelines to disrupt fuel shipments. Trade sanctions imposed some costs on the Russian economy; the other options were virtually costless. Russia should have been less willing to use trade sanctions against its allies. The case histories reveal that only two of the fifteen coercion attempts involving trade sanctions were directed against allies; thirteen of the fifteen were used against adversaries. Looking at the number of overall coercion events, Russia imposed moderate costs on itself in only 13 percent of its coercion attempts against allies. Against adversaries, the figure climbs to 54 percent. Chisquare tests reveal a positive relationship between conflict expectations and Russia's costs of coercion that is significant at the 5 percent level.

The conflict expectations model makes two predictions about the pattern of sanctions success. First, economic coercion should generate more substantial concessions when the gap in the opportunity costs of deadlock is greater. Second, the target will concede more if conflict expectations between the target and sender are low.

Tables 7.4 and 7.5 confirm these hypotheses. Target states allied with Russia granted significant concessions almost three-quarters of the time; for adversaries, the success rate falls to less than one-fifth. Opportunity costs also affected the rate of success, although the difference is not as substantial. Counting both significant and moderate concessions as successes, the importance of opportunity costs becomes more apparent. Target states with a large gap in opportunity costs agreed to significant or moderate concessions 73.7 percent of the time; the rate drops to 50.0 percent for target states with only moderate costs of coercion. The difference in success rates between allies and adversaries remains robust. Chi square tests attest to the statistical significance of these results. The conflict expectations variable was found to be positively correlated with a moderate or

Table 7.3. *The pattern of Russia's coercion attempts*

	Low expectations of future conflict	High expectations of future conflict
Large opportunity costs of coercion	*8 coercion attempts* 2 countries in category = 4.0 attempts per country	*11 coercion attempts* 3 countries in category = 3.7 attempts per country
Moderate opportunity costs of coercion	*7 coercion attempts* 5 countries in category = 1.4 attempts per country	*13 coercion attempts* 4 countries in category = 3.3 attempts per country

Table 7.4. *The pattern of significant concessions from the NIS*

	Low expectations of future conflict	High expectations of future conflict	Success rate for significant concessions
Large gap in opportunity costs of coercion	6 significant concessions 2 moderate concessions	3 significant concessions 3 moderate concessions 4 minor concessions 1 coercion failure	9/19 = 47.4%
Moderate gap in opportunity costs of coercion	5 significant concessions 2 moderate concessions	1 significant concession 2 moderate concessions 7 minor concessions 3 coercion failures	6/20 = 30.0%
Success rate for significant concessions	11/15 = 73.3%	4/24 = 16.7%	15/39 = 38.5%

significant concession and significant at the 1 percent level. The measure of opportunity costs was found to be positively correlated with a moderate or significant concession and significant at the 10 percent level. The aggregate figures clearly support the conflict expectations model.

In sharp contrast to the empirical support for the conflict expectations model, neither of the alternative explanations would appear to have an independent affect on the sanctions outcomes. Russia extracted significant or moderate concessions from politically weak

Table 7.5. *The pattern of significant and moderate concessions from the NIS*

	Low expectations of future conflict	High expectations of future conflict	Success rate for significant concessions
Large gap in opportunity costs of coercion	6 significant concessions 2 moderate concessions	3 significant concessions 3 moderate concessions 4 minor concessions 1 coercion failure	14/19 = 73.7%
Moderate gap in opportunity costs of coercion	5 significant concessions 2 moderate concessions	1 significant concession 2 moderate concessions 7 minor concessions 3 coercion failures	10/20 = 50.0%
Success rate for significant or moderate concessions	15/15 = 100%	9/24 = 37.5%	24/39 = 61.5%

target regimes 53.3 percent of the time; its success rate was 62.5 percent with target states that had strong and stable regimes. The use or threat of military power had a negative effect on sanctions success. When military power was threatened or exercised, Russia succeeded only 35.7 percent of the time; when economic statecraft was the sole coercive mechanism, the success rate was 80.0 percent. Chi square tests affirm the absence of any significant and positive correlation between these causes and a moderate or significant concession. Indeed, these tests reveal that the threat or use of military force is *negatively* correlated with a successful outcome and significant at the 1 percent level. The aggregate data suggests that Russia was better off when it refrained from using its military power.

Finally, Table 7.6 shows the results from an ordered probit regression for all of the coercion events.[1] These results support the other findings in this section. The only statistically significant variable in the regression is the expectations of future conflict. When conflict expectations are present, the magnitude of concessions made to Russia decreases. As predicted, the opportunity cost measure is positively

---

[1] The dependent variable was coded as significant = 3; moderate = 2; minor = 1; failure = 0.

Table 7.6. *The statistical determinants of NIS concessions*

Independent variable	Estimated coefficient	*t*-statistic
Absence of conflict expectations	1.709	3.531**
Cost differential	0.758	1.483
Threat or use of force	−0.280	−0.630
Instability of target regime	−0.433	−0.870
Log likelihood	−38.94	
Number of observations	39	

Note: ** Significant at 1%.

correlated with a successful outcome. It falls short of statistical significance, but performs better than the set of alternative explanatory variables. Neither the stability of the target regime nor the threat or use of force trends in the predicted direction, and more importantly, neither variable comes close to statistical significance.

A Boolean analysis

Although the overall support for the conflict expectations model is encouraging, the case histories show that the alternative explanations helped to determine some of the outcomes. In certain instances, Russia used military action to help secure acquiescence to economic pressure. In other situations, target regimes were as concerned about their domestic stability as they were with the foreign policy implications of noncompliance. In these situations, it is unclear what was driving the outcome; the result is overdetermined. It is possible that while an absence of conflict expectations is the primary mechanism for economic coercion to generate concessions, there are other causes. As a further test of the model's predictive power, the Boolean method of comparative analysis is used to document the effect of different combinations of independent variables.

The Boolean approach to determining causality is based upon the premise that outcomes have multiple causal mechanisms. The problem with a statistical approach is that it assumes that causality is additive; variable x_1 explains 5 percent of the variance, variable x_2 explains 10 percent, etc. A truly comparative method must take into account the possibility that the interaction of different independent variables determine the outcome. For example, while military statecraft and target regime instability do not appear to independently influence the outcome, the combination of the two causes may generate significant concessions. Regression techniques are limited in their ability to observe these interaction effects; just four independent variables can produce eleven different linear interaction terms. The advantage of Boolean analysis is that it can test all possible causal combinations and eliminate extraneous variables. It determines whether conditions are necessary, sufficient, or neither.

Until now, I have presented the conflict expectations, signaling, and domestic politics approaches as competing explanations of economic coercion. It is possible, however, that each of these approaches is neither a necessary nor a sufficient condition for generating concessions. These approaches may be part of a larger causal mechanism. The Boolean approach permits such a comparison of causal combinations. This is a more stringent test of the model presented here. If there are additional necessary or sufficient conditions for economic coercion to generate concessions, then it suggests that the conflict expectations model's explanatory power is more circumscribed than the previous chapters suggest.

The Boolean approach sets up a "truth table" that includes all possible combinations of the independent variables. It then lists all cases where the independent variables take those combinations of values and the number of instances where the coercion episode is judged successful, i.e. if the target made significant or moderate concessions. Set theory and DeMorgan's law eliminate explanatory factors as irrelevant when neither their presence nor their absence affects the outcome.

For example, consider two possible explanations for the creation of international regimes: the presence of a hegemon, and the presence of a unifying ideology. If international regimes are created when a hegemon exists and an ideology exists, but also when a hegemon exists and an ideology does not exist, then the latter variable has no causal effect and can be eliminated. In Boolean algebra, if A = the presence of a hegemon, a = the absence of a hegemon, and B and b represent similar values for ideology, then combination Ab represents a situation where a hegemon is present but an ideology is not. In this example, institutions are caused by $Ab + AB$. A is present for all the values of the second cause. Using DeMorgan's law, $Ab + AB$ can be reduced to just (A).

Table 7.7 sets out the truth table for significant concessions. The Boolean approach is not concerned with the frequency of each

Table 7.7. *Boolean truth table for significant concessions*

A Absence of conflict expectations	B Significant difference in opportunity costs	C Presence of military threat	D Target regime vulnerable to overthrow	Number of attempts	Number of significant concessions
no	no	no	no	3	0
no	no	no	yes	1	0
no	no	yes	no	5	0
no	no	yes	yes	4	1
no	yes	no	no	0	–
no	yes	no	yes	7	2
no	yes	yes	no	0	–
no	yes	yes	yes	4	1
yes	**no**	**no**	**no**	5	4
yes	**no**	**no**	**yes**	1	1
yes	no	yes	no	0	–
yes	no	yes	yes	1	0
yes	**yes**	**no**	**no**	3	3
yes	**yes**	**no**	**yes**	5	3
yes	yes	yes	no	0	–
yes	yes	yes	yes	0	–

combination, but rather the likelihood that such a combination of variables will produce a success. If a majority of the observed events in a category produce success, then that combination of independent variables represents a causal mechanism. There is a distinct gap in success rates between the four highlighted causal combinations and the other categories.[2]

Let A = the absence of conflict expectations, B = the presence of a significant gap in opportunity costs, C = the articulation of a military threat or military action in addition to economic sanctions, and D = the presence of instability within the target regime. The lower-case letters represent the opposite conditions: a = the presence of conflict expectations, b = the absence of a significant gap in opportunity costs, c = the absence of military coercion, and d = the presence of a stable

---

[2] Some other combinations produce no observations and are not classified as possible causal mechanisms. The lack of their appearance suggests that under such conditions, coercion is not likely to be attempted. Economic coercion cannot succeed if it is not considered, so logically it should not be included as a causal combination. See Ragin (1987), chapter 7 for further discussion.

target regime. Using Boolean algebra, one gets the following causality equation:

$$Abcd + AbcD + ABcd + ABcD = \text{significant concessions.} \quad (7.1)$$

Using DeMorgan's law, equation 5.1 can be simplified to:

$$Abc + ABc + Acd + AcD = \text{significant concessions.} \quad (7.2)$$

Reducing further:

$$Ac = \text{significant concessions.} \quad (7.3)$$

This causal combination is both necessary and sufficient for economic sanctions to produce significant concessions. Equation 7.3 reveals two interesting facts. First, contrary to previous claims in the literature, neither the threat of military force nor the absence of domestic political costs is a necessary or sufficient condition for economic coercion to succeed. Second, if the target is a close ally and the sender does not threaten military force, then economic coercion will generate significant concessions.

This result provides strong support for the conflict expectations model. The only possible causal combination for sanctions success is if the target is an ally and the sender does not threaten military force. The absence of conflict expectations is thus a necessary condition for economic coercion to extract significant concessions. Explanatory factors outside the conflict expectations logic, such as the target's domestic political situation, or the use of more violent measures, are either irrelevant or counterproductive for generating significant political concessions. This result buttresses the statistical findings and confirms that the conflict expectations model is not a stalking horse for other explanations.

With success defined as only a significant concession, the conflict expectations model performs as predicted. If the definition of success is widened to include moderate concessions as well, then the model would predict a success even with the presence of conflict expectations, provided the gap in opportunity costs is high as well. In Boolean terms, one would expect $(A + aB)$ to lead to a successful outcome. Using this expanded criterion, one gets the truth table shown in table 7.8. Seven categories clearly led to a successful outcome. This leads to the following causality equation:

$$aBcD + aBCD + Abcd + AbcD + ABcd + AbCD + ABcD = \text{successful coercion.} \quad (7.4)$$

Table 7.8. *Boolean truth table for significant and moderate concessions*

A Absence of conflict expectations	B Significant difference in opportunity costs	C Presence of military threat	D Target regime vulnerable to overthrow	Number of attempts	Number of significant or moderate concessions
no	no	no	no	3	1
no	no	no	yes	1	0
no	no	yes	no	5	1
no	no	yes	yes	4	1
no	yes	no	no	0	–
no	**yes**	**no**	**yes**	7	**5**
no	yes	yes	no	0	–
no	**yes**	**yes**	**yes**	4	**2**
yes	**no**	**no**	**no**	5	**5**
yes	**no**	**no**	**yes**	1	**1**
yes	no	yes	no	0	–
yes	**no**	**yes**	**no**	1	**1**
yes	**yes**	**no**	**no**	3	**3**
yes	**yes**	**no**	**yes**	5	**5**
yes	yes	yes	no	0	–
yes	yes	yes	yes	0	–

Simplifying:

$$Ac + AbD + aBD + BcD = \text{successful coercion},\qquad (7.5)$$

which can also be expressed as:

$$A(c + bD) + BD(a + c) = \text{successful coercion}.\qquad (7.6)$$

The combinations in equation 7.6 are responsible for 88 percent of the successful outcomes in Table 7.8. Equation 7.6 also supports the conflict expectations model. In order for economic coercion to generate significant or moderate concessions, there must be either an absence of conflict expectations or a significant gap in opportunity costs. In other words, the conflict expectations model generates the necessary conditions for a successful coercion episode.

The model does not, however, generate sufficient conditions. If conflict expectations are absent, either the target regime must be unstable, or the sender cannot threaten military force for coercion to generate at least moderate concessions. If conflict expectations are present, then in addition to a significant gap in opportunity costs, the target regime must suffer from institutional weakness for coercion to be successful.[3] The Boolean approach shows that the conflict expectations approach is a necessary part of explaining economic coercion, but for a subset of the cases, the target country's domestic situation must also be taken into account.

While these results buttress the statistical results presented in chapter 4, a caveat is in order. First, the use of Boolean algebra requires that all variables be coded as binary. Each variable can only have high and low values. This is troublesome in measuring both alignment and whether the event should be judged a success. Some countries are clearly allies or adversaries. A number of states, however, hold intermediate positions that are more difficult to categorize. The same is true of the outcome. In several cases, the target made some concessions, but failed to meet all of Russia's demands. It is difficult to categorize these cases. The binary approach acts as a serious constraint on a model that permits a more diverse variation of data.

Second, this approach ignores the frequency of cases in arriving at its conclusions. This can cause the end result to be highly contingent on one or two deviant cases, and underemphasize those causal mechanisms responsible for the lion's share of positive outcomes.

These criticisms are by no means exhaustive, but merely offered as evidence of the problematic nature of the Boolean method. Ragin's comparative approach offers further evidence supporting the model presented here. For economic sanctions to produce significant concessions, the absence of conflict expectations is a necessary condition. If the target–sender relationship is adversarial, there must be a large gap

---

[3] I do not focus on the other conditions specified in equation 7.6 because one could argue that it should be simplified to $A(c + D) + BD$ = successful coercion. The reason equation 7.6 is more complex is that there were no sanctions attempts in the category $ABCD$ (absence of conflict expectations, large gap in opportunity costs, threat of military force, politically unstable target regime). This is not surprising; in the absence of conflict expectations, the presence of a large gap in opportunity costs and a politically vulnerable target regime, economic coercion should succeed. There would be no reason for the sender country to incur the costs of a military threat as well. All of the explanations for economic coercion would assume a successful episode in that situation. Assuming that such an attempt would in all likelihood succeed, the revised causality equation would be:

$aBcD + aBCD + Abcd + AbcD + AbCD + ABcd + ABcD + ABCD$ = successful coercion;

$Abc + Acd + AbD + AcD + ABc + ABD + ACD + aBD + BcD + BCD$ = successful coercion;

$A(c + D) + BD$ = successful coercion. $\qquad$ (7.6′)

in opportunity costs for sanctions to generate significant or moderate concessions.

Some final observations

The conflict expectations model receives strong support from the cases of Russian economic coercion. Consistent with the coercion condition, Russia coerced its adversaries more frequently than its allies, and it showed the greatest constraint in coercing allies that faced only moderate costs of coercion. It was also willing to incur greater costs in sanctioning adversaries. Consistent with the concession function, Russia reaped greater concessions when conflict expectations were absent with the target, or when the gap in opportunity costs was sizeable.

Boolean analysis was performed to see what combination of causes would lead to a successful outcome. It was shown that the absence of conflict expectations is a necessary condition for the sender to extract significant concessions. The presence of a military threat or domestic instability within the target country are neither necessary nor sufficient conditions. When the definition of success is widened, it was shown that in the presence of conflict expectations, there must be a significant gap in opportunity costs for sanctions to lead to a successful outcome.

The performance of the alternative explanations in the Boolean analysis was mixed. Neither the target regime's domestic stability nor the sender's willingness to use stronger measures independently affected the outcome in the expected way. The use of other coercive policies such as the threat of military force or covert action was found to backfire; significant concessions are possible only if no companion policies are used. The presence of domestic instability within the target country was more potent. In the statistical analysis, it had no significant effect. In the Boolean analysis, it was found to be a necessary condition for moderate concessions if the target and sender were adversaries. Thus, the Boolean analysis confirms the importance of the conflict expectations model, but it also suggests that in certain cases the domestic politics of the target country helps to determine the outcome.

One final observation: there is a clear connection between conflict expectations and public diplomacy. Those countries more closely allied to Russia were not only willing to concede more, but they conceded with less of a fight. For example, Russia pressured both

Ukraine and Belarus on the issue of nuclear weapons. In 1992, Belarus indicated mild discontent with the arrangement, but quickly agreed to Moscow's terms. By contrast, Ukraine resisted Russia's proposal for two more years, resisted overt attempts at economic coercion, and conceded only after Russia agreed to additional economic inducements. Moscow's coercion of Ukraine was far more noticeable because Kiev was willing to cry foul in public.[4] Allies will concede more and complain less.

This difference between the behavior of allies and adversaries in a coercion attempt suggests why previous studies of economic sanctions suffer from sample bias. Without clear process-tracing to divine target country preferences before facing the threat of coercion, it is difficult to observe the act of concession. Even when it is observed, it is frequently thrown in with other events of cooperative behavior. For example, Armenia, Kyrgyzstan, and Belarus all cooperated with Russia on a number of issue-areas, including defense policy and the treatment of ethnic Russians. It would be easy to include episodes of Russian coercion as examples of cooperative behavior, because the target countries changed their positions soon after Moscow implied that it would employ economic sanctions. Coercion episodes involving allies are less likely to be noticed than episodes involving adversaries, because adversaries are more likely to draw out the event to the point where it captures the attention of both the media and the scholarly community.[5]

This phenomenon also helps to explain why the existing sanctions literature argues that economic statecraft is only effective under special circumstances. As noted in chapter 1, the alternative set of explanations focuses on the more celebrated cases of coercion. For example, among the instances of Russian economic coercion, the cases that attracted the most attention were Russia's use of economic and

---

[4] As somewhat unscientific evidence of this, a Lexis/Nexis search reveals that between January 1, 1992 and July 1, 1996 the *New York Times* ran 113 articles that mentioned "Belarus", "Russia" and "nuclear weapons." It ran 274 articles during the same time period that mentioned "Ukraine", "Russia" and "nuclear weapons." If you subtract the articles common to both groups, the ratio becomes 2 articles on Belarus and 163 on Ukraine.

[5] This parallels McCubbins and Schwartz's (1984) metaphors of police patrols and fire alarms in Congressional oversight committees. In the international community, a coercion episode involving adversaries is more likely to be noticed, like a fire alarm. Coercion attempts between allies are not as likely to turn heads, particularly if the ally acquiesces quickly. Only an active "police patrol" can ferret out these episodes.

military pressure against Azerbaijan, Georgia, and Moldova. They garnered the most press attention, and were believed to be important for policy analysis. However, these cases are not a representative sample. They represent situations where the protagonists anticipated frequent conflicts and were therefore extremely concerned about relative gains and reputation. The model presented here predicts these cases should produce the fewest concessions. A research project focusing only on these cases would naturally conclude that economic statecraft was of limited use.

III   Choosing between carrots and sticks

8 Economic statecraft and nuclear proliferation on the Korean peninsula

Carrots and sticks

The conflict expectations model outperforms the existing theories of economic sanctions. This has been shown in a survey of previous empirical studies, new statistical tests, and Boolean analysis. Each of the tests has provided firm support for the model. To determine the causal mechanisms of a coercion attempt, a structured, focused comparison of case studies is needed. Case studies complement the previous analysis in two ways. First, cases permit a more thorough evaluation of different explanations. Statistical results can be spurious; a Boolean approach straightjackets the data into a world of absolute dichotomy. To determine whether the predicted independent variable actually *causes* the outcomes, it is necessary to trace the actor's decision-making process, and compare the conflict expectations approach with the possible alternatives. Second, cases provide theory illustration. Regardless of how many equations or regressions are used to demonstrate a hypothesis, there is always the need to understand the nuts and bolts of a model through case studies. To talk about conflict expectations and opportunity costs in the abstract is one thing; observing their effect in a narrative allows readers to see the theory through example.

This chapter will use congruence and process-tracing procedures to confirm the model's empirical support, and also to determine if the model can explain how the sender chooses among policy options. Until now, I have focused primarily on the dynamics of economic coercion and treated the other options in the policy-maker's tool kit with benign neglect. This does not obviate the model's explanatory power. Nevertheless, models created in a vacuum are only a useful first step. To increase explanatory power, they must be able to incorporate choices observed in the real world. For this book's purposes, this means explaining how states consider the threat of economic coercion as compared to other policy tools, such as economic inducements or military compellence.

The conflict expectations model predicts that between adversaries, conflict expectations make it difficult for either carrots or sticks to work. Sanctions are of limited use because of the target's concern for relative gains and reputation. This is particularly true if the demand cannot be compromised. If the sender and target disagree over an indivisible issue, then the sender may find that although economic coercion could produce a total concession with an allied target, it could not produce a similar concession from an adversary. In situations where demands have an all-or-nothing quality, economic coercion can succeed with allies but fail with adversaries. Carrots are rarely used because of the sender's concern about relative gains and reputation. Between adversaries, economic inducements are predicted only if very stringent conditions are satisfied. The demand must be non-negotiable, the bribe must be very lucrative for the target, and the bribe must be nearly costless for the sender.

These predictions are tested against US efforts to halt nuclear proliferation on the Korean peninsula. The United States used economic coercion to stop South Korea from going nuclear in 1975. In freezing North Korea's nuclear program in 1994, Washington considered both economic sanctions and military compellence, but ultimately decided to use financial inducements. These cases were selected because the outcomes vary, while many candidate explanatory variables do not. The United States made the same demand of both countries. The United States dwarfed both states by all conventional measures of aggregate power. There were minimal differences in culture between the two target states. If opportunity costs and regime stability were any guide, North Korea should have been more vulnerable to economic pressure. As will be shown, if sanctions had been implemented, North Korea would have incurred the greater costs, its elite would have suffered more, and its regime would have been more vulnerable to domestic instability.

Why did the United States choose to use the carrot with its enemy and the stick with its ally? The cases will show that with South Korea, the threat of economic coercion was the first, best and most potent strategy for the United States. The close alignment between

South Korea and the United States, combined with the costs of disrupting Seoul's nuclear energy program, proved to be sufficient leverage for Washington to extract a significant concession. In the North Korean case, although the United States first considered economic coercion, it was clear that the target's leadership viewed the situation in strictly conflictual terms. It was unwilling to make major concessions, despite the serious costs of a stalemate, because it feared the United States would exploit them in future interactions. Economic coercion by itself was capable of producing minor concessions, but the United States could not compromise in its demands because of the strong norm of nonproliferation and the need to renew the Nuclear Non-Proliferation Treaty. Sanctions were insufficient to produce such a significant concession. The United States had to choose between a military option or an economic inducement. Given the costs associated with all-out conflict, and the cost-free nature of the carrot, it chose the latter.

The preferred methodological approach to case studies in international relations is process-tracing. Alexander George and Timothy McKeown define process-tracing as consisting of "both an attempt to reconstruct actors' definitions of the situation and an attempt to develop a theory of action."[1] The strength of this procedure is its emphasis on analyzing the series of decisions within an event, and identifying the proximate causes behind each decision. This is extremely difficult to do for these cases, however. There remains a great deal of secrecy surrounding these events, and most of the relevant documents are classified. With limited testimony from the participants, how is it possible to process-trace the event?

Where process-tracing is impossible due to a lack of information, congruence procedures will be used.[2] While there may be little direct evidence of what happened in the negotiations, there is a great deal of information about the decision-making environment. The information on US–Korean relations, nuclear proliferation, and US foreign policy for both cases is considerable. Logical inference, combined with knowledge of the decision-making environment, can generate predictions and counterfactuals about what should and should not happen if a proximate cause is true. In addition to the actual outcome, ancillary effects can also be predicted. The validity of each proximate

---

[1] George and McKeown (1985), p. 35.
[2] For more on congruence procedures, see van Evera (1996), pp. 30–5.

cause can be tested by examining the difference between the predicted and actual observations. That is how the case studies will proceed. Each case maximizes the use of direct evidence, while paying close attention to any information that would support or discredit a proximate cause.

This chapter starts with discussing why the United States was able to economically coerce South Korea into dismantling its nuclear weapons program. It then analyzes why the United States rejected both economic and military coercion in favor of economic induce-ments to persuade North Korea to relinquish its weapons program.

The United States and South Korea's nuclear program

The chronology

The Republic of Korea (ROK) decided to start a nuclear weapons program following the articulation of the Nixon doctrine in July 1969. The doctrine stated that the United States would honor all treaty commitments and secure its vital interests, but, "In cases involving other types of aggression, the United States would furnish military and economic assistance when requested and appropriate, but nations directly threatened should assume primary responsibility for their own defense."[3] Given the increasing unpopularity of basing American troops abroad, South Korea seemed an ideal target for the new doctrine's application. In 1970, the United States had 63,000 troops stationed there, armed with approximately 600 tactical nuclear weapons to deter a North Korean invasion. President Nixon proposed to withdraw a third of the troops – one division – while simultane-ously increasing American aid to bolster the ROK military.

The South Korean reaction was far from sanguine. The Prime Minister threatened to resign, explaining, "We are not against the Nixon Doctrine in principle, but if North Korean (leader) Kim Il Sung miscalculates, the South Korean people will wonder if America will abandon its security treaty or come to our defense."[4] After intense negotiations, both countries agreed to a withdrawal of the division, a

---

[3] Quoted in Back (1988), p. 111. For more on South Korea's anxieties about US security assurances, see also Cha (1999), chapter 4.

[4] Ibid., p. 123.

redeployment of US troops away from the demilitarized zone, and a US appropriation of $1.5 billion for military aid.

ROK President Park Chung Hee made the decision that his country needed a nuclear deterrent after the Nixon doctrine was announced.[5] In 1970, he set up the Weapons Exploitation Committee, which was, in the words of a US House investigation committee, "a covert, ad-hoc government committee, responsible to the Blue House (the South Korean White House) for weapons procurement and production."[6] In the early 1970s this committee voted unanimously to develop nuclear weapons.

There are three prerequisites for a viable nuclear program: a sufficient level of technical knowledge, a delivery vehicle, such as a missile, and a suitable amount of fissile plutonium or highly enriched uranium. Seoul actively pursued all three requirements in the early 1970s. It was relatively successful in acquiring both the knowledge and the missile technology. In addition to training its own personnel, the ROK government made a discrete effort to recruit ethnic Koreans in the United States with nuclear, chemical, or engineering expertise. By 1976, South Korea had a sufficient cadre of trained personnel.[7] Seoul entered negotiations with Israel in 1972 to purchase its Gabriel surface-to-surface missile. The United States, after trying to dissuade the South Koreans, eventually assisted them in the development of a Nike-Hercules variant. Seoul's first successful missile test came in September 1978.[8]

Acquiring the fissile material proved more difficult. One way to procure it was to convert the radioactive waste products from a civilian nuclear reactor. South Korea already had an active nuclear energy program. At the time, Westinghouse was building a light-water reactor, scheduled for completion in 1978. Although the nuclear fuel for the plant was not weapons-grade, the radioactive waste generated by the reactor contained weapons-grade plutonium. In order to extract it from the waste, however, a recprocessing facility was necessary. In 1972, the South Koreans initiated negotiations with

---

[5] See Selig Harrison's op-ed article, "A yen for the Bomb?" *Washington Post*, October 31, 1993, p. C1. Oberdorfer (1997, p. 68) argues that a North Korean capture of a ROK patrol boat at the same time the Nixon doctrine was articulated spurred Park's decision.
[6] US House (1978), p. 80. The Blue House is the South Korean equivalent of the White House.
[7] See Oberdorfer (1997), p. 69, Meyer (1984), and Reiss (1988), p. 89.
[8] US House (1978), p. 79.

the French government for the purchase of such a plant. Negotiations were also initiated with Belgium to purchase a mixed-oxide reprocessing laboratory.

The United States paid little attention to these efforts until India announced its peaceful nuclear explosion in April 1974. India had created its fissile material by using its Canadian research reactor and reprocessing plant. The US intelligence community looked at other states to see if they were taking similar steps. South Korea's pattern of acquisitions fitted the Indian approach. The last piece of technology was the reprocessing plant. One arms control analyst notes:

> The reprocessing plant potentially would have given them fissionable material for weapons, but it was practically the last thing on the list of things they needed, from special machine tools to the non-nuclear component of weapons. They were running all over the world picking up material and equipment. It was enough to make everybody extremely suspicious.[9]

The South Korean motivation for the weapons had not diminished. As noted earlier, President Park decided on the weapon program because of a weakening US commitment to Seoul's defense. By 1975, Saigon had fallen, the United States had withdrawn from its bases in Thailand, and the aid program to Seoul was behind schedule.

Belgium cut off negotiations following the Indian explosion, but negotiations with France continued. The United States reacted to the ROK–French negotiations by placing pressure on both sides to cancel any transfer. In March, the US ambassador to Korea told his French colleague in Seoul that, "in effect ... the United States has no doubts that the Koreans have in mind putting to ulterior military ends what they can make use of, such as plutonium." The French rebuffed the American request, stating that the decision to cancel the agreement was up to South Korea. The same month, US Secretary of State Henry Kissinger reportedly threatened to cancel the US security commitment to Korea if the ROK weapons program continued.[10]

ROK reassurances to the US government temporarily defused the issue. A few months later, however, President Park commented publicly and explicitly about the need for a nuclear deterrent. In

[9] Quoted in Robert Gillette, "US squelched apparent South Korea A-bomb drive," *Los Angeles Times*, November 4, 1978, p. 1.
[10] Hayes (1990), p. 204. On Kissinger's threat, see also Harrison, "A yen for the bomb."

April, he said, "We maintain a defense alliance with the US. However we could encounter some terrible problems if we base our future solely on our confidence in this alliance." In a June 1975 interview, Park said, "If the US nuclear umbrella were removed, we have to start developing our own nuclear weapons capability."[11] By the summer of 1975, the deal with France had been signed. Although the contract included a safeguards agreement with the International Atomic Energy Agency (IAEA), the United States doubted South Korea's commitment to it. With the reprocessing plant, Seoul would have had all of the ingredients for nuclear weapons on its soil.

By the fall, the United States was showing an increased concern about proliferation. Kissinger, in a September address to the United Nations, said: "The greatest single danger of unrestrained nuclear proliferation resides in the spread under national control of reprocessing facilities for the atomic materials in nuclear power plants."[12] The Americans and South Koreans had consultations about the issue from November 1975 to January 1976. During the week of January 23, Acting Assistant Secretary of State for Oceans, Environment and Scientific affairs Myron Kratzer met with South Korean officials to discuss nuclear energy matters.[13] At the end of the week, Kratzer testified before Congress that the ROK had canceled plans to purchase the reprocessing plant. He refused to provide any additional information on the about-face. The South Koreans were also extremely reticent about the decision. One ROK diplomat commented, "The United States made the strongest possible representations to the Korean and French governments."[14] Following this decision, the South Koreans abandoned their nuclear weapons program.

The direct evidence strongly suggests that the United States threatened to halt all trade and exchange involving Seoul's civilian nuclear energy program and military procurement if the reprocessing plant was not canceled. In December 1975, the US ambassador to South Korea cabled his superiors that he asked a senior ROK official, "whether Korea (is) prepared (to) jeopardize availability of best

---

[11] The first quotation is from Sano (1977), p. 377. The second is from J. P. Smith, "Glenn asks probe of Korea arms plan," *Washington Post*, November 4, 1978, p. A16.

[12] Quoted in "French nuclear spread," *New York Times* editorial, October 29, 1975, p. 40.

[13] See Ha (1983), appendix 3.

[14] Quoted in "Seoul officials say strong pressure forced cancellation of plans to purchase a French nuclear plant," *New York Times*, February 1, 1976, p. 11.

technology and largest financing capability which only US could offer, as well as vital partnership with US, not only in nuclear and scientific areas but in broad political and security areas."[15] Multiple press reports about the January 1976 reversal quoted anonymous officials saying that if the South Koreans had not acquiesced, the United States would have halted loans worth $275 million and loan guarantees worth $227 million from the Export–Import Bank. Washington also made it clear that it would withhold export licenses and block the purchase of a second Westinghouse reactor. In addition, the United States persuaded the Canadians to suspend their own reactor deal with Seoul unless the reprocessing plant was canceled.[16] Other US officials stated that negotiators also threatened the South Koreans with stopping $275 million annually in US military aid if the reprocessing plant went ahead as scheduled.[17]

The US reaction in March 1975 also suggests the importance of economic coercion in the dispute. The threat to disrupt the nuclear program had worked earlier in the year. In March 1975, Congress had frozen a $79 million loan and a $157 million loan guarantee to finance an additional Westinghouse plant unless the South Koreans ratified the Non-Proliferation Treaty. Although the ROK had signed the treaty in 1968, its Parliament had not debated it seven years hence. The delay was suspicious given that South Korea under Park Chung Hee was hardly a paragon of checks and balances; with opposition movements suppressed, ratification should have been pro forma. The president of the Export–Import Bank reiterated Congress's message. He informed the South Korean government in March that "The availability of a reprocessing facility in Korea could be considered to create a potential for nuclear proliferation which could become an impediment to our final approval of this loan."[18] After Congress made its threat, the South Korean Parliament promptly approved the

---

[15] Quoted in Oberdorfer (1997), p. 72.

[16] On the reports of economic coercion, see David Burnham, "South Korea drops plan to buy a nuclear plant from France," *New York Times*, January 29, 1976, p. A1; Don Oberdorfer, "South Korea cancels A-plant," *Washington Post*, January 30, 1976, p. A1; "Seoul officials say strong pressure forced cancellation of plans to purchase a French nuclear plant"; Gillette, "US squelched apparent South Korea A-Bomb drive." On the amounts of US aid to South Korea, see Long (1977), pp. 56–7.

[17] Leslie H. Gelb, "Nuclear proliferation and the sale of Arms," *New York Times*, August 11, 1976, p. 3; Gelb, "Conflict continues over US effort to halt spread of nuclear weapons," *New York Times*, August 24, 1976, p. 4.

[18] Hayes (1990), p. 204.

Non-Proliferation Treaty, and in June the House and Senate approved the financing.

Furthermore, economic sanctions would have found legitimacy in treaty. The accord between the two countries on nuclear matters restricted the Koreans from reprocessing any US-supplied uranium without Washington's permission. The agreement allowed the United States to revoke export licenses if the fuel was reprocessed, which gave it a clear legal mechanism to impose sanctions. The Ford administration made it clear to Congress in the fall of 1975 that it was willing to take such action if necessary.[19]

Following the ROK decision, analysts praised the threat of economic coercion as a useful tool for nonproliferation. The US Office of Technology Assessment wrote: "Recent American pressure upon South Korea to forgo acquisition of a reprocessing plant illustrates that sanctions can be effective, at least in a situation where the target state is highly vulnerable." Stephen Meyer comments: "The threat of an economic cutoff was particularly potent. By playing on the special dependence of South Korea, the United States was able to produce a rapid change in the incentives and disincentives perceived by the South Korean government." Albert Wohlstetter notes:

> The effectiveness of the levers at our disposal can be illustrated by the extreme sensitivity of various programs in the non-weapon states of the Third World (where the impending spread is now most threatening) to simple alterations in the terms of financing. Korea, for example, has drastically cut back its nuclear program in response to a slight hardening in Canadian and American financial terms.[20]

In this episode, it would seem, the threat of sanctions forced the South Koreans to acquiesce.

Why did economic coercion work?

Three factors explain why economic coercion succeeded: South Korea's high opportunity costs of deadlock, low opportunity costs of deadlock to the United States, and the absence of serious conflict expectations between the two countries.

South Korea's immediate costs of sanctions would have been the disruption of the loans and loan guarantees. This was the equivalent

---

[19] US Senate (1975), pp. 224–6.

[20] Office of Technology Assessment (1977), p. 219; Meyer (1984), p. 126; Wohlstetter (1976), p. 168.

of 3.4 percent of its gross national product in 1975, a considerable sum. This figure understates the true costs, however. To properly understand Seoul's opportunity costs of deadlock, it is necessary to comprehend the expected importance of nuclear power to the country in 1975, as well as the inability of the Korean nuclear program to substitute away from US suppliers.

As early as 1967, a ROK government commission had determined that the growth in energy demand would soon outstrip its indigenous coal supply. From 1967 to 1976 the demand for electric energy was expected to increase sixfold, and Seoul would be forced to increase oil imports by 50 percent in order to meet those needs. These estimates were overstated, but table 8.1 shows that Korea's dependence on imports did increase substantially. This increase imposed a serious drain on its hard currency reserves, and heightened the vulnerability of its economy to disruptions in the international oil market. The 1973 energy shock, for example, reduced ROK reserves to just two weeks of oil.[21] To reduce its oil dependence, the Council for the Promotion of Nuclear Power Generation decided in 1968 to order two medium-sized reactors. South Korean plans included an expansion of its nuclear sector to forty-five plants by the year 2000. As table 8.2 shows, nuclear power was expected to provide Korea with over 60 percent of its electricity by the end of the millennium.[22]

Given the structure of the international nuclear industry at the time, the South Koreans had little choice but to depend on the Americans for plant construction and fuel supply. Although the US monopoly on nuclear power technology was waning, it was still the dominant player when Seoul decided to buy its reactors. The US-designed light-water reactor was the most cost efficient, its technology the most proven. Not surprisingly, three of the four bids for constructing the ROK's first plant came from American firms. When the United States threatened sanctions in 1975, that plant was still under construction, and contracts had been signed with Westinghouse to build another reactor.

The purchase of the nuclear facilities also implied that the Koreans would have to rely almost exclusively on the United States for fuel. The Westinghouse plant was a light-water reactor, and could not use

---

[21] Reiss (1988), p. 89.

[22] Ha (1983), chapter 3. Such a figure did not come to pass. As of 1991, the South Koreans had nine nuclear reactors in operation producing 7,871 megawatts of electricity, less than half the amount estimated in 1976 (Hayes, 1990, p. 55).

Table 8.1. *ROK energy imports, 1960–75*

Year	Coal imports (thousand tons)	Petroleum imports (thousand tons of coal equivalent)	Percentage dependence on imported energy
1960	46	1,410	7.9
1961	372	1,549	10.1
1962	233	1,930	10.7
1963	204	2,157	11.0
1964	214	2,139	10.5
1965	151	2,827	12.5
1966	117	4,192	16.8
1967	114	7,014	25.3
1968	85	10,084	33.5
1969	118	13,689	40.5
1970	102	18,011	46.6
1971	72	21,263	50.8
1972	42	22,776	52.3
1973	801	26,718	54.9
1974	1083	26,993	55.1
1975	965	29,278	56.7

Source: Ha (1982), p. 234.

Table 8.2. *ROK electric-generation capacity, 1956–2000*

Year	Hydroelectric in megawatts (% of total)	Fossil fuel in megawatts (% of total)	Nuclear power in megawatts (% of total)
1956	114 (32.5)	237 (67.5)	
1961	143 (24.0)	224 (61.0)	
1966	215 (28.0)	554 (72.0)	
1971	340 (12.9)	2,288 (87.1)	
1976	710 (14.8)	4,100 (85.2)	
1981[1]	1,202 (12.0)	8,247 (82.1)	587 (5.8)
1986[1]	3,005 (14.7)	11,125 (54.1)	6,416 (31.2)
1991[1]	4,605 (12.9)	14,325 (39.9)	16,916 (47.2)
1996[1]	7,405 (13.3)	15,875 (28.4)	32,516 (58.3)
2000[1]	11,205 (14.1)	20,075 (25.3)	48,116 (60.6)

Note: [1] Estimated in 1976.
Source: Ha (1982), p. 235.

natural uranium. The reactor types required low-enriched uranium. In 1970, the United States manufactured 62.8 percent of the world's enriched uranium. Discounting the Soviet Union and China (unlikely suppliers to South Korea), the figure jumps to 95.6 percent.[23] By 1976, when the coercion attempt was made, the US share had declined to 81.5 percent, but its market power was significant enough to impose costs on the South Koreans if they had tried to purchase their fuel elsewhere. The threat to suspend all trade in nuclear materials would have completely devastated ROK plans for energy autonomy.

The contrast between the asset-specific nature of the nuclear industry and the more flexible market in missile technology is particularly illuminating. As noted in the chronology, when South Korea wanted to acquire ground-to-ground missiles, the United States refused to supply them and threatened to disrupt its military aid program. The Koreans were able to get the same technology from the Israelis. Washington, realizing that Seoul would not have to acquiesce, eventually provided the technology itself.[24] Because the missile technology was widely available, US export controls and limited sanctions were insufficient to prevent the South Koreans from acquiring what they wanted. The threat to disrupt the nuclear program was more potent, because Seoul was hard pressed to find a substitute that could absorb its expected demand.

If implemented, the economic costs to the United States of sanctions would have been mild. The specific US threat was to cut off a mixture of outright loans and loan guarantees. This does not mean that the United States benefited economically from a coercion strategy; if the threat had been carried out, the United States would have incurred costs in the form of lost sales to Westinghouse and several defense contractors. Although the overall amount of money involved ($502 million in nuclear sales, and $300 million in military contracts) was insignificant compared to US gross domestic product, it could have disrupted strategic sectors. Nevertheless, the nuclear industry was growing at a furious pace in the mid-1970s. In 1975 alone, nuclear power commitments expanded by 34 percent.[25] Westinghouse would have had little difficulty finding other customers. Overall US costs were minimal.

---

[23] Ha (1983).   [24] US House (1978), p. 79.
[25] US House (1975), pp. 390–1.

Finally, conflict expectations between South Korea and the United States were extremely low. The Park regime perceived no threat from the United States. In 1975 the Korean Foreign Minister described the 1954 Mutual Security Treaty as the "mainstay of the Republic of Korea's security," and stated, "The most important and effective deterrent against any possible recurrence of major conflict on the Korean Peninsula is the firm commitment of the United States to the security of South Korea."[26] After the coercion event, Seoul was unwilling to comment publicly about US pressure for fear of disrupting the alliance. The Koreans were concerned about the extent of the US commitment, but at no time did they consider balancing against the United States. Of the five states with interests in the region (the United States, the Soviet Union, China, Japan, North Korea) the United States represented the lowest perceived threat to ROK security.

The United States anticipated few conflicts with South Korea. This made it difficult for Washington to satisfy the coercion condition on other issues. By 1975, US administrations were consistently unwilling to threaten human rights sanctions against Seoul because of its authoritarian regime.[27] Only the proliferation issue sparked any concern for relative gains, and even that concern was mostly indirect. Kissinger, in a cable to the US embassy in Seoul, mentioned three US concerns: "Any Korean effort to establish nuclear capability would have ... major destabilizing effect in area"; second, North Korea and possibly Japan would have responded by acquiring their own weapons; third, "This impact will be complicated by fact that ROK nuclear weapon effort has been in part reflection of lessened ROKG confidence in US security commitment, and consequent desire on Park's part to reduce his military dependence on US."[28] Because their expectation of serious political conflict was minimal, there was little reason for either side to think of the dispute in relative terms.

Alternative explanations

One of the intriguing elements of this coercion episode is its relative secrecy. In his testimony, Kratzer provided few details about the negotiations. No other American or Korean official was willing to

---

[26] Quoted in Kim (1976), p. 19.

[27] Fox Butterfield, "US facing a dilemma in its Korea policy," *New York Times*, August 31, 1976, p. 6. See also chapter 3.

[28] Quoted in Oberdorfer (1997), p. 70.

make an attributed statement about the decision. The State Department refused to provide any further information to congressional committees despite repeated entreaties. This secrecy makes it easy to suggest a number of contending hypotheses. To determine the precise causal mechanism in this event, within-case analysis is necessary to see if there are other explanations for American or Korean actions.

There are three plausible alternatives to explain why the South Koreans backed down. First, the ROK leadership could have decided to delay their plans for weapons development and cave in temporarily to appease the Americans. Thus, economic coercion did not really succeed. Second, the United States may have persuaded France to cancel its contract with South Korea. So, international cooperation explains the successful attempt. Third, the US could have offered up carrots in the form of an extended nuclear umbrella, or increased aid to the South Korean military. It was the carrot that created the concession, not the stick. Each of these possibilities is considered in turn.

The coercion attempt was not really successful

One potential explanation is that South Korea decoupled its weapons program from its civilian energy program but covertly continued its weapons program. In 1975, the ROK plan was to develop an entire nuclear fuel cycle – an enrichment plant, reactors, and a reprocessing plant – within the country. There were other ways of acquiring the necessary plutonium or enriched uranium. If Seoul focused on the non-nuclear aspects of the weapons, such as the engineering and delivery components, and then covertly procured the fissile plutonium, it could have acquired weapons without threatening its civilian energy program. Washington would have had a more difficult time tracing this approach, since there would be no pattern of acquisition to trace. It would also have been the cost-effective approach; the reprocessing facility was never viable solely for the purpose of recycling nuclear fuel.[29]

There is some evidence to support this explanation. Just six months after the reprocessing plant was dropped, US officials, including the Secretary of Defense, voiced concerns about the Koreans restarting their program. The South Korean Foreign Minister threatened to play the nuclear card a number of times after the Carter administration considered withdrawing American troops from Korea. In May 1977,

---

[29] Weinstein and Komiya (1980), Ha (1983).

he commented that weapons might be developed, "if and when US tactical nuclear weapons have been withdrawn." A month later, he refined the conditions: "If nuclear weapons are required for national safety and the people's survival, or if under special conditions international treaties are not observed." In 1978, two research reports, from Koryo and Hanyang universities, recommended the development of a small-scale nuclear deterrent. That same year, ROK officials allegedly approached the French about the reprocessing plant again. Anonymous US officials maintained that Seoul tried to acquire heavy-water facilities until 1980.[30]

This causal explanation, in its purest form, is impossible to falsify. If the South Koreans succeeded in a covert effort to acquire plutonium, no one should have detected it. However, this explanation is still suspect. First, having nuclear weapons is useless if the information is completely private. Successful deterrence rests upon the premise that one's opponent knows the price of attacking. If Seoul tried to acquire weapons, it would be in the tricky position of wanting to covertly inform the North Koreans without tipping off the Americans. Such a delicate distribution of information would be difficult to sustain.[31]

Second, neither the United States nor the IAEA officially detected any serious ROK effort to develop nuclear weapons after 1976. The US congressional report that described the Weapons Exploitation Committee did not detect any new effort between 1975 and 1978, when the Foreign Minister made his statements.[32] The IAEA has conducted full-scope safeguard inspections of ROK nuclear facilities since 1975, and has not detected any violations. In 1985, the Canadians rebuffed a ROK proposal for a joint program involving the separation of weapons-grade plutonium, which could have indicated an effort to restart its program. Beyond that, nothing. Peter Hayes concludes, "there is no hard evidence that South Korea is welching on its 1975 bilateral agreement with the United States to forgo nuclear weapons."[33] Following the January 1976 decision, no non-proliferation analyst included the South Koreans as a potential nuclear power.[34]

---

[30] The two quotations in the paragraph are from Weinstein and Komiya (1980), p. 113. For US worries that Seoul would restart its program, see Gelb, "Nuclear proliferation and the sale of arms," and Hayes (1990), p. 205. On the Korean attempt to reopen negotiations with the French, see Oberdorfer (1997), pp. 73–4.

[31] See Yager (1980), pp. 55–7.   [32] US House (1978), p. 80.

[33] Hayes (1990), pp. 209–10.   [34] Spector (1985), p. 85.

Another flaw in this explanation is South Korea's reaction to the US decision to withdraw its tactical nuclear weapons in late 1991. Despite an easing of tensions elsewhere on the globe, the North Koreans were still extremely belligerent, and as will be seen later, developing their own nuclear weapons program. With the collapse of the Soviet Union, Seoul had its greatest opportunity to obtain the plutonium it needed through illicit means. Instead, the South Korean reaction was to propose to Pyongyang that the Korean peninsula be a nuclear-free zone. The ROK president, Roh Tae Woo, suggested an open inspection of nuclear facilities, including US military bases, to ensure that the North Koreans were not pursuing their own weapons program. Thus, if the South Koreans continued to pursue alternative nuclear plans, they had abandoned those plans by 1991.[35]

Finally, nothing in this alternative explanation contradicts the hypothesis of economic coercion being a causal mechanism in 1976. The specific American demand was to cancel the reprocessing plant agreement with France, which the South Koreans did. Clearly, Seoul's preferred option in 1976 was to manufacture the plutonium from its civilian reactors. By canceling the reprocessing plant, the Koreans were forced to eliminate their preferred choice of a domestic ability to produce plutonium. It is possible that after 1976 Seoul made covert attempts to acquire the fissile material, but one could argue that it was in response to a new threat, specifically Carter's troop withdrawal decision. Furthermore, it is equally possible that the United States used covert economic pressure in those later instances to block the South Koreans.

The United States succeeded because of international cooperation

The Indian nuclear test in 1974 alerted all of the states exporting nuclear technology to the dangers of developing states exploiting their civilian nuclear programs to develop nuclear weapons. This threat was serious enough to cause those countries to meet twice in London during 1975 to craft an agreed set of rules governing nuclear exports. It was during this time that the French and Koreans were finalizing the deal on the reprocessing plant. It is likely that the

[35] Don Oberdorfer, "US decides to withdraw A-arms from S. Korea," *Washington Post*, October 19, 1991, p. A1; Steven R. Weisman, "South Korea to keep out all atom arms," *New York Times*, November 9, 1991, p. 3.

United States pressured France at these meetings to cancel the contract. Some of the direct evidence supports this explanation. South Korean statements after the decision noted the strong pressure the United States placed on both South Korea *and* France. Kratzer, in his testimony, went out of his way to praise the French stance on nonproliferation.[36] Finally, in May 1976, French President Valéry Giscard d'Estaing stated on the television program *Meet the Press* that Paris had already decided not to sell the facility to South Korea.[37] If this is true, then the apparent success of US economic coercion would be a mirage; the South Koreans caved in only because they knew that France would not honor its contract.

This explanation, beyond the statement of d'Estaing, is weak on both evidence and on logic. First, the evidence. The French and Americans were split at the July meeting in London. The United States believed that export controls were the best policy to halt the spread of weapons. France took a different stand, arguing that legal commitments to obey International Atomic Energy Association safe-guards were sufficient. The French IAEA representative wrote of his country's position: "France remained opposed to any form of nuclear embargo aimed at putting pressure on the energy policy of a country which refuses to submit its full fuel cycle to safeguards."[38] Further-more, the timing is off. There is a six-month gap between the July meeting in London and Kratzer's announcement that South Korea had canceled its purchase. If the French actually behaved as d'Estaing suggested, then the cancelation should have been sooner. Indeed, in late October a *New York Times* editorial excoriated the US administration for *failing* to pressure France:

> The prolonged efforts of American officials to discourage France ... from their nuclear deals undoubtedly would have had a far better chance of success if Secretary Kissinger or President Ford had not over-pessimistically refused to engage their own personal prestige, and the full influence of the United States, for fear of a pointless crisis with major allies.[39]

It does seem clear that the London meeting in July persuaded the French to add the safeguards agreement to the reprocessing deal. But this move was consistent with its preferred policy of legal restraints.

[36] US Senate (1976), p. 419.   [37] Ha (1983), p. 181.
[38] Goldschmidt (1977), p. 80. It should be remembered that in 1976, France was not a signatory to the Non-Proliferation Treaty, although it had agreed to act as if it was.
[39] "French nuclear spread," *New York Times*, October 29, 1975, p. 40.

As noted earlier, the United States did not think that legal agreements were sufficient. In agreeing to the reprocessing deal, even with the safeguards agreement, the French failed to cooperate with the United States.

There is also Kratzer's testimony. In response to queries by the Senate committee, he refused to provide details to most of the questions about how the US succeeded in its diplomacy. His answer to a question about France's involvement, however, was without reticence:

> *Senator Glenn*: Was this terminated at the request of the South Koreans, are you free to say, or did the French call off this deal?
> *Mr. Kratzer*: The South Korean Government reached its own decision that the cancellation of this plant was in its best interests. It decided not to proceed."[40]

Background evidence also fails to lend much credibility to d'Estaing's claim. During the mid-1970s, France was engaged in a bitter commercial rivalry with the United States to supply nuclear technology to developing countries. Between the 1973 oil shock and the Three Mile Island accident in 1979, nuclear power was thought to be a strategic growth industry. The United States, starting in the early 1960s, aggressively pursued market share so as to establish the industry standard. By May 1976, the United States had exported sixty nuclear reactors; fifty-seven of them came with financial assistance from the federal government.[41] France had repeatedly accused the United States of using the proliferation issue as a way of maintaining its near-monopoly on the industry. In the mid-1970s, US nonproliferation policy was suspect. After the May 1974 explosion of India's nuclear device, the Canadians, who had supplied reactor and technical support, suspended all further nuclear exchanges with India. The United States continued to supply nuclear fuel. Only a month after the Indian explosion, the Nixon administration offered to sell both Israel and Egypt 600-megawatt reactors. IAEA safeguards were guaranteed, but the timing of the proposal cast doubt on US nonproliferation policy. Five months after the Indian test, Secretary of State Henry Kissinger made a speech in India indicating that the United States was not bothered by New Delhi's actions. In 1976, one analyst wrote: "It is present US policy not to allow the export of reprocessing or enrichment plants, but there is concern in the nuclear

---

[40] US Senate (1976), p. 419.   [41] Long (1977), p. 55.

industry that the continued refusal to do so may put Americans at a commercial disadvantage."[42] It appeared that nonproliferation was not a high priority for the United States until the South Korean episode. It is unlikely that France would have switched its policies because of US moral suasion.

One more episode discounts this hypothesis. If the French had decided to halt exports to South Korea because of suspected nuclear proliferation, then the policy should have been implemented against all potential nuclear states. It was not. At the same time the South Korean plant was scrubbed, France and Pakistan also agreed to build a reprocessing plant. The United States and Canada reacted strongly to the agreement, with Canada halting all exports of uranium and heavy water for Pakistan's Canadian-built plant. Despite the identical patterns of combined Canadian–American diplomatic pressure, neither the French nor the Pakistanis yielded on the project.[43]

It was the carrot, not the stick

The South Koreans only decided to acquire nuclear weapons when the Nixon doctrine was announced. Statements from the ROK President and Foreign Minister indicated that the nuclear option would be pursued contingent on the withdrawal of US troops and tactical nuclear weapons. It is possible that South Korea agreed to cancel its weapons program because the United States extended ironclad security guarantees,[44] eliminating the need for nuclear weapons, as well as increased level of military aid.[45] US Secretary of Defense James Schlesinger made headlines in 1975 when he declared that the United States would defend South Korea with nuclear weapons if necessary. This could have convinced the South Koreans there was no need to develop the weapons.

There is no question that US policy-makers were conscious of the link between alliance commitments and the need for nuclear

---

[42] Quoted in Baker (1976), p. 204. See also Thomas Halsted, "The spread of nuclear weapons: is the dam about to burst?" *Bulletin of the Atomic Scientists*, May 1975, pp. 8–11.

[43] Goldschmidt (1977).

[44] Although the alliance between the United States and ROK was in place for twenty years by this time, the language of the security obligations was somewhat vague. See Sano (1977), pp. 380–2, and Reiss (1988).

[45] Sigal (1998, p. 20) makes this argument.

weapons. Fred Iklé, head of the Arms Control and Disarmament Agency, testified before Congress in late 1975:

> For the foreseeable future, our alliances are essential in preventing a massive spread of nuclear weapons. For many nations, protection through a strong alliance is now the only alternative to a desperate search for security by acquiring their own nuclear weapons. Indeed, several nations with the greatest potential for nuclear arms now refrain from building weapons because of our alliance commitments.[46]

Security guarantees might not have been enough. In December, while the two countries were in negotiations about the reprocessing plant, the South Koreans requested $1.5 billion in loans from the US government for a new force improvement program.[47] The United States might have decided to link the aid request to the cancelation of the reprocessing plant.

This potential causal mechanism is the most intriguing, because it suggests that the United States really used carrots to alter ROK policy. This possibility also highlights an interesting question: how can countries remain allies after a coercion episode? Assume for the moment that economic coercion was the causal mechanism. What incentive would the Koreans have to maintain their extremely close alignment with the United States after they had just been coerced by their ally? Intuition suggests that the United States must have used the carrot to appease the South Koreans, not the stick, otherwise the South Koreans would have pursued other allies.

Despite this intuition, the case for economic and security inducements is weak. First, it is highly unlikely that the security guarantees would have convinced the South Koreans to halt their program. The original motivation for the weapons program was suspicion about US intentions. Nothing between 1970 and 1975 could have possibly assuaged these worries. The Nixon Doctrine had already given the perception that the United States did not consider South Korea to be a strategic interest. The fall of South Vietnam in April 1975 further weakened the US reputation in Asia, despite statements from Ford, Kissinger, and Schlesinger reaffirming the Mutual Security Treaty. The

---

[46] US Senate (1975), p. 218.
[47] Don Oberdorfer, "Korea asks $1.5 billion in US loans for arms," *Washington Post*, December 29, 1975, p. A2.

US was in the process of pulling out of Thailand at the same time it was reassuring Seoul. John Oh wrote at the time,

> What loomed in the forefront of the psychological milieu of the South Koreans in 1975 were the decisive military victories in Indochina and the helter-skelter flight of South Vietnamese refugees ... The real or imagined changes in power alignments in Asia and the Pacific sometimes seem to depict South Korea as the next domino to fall.[48]

By this point, the South Koreans had also been frustrated by US docility towards North Korean aggressions. For the previous seven years, South Korea observed mild US reactions to North Korean provocations. The United States, preoccupied with Vietnam, did not respond forcefully to the 1968 guerrilla attack on the Blue House; to the seizure of the USS *Pueblo*, just two days later; to the shooting down of an EC-121 reconnaissance plane in April 1969; to the repeated North Korean provocations at the DMZ; to the discoveries of North Korean tunnels crossing the DMZ into South Korean territory; and to the heightened rhetoric of North Korean President Kim-Il Sung after the fall of Saigon.[49]

The only tangible evidence of extended security guarantees is Schlesinger's statement, but it is suspect. First, the timing is again off; the statement was made in May 1975, but the deal with France was not scrubbed until the following January. Second, Schlesinger's statement was sandwiched by other US statements that threatened to disrupt the security relationship. Kissinger threatened to withdraw all security assurances two months before the Schelsinger statement. In May 1976, Schlesinger's replacement as Secretary of Defense, Donald Rumsfield, threatened his ROK counterpart with a "review of the entire spectrum of its relations with the ROK." Reviewing the entire episode, the US ambassador to Seoul noted that, "given US attitudes, one had to admit that (the) South Koreans had some reason for their concern over their future security."[50] Seen in this context,

[48] Oh (1976), p. 72. See also Cha (1999), chapter 4, and Yager (1980), pp. 313–14.

[49] *Economist*, "In the front line," July 5, 1975, p. 70; Chung (1984), and Back (1988).

[50] Oberdorfer (1997), pp. 72–3. The repeated US threats also lead to the opposite hypothesis: South Korea backed down because of security threats and not economic coercion. Peter Hayes (1990) and Selig Harrison ("A yen for the bomb?") have written that the South Koreans backed down because of Kissinger's threat to withdraw security guarantees in March 1975. This hypothesis fails on both empirical and theoretical grounds. First, it does not fit the data after the spring of 1975. If Seoul agreed to back down in March, why did it take another ten months to cancel the reprocessing plant? If

Schlesinger's statements seem less like a carrot and more like an attempt to reassure South Korea of the status quo.

Finally, Schlesinger's statements, although interpreted in the press to mean a nuclear guarantee, were in fact more qualified. In all of his public comments and press conferences on his August 1975 trip to Korea and Japan, he indicated his belief that conventional deterrence would be sufficient, and was reluctant to discuss the question of nuclear deterrence. When pressed on the issue by the media, his responses could not have been all that comforting to the South Koreans:

> *Reporter*: If you're saying that we're not going to fall beyond Seoul, we would use firepower to save Seoul. I presume that includes nuclear weapons. Am I correct?
> *Schlesinger*: No, I think that is stretching the presumption a little too far. What we are prepared to do is to apply conventional firepower, massively. Under those circumstances, of course, if there were the danger of a catastrophic defeat, which I do not expect in view of the force balance, I think that the President would then have to consider the situation.[51]

If the United States was willing to lose Seoul before using nuclear weapons, Schlesinger's statement would have been of little value to South Korea. It is possible that the private consultations conveyed a firmer message. Nevertheless, these statements surely introduced some element of uncertainty into a private US guarantee. This uncertainty, combined with previous actions, devalued any security guarantee that was proffered.

Finally, while the South Koreans wanted a firmer security guarantee, they could not have been blind to the Ford administration's

Kissinger threatened to withdraw the security assurance, why did Schlesinger strengthen the commitment in the summer? Finally, while Kissinger's March threat failed to move South Korea, the December threat, which emphasized the economic dimension, did succeed in getting the South Koreans to acquiesce.

Theoretically, the security threat does not work. The original motivation for the South Korean nuclear program was uncertainty regarding US security assurances. Furthermore, both Cha (1999, chapter 4) and Oberdorfer (1997, pp. 68–74) note that the United States was aware that its standoffish behavior was increasing Korean insecurity. Since a wavering security commitment from the United States caused the initiation of the weapons program, why would an additional flipflop have caused it to stop? Why would the United States have believed that such a threat would have worked?

[51] Press conference, Andrews Air Force Base, Maryland. September 1, 1975. In *Public Statements of the Secretaries of Defense; The Nixon and Ford Administrations* (Frederick, MD: University Publications of America, 1982).

domestic weaknesses. The negotiations over the processing plant were held as the 1976 presidential race was starting. Ford faced a tough primary fight, and the odds on his election after Watergate were not good. Any guarantees or promises of aid would not have been likely to last beyond his administration. Throughout the fall and winter of 1975, Congress was more concerned with the Park regime's human rights record, as well as ROK lobbying efforts in Washington.[52] Multiple amendments were attached to foreign assistance bills requiring that such aid be severed if a government engaged in a consistent pattern of human rights abuses.[53] It would have been impossible for the administration to pass any increase in ROK assistance given that political climate. Furthermore, after Vietnam, public opinion was staunchly opposed to US involvement in South Korea. In one poll published in 1975, only 14 percent favored US military involvement if North Korea attacked South Korea. Of the elites polled, the figure was 19 percent. Other polls taken during the same time also suggested a strong isolationist streak with regard to Asia.[54] These figures suggest that no security guarantee would have been worth much at the time of the coercion event.

The possibility of increased military aid is more intriguing, because if true, it would show that the United States extracted more concessions with the carrot than the stick. The direct evidence for this argument is not strong, however. First, a key element of the December 1975 ROK aid request was to have the ability to co-produce the M-60 tank as well as fighter and interceptor aircraft. The United States refused these requests, fearing it would destabilize the balance of power in the region. It also refused to sell F-16 aircraft and advanced rocket technology.[55] South Korea did not receive a *quid pro quo* offer of increasing its conventional production of arms in exchange for halting its nuclear plans.

It is still possible that Korea received more aid in exchange for not buying the reprocessing plant. If the offer of military aid convinced Seoul to drop its nuclear program, then the US contribution to the Korean defense budget should have risen after 1976. Table 8.3 shows the percentage contribution to South Korean military expenditures

---

[52] See US House (1978).   [53] See Sano (1977), p. 387.

[54] Michael Getler, "Number, location of US troops in South Korea stir concern," *Washington Post*, May 24, 1995, pp. A13–A14. See also Sano (1977), pp. 389–90.

[55] See Back (1988), pp. 176–80, and Oberdorfer, "Korea asks $1.5 Billion in loans for arms."

273

Table 8.3. *Contributions to ROK military expenditures, 1969–79*

Year	Domestic sources (%)	US defense budget support (%)	US direct military assistance (%)
1969	53.5	14.2	32.3
1970	56.8	12.7	30.5
1971	50.3	4.6	45.1
1972	65.2	2.8	32.0
1973	72.4	1.1	26.5
1974	87.7	–	12.3
1975	91.4	–	8.6
1976	95.9	–	4.1
1977	99.7	–	0.3
1978	100.0	–	–
1979	100.0	–	–

Source: Ha (1984), p. 119.

between 1960 and 1980. Starting in 1963, there was a slow decrease in US contributions. The pattern did not change after 1976. Table 8.4 shows the levels of US assistance to South Korea from 1971 to 1979. During the 1970s, US assistance to Korea shifted from grants to loans, as the Korean economy became capable of sustaining its defense budget and foreign aid became less popular in Congress. The United States was increasingly unwilling to bankroll the Korean military buildup on concessionary terms. Less than a week before Kratzer's testimony, Ford announced an end to all free military assistance to South Korea, replacing it with loans.[56] The grant aid was never re-established, suggesting that the timing of the statement was not designed to increase the attractiveness of the aid carrot.

Table 8.4 does show an overall increase in loans from 1976 and 1977; it is possible that the increase could have been in exchange for the ROK change in policy. However, neither the South Korean nor the American statements about the affair viewed the aid lever as a carrot. Rather, both saw it as a stick. The South Koreans talked of "pressures bordering on threats" when discussing the incident. A State Department official described the US bargaining strategy as follows: "We simply made the negative clear to them, that if they went forward with the reprocessing plant, Congress would insist on the termination

[56] "Ford plans to cut military aid grants," *New York Times*, January 21, 1976, p. 29.

Table 8.4. *US military assistance to ROK 1971–9*

Year	Grants ($ million)	Loans ($ million)	Total ($ million)
1971	541.2	15.0	556.2
1972	515.2	17.0	532.2
1973	338.8	24.2	363.0
1974	100.6	56.7	157.3
1975	82.6	59.0	141.6
1976	62.1	126.0	188.1
1977	4.1	286.5	290.6
1978	1.9	275.0	276.9
1979	1.7	190.0	191.7

Source: US House (1978), p. 380; Black (1988), p. 174.

of further military credit sales. And they understood this."[57] What comes through in these statements is that both the Koreans and Americans perceived the status quo as involving some sort of US assistance. Any threat to disrupt this aid was perceived as a coercive policy.

A review of the 1975–6 episode shows that the South Koreans backed down because of US threats to disrupt exchange in the nuclear technology and military arms sectors. In both sectors, the Koreans were extremely dependent on American suppliers, and would have incurred significant costs if the threat had been executed. The United States would have suffered minimal costs if the threat had been carried out. Alternative explanations, such as the use of economic incentives or the necessity of international cooperation, do not have much empirical support.

The United States and North Korea's nuclear program

The chronology

The end of the cold war put extraordinary economic and political pressure on the Democratic People's Republic of Korea (DPRK), providing the incentive to develop nuclear weapons. The economic

[57] Gelb, "Nuclear proliferation and the sale of arms." On the South Korean reaction, see "Seoul officials say strong pressure forced cancellation of plans to purchase a French nuclear plant." *New York Times*, February 1, 1976, p. 11.

pressure came from the collapse of North Korea's trading relationship with Russia and China. Both countries stopped trading on concessionary terms and insisted on hard-currency payments. Pyongyang had been running large current account deficits with both countries, and was forced to cut its imports drastically once the switch to hard currency was made. From 1987 to 1993, DPRK oil imports from China and Russia/USSR fell by more than 50 percent. Despite the North Korean ideology of *juche*, or self-reliance, Pyongyang relied on energy and grain imports from both China and Russia in order to fuel its economy and feed its population. The shift to hard currency and the resulting drop in energy imports caused the North Korean economy to shrink in the early 1990s, as can be seen in table 8.5. The contrast with a robust South Korean economy was particularly disturbing to the DPRK.

Diplomatically, the DPRK also suffered serious reversals. South Korea's *Nordpolitik* strategy of engaging both China and the Soviet Union in the late 1980s was a great success; the USSR established diplomatic relations in 1990, the Chinese two years later. North Korea did not react well to these diplomatic maneuverings. When Soviet Foreign Minister Eduard Shevardnadze went to Pyongyang to inform the DPRK leadership of Moscow's decision to recognize South Korea, the North Koreans responded by threatening to develop nuclear weapons.[58] The fate of its close ally East Germany did nothing to alleviate the DPRK leadership; it did not want to be absorbed by the ROK.

As its incentives increased, the DPRK nuclear program accelerated. It is impossible to date the precise moment when North Korea's bomb program started. In 1965, the Soviet Union supplied North Korea with a small, 5-megawatt research reactor, located in the town of Yongbyon. The South Korean effort to acquire weapons in the mid-1970s was obviously a cause for concern, but this in itself meant little. In the late 1980s, however, US satellite reconnaissance showed the construction of two larger gas-graphite reactors. None of these facilities were connected to the North Korean power grid, suggesting that they were not built for generating electricity. More disturbingly, the photographs also showed a reprocessing plant under construction. Once finished, Pyongyang would have had the ability to convert its nuclear waste into fissile plutonium. Furthermore, the gas-graphite reactor used

---

[58] Mazarr (1995), pp. 55–6.

Table 8.5. *North Korea's economic health, 1990–4*

Year	Real GNP growth	Rice output (1,000 tons)	External debt ($ billion)	Exports ($ million)	Imports ($ million)
1990	−3.7	5,900	n/a[1]	1,960	2,760
1991	−5.2	5,300	4.7	1,010	1,710
1992	−5.0	n/a[1]	n/a[1]	1,020	1,640
1993	−3.5	1,330	n/a[1]	1,020	1,620
1994	−3.0	n/a[1]	9.8	840	1,270

Note: [1] Not available.
Source: Economist Intelligence Unit (1995), p. 33.

natural uranium, which North Korea had in abundance. Once the reprocessing plant was completed, the DPRK would have possessed a completely indigenous fuel cycle to manufacture fissile material. The small research reactor could produce enough plutonium for one or two atomic bombs a year; the larger facilities, up to a dozen.[59]

In addition to the fissile material, a complete nuclear program needs a certain level of engineering competence and a delivery mechanism. After thirty years of Soviet assistance and twenty years of IAEA assistance, the North Koreans did have sufficient skill to attempt the indigenous construction of both the reactors and the reprocessing plant, a strong indicator that it had the technical knowledge to make the components of a bomb. Indeed, in 1990, the United States detected an explosion at Yongbyon consistent with the blast necessary to detonate a nuclear device.[60] As for the delivery mechanism, North Korean missiles were of sufficient quality to be exported to Iran and Libya. In the 1980s it had two variants of the Soviet Scud missile, capable of striking only the Korean peninsula. By 1994, however, it had test-fired its Rodong-1 missile, which had the range to strike western Japan.[61]

Thus, by 1991, North Korea had both the incentive and the means to acquire nuclear weapons. By 1991, the North Koreans had shut down its operational reactor three times in the past three years to remove spent fuel – the first step to reprocessing plutonium. All of the

[59] *Economist*, "Dedicated followers of fission," May 28, 1994, p. 20.
[60] Sigal (1998), p. 26. Mazarr (1995) provides conflicting reports on North Korea's technical ability.
[61] The Rodong-2, in development, has the capability to strike all of the Japanese islands as well as Taiwan. *Economist*, "A dangerous game," May 28, 1994, p. 22.

countries with a stake in the region – South Korea, Japan, China, the United States, and Russia – were aware of the problem.

The United States, after consulting with Seoul, decided to remove North Korea's incentive to build the weapons through a two-pronged approach. First, Washington would offer negative security guarantees, i.e. a pledge not to attack the DPRK, in the hopes of reducing North Korean insecurity. Second, Washington also urged the other great powers in the region to pressure Pyongyang into fully implementing the Non-Proliferation Treaty. Both the Russians and the Chinese had successfully pressured Pyongyang in the past. In 1975, Beijing vetoed a North Korean proposal to invade South Korea. In 1985, the Soviets held up signing a new trade agreement to pressure the DPRK into signing the Non-Proliferation Treaty.[62]

The diplomatic blitzkrieg started in late 1991. In October, President Bush announced the withdrawal of US nuclear weapons from the ROK. Weeks later, South Korean President Roh Tae Woo proposed making the peninsula a nuclear-free zone. Both Seoul and Washington offered to open up US military bases for North Korean inspection. In the same month, China put pressure on North Korean President Kim-Il Sung to cut a deal with Seoul during his October 1991 visit to Beijing.[63]

The combined diplomatic assault appeared to work. Kim convened a Politiburo meeting immediately after the Beijing visit to switch to a more accommodating policy towards South Korea and the United States. The Koreas signed two historic joint declarations in December 1991. The first agreement was a general pledge towards reconciliation and nonaggression; the second agreement dealt specifically with nuclear matters. Both countries pledged not to "test, manufacture, produce, receive, possess, store, deploy or use nuclear weapons." The agreement also included a section promising not to "possess nuclear reprocessing and uranium enrichment facilities." In January 1992 Pyongyang signed a safeguards agreement with the IAEA. On paper at least, North Korea had agreed not to pursue any weapons program.

The diplomacy of early 1992 contrasted sharply with DPRK actions

---

[62] Oberdorfer (1997), p. 254. After signing, there was some delay in reaching a safeguards agreement with the IAEA. Without the agreement, the IAEA could not monitor or record any efforts to reprocess plutonium. As of 1991, an agreement had yet to be signed.

[63] Edward Neilan, "China's rebuke to North Korea raises disarmament hopes," *Washington Times*, October 21, 1991, p. A1.

for the rest of the year. The ROK–DPRK deal was never implemented, as a result of renewed friction between the two countries. The IAEA also encountered problems. US intelligence supplied to the IAEA indicated that in 1989, the North Koreans had extracted enough plutonium from the research reactor to manufacture one or two atomic weapons. The extracted plutonium was stored in the reprocessing facility. North Korea did not list that plant on its declared list of facilities open to inspection. In February 1993 the IAEA inspection of the declared facilities partially confirmed US allegations. The IAEA then requested special inspections of the suspected plutonium sites. The North Koreans refused, and shocked everyone by announcing in March 1993 that they would withdraw from the NPT in three months. No country had ever attempted to pull out of the treaty. If it withdrew, it would have been impossible to stop any future DPRK weapons program.

The immediate US response was to threaten economic coercion. Immediately following the DPRK announcement, US Secretary of State Warren Christopher was quoted in the press stating that sanctions would be the result if North Korea continued on its present path.[64] Despite this initial reaction, Washington calibrated its approach after consultations with its allies. There was good reason for this. The United States had no trade to interrupt with North Korea; unilateral sanctions would have been meaningless. If economic coercion was to be effective, it needed international cooperation. While China, Russia, Japan, and South Korea all preferred the North Koreans not to have nuclear weapons, they also preferred an attempt at negotiations rather than an immediate rush to sanctions. After consultations with Seoul and Tokyo, the Clinton administration agreed to direct talks with the North Koreans to resolve the impasse.

In June 1993, barely a week before the North Koreans were to withdraw from the NPT, the American and North Korean delegations met. The talks were fruitful enough for Pyongyang to "suspend" its declaration and permit continued IAEA inspection of its declared facilities, but not the special inspections that triggered the crisis. It also pledged to restart working-level contacts with South Korea. In return, the United States reiterated its pledge not to attack North Korea and to hold further talks.

Two rounds of negotiations made little headway. At these meetings,

---

[64] See Mazarr (1995), p. 111.

the United States continued to offer limited carrots, such as a recycled guarantee against an attack. On the whole, however, US policy-makers preferred more coercive tactics. One US official noted, "To some extent the diplomatic effort was forced on us by tactical considerations. The only way we could build a consensus at the UN Security Council to impose sanctions was to demonstrate that the North Koreans were unwilling to make a deal."[65] During the negotiations, North Korea repeatedly signaled that it was willing to accept a "package deal"; the North Koreans would stop work on the reprocessing plant and its gas-graphite reactors in return for the construction of light-water reactors of commensurate size. Since Pyongyang was unable to pay for the reactors, they were essentially asking for a carrot.

The United States was resistant to the carrot option for two reasons. First, South Korea objected vociferously that the DPRK had not returned to the negotiating table with Seoul. The ROK government was paranoid about any cooperation between Washington and Pyongyang. Second, there was considerable reluctance about the cost of the carrot, which was in the billions.[66] Discussions continued, but little headway was made. By March 1994, the IAEA informed the United Nations Security Council that it could not ensure the continuity of its inspections. If the North Koreans tried to extract more plutonium from their research reactor, it would go unobserved by the IAEA. Before the third round of talks was to be held, IAEA inspectors were unable to examine all of the declared facilities. The United States, in response, halted negotiations. The North Koreans reacted by breaking off parallel negotiations with the ROK, but not before the DPRK delegate excoriated the South Korean delegates with a planned outburst, ending with the observation, "Seoul is not far from here. Should war erupt, Seoul will become a sea of fire."[67]

Following the cessation of talks, the UN Security Council unanimously approved a statement in early April requesting the North Korean regime to resume cooperating with the IAEA inspectors, and gave them a deadline of six weeks to do so. The statement was not as diplomatically strong as a resolution, but was noteworthy because China largely agreed to the US language, participated in the drafting, and was willing to approve a document that threatened sanctions at a

---

[65] Quoted in Sigal (1998), p. 59.   [66] Sigal (1998), pp. 69, 84–90.
[67] Quoted in Koh (1994), p. 66, n. 30.

later date. The United States began to bolster its military presence on the Korean peninsula, including the placement of Patriot missiles. The DPRK Foreign Minister issued a boiler-plate rejection, but Pyongyang also indicated some flexibility. Before the six-week deadline, it informed the IAEA that it would extract spent fuel rods from the research reactor and would permit its inspectors to observe the process. A third round of US–DPRK negotiations was scheduled.

Just when negotiations seemed on track again, another crisis erupted. North Korea refused to allow the IAEA to examine the fuel rods at the research reactor to see if prior extractions had occurred. On June 10, the agency cut off all nuclear assistance and threatened to withdraw all of its inspectors. DPRK intransigence caused the United States to push harder for the sanctions option in the Security Council. Pyongyang withdrew from the IAEA, and reiterated that the implementation of sanctions was equivalent to war. A day later, the United States, South Korea, and Japan issued a joint pledge to impose sanctions regardless of the Security Council's decision. Washington also took steps to reinforce its troops in South Korea with an additional 10,000 men, more sophisticated weaponry, and ships prepared to enforce a naval embargo.

North Korea's response was mixed. Publicly, it reiterated the theme that sanctions would mean war. Privately, however, Pyongyang indicated to Washington its willingness to accept a package deal; it would eliminate its existing nuclear program in exchange for modern light-water reactors and diplomatic relations with the United States. Kim-Il Sung made this exact offer to two different US policy analysts visiting North Korea in early June, to signal his terms to Washington.[68] Another message was sent via Cambodia's King Norodom Sihanouk, expressing a wish to avoid a military conflict.[69] Then, on June 16th, former President Jimmy Carter traveled to Pyongyang. He received the same offer from Kim-Il Sung, as well as an agreement to meet ROK President Kim Young Sam at the earliest convenience. Unlike the other intermediaries, Carter had direct access to the Clinton administration's foreign-policy team. He communicated the DPRK proposal to Washington. After receiving written confirmation on June 22, the United States suspended its sanctions efforts at the United Nations and went back to the negotiating table. Despite the death of Kim-Il

---

[68] Mazarr (1995), chapters 1 and 8.
[69] "Nude, absolutely naked," *Far Eastern Economic Review*, June 23, 1994, p. 15.

Sung less than a month later, US–DPRK negotiations continued into the fall, and sanctions were not imposed.

In October 1994, a Framework Agreement was signed between the two countries. The agreement consisted of a series of reciprocal actions that could be broken off at any time if the other side failed to cooperate. In sequence, it worked as follows:

1. North Korea remains in the NPT, freezes all activity in its existing nuclear facilities, and suspends construction of its 50 MW and 200 MW reactors. The IAEA monitors this halt.
2. The United States supplies heavy oil in lieu of the lost energy from the reactors. The Korean Peninsula Energy Development Organization (KEDO), a consortium of Japan, South Korea, and the United States, contracts out for a light-water reactor. Trade and investment barriers between the United States and North Korea are reduced.
3. The IAEA resumes routine inspections of "non-frozen" activities.
4. Construction of the first light-water reactor commences.
5. Before the delivery of key nuclear components of the reactor, North Korea complies fully with IAEA safeguards. This includes allowing special inspections of the reprocessing plant.
6. The components are delivered.
7. North Korea ships its spent fuel to the United States and starts to dismantle its existing facilities.
8. The first reactor is finished; heavy oil shipments cease.
9. All existing DPRK facilities are dismantled.
10. The second light-water reactor is built.[70]

US officials have stated repeatedly since October 1994 that the agreement is not based on trust. A glance at the timetable bears this out. The agreement forces North Korea to make a concession for every incentive. Nevertheless, the DPRK benefits enormously from this arrangement. The cost of the framework agreement was estimated by US Secretary of Defense William Perry at $5 billion, by far the largest

[70] For a copy of the unclassified portions of the agreement, see Council on Foreign Relations (1995), appendix 1. The classified portion of the agreement is a two-page minute containing the exact timetable of the special inspections (Reiss 1995, p. 276).

foreign investment in North Korea's history.[71] Averaged out over the agreement's eight years, the deal injects capital investment equal to 2.8 percent of its gross domestic product. The electrical power from the reactors boosts electricity output by 27.4 percent.[72]

This was, needless to say, a substantial carrot. This episode would seem to contradict the conflict expectations model. Given the adversarial relationship between the United States and North Korea, why did the former decide on economic inducements instead of implementing sanctions?

The threat of economic sanctions was unsuccessful in generating all the desired concessions for two reasons. First, North Korea's expectations of future conflict were so extreme that it preferred stalemate to total acquiescence. Although Pyongyang was willing to make some concessions to avert sanctions, its expectation of future political conflicts made conceding doubly painful; it was afraid the United States would exploit a favorable settlement in later interactions. Second, the United States could not compromise its demands due to the normative importance it placed on nonproliferation issues. Faced with a choice of economic inducements, military compellence, or stalemate, it chose the former because of the costs associated with the latter options.

The next few sections will support this explanation by considering alternative explanations. The first section argues that North Korea's expectations of future conflict made it unwilling to acquiesce to large concessions, although the threat of sanctions was sufficient to induce smaller concessions. The next section evaluates alternative theories for why the North Koreans were so obstinate. The final section analyzes US options in June 1994 to end the crisis. It argues that the carrot was selected because Washington was unwilling to scale back its demands, sanctions were insufficient to extract the required concessions, and the costs of military compellence were far too high.

Why did coercion fail?

Despite the potential cost of sanctions, North Korea's overriding concern for relative gains and reputation made it prefer deadlock rather than acquiescence to all of Washington's demands. DPRK expectations of future conflict dictated that the costs of stalemate were

---

[71] US Senate (1995), p. 18.
[72] Council on Foreign Relations (1995), p. 7.

less than those of conceding to the United States. It treated the negotiations as a zero-sum game. The source of this concern was both the high degree of threat the country felt following its diplomatic isolation, and its fear of losing its sovereignty through future conflicts with the United States and South Korea.

As noted in the chronology, the North Korean regime was preoccupied with the fate of East Germany. The DPRK elite was particularly surprised by the fall of communism in Mongolia, an Asian neighbor. They expressed this surprise in private to US officials.[73] South Korea's diplomacy left Pyongyang asymmetrically isolated; all of the great powers recognized and traded with the ROK, but Japan and the United States did not recognize the DPRK. As South Korea's economy grew in size, it became an unstated assumption among the region's players that the North would eventually be absorbed. David Kang observes, "The dominant North Korean emotion underlying its foreign policy is fear – fear of encirclement, fear of invasion, and fear of foreign influences directing its actions ... with a high security dilemma and indistinguishable offensive and defensive deployments, North Korea will hold an acute threat perception."[74]

North Korea was extremely concerned about relative gains because of its expectations of future political conflict. Conceding on the nuclear issue meant, in the long run, weakening themselves in the zero-sum game of state survival it played with South Korea. Paul Bracken touched on this issue in observing:

> there are two "games" being played on the Korean peninsula. The first game is non-zero sum in character. It amounts to bargaining around a military and nuclear negotiation where the gains of one side do not necessarily come at the expense of the other. The second, and more important game, is zero sum. It is a game of control, and only one state can gain control of the entire Korean peninsula ... it is the state-survival competition, rather than the one concerning non-proliferation and arms control, that shapes the dynamics of inter-state relations among all affected parties.[75]

The official DPRK press organs provided a remarkably consistent stream of statements in June 1994 indicating their view on US demands. The statements are consistent with fears of conceding anything to the United States, and demonstrate that they viewed the political conflict as a zero-sum issue:

---

[73] US House (1990), pp. 21–2.
[74] Kang (1995), pp. 260–1.   [75] Bracken (1990), p. 86.

June 7: "The demand for 'a special inspection' is a gross infringement upon our sovereignty and a graphic expression of the policy of stifling the DPRK."

June 10: "This demand reveals its intention to disarm the DPRK. It is a wanton violation of our sovereignty of the DPRK and a graphic expression of the policy of stifling it to demand 'a special inspection'. This can never be allowed."

June 16: " . . . it does not want to truly solve the nuclear issue on the Korean peninsula, but is trying to stifle the DPRK militarily on the pretext of 'nuclear development'."

June 18: " . . . this is an unreasonable act to stifle anti-imperialist independent countries including the Democratic People's Republic of Korea under the unjustifiable pretext of 'non-proliferation' of nuclear and other mass destruction weapons."[76]

Obviously, official propaganda should be discounted somewhat as a source for DPRK preferences. Still, these statements are consistent with its backdoor signals. One of Kim-Il Sung's messages to the United States, relayed through King Sihanouk of Cambodia, reveals much about the security concerns and expectations of future conflict that guided North Korean preferences:

The reason we refuse inspection in depth is just this: we only have secret defense systems and organizations and the Americans know, perhaps, that we have no nuclear weapons, but they want to know what exactly our defense system with conventional weapons is. That is the reason they want the UN atomic agency to make inspections in depth. Besides the question of our sovereignty and national dignity and pride, we have our secrets.

Please compare us to a man: They want us to take off our shirt, our coat, and now our trousers, and after that we will be nude, absolutely naked. What they want us to be is a man without defense secrets, just a naked man. We cannot accept that. We would rather accept a war."[77]

---

[76] " 'Special' inspection said 'out of question,'" in FBIS-EAS-94–110, June 8, 1994, p. 22; " 'Heinous political aim alleged,'" in FBIS-EAS-94–112, June 10, 1994, p. 18; "US 'military pressure', 'scheming' rejected," in FBIS-EAS-94–116, June 16, 1994, p. 15; "US uses NPT to dominate other nations," in FBIS-EAS-94–118, June 20, 1994, p. 20. All quotations are from the official North Korean press agency, KCNA.

[77] Quoted in *Far Eastern Economic Review*, "Nude, absolutely naked," June 23, 1994, p. 15.

Kim-Il Sung's logic would sound odd except for two important facts. First, during its existence, North Korea has been the subject of no less than seven nuclear threats from the United States. In late 1991, as the crisis was heating up, Joint Chief of Staff Chair Colin Powell told reporters about North Korea, "If they missed Desert Storm, this is a chance to catch a re-run." Pyongyang had every reason to anticipate future clashes with Washington. Second, during a January 1992 trip to the DMZ, Bush administration officials told reporters that to answer the nuclear question, they would need a "mandate to roam North Korea's heavily guarded military sites."[78] This fits very well with DPRK characterizations of the inspections as a fishing expedition for US intelligence. Just because North Korea was paranoid did not mean that other countries were not out to get it.

Pyongyang was concerned that conceding on the nuclear issue would give the United States greater leverage in future disputes. North Korea believed that the United States would be able to exploit concessions in the present in any militarized dispute down the road. Because Pyongyang's expectations of future conflict with Seoul and Washington were obviously high, it had to think of any concession in terms of relative gains and reputation.

Once this substantive preference becomes clear, North Korea's actions make more sense. Scott Snyder comments:

> In order to claim that North Korean principles of sovereignty and self-reliance had been preserved, it had become inevitable that Pyongyang, when faced with a demand from the United States, would choose to take exactly the opposite action – even if that action appeared to damage North Korean national interests – rather than be seen as capitulating on its core principles.[79]

Bracken notes,

> the immediate threat to North Korea is ... strategic isolation leading to greater economic isolation, and opportunities for international intervention in Korean affairs. This is what is now happening, most notably with the pressure on the North to open suspect nuclear facilities to inspection by the IAEA. But such demands must surely be seen as only the first moves to open up the entire North Korean state."[80]

---

[78] Powell quoted in Sigal (1998), p. 31. Bush officials quoted in Cumings (1997), p. 469. On US nuclear threats against North Korea, see Cumings (1997), pp. 450–70.
[79] Snyder (1995), p. 17.
[80] Bracken (1990), p. 91.

The North Koreans were vitally concerned about the distribution of gains. They worried that any concessions about inspections would give the United States additional leverage in the future. Pyongyang believed that the transfer of intelligence information, and the general opening of the DPRK to outside influences, would weaken the regime's bargaining position in future conflicts. It was willing to suffer the formidable costs of deadlock rather than acquiesce to all of the US demands.

Even with such extreme concern about relative gains, the chronology indicates that North Korea was willing to make some concessions in exchange for avoiding deadlock. DPRK negotiators divided the proliferation issue into two categories: complying with IAEA safeguards against the development of weapons in the future, and agreeing to special inspections to trace past nuclear efforts. During the June 1993 standoff, both US and South Korean negotiators indicated that unless Pyongyang backed down, sanctions would be implemented. Pyongyang then agreed to suspend its withdrawal from the NPT and permit IAEA inspections of its declared facilities. Washington agreed not to attack Pyongyang, but this was a "recycled" carrot; the United States conceded nothing new. The chief benefit to North Korea was the delay of sanctions. Michael Mazarr writes, "Although US and South Korean negotiators would not know it at the time, this same series of events would repeat itself over the coming year. North Korea would agree to a small portion of the IAEA and US demands, thus putting off sanctions and prolonging the nuclear dispute, while leaving the most important issues on the table." Mitchell Reiss comments, "In 1993–94, whenever economic sanctions even appeared on the horizon, North Korea found some way to reengage the United States. If this option had been pursued sooner, it is possible that the North would have been forthcoming sooner as well."[81]

US policy-makers also believed that the threat of sanctions led to greater DPRK flexibility at the negotiating table. Secretary of State Warren Christopher told Congress: "The North Korean leadership made this decision because it understood that if it did not, the United States would pursue sanctions and was prepared to deal with the consequences." The principal American negotiator, Robert Gallucci, was convinced that the tangible threat of sanctions led the DPRK to be

[81] Mazarr (1995), p. 121; Reiss (1995), p. 283.

more accommodating after the June crisis.[82] For example, the DPRK offer in June to freeze its nuclear program left unclear whether reprocessing was included. The United States insisted on a total freeze before the sanctions drive was called off. The North Koreans quickly agreed to the specific US terms.

There is also evidence that the June 1994 threat of economic coercion did modify the package deal between the two countries in favor of the United States. As the US position became more belligerent, North Korea increased the number of private messages that it was ready to cut a deal. Furthermore, the DPRK offer relayed through private intermediaries in the first week of June 1994 differs somewhat from the final arrangement. The early June proposal suggested that the US-led consortium underwrite the purchase of a Russian light-water reactor; it also linked special inspections to a normalization of relations between the United States and North Korea. In the final agreement, normalization and special inspections were not explicitly linked. More important, it was made clear to the North Koreans that South Korea would build the light-water reactor. The asset-specific nature of the nuclear reactors made this change a significant concession, because it created a North Korean dependency on South Korean technology. In the end, the threat of sanctions forced North Korea into compromising its position on some of the issues.

US leverage was constrained by the DPRK's expectations of future conflict. The threat of economic coercion was capable of producing a certain number of concessions. Pyongyang would have been willing to acquiesce if the United States had reduced its demand to allowing the IAEA to maintain safeguards on all of its declared nuclear facilities, preventing any future proliferation effort. By contrast, the DPRK preferred deadlock, and even war, to making the additional concession of permitting the United States to investigate previous efforts to develop nuclear weapons. Only with the proffering of the carrot was North Korea prepared to agree to all of Washington's demands.

Alternative explanations

Before examining the US decision to use the carrot, it is worth exploring alternative explanations for why economic coercion failed.

---

[82] Christopher quoted in Sigal (1998), p. 199; Gallucci observations in Oberdorfer (1997), p. 353.

There are two other candidate explanations. First, sanctions would have imposed minimal costs on the DPRK. This was the result of either the autarkic nature of North Korea's economy or the inability of the United States to generate the necessary international cooperation. Second, the North Korean leadership was irrational and therefore was incapable of responding to cost–benefit analysis. These alternatives will be considered in turn.

The target's opportunity costs were insignificant

At first glance, it appears that the sanctions would not have sufficiently damaged the DPRK economy. North Korea was built on the ideology of *juche*, or self-reliance. Economic autarky flowed from this ideology. An economy built on this ideology would appear to be invulnerable to sanctions. There was considerable pessimism among some of the protagonists about whether sanctions would have imposed severe costs on the North Korean regime. One Japanese official, for example, commented, "even if we can get them passed [in the Security Council], sanctions probably won't do much good." A United States official was more explicit: "all policy options stink."[83]

The claim that *juche* protected North Korea from sanctions can be quickly discarded. Despite the DPRK claims about self-reliance, it was dependent upon foreign trade and exchange. The cutoff of Soviet aid and trade credits caused the North Korean economy to shrink drastically during the early 1990s. Trade levels also decreased as more countries insisted on hard-currency payments. In December 1993, even the OPRK Worker's Party central committee blamed its economic downturn on, "the collapse of socialist countries and the socialist market of the world."[84] At the same meeting, the party announced its new economic plan, in which top priority would be given to foreign trade – a sure sign that *juche* was an economic dead letter.[85] Most commentators agreed that United Nations sanctions could have imposed serious damage to the DPRK economy.[86]

Another possible explanation is that the United States could not generate the necessary international cooperation for sanctions to have any bite. The conventional wisdom was that they would have been

---

[83] The Japanese quote is from Mazarr (1995), p. 118; the US official is from *Economist Intelligence Unit, Country Report: South Korea, North Korea,* 1st quarter 1994, p. 30.
[84] Quoted in Cumings (1997), p. 426.
[85] Mazarr (1995), pp. 130–1; Oberdorfer (1997), p. 297.
[86] See, for example, *Economist,* "A dangerous game," May 28, 1994, p. 22.

ineffective without Chinese cooperation. By 1994, China was Pyongyang's largest trading partner, with 34 percent of its total trade. Beijing exported oil as well as staple goods such as rice and corn. In 1991, Chinese staple exports accounted for 13 percent of North Korean aggregate demand; by 1993, that figure had climbed to 43 percent.[87] Most analysts assumed that if the Chinese failed to participate in the sanctions effort, the disruption would not have been costly enough to force acquiescence. However, as the crisis came to a head in June 1994, China hinted that it would either veto or ignore a sanctions resolution. Michael Mazarr comments: "Had China been an advocate rather than a staunch opponent of economic sanctions, the course of US and international diplomacy ... might have been entirely different.[88] In addition to Chinese recalcitrance, the United States was having difficulty getting even Japan and South Korea on board.[89]

There are two responses to this claim. First, although China was not predisposed to sanctions, a veto was not necessarily forthcoming. There is no question that China wanted the DPRK to abandon its weapons program and adhere to the NPT. By June 1994, it was far from clear that it would do this. It is telling that China abstained rather than voted against the IAEA sanctions. With the June 14 pledge by the United States, Japan, and South Korea to impose sanctions regardless of the Security Council vote, China's veto held less influence. Rather than be seen as obstructionists, it was entirely possible that Beijing would have abstained. This would be consistent with Don Oberdorfer's claim that Chinese diplomats in Beijing and Pyongyang told North Korea that although it opposed sanctions, the strength of international opinion would prevent a veto.[90] US willingness to lobby the other Security Council members is evidence that the Clinton administration did not think the Chinese position was cast in stone.

At the absolute minimum, the United States, Japan, and South Korea were pledged to attempt economic coercion. Which leads to the second point: economic sanctions would have hurt the DPRK elite regardless of Chinese participation. This is because of the dual structure of the North Korean economy.[91] Korean, American, and Russian analysts have all observed a second, "court" economy, run by

---

[87] Figures from Han (1994). [88] Ibid. See also Mazarr (1995), p. 115.
[89] Reiss (1995), p. 282. [90] Oberdorfer (1997), pp. 320–1.
[91] See Kim (1993); Mikheev (1993); Perry (1990); *Economist*, "South Korea: a survey," June 3, 1995, p. 6; and Economist Intelligence Unit, *Country Report: South Korea and North Korea*, 2nd quarter, 1995, pp. 40–3.

and for the DPRK elite, particularly the military.[92] The official, centrally planned economy is run by the civilian government, and performs dismally. It is generally believed that the court economy is both more efficient and more entrepreneurial. It is responsible for military exports to Iran, Syria, and Libya, as well as a textile industry that generates considerable export revenue from Japan and South Korea. Russian analysts estimate that the court economy is responsible for 15 percent of DPRK industrial production, and up to 40 percent of its export revenue.[93]

This type of economic structure would be unremarkable except for two considerations. First, the court economy would have been extremely vulnerable to economic coercion regardless of Chinese participation. It relied heavily upon capital inflows from the Cho'chong'ryun, an association of ethnic Koreans who live in Japan and have relatives in the DPRK. The hard-currency transfers are estimated to range from $600 million to $1.8 billion annually. The Japanese also represent North Korea's largest hard-currency export market; for example, 10 percent of Japanese business suits are stitched in the DPRK.[94] By 1994, South Korea was also a significant export market. Roughly $200 million worth of goods were shipped to the ROK, making it Pyongyang's fourth largest trading partner. Sanctions would have disrupted this exchange. It would have also frustrated the court economy's oil-for-arms trade with Iran and Libya. By the mid-1990s the DPRK military was selling roughly $500 million in ballistic missile technology to Middle Eastern customers.[95] It is highly unlikely that China would have been willing to allow the DPRK to transport these goods across their territory during an embargo. Besides the obvious reputational costs, such a move would have required China to assist North Korea in eroding its own share of the international textile and arms market. Beijing's behavior during the episode suggests that while it did not wholeheartedly favor sanctions, it would not have blindly supported Pyongyang at its own expense.

Applying the most conservative estimate to Japanese transfers and

[92] For example, Cumings (1997, p. 427) notes that the head of the Najin-Sonbong free economic and trade zone was Kim Jong U, a relative of Kim-Il Sung.
[93] Mikheev (1993), pp. 87–8.
[94] For more on the Cho'chong'ryun, see Lind (1997); *Time*, "Kim Il Sung's money pipeline," June 13, 1994, p. 27, and David E. Sanger, "North Koreans in Japan are seen as cash source for nuclear arms," *New York Times*, November 1, 1993, p. 1.
[95] Reiss (1995), pp. 232–3.

exports, sanctions applied by Japan alone would have been the equivalent of 3.6 percent of North Korea's GDP. Adding in exports to South Korea, the figure jumps to 4.5 percent; a cutoff of the missile sales would have increased the amount to almost 7 percent. Relative to the sanctions episodes described in HSE, this is a sizable sum. It is larger than South Korea's estimated costs of coercion in 1975.

The second fact to consider is the political calculus behind the court economy. The military elite was the most powerful interest group in North Korea. The second economy was set up largely to service the interests of that elite. Bureaucratically, its finances were organized separately from the civilian sector. Its demands were fulfilled before resources were committed to the official economy. Even in times of economic crisis, that sector remained in operation. This was consistent with the efforts of Kim-Il Sung and Kim's successor and son, Kim Jong-Il to provide the army with access to consumer goods and opportunities for hard currency, as well as their concerns about losing power. High-ranking defectors claimed that the younger Kim relied on handouts of high-priced luxury goods to ensure this fealty.[96] The organization of the DPRK military seemed designed less to fight a war than to thwart any one group from overthrowing the Kims. If the leadership was willing to sacrifice military efficiency to protect itself, it indicates the strong concern of a coup.[97]

Sanctions would have threatened the court economy most of all, eliminating access to hard currency and luxury goods. Economic sanctions would have crippled the upper echelons of the North Korean government and promoted instability within the target regime. As noted in chapter 1, one of the arguments in the sanctions literature is that acquiescence becomes more likely when the economic sanctions hurt the country's elite and lead to domestic political instability. This is usually difficult to arrange, but this case provides a near-ideal type. Economic coercion, even without Chinese help, would have devastated the DPRK elite.

The North Korean leadership was not rational

In the early 1990s, the dominant adjectives used to describe DPRK foreign policy were erratic, illogical, inconsistent, unpredictable, and

---

[96] See US House (1990), p. 35; Perry (1990); *Economist*, "The North Korean enigma," October 21, 1995, p. 37.
[97] Bracken (1990), pp. 94–5.

unrealistic.[98] Mazarr argues that, "North Korea's pride, paranoia, and unpredictability meant that sanctions would probably not have the desired effect." In 1992, a US embassy official in Seoul asserted, "Kim Il Sung is not rational." The principal negotiator for the United States, Robert Gallucci, testified before Congress in June 1994 that, "I have frequently said that why the North Koreans do things is a mystery to me." After the crisis, the *Financial Times* wrote, "North Korea's opaque system, its hermit-like leadership, and its weird responses on many international issues make it difficult to predict which course Pyongyang might follow."[99]

This assertion of irrationality was backed up by personality profiles of the DPRK leaders Kim-Il Sung and his son Kim Jong-Il. Information on the DPRK leadership was scarce, mostly the product of diplomatic rumors and unverifiable reports from North Korean defectors. Given the incentive of defectors to paint the DPRK regime in desperate colors, these reports cannot be taken at face value. The available information was nevertheless troubling. It reinforced the belief that both Kims were so far removed from reality that they were incapable of accurately weighing the costs and benefits of their foreign policy. One assessment of the younger Kim argued that he had lived his adult life "in an artificial world where he is praised, flattered, and patronized ... he may be even more narrow and impatient, more rigid and doctrinaire, and less informed and objective about the outside world than his father."[100] Others contended that the younger Kim was a callow playboy more concerned with personal gratification than issues of state importance.[101]

The claim of irrationality cannot be lightly dismissed, and is difficult to falsify, in part because irrationality could take myriad forms. However, there are facts that are consistent with the conflict expectations model and inconsistent with an irrationality hypothesis. First, the chronology shows that DPRK was willing to make concessions when faced with pressure from either the Soviet Union or China. In 1985 North Korea signed the NPT in response to Soviet pressure; in

---

[98] See Roy (1994), pp. 130–3.

[99] The quotes are from Mazarr (1995), p. 131; Kang (1995), p. 264; US House (1994), p. 20; Tony Walker, "Hungry North Korea on short fuse," *Financial Times*, February 7, 1996, p. 6.

[100] Quoted in Roy (1994), p. 131.

[101] "What kind of man drinks Hennessy? Excellent question," *Wall Street Journal*, August 5, 1994, p. A1.

1991 it agreed to negotiations with South Korea in response to Chinese pressure. Why would a decision-maker divorced from reality consistently accede to allied pressure but resist similar pressure from adversaries?

Second, the chronology also shows a consistent pattern of offering minor concessions just before sanctions were about to be implemented. This pattern is peculiarly regular for an irrational actor. However, it is consistent with an aggressive bargaining strategy. Other analysts concur on this point. Leonard Spector commented in June 1994, "The pattern of North Korean negotiation is to create a looming sense of danger, and then extract concessions."[102] South Korean evaluations of DPRK bargaining tactics argue that although North Korean negotiators are consistently belligerent, they respond to changes in the costs and benefits of stalemate.[103] Once economic sanctions were perceived as imminent, the DPRK negotiators were prepared to make minor concessions consistent with the conflict expectations model.

Finally, if the irrationality claim is correct, then one would have expected to see some change in policy after Kim-Il Sung died in July 1994. Of the two leaders, it was suspected that the younger Kim was the more erratic. If he was irrational, one would anticipate a more inconsistent foreign policy. This did not happen. After a brief hiatus, the negotiations between North Korea and the United States continued as before. The pattern of tough bargaining, DPRK inflexibility, and concessions at the last minute also continued as before.[104] It is possible that Kim Jong-Il was already the primary decision-maker prior to the elder Kim's death, but this would contradict several other pieces of the chronology. In particular, Carter met Kim-Il Sung, not Kim Jong-Il. Carter described the elder Kim as "vigorous, alert, intelligent, and remarkably familiar with the issues."[105]

Overall, the pattern of DPRK behavior is too consistent for the irrationality claim to hold. The recurrent nature of these accusations highlights the difference between subjective and instrumental rationality. Subjective rationality claims that all actors have the same ordering of preferences; instrumental rationality argues that given a set of preferences, actors will act strategically to maximize those

---

[102] *Far Eastern Economic Review*, "Point-counterpoint," June 2, 1994, p. 16.
[103] Heo (1996). [104] Sigal (1998), pp. 172–204.
[105] Quoted in Kihl (1994), p. 114.

preferences. From an American perspective, it is easy to accuse the DPRK regime of being subjectively irrational. In its fifty-year existence North Korea has repeatedly violated several international norms, including terrorism and state-sponsored assassination. It has continued operating a Stalinist economy despite the collapse of communism as a viable system. Violating the norm of nonproliferation was merely the latest action that was in conflict with US preferences. Clearly the United States and North Korea do not value the same things. Given what is important to the DPRK elite, however – staying in power, maintaining sovereignty – the regime acted in a manner consistent with instrumental rationality. Scott Snyder concurs: "Rational self-interest in the North Korean context was measured overwhelmingly by political and ideological considerations; from the outside North Korean choices appeared irrational and self-defeating."[106] Once conflict expectations are factored in, it is easy to understand why Pyongyang would have cared so much about its reputation and the relative distribution of gains.

Choosing the carrot

Public statements suggest that the Clinton administration was well aware of the damage sanctions would have inflicted on North Korea even if China was not a participant. Press reports indicated that in June 1993, Secretary of State Warren Christopher believed that sanctions would be effective despite China's lack of cooperation. Defense Secretary William Perry observed in April 1994 that, "various financial sanctions ... could be imposed only with the agreement and actions of a relatively few countries."[107] The North Koreans were also made fully aware that sanctions would be implemented without the Security Council's approval.[108] Despite this knowledge, the United States acceded to negotiations because it needed the cooperation of Japan and South Korea and wanted the cooperation of China. All three countries wanted to see an attempt at dialogue before sanctions were implemented.

The United States was willing to negotiate, but it viewed these negotiations as a way to satisfy its allies' qualms about sanctions, and

---

[106] Snyder (1995), p. 8.

[107] Mazarr (1995), p. 114; *Far Eastern Economic Review*, "No compromise," April 14, 1994, pp. 17–18.

[108] See "Gallucci's remarks on sanctions reported," in FBIS-EAS-94–114, June 14, 1994, p. 18.

to brandish the possibility of sanctions as the outcome if North Korea failed to concede. Washington's strategy during the first round of negotiations, according to a State Department official, was one of "showing the sticks first, and holding the carrots in reserve ... the carrots were in a basket, and the basket was kept squarely on the floor behind him." Most of these carrots, furthermore, were nothing new. They consisted mostly of negative security assurances, which had been made in previous negotiations.[109] Even after North Korea suspended withdrawal from the NPT, the United States retained a belligerent tone. On a visit to Seoul in July 1993, President Clinton warned Pyongyang that if North Korea developed nuclear weapons, "it would be the end of their country." Other US officials made similar noises throughout the summer. In October, Defense Secretary Les Aspin told Japanese officials that negotiations would likely fail, and the result would be a sanctions attempt.[110] Even after Carter's message in mid-June that the North Koreans were ready to accept a package deal, Secretary of State Warren Christopher met with Russian Foreign Minister Andrei Kozyrev to hammer out the exact sequencing of UN sanctions. It was not until President Clinton received a written communication from North Korea confirming Carter's statement that the sanctions machinery halted.[111]

Even though the United States was willing to coerce, it decided to proffer the carrot instead. Why? I argued in chapter 2 that in a situation where two states are adversaries, the expectation of frequent conflicts constrains the ability of the sender to make too large a demand. This concern for relative gains placed a severe constraint on what the United States could demand, despite the DPRK's costs of deadlock. If the demand has an all-or-nothing quality, then economic coercion in itself is insufficient to obtain the necessary concessions. The previous section showed that Pyongyang was willing to compromise on reduced concessions to avert sanctions, but would not acquiesce to all of the US demands. In this instance, the United States could not compromise its demands because of the importance it attached to the norm of nonproliferation. Forced to choose between a sustained deadlock, a military strike, and economic inducements, Washington chose the carrot because of conditions unique to this case.

[109] Snyder (1995), p. 12.
[110] Koh (1994), p. 63. See also Mazarr (1995), pp. 126–7.
[111] See *Economist*, "Korea's bomb stops ticking," June 25, 1994, p. 31.

US statements during the crisis made its demands clear: Washington wanted a complete termination of North Korea's nuclear program. Both before and after the framework agreement, high-level officials publicly confirmed this all-or-nothing demand. In November 1993, Clinton stated on *Meet the Press*: "North Korea cannot be allowed to develop a nuclear bomb. We have to be very firm about it." A month later, Aspin confirmed that Clinton's statement was an ultimatum, and noted, "We will not let the North Koreans become a nuclear power ... nuclear weapons in the hands of North Korea is unacceptable." Announcing the package deal in June 1994, Clinton said, "In response to North Korea's nuclear activities, we have consistently pursued two goals: a non-nuclear Korean Peninsula and a strong international non-proliferation regime." Testifying before Congress in January 1995, Perry said, "Our policy, from the beginning, is that we could not accept a nuclear program in North Korea ... That had been our objective from the beginning, to stop that program."[112]

To understand why the United States was so adamant about its position, it is necessary to understand the precarious future of the Non-Proliferation Treaty during the crisis. Inspections following the Gulf War revealed that the standard IAEA inspections had failed to uncover Iraq's massive program. This failure weakened the IAEA's reputation, and made North Korea's program a test case of the US commitment to nonproliferation. The renewal of the NPT was in 1995; in the run-up to that date, several developing countries expressed reservations about its extension.[113] The breakup of the Soviet Union created three new nuclear states. As was discussed in the last chapter, Kazakhstan and Ukraine were reluctant to transfer their weapons to Russia. The collapse of the Soviet nuclear infrastructure greatly reduced the barriers to acquiring the necessary atomic material and technical expertise.[114]

With the end of the cold war, nonproliferation became a high priority for the United States. In the 1993 Department of Defense Bottom Up Review, proliferation was considered to be the greatest defense policy challenge for this decade. In 1994, the US Joint Chiefs

---

[112] Mazarr (1995), pp. 134, 144; "North Korean nuclear situation," *US Department of State Dispatch*, June 27, 1994, p. 421; US Senate (1995), p. 38.

[113] *Economist*, "Nuclear non-proliferation: between the bomb and a hard place," March 25, 1995, pp. 23–6.

[114] The North Koreans tried to exploit this opportunity by hiring several Russian nuclear technicians full time. They were detained prior to entering the DPRK.

of Staff National Military Strategy identified the same issue as the top military threat facing the United States.[115] A linchpin of the US nonproliferation strategy was to ensure the renewal of the NPT. It was at this juncture that the North Korean crisis emerged. Young Wahn Kihl writes, "The impending reform of the NPT in 1995 gave North Korea a window of opportunity to play its nuclear card correctly to its advantage." Reiss notes, "US policy labored under a powerful 'disadvantage' – its traditional opposition to nuclear proliferation and its long-standing support for the integrity of the IAEA and NPT regimes."[116] To American policy-makers, it was imperative that the DPRK program be completely eliminated, to demonstrate US preferences on the issue. Hence its absolutist position. It was not enough to guarantee that the North Koreans would not be able to make nuclear weapons in the future; the US had to ensure that all previous attempts were exposed.

The threat of sanctions was sufficient to coerce North Korea into making some concessions, as noted previously. Its expectation of future conflicts *vis-à-vis* the United States, however, made total acquiescence unpalatable. It preferred deadlock to acquiescence given US demands; indeed, there was evidence to suggest it preferred war. Policy-makers in Washington were aware of this conundrum. Secretary Perry's testimony in January 1995 reveals the Clinton administration's thinking on the issue:

> While the United States and the international community were prepared to resort to sanctions if all other diplomatic remedies had failed, the outcome of a sanctions regime would have been highly unpredictable. Certainly, sanctions would have heightened tensions on the peninsula and would have obligated the United States and South Korea to take measures to prepare for military hostilities, especially in light of North Korean assertions that sanctions were tantamount to war.
>
> In general, our past experience shows that the North does not usually respond well to such blunt applications of pressure and, given the North's need to nurture its national pride, it is unlikely that the North would have acquiesced to US demands after sanctions had been imposed.[117]

Sanctions were insufficient to extract the necessary concessions from

---

[115] Mazarr (1995), pp. 4–5.
[116] Kihl (1994), p. 128; Reiss (1995), p. 281.
[117] US Senate (1995), p. 94.

the DPRK, and by June 1994 US policy-makers were aware of it.[118] This left the United States with three options: military action, economic inducements, or stalemate.

The cost of a military strike to the United States would have been considerable, since it would have undoubtedly triggered a North Korean attack.[119] The price of such a conflict was not worth the combined benefits of nonproliferation and the damage inflicted on North Korea. Mazarr notes that the United States was never willing to go to war over a possible NPT violation, even when the violator was considered a "rogue" state. In the case of North Korea, both Secretary Perry and General Luck, the commander of US forces in Korea, indicated in their testimony to Congress that the costs of the military option were exorbitant. General Luck estimated that a ground war would have cost over a trillion dollars to all the combatants. The United States would have incurred over $100 billion in damages. US casualties were estimated at 80,000 to 100,000 soldiers killed. Furthermore, a quick victory was far from assured. The DPRK had 65 percent of their armed forces, including 8,400 artillery pieces and 2,400 multiple rocket launchers, within sixty miles of the demilitarized zone. Nearly all of the military experts agreed that Seoul would have been destroyed in a war no matter which side won. Although most US commanders were confident of victory, a 1991 Pentagon simulation had the North Koreans winning in four weeks if they launched an all-out attack.[120] The prospect of Chinese intervention injected even greater uncertainty into this scenario.

Even if the United States was capable of defeating the North Korean regime, it would have been more costly to the United States than the DPRK. Washington would have had to bankroll some of the damage suffered by Seoul, as well as some of the costs of reunification. In a war, North Korea's costs would have eventually boomeranged back

---

[118] Reiss (1995, p. 271) argues that this was why Clinton approved Carter's trip to Pyongyang: "Clinton's consent evidenced not only a disdain for his foreign policy team but also his doubts about the wisdom of such a strategy – UN sanctions in response to the North's nuclear stonewalling – that he had approved and directed since his first days in office."

[119] A 1992 RAND report recommended military strikes if and only if South Korea and the United States were "willing and able to wage a full-scale war against North Korea." Reiss (1995), p. 259.

[120] Ibid., pp. 22–3. See also *Time*, "What if war breaks out in Korea?" June 13, 1994, p. 32, and Kihl (1994), p. 114.

into the lap of South Korea and the United States.[121] Nonproliferation was a high priority for the United States, but the costs were far too high to pay, given the demand. The United States was also unwilling to go to war just to weaken Pyongyang, because Washington would have incurred the greater costs.

The costs of war also made sustained deadlock an unattractive option. North Korea had made repeated statements in the spring of 1994 stating that the imposition of sanctions would be interpreted as a declaration of war. This increased the costs and risks to the United States of a sustained deadlock. Furthermore, the DPRK decision to refuel its reactors in May 1994 meant that while the United States did nothing, North Korea would continue to reprocess its spent fuel and extract more plutonium.

Economic coercion was not enough to produce the necessary concessions, military statecraft would have incurred tangible costs greater than the benefit of a nuclear-free Korea, and sustained deadlock included the possibility of war. The only option left was to use economic inducements. Despite the lack of other options, the Clinton administration was reluctant to turn to the carrot. There was significant opposition within the United States for the bribe. In the first half of June, prominent policy experts in and out of the Clinton administration preferred the hardline option.[122] After Clinton called off the sanctions campaign, the administration received considerable editorial flak for its decision. Several commentators described it as an American retreat; Albert Wohlstetter blasted the administration for repeated flip-flopping.[123]

The harshest criticism directed against the decision concerned the erosion of US reputation. Lally Weymouth wrote: "If and when President Clinton is willing to draw a line in the sand, how will he persuade North Korea's brutal dictator, Kim Il Sung, that this time America is serious?" Charles Krauthammer observed: "After this display, what allies are going to join a US-led coalition the next time

---

[121] See John Burton, "Seoul on hook of unattractive options," *Financial Times*, June 6, 1994, p. 6.

[122] See Mazarr (1995), p. 161, and Sigal (1998), p. 163; the hardline stance was typified by Brent Scowcroft and Arnold Kanter, "Korea: time for action," *Washington Post*, June 15, 1994, p. A25.

[123] Albert Wohlstetter, "Too many flip-flops," *Washington Post*, June 26, 1994, p. C7. See also Philip Zelikow, "Can talks with North Korea succeed?" *New York Times*, June 24, 1994.

talks break down or Kim crosses the line?"[124] These criticisms confirm the model's prediction that a sender country will be extremely reluctant to use the carrot with an adversarial target because it will weaken the sender's reputation for toughness.

Despite these concerns, the Clinton administration opted for the carrot for three reasons. First, the deal went much further than adherence to the NPT, satisfying the non-negotiable demands of the United States. In agreeing to trade its gas-graphite reactors for light-water reactors, the North Koreans lost two links in their ability to manufacture fissile plutonium. Light-water reactors need enriched fuel to operate; gas-graphite reactors can use natural uranium. Because the DPRK has no enrichment capability, it will have to import the fuel. This, combined with the destruction of the reprocessing facility, eliminated North Korea's proliferation potential. Testifying before Congress, Leonard Spector emphasized the totality of the arrangement: "If this agreement is implemented, I would say that with the exception of the involuntary denuclearization that was imposed on Iraq after the 1991 gulf war, there has never been an international agreement that goes so far to eliminate an emergent nuclear weapons capability."[125]

Second, the primary sender paid a very low price for the inducement. When North Korea originally proposed the package deal in June 1993, the United States balked because of the large price tag involved. The carrot option was eventually feasible only because South Korea was willing to shoulder most of the costs. The annual US contribution to the Framework Agreement was estimated to be between $20 and $30 million, far less than the $5 billion total.[126] As carrots go, this was an extremely inexpensive one for the United States. Yet even these costs were contested within the country. Both Congress and the administration were upset about reports that North Korea was diverting the heavy oil from the United States to power a

---

[124] Lally Weymouth, "What good did Carter do?", *Washington Post*, June 21, 1994, p. A17; Charles Krauthammer, "'Peace in our time,'" *Washington Post*, June 24, 1994, p. A27. Both reputation and relative gains concern also explain why the Framework Agreement forced a possible collapse in late 1998. Congressional reluctance to fund KEDO led to delays in the construction of the light-water reactors, promised fuel oil not being shipped, and no normalization of relations between the United States and North Korea. In response, Pyong yang has been observed taking steps to restart its weapons program. See Robert Manning, "Time Bomb," *The New Republic*, November 30, 1998, pp. 27–31.

[125] US House (1995), p. 44.   [126] Ibid., p. 120.

steel plant.[127] Washington was extremely concerned about the relative distribution of payoffs in this case.

Finally, the agreement gave the United States something it never had before; economic leverage over North Korea. That leverage was on display when North Korea tried to prevent a South Korean firm from building the light-water reactors in early 1995. Ambassador Gallucci replied by observing that there would be no financing for any project other than a South Korean reactor. Pyongyang, forced to choose between deadlock and accepting the carrot, conceded.[128] As the Framework Agreement is implemented, the United States and South Korea will have increased leverage over the North. The Economist Intelligence Unit noted, "Externally, as Pyongyang becomes dependent for oil and grain on powers that it still treats as enemies, so the donors acquire the leverage to cut off the flow unless the north proves more accommodating on other matters."[129] The need for low-enriched uranium will only increase the extent of North Korean dependence upon the members of KEDO. The dominant market share of the United States in enriched uranium will give it significant influence over the Korean energy sector. Furthermore, the Framework Agreement assumes a lowering of trade and investment barriers between the two countries. If North Korea's pattern of trade with South Korea and Japan is any indication, the United States will acquire additional leverage. In this sense, the carrot can become a future stick. Of course, the utility of such a stick will remain dependent upon whether North Korea continues to anticipate frequent conflicts in its relations with the United States.

In conclusion, process-tracing of this episode shows that the United States rationally chose to offer economic inducements to the North Korean regime because it was the most attractive option, given the constraints of economic and military coercion. The economic coercion of North Korea, even if limited to trade with Japan and South Korea, would have inflicted serious damage. Despite the high opportunity costs of deadlock, the DPRK regime was so concerned about the relative distribution of payoffs that it was willing to accept deadlock and go to war rather than completely acquiesce to the United States.

---

[127] Snyder (1995), n. 43.
[128] See US House (1995), pp. 26–7, and *Economist*, "North Korea: battling on," June 17, 1995, p. 37.
[129] Economist Intelligence Unit, *Country Report: South Korea and North Korea*, 3rd quarter, 1995, p. 43.

Pyongyang was willing to make some concessions in the face of economic pressure, but it would not completely surrender. The United States was aware of the DPRK preferences, but could not compromise its demands. Washington's attachment to the NPT regime was too great. Faced with a choice of either brandishing the gun or proffering the carrot, it chose the latter. It was less expensive and achieved the desired end.

Implications

This chapter provides strong empirical support for the conflict expectations model. The costs of military compellence and economic inducements make economic coercion the preferred policy option for the sender, yet its usefulness is bounded. Because adversarial targets anticipate frequent conflicts, the sender will be constrained in its ability to make significant demands. If the sender is unable to compromise its demands, it will be forced to choose between military compellence or economic inducements to extract concessions from the target country. If the carrot is sufficiently cheap to the sender and lucrative to the target, the sender can successfully use carrots with adversaries.

Process-tracing and congruence procedures support this explanation. This chapter has shown why the United States was able to use economic coercion to force South Korea into abandoning its nuclear program in 1976 but had to use economic inducements to convince its adversary, North Korea, to abandon its program eighteen years later. Although the target's potential damage from sanctions was greater in the North Korean case, the concern for the distribution of gains was also greater. North Korea's security and sovereignty preferences made its interactions with the United States a zero-sum game. The extreme distributional concerns made it unwilling to completely acquiesce in the face of economic pressure. The United States was incapable of modulating its demand, and reluctantly decided that its best option was to use the threat of coercion combined with economic inducements to get what it wanted. The imposing costs of military intervention were also a factor. South Korea, by contrast, anticipated few conflicts with the United States and was thus willing to make concessions rather than suffer the short-run costs of stalemate. Because its costs of coercion were minimal, the United States could satisfy the coercion condition.

One other observation emerges from these case studies. In part II, coercion attempts between Russia and its allies were publicly downplayed by both the sender and target. The South Korean episode shows a series of high-level talks between the United States and the Republic of Korea. When the decision was announced, it was done with little fanfare. No American or South Korean official was willing to publicly confirm what exactly happened during the negotiation sessions. This lack of public discourse eliminated some of the reputational costs. Although South Korea was obviously displeased by the coercion, the level of public rancor was minimal. By contrast, the crisis between the two adversaries resulted in more overt claims of coercive strategies. Much of the diplomacy in the North Korean episode was public. Both sides made inflammatory statements that occupied much of the private negotiations. The lack of multiple negotiating channels forced the DPRK to rely on private intermediaries and third-party countries to relay messages to Washington. Had the United States been willing to send a high-level delegation to Pyongyang, the conflict could have been resolved much earlier. This shows yet again that it is easier to detect coercion events between adversaries than allies, because adversarial targets are more likely to publicly claim they are being pressured.

IV   Conclusion

9 Conclusions, implications, speculations

Theories can never be proven true, but they can amass support. This support is more robust if the evidence varies across time and place. The evidence has ranged in place from the corridors of power in Washington to the oil fields of the Caspian Sea to the demilitarized zone on the Korean peninsula. It has moved in time from the Peloponnesian war to the present day.

This chapter summarizes what has been learned about economic coercion in international relations. It first reviews the predictions and performance of the conflict expectations model, and summarizes additional insights gained from the empirical record. It then offers up a critique of the theories and methodologies developed in the previous chapters. These conclusions have ramifications for the study and practice of foreign policy. This chapter concludes by discussing the model's policy implications, and then considering the broader implications for international relations theory and future research.

A review

When states decide whether to threaten economic coercion, or how to respond to such a threat, they care about the immediate costs and benefits of sanctions implementation, but they also care about the likelihood of future political conflicts. Concessions made in the present can be translated into future leverage, or can blemish a reputation for tough bargaining. When states anticipate frequent conflicts in the future, they will care more about the relative gains implications of the immediate outcome.

The effect of conflict expectations on the incidence and outcome of economic sanctions is contradictory. If the sender and target are adversaries, then the sender will be willing to impose sanctions under conditions that would be rejected if the two states were allies. However, the sender's eagerness does not translate into significant concessions. Heightened conflict expectations limit the number of concessions the target will make. The target will be more reluctant to acquiesce if it anticipates multiple disputes, because its concessions represent a transfer of political leverage to the sender country, magnifying the impact of the concession in the target's eyes. With non-negotiable demands, sustained deadlock is a distinct possibility. If the target is an ally, then the sender will prefer to sanction only if the costs to itself are minimal and the costs to the target are significant. Although the sender is more reluctant to coerce, it reaps significant benefits when it threatens sanctions. Because the target does not anticipate frequent conflicts, it will care more about the immediate costs and benefits of a stalemate than the long-run implications of any transfer of leverage. Ironically, the sender will extract the greatest redistribution of political assets when it cares the least about such a distribution.

This theory of state behavior suggests that previous explanations of economic sanctions are incomplete because of selection bias. The most celebrated cases of economic coercion are frequently those where conflict expectations are the greatest. By selecting cases that take such extreme values of various independent variables for in-depth analysis, scholars have unwittingly reduced the variance of the dependent variable. As a result, they suppress the causal effects of conflict expectations and magnify the effects of less relevant variables.

The empirical record supports the theory's assertions. Chapter 3 reviewed the existing evidence on the causes of sanctions initiation and outcomes and showed that the alternative approaches did a poor job of explanation. The statistical evidence in chapter 4 buttressed these findings.

Part II of the book tested the model on recent Russian efforts to coerce the NIS of the former Soviet Union. The evidence from these cases confirmed the model's prediction. In dealing with its adversaries, Russia was willing to incur greater costs in using economic coercion, and it coerced its adversaries more often than its allies. In analyzing the outcomes, however, allies granted far more concessions than adversaries, even though Russia dwarfed all of the NIS in terms of aggregate power. Boolean analysis revealed that an absence of conflict expectations, combined with the absence of a military threat, was a necessary and sufficient condition to generate significant concessions.

Chapter 8 compared the US response to South Korean and North Korean efforts to develop nuclear weapons. In the end, the United States chose to offer economic inducements to halt North Korean efforts, but economically coerced its ally, South Korea, when it attempted to develop weapons. The case histories reveal that the threatened sanctions would have been painful to both countries. Because South Korea did not perceive the United States as a threat, it was willing to make the concession. By contrast, North Korea's expectations of future conflict were so high that it was unwilling to accede to all of the US demands without significant compensation. The United States could not compromise its demands because of the importance attached to the NPT regime and the norm of nonproliferation. Although economic coercion was capable of producing limited concessions, the United States had to offer carrots to secure its demands.

The alternative explanations generate more marginal support. Statistically, the signaling explanation cannot explain the variation in the target's concessions. The case studies reveal that military statecraft is useful only when regular force is used; threats alone are insufficient. The domestic politics approach has a more mixed record. The statistical results show that it cannot explain when economic coercion is initiated. It fares somewhat better in explaining the outcome. The case study evidence reveals that while an unstable target regime can contribute to a successful sanctions episode, it is neither necessary nor sufficient. A weak target regime has a knife-edge property. It can lead to acquiescence, but it can also lead the regime to harden its position *vis-à-vis* the sender so as to bolster its domestic support. The conflict expectations model does a superior job of explaining both the initiation and the outcome of economic coercion.

Additional insights

This book has also revealed additional insights about economic coercion that go beyond the model developed here. First, the coercion of adversaries is far more public than the coercion of allies. This was true of both senders and targets. The US pressure of South Korea was applied without public notification until after the fact. The South Korean regime, in response, refused to comment about the issue. By contrast, the call for sanctions in dealing with North Korea involved high-profile public deliberations within the Clinton administration and the United Nations Security Council. North Korea issued constant press releases lambasting the United States for its coercive diplomacy. This phenomenon was also true in the instances of Russian coercion. Russian President Boris Yeltsin announced the use of economic pressure to coerce Ukraine on national television; there were similar public pronouncements about applying sanctions to the Baltic states. Each of these target regimes also publicized the events as acts of economic coercion. In contrast, the use of economic pressure against Belarus and the Central Asian states was less trumpeted by Moscow, even though it was far more effective. These target states generally refrained from publicly complaining about Russia's economic pressure.

This tendency for coercion episodes involving adversaries to be more public explains much of the conventional wisdom in the sanctions literature. I suggested in the first chapter that many of the best known episodes of economic sanctions were atypical. This is borne out by the evidence. Previous studies of sanctions have usually analyzed high-profile cases involving adversaries and extensive multi-lateral cooperation. The model and the empirical evidence suggest that these cases are the most likely to involve two adversaries, and produce minimal concessions at best. By focusing only on these cases, these studies came to the conclusion that sanctions were ineffective. This book has demonstrated that the universe of cases is more diverse than was previously suspected.

Second, the evidence reveals that target states adopt several strategies to avoid acquiescing under economic pressure. Realignment certainly reduces the number of concessions a target state will be expected to make, but it also increases the risk of constant coercion attempts. States can also attempt to bandwagon. By allying themselves closely to the sender country, the target can reduce the sender's incentive to use sanctions. However, the large-N data show few cases of balancing and virtually no cases of bandwagoning. Indeed, the case evidence from the former Soviet Union reveals a third strategy: the use of international institutions as a way to bind the sender's hands. Several of the NIS pushed for strong international institutions that would lead to greater integration with Russia, but also prevent Russia from using its foreign economic policies in a coercive manner. Somewhat surprisingly, states preferred to use international institutions rather than balance-of-power strategies to ward off economic coercion.

A critique

Although the explanation for economic coercion developed here appears promising, it is far from complete. Despite its strength, there are theoretical and methodological limits to this book. This section is not intended to be a *mea culpa* as much as an honest inventory of the hurdles that still nead to be cleared.

Theoretically, I usually chose tractability over complexity in presenting the conflict expectations model. This choice carries a price. For example, I assumed that conflict expectations were exogenous to the statecraft game. It is possible, however, that conflict expectations are endogenous to sanctions disputes. Such a possibility would require a more complex game that incorporates wider time horizons. Another criticism can be found in the notion of conflict expectations itself. I have generally argued that alignment can act as a real-world proxy for conflict expectations, and with formal allies or enduring rivals, such an approach is satisfactory. Dyads that do not fall into either category are more nebulous. There is a danger that such ambiguous dyads might be vulnerable to *post hoc* data fitting. More stringent codings might be needed.

Another theoretical criticism is that the conflict expectations model largely avoids the relationship between economic and military coercion. The evidence presented here suggests that economic coercion is a viable alternative to the use of force in political disputes, and does not act merely as a signal for military statecraft. That does not exhaust the set of possible relationships between the two forms of statecraft, however. As David Baldwin has pointed out, economic statecraft needs to be judged in relation to other means of influence.[1] While this book has avoided linking the causes of economic coercion with the causes of war, later work will need to pay attention to this dynamic.

Empirically, the book is also open to criticism. The statistical sections rely on sanctions data that have been the subject of numerous criticisms. The bulk of the observations occurred during the cold war. It is possible that bipolarity profoundly affected the statistical results in ways that will be impossible to tell until a sufficient number of

[1] Baldwin (1985).

post-cold war observations are coded. I tried to address this problem in the later parts of the book, but they are also not free of criticism. The recent nature of the post-Soviet cases of economic coercion make the outcomes of Russian attempts at economic coercion provisional. Finally, the cases of nuclear proliferation on the Korean peninsula are necessarily incomplete. The classified nature of US decision-making, combined with the xenophobic mentality of the North Korean regime, makes it impossible at the present time to ascertain the mindset of the American and Korean decision-makers.

The theory and evidence are incomplete. The model does not describe every iteration of the bargaining process. It does not explain all the variation in the occurrence or outcomes of sanctions episodes. The alternative explanations play some role in the adjudication of coercion disputes. Nevertheless, this project is a significant step forward in explaining the dynamics of economic coercion. It presents a unified theory that explains both the likelihood of observing economic diplomacy as well as the likelihood of its success. It presents empirical evidence using multiple methodologies that strongly support the model's hypotheses. It leads to new interpretations of old cases, and generates new facts about more recent coercion episodes. The model developed here represents an improvement over existing explanations.

Policy implications

It is a wonderful cliché in foreign affairs that academics make grandiose and unrealistic generalizations, inviting the scorn of policy-makers for overlooking the complexity and the politics of the situation. With regard to sanctions, however, the cliché has been reversed. Prominent policy-makers are fond of dismissing economic statecraft as a useless and counterproductive option. Academics recognize that the situation is not that simple.

What is the optimal way to utilize economic coercion? The theory and evidence from this book offer several suggestions on the use of economic coercion in the conduct of US foreign policy.[2] Threaten to

---

[2] A word of caution is in order. It is somewhat awkward for a social scientist to make observations about policy that are actually useful. Social science theories simplify the world in order to explain it; policy-makers want as much information about a particular crisis or interaction as possible. These two goals can conflict. Hans Morgenthau observed in *Politics Among Nations*: "The first lesson the student of international politics

impose the most damaging sanctions as soon as possible. Delay on this issue gives the target country the chance to defray the long-run opportunity costs. Be wary of devoting resources to securing multilateral cooperation in implementing sanctions. The statistical evidence suggests that cooperation is far from a prerequisite of successful sanctions. Most important, calibrate the demand to the expectations of future conflict. All else being equal, China, North Korea, or Cuba will not make the same concessions to the United States as Japan, South Korea, or El Salvador. The first group of countries view the United States as a threat, and are reluctant to make concessions that they believe will be exploited in the future. Diplomacy and rhetoric can alter these perceptions only at the margins.

Over the longer run, the model developed here shows that the engagement versus containment debate is sterile and unproductive. An ongoing argument in policy circles is whether it is better to compel other states to change their policies through increased trade and exchange or through a long-term trade boycott.[3] In theory, the engagement option works in two ways. First, by increasing interdependence, engagement makes it costly for the target regime to adopt policies that conflict with the sender. Second, increased trade fosters a powerful domestic bloc within the target country that undercuts the regime's grip on power. In theory, the containment option works by punishing the target so that it has the incentive to change its existing policies.

In the United States, this debate has lasted for at least thirty years; only the target countries have changed. In the 1970s, the argument was about the Soviet Union. In the 1980s, the debate was about Cuba and South Africa. In the 1990s, controversy has surrounded US foreign economic policies towards China and the group of rogue states: Iran, Iraq, Libya, Cuba, and North Korea.

What all of these states have in common is that they anticipate frequent conflicts with the United States over a broad array of policies. The theory and evidence presented in this book suggest that neither strategy will be particularly successful in the long run. The containment option will generate few concessions from adversaries, even if the target's opportunity costs of containment are high. None of the

must learn and never forget is that the complexities of international affairs make simple solutions and trustworthy prophecies impossible. Here the scholar and the charlatan part company." The reader is thus forewarned. Morgenthau quoted in Newsom (1996), p. 59.

[3] See Lavin (1996) for a recent discussion.

outlaw states has made any concessions to the United States because of economic pressure.

The engagement option would seem to be more attractive. Increased trade would increase the target's costs of any coercion attempt. There is the additional argument that increased trade undercuts the target regime's domestic base by creating a new interest group that prefers acquiescing to the sender. Furthermore, the North Korean case discussed in chapter 8 shows that economic inducements can lead to acquiescence in the present and enhanced leverage for the future.

A closer look at these arguments suggests that the engagement option is only marginally superior to the containment option. First, the benefits of engagement appear only when the sender is willing to threaten the disruption of economic exchange. Adversaries anticipate the probability of future conflicts and will act to minimize their trade vulnerabilities.[4] Unless conflict expectations change, this threat will not produce many more concessions. Even if trade levels were to rise, the model developed here has shown that increasing an adversarial target's costs of coercion increases the concession size by only a marginal amount.

Second, the evidence presented here shows that the domestic politics standpoint cuts both ways: an engagement strategy can lead to a less responsive target. Assume that increased trade generates a faction in the target's ruling coalition that prefers accommodating the sender. The regime could react in several ways. It could indeed shift its policies in line with the sender's preferences, reflecting the shift in the median preferences of the ruling coalition. However, a second possibility would be to increase cleavages within the old ruling coalition, leading to the formation of a new, narrower coalition by removing the accommodationist faction. A new coalition would include previously excluded harder-line elements, leading to a more aggressive stance towards the sender. An engagement strategy has just as much potential to backfire as a containment strategy.

The case study of the US–DPRK conflict highlights the success of the carrot option, but it also reveals that the United States chose the carrot because its nonproliferation policy was non-negotiable and the cost of the carrot was cheap. The Clinton administration considered economic and military coercion before reluctantly agreeing to the

---

[4] See Holsti (1982) and Gowa (1994) on how states try to protect themselves against the prospect of economic coercion.

carrot. One policy analyst commented during the crisis, "all policy options stink." In a nutshell, that describes the problem of the engagement/containment dilemma. This debate inevitably deals with adversaries. Due to heightened conflict expectations, no policy option will produce significant concessions and therefore all of them will be frustrating. In dealing with adversaries, neither option will reap what its supporters claim.

Finally, as noted in chapter 1, the end of the cold war has led to several innovations in the use of economic coercion from the United States.[5] These innovations include congressionally mandated sanctions, extraterritorial sanctions, and sanctions imposed by states and localities. These developments merit some discussion.

Single-issue lobbies for the war on drugs, terrorism, religious freedom, human rights, fair trade, and nonproliferation have tried to influence policy through the application of mandatory economic sanctions. These categorical mandates, established by Congress, have been responsible for the lion's share of threatened or applied sanctions since 1990. Activists argue that congressional mandates create an automatic trigger within the United States government that cannot be deactivated. Targeted countries, including close allies, will recognize that the executive branch has little discretionary power. This makes the US threat of sanctions more credible and therefore induces these countries to alter their policies. As in a game of chicken between two cars, the driver who throws the steering wheel out of the window should win every time.

The problem with this logic is that even with congressional mandates, the executive branch still controls the steering wheel. All of these laws include at least two ways for the executive branch to circumvent sanctions. First, most of these laws rely on an executive agency to determine if the relevant countries are complying with American standards. This gives the president the bureaucratic muscle to avert sanctions by refusing to follow the spirit of the laws. For example, as noted in chapter 3, the Carter administration, although concerned with human rights, refused to brand any country as a

---

[5] In the past five years, several US states and localities have also attempted to employ economic coercion against other countries. These will not be discussed in depth for two reasons. Practically, they are useless. For example, it is doubtful that Myanmar will acquiesce due to the economic costs imposed by Santa Cruz, California. Legally, these kinds of sanctions rest on dubious constitutional grounds (Schmahmann and Finch 1997).

"gross violator" of human rights because it did not want to trigger automatic sanctions. More recently, the Clinton administration certified Mexico as a responsible partner on drug prevention while denying the same status to Colombia, despite the marked similarities between the two countries on the drug issue. In explaining the effect of mandated sanctions on US foreign policy, Clinton was remarkably candid in his appraisal:

> What always happens if you have automatic sanctions legislation is it puts enormous pressure on whoever is in the executive branch to fudge an evaluation of the facts of what is going on. And that's not what you want. What you want is to leave the President some flexibility, including the ability to impose sanctions, some flexibility with a range of appropriate reactions.[6]

Second, even if executive agencies are completely candid in their reports to Congress, almost every piece of legislation regarding sanctions has a "national interest" waiver attached to it. This gives the president the authority to waive any sanctions where other foreign policy considerations indicate. Congress, for example, would have been willing to accept drug certification of Mexico had the Clinton administration invoked the national interest waiver. Obviously, the national interest argument can be used to exempt US allies from sanctions. The result is the same pattern predicted by the conflict expectations model; sanctions are targeted against adversaries and few concessions are granted. Far from being an example of throwing out the steering wheel, congressional mandates are about as effective as honking the horn.

Another type of economic pressure that has recently captured attention is the use of extraterritorial, or secondary, sanctions. In these situations, the United States threatens to sanction firms or countries that trade or invest in a country that it has already sanctioned. The pipeline sanctions discussed in chapter 3 fall under this category. So do attempts by the Carter administration to widen the freeze on Iranian financial assets in European branches of US banks. More recently, any sanctions generated by laws punish corporations and executives that do business with Cuba, Iran, and Libya fall under this category.

It would be easy to label this kind of economic pressure as political

---

[6] Elaine Sciolino, "On sanctions, Clinton details threat to truth," *New York Times*, April 28, 1998, pp. A1, A7.

showboating. The truth is a little more complex. Extraterritorial sanctions force firms to choose between the US market or the target country's market, which is usually less important to the corporation. In addition, even the threat of extraterritorial sanctions introduces uncertainty into the business climate, reducing the value of continued trade with the target state. US sanctions against foreign firms have often succeeded in getting firms to acquiesce. In the Iranian case, the foreign subsidiaries cooperated with the United States in freezing the Iranian assets. In the pipeline case, most of the foreign firms valued their business with the United States more than with the Soviet Union. Even the Helms–Burton Act slowed the pace of foreign investment in Cuba.[7]

The problem, of course, is that sanctions against foreign firms are usually transformed into sanctions against the countries that host these firms. The host countries inevitably see extraterritorial sanctions as a violation of their sovereignty. They stiffen the backbone of corporations, and turn the situation into an interstate dispute. This is where the conflict expectations model predicts that extraterritorial sanctions will fail. When host countries turn these sanctions into a potential trade war, the sender faces the prospect of incurring significant costs. Because these host countries are usually allies (i.e. Canada and Western Europe for the United States), the coercion condition is rarely satisfied. The sender country will prefer to back down. Host countries have an incentive to up the stakes because it forces the United States to back down. This dynamic appears to explain the reluctance of the United States to implement extraterritorial sanctions in the 1980s,[8] and the Clinton administration's deal with the European Union not to implement Helms–Burton and other extraterritorial sanctions.

Questions for future research

The model's validity in explaining the occurrence and outcome of economic coercion attempts has broader implications for theories of international relations. One conclusion is that because of conflict expectations, the concern for relative gains matters, and it matters in

---

[7] See Alerassool (1993) on the Iranian case, Martin (1992), chapter 8, on the pipeline sanctions, and the *Economist*, "Saying boo to Helms–Burton," October 19, 1996, p. 49, on Cuba. More generally, see Shambaugh (1999).
[8] Rodman (1995).

unexpected ways. The model shows that senders will be more eager to sanction when they care about relative performance. What is surprising is that the sender's eagerness does not translate into larger concessions. Instead, senders can expect fewer concessions, because the target will wish to minimize the disutility of transferring political advantages to the sender. Therefore, the concern for relative gains makes the use of economic sanctions more frequent and more futile.

This result is distinct from either the neoliberal or neorealist paradigms. Neoliberals are incorrect in downplaying the effect of conflict expectations on the pattern of trade and economic exchange. Nation-states must consider the prospect of economic manipulation when they engage in trade and exchange. Neorealists must also deal with significant anomalies. Realists argue that states are concerned with the distribution of power, and that compels them to act as if they care about relative gains. The evidence presented here contradicts that story, however. All of the evidence confirms that conflict expectations affects the behavior of small target countries even when dealing with great powers. This should not happen in a neorealist world, since the differences in power are already so great. Furthermore, the presence of relative gains concern reduces rather than enhances the capabilities of great powers. Power is exercised through the ability to impose significant opportunity costs on the target country, but it is also mitigated by the target's conflict expectations. The preferences of small states, and their choice of alliance partners, matter more than neorealists would care to admit. These anomalies suggest that a synthesis of these two paradigms would prove more useful than continued attempts to declare one better than the other.

A good research project should start with a set of clearly defined research puzzles, answer them, and develop new questions from the answers. The results from this book provoke at least four research questions.

What is the effect of domestic politics on coercion attempts? This book has shown that there is no theory of domestic politics in international relations that can explain the initiation and outcome of economic coercion. One could argue that this says more about the state of second-image theories in international relations theory than it does about economic statecraft. The two-level games literature has focused on the effect of domestic political forces on international cooperation. Less attention has been given to the role domestic groups and institutions play in coercive bargaining. There have been some recent attempts to flesh out domestic or two-level approaches on this issue, but further work is needed.[9] One possibility, touched on only briefly here, is that domestic groups and institutions act as intervening variables between the expectations of future conflict and the outcome. For example, it is possible that between adversaries, domestic groups in both the target and sender will have a greater incentive to adopt belligerent positions in an attempt to enhance their respective standing. Between allies, such an approach would not be as fruitful. If this is true, then the effect of domestic politics would be to reinforce the effect of the conflict expectations model.

How do sender countries choose among their influence policies? This book has touched on the issue of choosing between economic sanctions and economic inducements, but has largely skipped the choice between sanctions, war, or a combination of policies. The relationship between the two forms of statecraft is more complicated than one of pure substitutes or pure compliments. Although the hypothesis that economic sanctions act as signals for the use of force has found little empirical support in this book, there are other possibilities. For example, economic coercion may be a substitute for force in conflicts between democracies, but not between other dyads. Another possibility is that the implementation of economic coercion accidentally or purposefully increases the chances of war. Is economic coercion prone to "mission creep" or is it part of a conscious strategy that leads to war?

What is the role international institutions play in constraining the possibility of economic coercion? In theory, regimes such as the World Trade Organization, the European Union, and the CIS limit the ability of nation-states to coerce other members. Weaker states have an obvious motivation for encouraging such institutions; they reduce the probability of great power coercion. A more intriguing question is why great powers are willing to go along. One possibility is that international institutions allow great powers to engage in displays of credible commitment. The catch, of course, is that great powers frequently violate or manipulate institutional norms. The CIS has failed to prevent the Russian Federation from using economic coercion as an instrument of foreign policy. The United States has used tools of economic statecraft that violate the General Agreements on Tariffs and

---

[9] Kirshner (1997) provides a particularly promising approach to analyzing the domestic politics of the target country.

Trade. Great powers try to use international organizations as instruments of economic coercion. There is an underlying tension between needing institutions to ensure the long-run stability of the global political economy and violating institutional constraints to secure the national interest. How do great powers manage this tradeoff?

How do states trade with each other, given the prospect of economic coercion? This book has focused on the immediacy of the coercion event. It has shown that economic coercion is a constant possibility in the international system. Countries must cope with the Faustian bargain of enhancing their welfare through increased trade and exchange while increasing their vulnerability to potential economic coercion. This fact has larger implications for the study of international political economy. First, how does the possibility of coercion force potential targets to alter their trade patterns? What other strategies can weak powers pursue in order to avoid this possibility? Stephen D. Krasner and Peter Katzenstein have investigated how states use external and internal resources to protect their sovereignty from the vagaries of the international marketplace.[10] Less work has been done on how states act to protect themselves against great power manipulation of these markets.

Senders face different tradeoffs in choosing to threaten economic coercion. Target states can reduce the number of equilibrium concessions if they engage in balancing behavior. A glance at the data suggests that states rarely realign themselves in response to sender's attempt at economic coercion, but it exists as a possibility. Senders must be concerned about the quality of their long-term relationship with the target following a coercion attempt. Senders that frequently coerce can create the reputation of being unreliable partners.[11] As seen in chapter 6, Russia alienated many of its erstwhile allies by exploiting its economic leverage as well as disregarding institutional norms when they impeded its quest for short-term gains. How do senders balance the long-run damage to their credibility with the short-run

---

[10] See Krasner (1985) on the use of international organizations to regulate the market, and Katzenstein (1985) on the use of domestic arrangements to do the same.

[11] For example, when President Carter decided to impose a grain embargo on the Soviet Union, he exempted the first 8 million tons because he did not want to break an existing contract (Paarlberg, 1980). Similarly, after the success in freezing Iranian assets in the United States during the hostage crisis, commentators were worried about the long-run implications for property rights in financial markets (Miyagawa 1992).

gains of coercion? This is a constraint of economic coercion that needs to be explored further.

This book demonstrates that the range and utility of economic coercion is more varied than previously thought. Sanctions do not always fail; sometimes they reap notable successes. There is an explanation for the bias in the conventional wisdom. Economic coercion between adversaries is likely to be more public, more costly to the sanctioner, and less successful at forcing concessions. This is because adversaries anticipate frequent conflicts with each other and will care more about relative gains and reputation, making sanctions more likely but less profitable. Economic coercion between allies, although rarer, is considerably more effective. States will be understandably reluctant to coerce allies. Once they do, however, the absence of conflict expectations will make the sanctioned country more willing to concede. Therefore, in observing the entire range of coercion episodes, one sees a majority of noisy sanctions disputes between adversaries with limited success, and a minority of quiet sanctions disputes between allies, with greater success. The standard explanation of sanctions fails to see the entire picture. If nothing else, this book broadens the canvas.

References

Achen, Christopher, and Duncan Snidal. 1989. Rational deterrence theory and comparative case studies. *World Politics* 41: 143–69.

Adler-Karlsson, Gunnar. 1968. *Western Economic Warfare, 1947–1967: a Case Study in Foreign Economic Policy*. Stockholm: Almqvist and Wiksell.

Alerassool, Mahvash. 1993. *Freezing Assets: the USA and the Most Effective Economic Sanction*. New York: St. Martin's.

Alieva, Leila. 1995. The institutions, orientations, and conduct of foreign policy in post-Soviet Azerbaijan. In Adeed Dawisha and Karen Dawisha, eds., *The Making of Foreign Policy in Russia and the New States of Eurasia*. Armonk, NY: M. E. Sharpe.

Alves, Maria. 1985. *State and Opposition in Military Brazil*. Austin, TX: University of Texas Press.

Arbatov, Alexei. 1994. Russian foreign policy priorities for the 1990s. In Stephen Miller and Teresa Pelton Johnson, eds., *Russian Security After the Cold War: Seven Views From Moscow*. CSIA Studies in International Security 3. Brassey's: Washington, DC.

Arens, Moshe. 1995. *Broken Covenant: American Foreign Policy and the Crisis between the US and Israel*. New York: Simon and Schuster.

Axelrod, Robert. 1984. *The Evolution of Cooperation*. New York: Basic Books.

Axelrod, Robert, and Robert Keohane. 1986. Achieving cooperation under anarchy: strategies and institutions. In Kenneth Oye, ed., *Cooperation Under Anarchy*. Princeton: Princeton University Press.

Back, Kwang-Il. 1988. *Korea and the United States*. Seoul: Research Center for Peace and Unification of Korea.

Baker, James. 1995. *The Politics of Diplomacy: Revolution, War and Peace, 1989–1992*. New York: G. P. Putnam's Sons.

Baker, Steven. 1976. Monopoly or cartel? *Foreign Policy* 23: 202–20.

Baldwin, David. 1985. *Economic Statecraft*. Princeton: Princeton University Press.

Barber, Benjamin. 1995. *Jihad vs. McWorld*. New York: Times Books.

Barber, James. 1979. Economic sanctions as a policy instrument. *International Affairs* 55: 367–84.

Bayard, Thomas, Joseph Pelzman, and Jorge Perez-Lopez. 1983. Stakes and risks in economic sanctions. *World Economy* 6(1): 73–87.

Bienen, Henry, and Robert Gilpin. 1980. Economic sanctions as a response to terrorism. *Journal of Strategic Studies* 3: 89–98.

Blank, Stephen. 1995. Energy, economics, and security in Central Asia: Russia and its rivals. *Central Asian Survey* 14: 373–406.

Blessing, James. 1975. The suspension of foreign aid by the United States, 1927–1948. PhD dissertation, State University of New York at Albany.

1981. The suspension of foreign aid: a macro-analysis. *Polity* 13: 524–35.

Bracken, Paul. 1990. The North Korean nuclear program as a problem of state survival. In Andrew Mack, ed., *Asian Flashpoint: Security and the Korean Peninsula*. Canberra: Allen and Unwin.

Bremmer, Ian. 1994. Nazarbayev and the North: State-building and ethnic relations in Kazakhstan. *Ethnic and Racial Studies* 17: 619–35.

Brzezinski, Zbignew. 1983. *Power and Principle*. New York: Farrar, Strauss & Giroux.

1994. The premature partnership. *Foreign Affairs* 73(2): 67–82.

Brzezinski, Zbigniew, and Paige Sullivan, eds. 1997. *Russia and the Commonwealth of Independent States: Documents, Data, and Analysis*. Armonk, NY: M. E. Sharpe.

Buck, Lori, Nicole Gallant and Kim Richard Nossal. 1998. Sanctions as a gendered instrument of statecraft: the case of Iraq. *Review of International Studies* 24: 69–84.

Bueno de Mesquita, Bruce. 1981. *The War Trap*. New Haven: Yale University Press.

Buzan, Barry. 1984. Economic structure and international security. *International Organization* 38: 597–624.

Cannon, Lou. 1991. *Reagan: The Role of a Lifetime*. New York: Simon and Schuster.

Carter, Jimmy. 1982. *Keeping Faith*. New York: Bantam Books.

Cha, Victor. 1999. *Alignment Despite Antagonism: The United States–Korea–Japan Security Triangle*. Stanford, CA: Stanford University Press.

Chayes, Abram, and Antonia Handler Chayes. 1995. *The New Sovereignty: Compliance with International Regulatory Agreements*. Cambridge, MA: Harvard University Press.

Chung, Chin-Wee. 1984. American–North Korean relations. In Youngnok Koo and Dae-Sook Suh, eds., *Korea and the United States: a Century of Cooperation*. Honolulu: University of Hawaii Press.

Clinton, W. David. 1994. *The Two Faces of National Interest*. Baton Rouge, LA: Louisiana State University Press.

Cohen, Stephen. 1982. Conditioning US security assistance on human rights practices. *American Journal of International Law* 76: 246–79.

Collier, David, and James Mahoney. 1996. Insights and pitfalls: selection bias in qualitative research. *World Politics* 49: 56–91.

Congressional Research Service. 1979. *Human Rights and US Foreign Assistance:*

Experiences and Issues in Policy Implementation. Prepared for the US Senate Committee on Foreign Relations, 96th Congress, 1st session. Washington, DC: US Government Printing Office.

Cortright, David, and George Lopez, eds. 1995. *Economic Sanctions: Panacea or Peacebuilding in a Post-Cold War World?* Boulder, CO: Westview Press.

Council on Foreign Relations. 1995. *Success or Sellout? The US–North Korean Nuclear Accord*. New York: Council on Foreign Relations.

Crahan, Margaret. 1982. National security ideology and human rights. In Margaret Crahan, ed., *Human Rights and Basic Needs in the Americas*. Washington, DC: Georgetown University Press.

Crawford, Beverly. 1994. The new security dilemma under international economic interdependence. *Millennium: Journal of International Studies* 23: 25–55.

Cumings, Bruce. 1997. *Korea's Place in the Sun: a Modern History*. New York: W. W. Norton.

D'Anieri, Paul. 1995. Economic interdependence in Ukrainian foreign policy. Presented at the 1995 Annual Meeting of the American Political Science Association, Chicago, IL.

Daoudi, M.S., and M. S. Dajani. 1983. *Economic Sanctions: Ideals and Experience*. Boston: Routledge and Kegan Paul.

Dashti-Gibson, Jaleh, Patricia Davis, and Benjamin Radcliff. 1997. On the determinants of the success of economic sanctions: an empirical analysis. *American Journal of Political Science* 41: 608–18.

Dassel, Kurt, and Eric Reinhardt. 1999. Domestic strife and the initiation of violence at home and abroad. *American Journal of Political Science* 43: 56–85.

David, Stephen. 1991. *Choosing Sides: Alignment and Realignment in the Third World*. Baltimore, MD: Johns Hopkins University Press.

Dawisha, Adeed, and Karen Dawisha, eds. 1995. *The Making of Foreign Policy in Russia and the New States of Eurasia*. Armonk, NY: M. E. Sharpe.

Dawisha, Karen, and Bruce Parrott. 1994. *Russia and The New States of Eurasia*. Cambridge: Cambridge University Press.

Diehl, Paul. 1985. Arms races to war: some empirical linkages. *Sociological Quarterly* 26: 331–49.

Diehl, Paul, and Gary Goertz. 1993. Enduring rivalries: theoretical constructs and empirical patterns. *International Studies Quarterly* 37: 147–71.

Dobrynin, Anatoly. 1995. *In Confidence*. New York: Random House.

Dorian, James, Ian Sheffield Rosi, and Tony Indriyanto. 1994. Central Asia's oil and gas pipeline network: current and future flows. *Post-Soviet Geography* 35: 412–30.

Dorian, James, Shakarim Zhanseitov, and Tony Indriyanto. 1994. The Kazakh oil industry. *Energy Policy* 22: 685–98.

Doxey, Margaret. 1980. *Economic Sanctions and International Enforcement*, 2nd edn. London: Macmillan.

1987. *International Sanctions in Contemporary Perspective*. New York: St. Martin's Press.

Doyle, Michael. 1986. Liberalism and world politics. *American Political Science Review* 80: 1151–67.

Drew, Elizabeth. 1977. A reporter at large: human rights. *The New Yorker* (July 18): 36–62.

Drezner, Daniel. 1997a. Counterproductive cooperation: coalition building in sanctions disputes. Presented at the International Studies Association annual meeting, Toronto, Canada.

1997b. Allies, adversaries, and economic coercion: Russian foreign economic policy since 1991. *Security Studies* 6: 65–111.

1998. Preference formation in reduced-form and extended-form games of international interactions. Working Paper, University of Colorado at Boulder.

Drury, A. Cooper. 1997. Economic sanctions and presidential decisions: models of political rationality. PhD dissertation, Arizona State University.

Eaton, Jonathan, and Maxim Engers. 1992. Sanctions. *Journal of Political Economy* 100: 899–928.

Eland, Ivan. 1995. Economic sanctions as tools of foreign policy. In David Cortright and George Lopez, eds., *Economic Sanctions: Panacea or Peacebuilding in a Post-Cold War World?* Boulder, CO: Westview Press.

Ellings, Richard. 1985. *Embargoes and World Power: Lessons From American Foreign Policy.* Boulder, CO: Westview Press.

Elliott, Kimberly, and Peter Uimonen. 1993. The effectiveness of economic sanctions with application to the case of Iraq. *Japan and the World Economy* 5: 403–9.

Fearon, James. 1994. Domestic political audiences and the escalation of international disputes. *American Political Science Review* 88: 577–92.

1995. Rationalist explanations for war. *International Organization* 49: 379–414.

Forsythe, Rosemary. 1996. *The Politics of Oil in the Caucasus and Central Asia.* Adelphi Paper 300. London: International Institute for Strategic Studies.

Galtung, Johan. 1967. On the effects of international economic sanctions, with special reference to Rhodesia. *World Politics* 19: 378–416.

Gardner, Grant, and Kent Kimbrough. 1990. The economics of country-specific tariffs. *International Economic Review* 31: 575–88.

Gardner, H. Stephen. 1984. Assessing the costs to the US economy of trade sanctions against the USSR. In Gordon Smith, ed., *The Politics of East-West Trade.* Boulder, CO: Westview Press.

George, Alexander. 1993. *Bridging the Gap: Theory and Practice in Foreign Policy.* Washington, DC: United States Institute of Peace Press.

George, Alexander, and Timothy McKeown. 1985. Case studies and theories of organizational decision-making. In R. Coulam and R. Smith, eds., *Advances in Information Processing in Organizations.* Greenwich, CT: JAI Press.

Goldschmidt, Bertrand. 1977. A historical survey of nonproliferation policies. *International Security* 2: 69–87.

References

Goltz, Thomas. 1993. Letter from Eurasia: the hidden Russian hand. *Foreign Policy* 92: 92–116.

Gowa, Joanne. 1986. Anarchy, egoism, and third images: the evolution of cooperation and international relations. *International Organization* 40: 167–86.

——— 1994. *Allies, Adversaries, and International Trade*. Princeton: Princeton University Press.

Green, Donald, and Ian Shapiro. 1994. *Pathologies of Rational Choice Theory*. New Haven: Yale University Press.

Greene, William. 1990. *Econometric Analysis*. New York: Macmillan.

Grieco, Joseph. 1988. Anarchy and the limits of cooperation. *International Organization* 42: 485–507.

——— 1990. *Cooperation Among Nations*. Ithaca, NY: Cornell University Press.

Gromyko, Andrei. 1989. *Memoirs*. New York: Doubleday.

Ha, Young-Sun. 1982. Republic of (South) Korea. In James Katz and Onkar Marwah, eds., *Nuclear Power in Developing Countries*. Toronto: Lexington Books.

——— 1983. *Nuclear Proliferation, World Order, and Korea*. Seoul: Seoul National University Press.

——— 1984. American–Korean military relations: continuity and change. In Youngnok Koo and Dae-Sook Suh, eds., *Korea and The United States: a Century of Cooperation*. Honolulu: University of Hawaii Press.

Haass, Richard. 1997. Sanctioning madness. *Foreign Affairs* 76(6): 74–95.

Haass, Richard, ed. 1988. *Economic Sanctions and American Diplomacy*. Washington, DC: The Brookings Institution.

Haig, Alexander. 1984. *Caveat: Realism, Reagan and Foreign Policy*. New York: Macmillan.

Han, Yong-Sup. 1994. China's Leverages over North Korea. *Korea and World Affairs* 18: 233–49.

Hanson, Stephen. 1996. Finding the "Russia" behind Russian foreign policy. Presented at the 1996 Western Political Science Association Annual Meeting, San Francisco, CA.

Harris, Chauncy. 1994. Ethnic tensions in the successor republics in 1993 and early 1994. *Post-Soviet Geography* 35: 185–203.

Hayes, Peter. 1990. *Pacific Powderkeg: American Nuclear Dilemmas in Korea*. Toronto: Lexington Books.

Heleniak, Tim. 1997. The changing nationality composition of the Central Asian and Transcaucasian States. *Post-Soviet Geography and Economics* 38: 357–78.

Hendrickson, David. 1994. The democratist crusade. *World Policy Journal* 11: 18–30.

Heo, Man-Ho. 1996. The characteristics of the North Korean negotiating activities: a theoretical deviation or its regularity. Presented at the 1996 annual meeting of the American Political Science Association, San Francisco, CA.

Hill, Fiona, and Pamela Jewett. 1994. *"Back in the USSR": Russia's intervention* in the Internal Affairs of the Former Soviet Republics and the Implications for United States Policy Toward Russia. Cambridge, MA: Strengthening Democratic Institutions Project, John F. Kennedy School of Government, Harvard University.

Hirschman, Albert O. 1945. *National Power and the Structure of Foreign Trade*. Berkeley, CA: University of California Press.

Hoffman, Fredrik. 1967. The function of economic sanctions: a comparative analysis. *Journal of Peace Research* 2: 140–60.

Holsti, Kal, ed. 1982. *Why Nations Realign: Foreign Policy Restructuring in the Postwar World*. London: Allen and Unwin.

Hufbauer, Gary, Kimberly Elliott, Tess Cyrus, and Elizabeth Winston. 1997. *US Economic Sanctions: Their Impact on Trade, Jobs, and Wages*. Working Paper, Institute for International Economics.

Hufbauer, Gary, Jeffrey Schott, and Kimberly Elliott. 1990a. *Economic Sanctions Reconsidered: History and Current Policy*, 2nd edn. Washington: Institute for International Economics.

1990b. *Economic Sanctions Reconsidered: Supplemental Case Histories*, 2nd edn. Washington: Institute for International Economics.

Hunter, Shireen. 1996. *Central Asia Since Independence*. London: Praeger.

International Monetary Fund. 1994. *The Russian Federation in Transition: External Developments*. Washington, DC: International Monetary Fund.

Irwin, Douglas. 1991. Mercantilism as strategic trade policy: the Anglo-Dutch rivalry for the East India trade. *Journal of Political Economy* 99: 1296–314.

Jackson, William. 1994. Imperial temptations: ethnics abroad. *Orbis* 38: 1–17.

Jentleson, Bruce. 1986. *Pipeline Politics: the Complex Political Economy of East–West Energy Trade*. Ithaca, NY: Cornell University Press.

Kaempfer, William, and Anton Lowenberg. 1988. The theory of international economic sanctions: a public choice approach. *American Economic Review* 78: 786–93.

1997. Unilateral versus multilateral international sanctions: a public choice perspective. Unpublished MS, University of Colorado at Boulder.

Kang, David. 1995. Rethinking North Korea. *Asian Survey* 35: 253–67.

Kasenov, Ourmirseric. 1995. The institutions and conduct of the foreign policy of postcommunist Kazakhstan. In Adeed Dawisha and Karen Dawisha, eds., *The Making of Foreign Policy in Russia and the New States of Eurasia*. Armonk, NY: M. E. Sharpe.

Katzenstein, Peter. 1985. *Small States in World Markets*. Ithaca, NY: Cornell University Press.

Kennan, George. 1977. *The Cloud of Danger: Current Realities of American Foreign Policy*. Boston: Little, Brown.

Kennedy, Paul. 1987. *The Rise and Fall of the Great Powers*. New York: Vintage Press.

Keohane, Robert. 1993. Institutional theory and the Realist Challenge After the Cold War. In David Baldwin, ed. *Neorealism and Neoliberalism: The Contemporary Debate*. New York: Columbia University Press.

327

Keohane, Robert, and Lisa Martin. 1995. The promise of institutionalist theory. *International Security* 20: 39–51.

Keohane, Robert, and Joseph Nye. 1978. *Power and Interdependence*. Boston: Scott Foresman.

Kihl, Young Wahn. 1994. Confrontation or compromise on the Korean peninsula: the North Korean nuclear issue. *Korean Journal of Defense Analysis* 6: 101–28.

Kim, Se-Jin, ed. 1976. *Documents on Korean–American Relations, 1943–1976*. Seoul, Research Center for Peace and Unification.

Kim, Sungwoo. 1993. Recent economic policies of North Korea. *Asian Survey* 23: 864–78.

King, Gary. 1989. *Unifying Political Methodology: the Likelihood Theory of Statistical Inference*. Cambridge: Cambridge University Press.

King, Gary, Robert Keohane, and Sidney Verba. 1994. *Designing Social Inquiry*. Princeton: Princeton University Press.

Kirshner, Jonathan. 1997. The microfoundations of economic sanctions. *Security Studies* 6: 32–64.

Klein, B., R. Crawford, and A. Alchian. 1978. Vertical integration, appropriable rents, and the competitive contracting process. *Journal of Law and Economics* 21: 297–326.

Klotz, Audie. 1996. Norms and sanctions: lessons from the socialization of South Africa. *Review of International Studies* 22: 173–90.

Knorr, Klaus. 1975. *The Power of Nations: the Political Economy of International Relations*. New York: Basic Books.

Koh, Byung Chul. 1994. Confrontation and cooperation on the Korean peninsula: the politics of nuclear nonproliferation. *Korean Journal of Defense Analysis* 6: 53–83.

Konovalov, Alexander, Sergey Oznobistchev, and Dmitry Evstafiev. 1995. A review of economic sanctions: a Russian perspective. In David Cortright and George Lopez, eds., *Economic Sanctions: Panacea or Peacebuilding in a Post-Cold War World?* Boulder, CO: Westview Press.

Krasner, Stephen D. 1978. *Defending the National Interest: Raw Materials Investments and US Foreign Policy*. Princeton: Princeton University Press.

1985. *Structural Conflict: the Third World Against Global Liberalism*. Berkeley, CA: University of California Press.

Krasnov, Gregory, and Joseph Brada. 1997. Implicit subsidies in Russian–Ukrainian energy trade. *Europe-Asia Studies* 49: 825–43.

Lam, San Ling. 1990. Economic sanctions and the success of foreign policy goals. *Japan and the World Economy* 2: 239–48.

Lamulin, Murat. 1995. Kazakhstan's nuclear policy and the control of nuclear weapons. In George Quester, ed., *The Nuclear Challenge in Russia and the New States of Eurasia*. Armonk, NY: M. E. Sharpe.

Lavin, Franklin. 1996. Asphyxiation or oxygen? The sanctions dilemma. *Foreign Policy* 104: 139–54.

Leigh-Phippard, Helen. 1995. US strategic export controls and aid to Britain, 1949–58. *Diplomacy & Statecraft* 6: 719–52.

Leng, Russell. 1983. When will they ever learn? Coercive bargaining in recurrent crises. *Journal of Conflict Resolution* 27: 379–419.

Lenway, Stefanie Ann. 1988. Between war and commerce: economic sanctions as a tool of statecraft. *International Organization* 42: 397–426.

Leyton-Brown, David, ed. 1987. *The Utility of International Economic Sanctions.* London: Croom Helm.

Li, Chien-Pin. 1993. The effectiveness of sanctions linkages: issues and actors. *International Studies Quarterly* 37: 349–70.

Liberman, Peter. 1996. Trading with the enemy: security and relative economic goals. *International Security* 21: 147–75.

Licht, Sonja. 1995. The use of sanctions in former Yugoslavia: can they assist in conflict resolution? In David Cortright and George Lopez, eds., *Economic Sanctions: Panacea or Peacebuilding in a Post-Cold War World?* Boulder, CO: Westview Press.

Lijphart, A. 1971. Comparative politics and the comparative method. *American Political Science Review* 65: 682–93.

Lind, Jennifer. 1997. Gambling with globalism: Japanese financial flows to North Korea and the sanctions policy option. *The Pacific Review* 10: 391–406.

Lindsay, James. 1986. Trade sanctions as policy instruments: a re-examination. *International Studies Quarterly* 30: 153–73.

Long, Clarence. 1977. Nuclear proliferation: can Congress act in time? *International Security* 1(4): 53–76.

Lopez, George, and David Cortright. 1997. Economic sanctions and human rights: part of the problem or part of the solution? *The International Journal of Human Rights* 1: 1–25.

Losman, Donald. 1979. *International Economic Sanctions: the Cases of Cuba, Israel and Rhodesia.* Albuquerque, NM: University of New Mexico Press.

Mansfield, Edward. 1995. International institutions and economic sanctions. *World Politics* (47): 575–605.

Martin, Lisa L. 1992. *Coercive Cooperation: Explaining Multilateral Economic Sanctions.* Princeton: Princeton University Press.

Martin, Lisa L., and Kathryn Sikkink. 1993. US policy and human rights in Argentina and Guatemala, 1973–1980. In Peter Evans, Harold Jacobson, and Robert Putnam, eds., *Double-Edged Diplomacy.* Berkeley, CA: University of California Press.

Mastanduno, Michael. 1992. *Economic Containment: COCOM and the Politics of East–West Trade.* Ithaca, NY: Cornell University Press.

Matthews, John. 1996. Current gains and future outcomes. *International Security* 21: 112–46.

Mayall, James. 1984. The sanctions problem in international economic relations: reflections in the light of recent experience. *International Affairs* 60: 631–42.

Mazarr, Michael. 1995. *North Korea and the Bomb: a Case Study in Nonproliferation.* New York: St. Martin's Press.

McCubbins, Matthew, and Thomas Schwartz. 1984. Congressional oversight overlooked: police patrols versus fire alarms. *American Journal of Political Science* 2: 165–79.

McFaul, Michael. 1995. Revolutionary ideas, state interests, and Russian foreign policy. In Vladimir Tismaneanu, ed., *Political Culture and Civil Society in Russia and the New States of Eurasia*. London: M. E. Sharpe.

McKelvey, R., and W. Zavoina. 1975. A statistical model for the analysis of ordinal level dependent variables. *Journal of Mathematical Sociology* 4: 103–20.

Mearsheimer, John. 1995. The false promise of international institutions. *International Security* 19: 5–49.

Mercer, Jonathan. 1996. *Reputation and International Politics*. Ithaca, NY: Cornell University Press.

Meyer, Stephen. 1984. *The Dynamics of Nuclear Proliferation*. Chicago: University of Chicago Press.

Mikheev, Vasily. 1993. Reforms of the North Korean economy: requirements, plans and hopes. *Korean Journal of Defense Analysis* 5: 81–95.

Miller, Judith. 1980. When sanctions worked. *Foreign Policy* 39: 118–29.

Miyagawa, Makio. 1992. *Do Economic Sanctions Work?* London: St. Martin's Press.

Moravscik, Andrew. 1993. Integrating international and domestic theories of international bargaining. In Peter Evans, Harold Jacobson, and Robert Putnam, eds., *Double-Edged Diplomacy: International Bargaining and Domestic Politics*. Berkeley, CA: University of California Press.

Morgan, T. Clifton, and Valerie Schwebach. 1996. Economic sanctions as an instrument of foreign policy: the role of domestic politics. *International Interactions* 21: 247–63.

——— 1997. Fools suffer gladly: the use of economic sanctions in international crises. *International Studies Quarterly* 41: 27–50.

Morrison, John. 1993. Pereyaslav and after: the Russian–Ukrainian relationship. *International Affairs* 69: 677–703.

Morrow, James D. 1994. *Game Theory for Political Scientists*. Princeton: Princeton University Press.

Muravchik, Joshua. 1986. *The Uncertain Crusade: Jimmy Carter and the Dilemmas of Human Rights Policy*. New York: Hamilton Press.

Nelson, Harold, and Irving Kaplan, eds. 1981. *Ethiopia: a Country Study*. Washington: US Government Printing Office.

Newsom, David. 1996. Foreign policy and academia. *Foreign Policy* 101: 52–67.

Nye, Joseph. 1990. Soft power. *Foreign Policy* 80: 153–71.

Oberdorfer, Don. 1997. *The Two Koreas: a Contemporary History*. Reading, MA: Addison-Wesley.

Office of Technology Assessment. 1977. *Nuclear Proliferation and Safeguards*. Washington: US Government Printing Office

——— 1994. *Proliferation and the Former Soviet Union*. Washington: US Government Printing Office.

Oh, John K. C. 1976. South Korea 1975: a permanent emergency. *Asian Survey* 14: 72–81.

Olcott, Martha Brill. 1997. Kazakhstan. In Glenn Curtis, ed., *Kazakhstan, Kyrgyzstan, Tajikistan, Turkmenistan, and Uzbekistan: Country Studies*. Washington: Federal Research Division, Library of Congress.

Olson, Richard Stuart. 1979. Economic coercion in world politics: with a focus on North–South relations. *World Politics* 31: 471–94.

Oye, Kenneth. 1986, ed. *Cooperation under Anarchy*. Cambridge: Harvard University Press.

Paarlberg, Robert. 1980. Lessons of the grain embargo. *Foreign Affairs* 59(3): 144–62.

———. 1987. The 1980–81 US grain embargo: consequences for the participants. In David Leyton-Brown, ed., *The Utility of International Economic Sanctions*. London: Croom Helm.

Pape, Robert. 1997. Why economic sanctions do not work. *International Security* 22: 90–136.

Pastor, Robert. 1988. The Carter administration and Latin America: a test of principle. In John D. Mortz, ed., *United States Policy in Latin America*. Lincoln, NE: University of Nebraska Press.

Paznyak, Vyachislav. 1995. Belarusian denuclearization policy and the control of nuclear weapons. In George Quester, ed., *The Nuclear Challenge in Russia and the New States of Eurasia*. Armonk, NY: M. E. Sharpe.

Perry, John Curtis. 1990. Dateline North Korea: a communist holdout. *Foreign Policy* 80: 172–91.

Pollins, Brian M. 1994. Cannons and capital: the use of coercive diplomacy by major powers in the twentieth century. In Paul Diehl and Frank Wayman, eds., *Reconstructing Realpolitik*. Ann Arbor, MI: University of Michigan Press.

Porter, Bruce, and Carol Saivetz. 1994. The once and future empire: Russia and the "near abroad." *The Washington Quarterly* 17(3): 75–90.

Powell, Robert. 1991. The problem of absolute and relative gains in international relations theory. *American Political Science Review* 85: 1303–20.

———. 1994. Anarchy in international relations theory: the neorealist–neoliberal debate. *International Organization* 48: 313–44.

Ragin, Charles. 1987. *The Comparative Method*. Berkeley, CA: University of California Press.

Reagan, Ronald. 1990. *An American Life*. New York: Simon and Schuster.

Reiss, Mitchell. 1988. *Without the Bomb: the Politics of Nuclear Proliferation*. New York: Columbia University Press.

———. 1995. *Bridled Ambition: Why Countries Constrain their Nuclear Capabilities*. Washington, DC: The Woodrow Wilson Center Press.

Rengger, N. J. 1990. *Treaties and Alliances of the World*. Detroit: Longman.

Renwick, Robin. 1981. *Economic Sanctions*. Harvard Studies in International Affairs 45. Cambridge: Center for International Affairs.

Reuther, David. 1995. UN sanctions against Iraq. In David Cortright and George Lopez, eds. *Economic Sanctions: Panacea or Peacebuilding in a Post-Cold War World?* Boulder, CO: Westview Press.

References

Richardson, Neil, and Charles Kegley. 1980. Trade dependence and foreign policy compliance. *International Studies Quarterly* 24: 191–222.

Rodman, Kenneth. 1995. Sanctions at bay? Hegemonic decline, multinational corporations, and US economic sanctions since the pipeline case. *International Organization* 49: 105–37.

Rogers, Beth. 1996. Using economic sanctions to control regional conflicts. *Security Studies* 5: 43–72.

Rosecrance, Richard. 1986. *The Rise of the Trading State: Commerce and Conquest in the Modern World*. New York: Basic Books.

Rousso, Alan. 1996. Inequality, relative gains, and realism. Presented at the 1996 annual meeting of the American Political Science Association, San Francisco, CA.

Rowe, David. 1993. Surviving economic coercion: Rhodesia's responses to international economic sanctions. PhD dissertation, Duke University.

Roy, Denny. 1994. The myth of North Korean "Irrationality." *Korean Journal of International Studies* 25: 129–45.

Rubinstein, Alvin. 1994. The geopolitical pull on Russia. *Orbis* 38: 567–83.

Russell, Wynne. 1995. Russian relations with the "near abroad." In Peter Sherman, ed., *Russian Foreign Policy Since 1990*. Boulder, CO: Westview Press.

Sabonis-Chafee, Theresa. 1995. The Russian–Lithuanian energy relationship: a case study in power politics. Presented at the 1995 Annual Meeting of the American Political Science Association, Chicago, IL.

Sagers, Matthew J. 1993. The energy industries of the former USSR: a mid-year survey. *Post-Soviet Geography* 34: 341–418.

1994. The oil industry in the southern-tier former Soviet republics. *Post-Soviet Geography* 35: 267–98.

Sano, John. 1977. United States foreign policy towards South Korea. *Korea and World Affairs* 1: 375–96.

Schelling, Thomas. 1960. *The Strategy of Conflict*. Cambridge, MA: Harvard University Press.

Schlesinger, James. 1997. Fragmentation and hubris. *The National Interest* 49: 3–10.

Schmahmann, David, and James Finch. 1997. The unconstitutionality of state and local enactments in the United States restricting business ties with Burma (Myanmar). *Vanderbilt Journal of Transnational Law* 30: 175–207.

Schmidt, Josephine, ed. 1995. *Building Democracy: The OMRI Annual Survey of Eastern Europe and Former Soviet Union*. Armonk, NY: M. E. Sharpe.

Schmiedeler, Brian. 1995. Kazak foreign policy after the collapse of the Soviet Union: forging a new state. Presented at the 1995 Annual Meeting of the American Political Science Association, Chicago, IL.

Schneider, Jeffrey. 1993. Republic energy sectors and inter-state dependencies of the Commonwealth of Independent States and Georgia. In United States Congress, Joint Economic Committee, *The Former Soviet Union in Transition, Vol. II*. Washington, DC: US Government Printing Office.

Schoultz, Lars. 1980. US Economic aid as an instrument of foreign policy: the case of human rights in Latin America. In Jack Nelson and Vera Green, eds., *International Human Rights: Contemporary Issues*. Stanfordville, NY: Human Rights Publishing Group.

——— 1981. *Human Rights and United States Policy Towards Latin America*. Princeton: Princeton University Press.

——— 1982. The Carter administration and human rights in Latin America. In Margaret Crahan, ed., *Human Rights and Basic Needs in the Americas*. Washington, DC: Georgetown University Press.

Schreiber, Anna. 1973. Economic coercion as an instrument of foreign policy: US economic measures against Cuba and the Dominican Republic. *World Politics* 25: 387–413.

Shambaugh, George. 1996. *States, Firms, and Power: Successful Sanctions in US Foreign Policy*. Albany: State University of New York Press.

Sherr, James. 1997. Russia–Ukraine *rapprochement?*: the Black Sea fleet accords. *Survival* 39: 33–50.

Shultz, George. 1993. *Turmoil and Triumph: My Years as Secretary of State*. New York: Charles Scribner's Sons.

Sigal, Leon. 1998. *Disarming Strangers: Nuclear Diplomacy with North Korea*. Princeton: Princeton University Press.

Sikkink, Kathryn. 1993. The power of principled ideas: human rights policies in the United States and Western Europe. In Judith Goldstein and Robert Keohane, eds., *Ideas and Foreign Policy*. Ithaca, NY: Cornell University Press.

Simon, Marc. 1997. Coercion or nonviolence: improving the effectiveness of international economic sanctions in cases of human rights. Paper presented at the annual meeting of the International Studies Association, Toronto, Canada.

Sislin, John. 1994. Arms as influence: the determinants of successful influence. *Journal of Conflict Resolution* 38: 665–89.

Small, Melvin, and J. David Singer. 1969. Formal alliances, 1816–1965: an extension of the basic data. *Journal of Peace Research* 3: 257–82.

Smith, Alistair. 1996. The success and use of economic sanctions. *International Interactions* 21: 229–45.

Snidal, Duncan. 1991. Relative gains and the pattern of international cooperation. *American Political Science Review* 85: 701–26.

Snyder, Scott. 1995. Dealing with North Korea's nuclear program: the role of incentives in preventing deadly conflict. Unpublished MS, United States Institute for Peace, Washington, DC.

Sokov, Nikolai. 1997. Managing a crisis of the nuclear non-proliferation regime in the former Soviet Union. Paper presented at the International Studies Association annual meeting, Toronto, Canada.

Spector, Leonard. 1985. *The New Nuclear Nations*. New York: Vintage Books.

Stohl, Michael, David Carleton, and Steven Johnson. 1984. Human rights and US foreign assistance from Nixon to Carter. *Journal of Peace Research* 21: 215–26.

References

Thucydides. 1972. *History of the Peloponnesian War.* Translated by Rex Warner. New York: Penguin Books.

Tsebelis, George. 1990. Are sanctions effective? a game-theoretic analysis. *Journal of Conflict Resolution* 34: 3–28.

Twining, David. 1993. *Guide to the Republics of the Former Soviet Union.* Westport, CT: Greenwood Press.

Ullman, Richard. 1978. Human rights and economic power: the United States versus Idi Amin. *Foreign Affairs* 56(3): 529–43.

US House, Committee on Foreign Affairs. 1994. *Developments in North Korea.* Hearings, 103rd Congress, 2nd session. Washington, DC: US Government Printing Office.

1990. *Korea: North–South Nuclear Issues.* Hearings, 101st Congress, 2nd session. Washington, DC: US Government Printing Office.

US House, Committee on International Relations. 1975. *Nuclear Proliferation: US Foreign Policy Implications.* Hearings, 94th Congress, 1st session. Washington, DC: US Government Printing Office.

1978. *Investigations of Korean–American Relations.* Washington, DC: US Government Printing Office.

1995. *The North Korean Military and Nuclear Non-Proliferation Threat: Evaluation of the US–DPRK Agreed Framework.* Hearings, 104th Congress, 1st session. Washington, DC: US Government Printing Office.

US Senate, Committee on Armed Services. 1995. *The Security Implications of the Nuclear Non-Proliferation Agreement with North Korea.* Hearings, 104th Congress, 1st session. Washington, DC: US Government Printing Office.

US Senate, Committee on Government Operations. 1975. *The Export Reorganization Act.* Hearings, 94th Congress, 1st session. Washington, DC: US Government Printing Office.

1976. *The Export Reorganization Act of 1976.* Hearings, 94th Congress, 2nd session. Washington, DC: US Government Printing Office.

Van Bergeijk, Peter A. G. 1989. Success and failure of economic sanctions. *Kyklos* (42): 385–404.

1994. *Economic Diplomacy, Trade, and Commercial policy: Positive and Negative Sanctions in a New World Order.* Brookfield, VT: Edward Elgar.

Van Evera, Stephen. 1996. *Guide to Methodology for Students of Political Science.* Cambridge, MA: Defense and Arms Control Studies Program, Massachusetts Institute of Technology.

Vance, Cyrus. 1983. *Hard Choices: Critical Years in American Foreign Policy.* New York: Simon and Schuster.

Vares, Peeter. 1995. Baltic foreign and security policies. In Adeed Dawisha and Karen Dawisha, eds., *The Making of Foreign Policy in Russia and the New States of Eurasia.* Armonk, NY: M. E. Sharpe.

Viner, Jacob. 1948. Power versus plenty as objectives of foreign policy in the seventeenth and eighteenth centuries. *World Politics* 1: 1–29.

Von Amerongen, Otto Wolff. 1980. Economic sanctions as a foreign policy tool? *International Security* 5: 159–67.

Wagner, R. Harrison. 1988. Economic interdependence, bargaining power, and political influence. *International Organization* 42: 461–83.

Wallensteen, Peter. 1968. Characteristics of economic sanctions. *Journal of Peace Research* 5: 248–67.

Walt, Stephen M. 1987. *The Origins of Alliances.* Ithaca, NY: Cornell University Press.

Waltz, Kenneth. 1979. *Theory of International Politics.* New York: McGraw-Hill.

Webber, Mark. 1996. *The International Politics of Russia and the Successor States.* New York: Manchester University Press.

Weinstein, Franklin, and Fuji Komiya, eds. 1980. *The Security of Korea: US and Japanese Perspectives on the 1980s.* Boulder, CO: Westview Press.

Werleigh, Charlotte. 1995. The use of sanctions in Haiti: assessing the economic realities. In David Cortright and George Lopez, eds. *Economic Sanctions: Panacea or Peacebuilding in a Post-Cold War World?* Boulder, CO: Westview Press.

Wesson, Robert. 1981. *The United States and Brazil: the Limits of Influence.* New York: Praeger.

Wiarda, Howard. 1995. *Democracy and its Discontents.* New York: Rowman and Littlefield.

Willett, Thomas, and Mehrdad Jalalighajar. 1983. US trade policy and national security. *Cato Journal* 3: 717–27.

Wohlstetter, Albert. 1976. Spreading the bomb Without Quite Breaking the Rules. *Foreign Policy* 25: 88–96, 145–79.

Wolf, Bernard. 1987. Economic impact on the United States of the pipline sanctions. In David Leyton-Brown, ed., *The Utility of International Economic Sanctions.* London: Croom Helm.

Woodward, Susan. 1995. The use of sanctions in former Yugoslavia: misunderstanding political realities. In David Cortright and George Lopez, eds. *Economic Sanctions: Panacea or Peacebuilding in a Post-Cold War World?* Boulder, CO: Westview Press.

Yager, Joseph A., ed. 1980. *Nonproliferation and US Foreign Policy.* Washington: The Brookings Institution.

Index

CAMBRIDGE STUDIES IN INTERNATIONAL RELATIONS

Made in the USA
Lexington, KY
01 December 2018